CW01418326

Civil–Military Cooperation in Post-Conflict Operations

Civil–Military Cooperation (CIMIC) is the relationship between militaries and humanitarians. Largely conducted in post-conflict environments, CIMIC has become a key characteristic of military operations in the twenty-first century. However, the field is mostly understood through stereotype rather than clear, comprehensive analysis. The range and scope of activities which fall under the wider rubric of CIMIC is huge, as are the number of differing approaches, across situations and national armed forces. This book will demonstrate the wide variety of national approaches to CIMIC activities, and introduce some theoretical and ethical considerations into a field that has largely been bereft of this type of debate.

This volume contains several case studies of recent CIMIC (in the Balkans and Afghanistan) along with theoretical analyses, and will assist scholars, practitioners, and decision-makers to become more aware of the "state of the art" in this field.

This book will be of much interest to all students of military studies, humanitarian operations, peace operations and security studies in general.

Christopher Ankersen has acted as a consultant to governments, militaries, and firms on issues of policy, management and security in Canada, the United Kingdom, and the United States. From 2001 to 2004, he was Ralf Dahrendorf Scholar at the London School of Economics and Political Science. He is editor of *Understanding Global Terror*.

Cass military studies

Intelligence Activities in Ancient Rome
Trust in the gods, but verify
Rose Mary Sheldon

Clausewitz and African War
Politics and strategy in Liberia and Somalia
Isabelle Duyvesteyn

Strategy and Politics in the Middle East, 1954–60
Defending the northern tier
Michael Cohen

The Cuban Intervention in Angola, 1965–1991
From Che Guevara to Cuito Cuanavale
Edward George

Military Leadership in the British Civil Wars, 1642–1651
'The genius of this age'
Stanley Carpenter

Israel's Reprisal Policy, 1953–1956
The dynamics of military retaliation
Ze'ev Drory

Bosnia and Herzegovina in the Second World War
Leaders in war
Enver Redzic

West Point Remembers the 1991 Gulf War
Edited by Frederick Kagan and Christian Kubik

Khedive Ismail's Army
John Dunn

Yugoslav Military Industry 1918–1991
Amadeo Watkins

Corporal Hitler and the Great War 1914–1918
The list regiment
John Williams

Rostóv in the Russian Civil War, 1917–1920
The key to victory
Brian Murphy

The Tet Effect, Intelligence and the Public Perception of War
Jake Blood

Civil–Military Cooperation in Post-Conflict Operations

Emerging theory and practice

Edited by Christopher Ankersen

Routledge
Taylor & Francis Group

LONDON AND NEW YORK

First published 2008
by Routledge
2 Park Square, Milton Park, Abingdon, Oxon OX14 4RN

Simultaneously published in the USA and Canada
by Routledge
270 Madison Ave, New York, NY 10016

Routledge is an imprint of the Taylor & Francis Group, an informa business

© 2008 Selection and editorial matter Christopher Ankersen; individual
chapters the contributors

Typeset in Times by Wearset Ltd, Boldon, Tyne and Wear
Printed and bound in Great Britain by TJI Digital, Padstow, Cornwall

All rights reserved. No part of this book may be reprinted or reproduced or
utilized in any form or by any electronic, mechanical, or other means, now
known or hereafter invented, including photocopying and recording, or in
any information storage or retrieval system, without permission in writing
from the publishers.

British Library Cataloguing in Publication Data
A catalogue record for this book is available from the British Library

Library of Congress Cataloging in Publication Data
A catalog record for this book has been requested

ISBN10: 0-415-42884-X (hbk)
ISBN10: 0-203-96492-6 (ebk)

ISBN13: 978-0-415-42884-2 (hbk)
ISBN13: 978-0-203-96492-7 (ebk)

Contents

Contributors

Christopher Ankersen has written on a wide array of defence and security topics. He was Lord Dahrendorf Scholar at the London School of Economics and Political Science (LSE) from 2001 to 2004 and a Canadian Security and Defence Forum Scholar and Fellow from 2002–2005. He has taught at the LSE, King's College London, the London Centre for International Relations, and Carleton University. He is editor of *Understanding Global Terror*, a collection of scholarly essays from the UK, North America, and Israel. Christopher was an officer in Princess Patricia's Canadian Light Infantry, serving in Croatia (as a part of the United Nations Protection Force) and Kosovo (as a part of NATO's 'KFOR').

Yann Braem is PhD candidate at the Institut Français de Géopolitique (French Institute of Geopolitics), University of Paris VIII. He is researching the interactions between humanitarianism and military action in peace operations, based on fieldwork conducted in Kosovo (2001–2002) and Afghanistan (2003). He has also studied gendarmerie type forces and CIVPOL in peace operations. Yann regularly contributes to research projects led by the French Ministry of Defence, notably through le Centre d'Etudes en Sciences Sociales de la Défense and has been an assistant professor of political science at the Institut d'Etudes Politique of Toulouse and the University of Clermont Ferrand.

Cedric de Coning is a Research Fellow at the African Centre for the Constructive Resolution of Disputes (ACCORD) and Norwegian Institute of International Affairs (NUPI) and a consultant for the United Nations Office for the Coordination of Humanitarian Affairs (OCHA). He started his career in the South African Foreign Ministry where he was posted to Washington DC and Addis Ababa. He served with the United Nations Transitional Administration in East Timor and with the UN Department of Peacekeeping Operations (DPKO). Cedric holds a M.A. in Conflict Management and Peace Studies from the University of KwaZulu-Natal and is a DPhil candidate at the University of Stellenbosch.

Dr Andy Knight is Professor of International Relations at the University of Alberta. He co-edited the Journal, *Global Governance*, from 2000 to 2005, was Vice Chair of the Academic Council on the United Nations System, and is currently a member of the Board of Directors of the John Humphrey Centre for Peace and Human Rights and an Executive Board member of the Canadian Consortium on Human Security (CCHS), the Canadian Association for Security and Intelligence Studies (CASIS), the Canadian Consortium for Peace Studies (CCPS), and the Education for Peace Academic and Research Council (EPARC). Andy's most recent books are the second edition of the edited volume *Adapting the United Nations to a Postmodern Era: Lessons Learned* and a co-edited book titled *Building Sustainable Peace*.

Michael McNerney is Director of International Capacity-Building – Partnership Strategy in the Office of the Secretary of Defense, providing policy oversight for US military efforts to educate, train, and equip foreign militaries, assist defense reform efforts, and provide humanitarian assistance. Previous assignments involved stability operations policy, Afghanistan, and environmental issues. He spent 2004/5 on the faculty of the Marshall Center for Security Studies in Germany. Michael's publications include book chapters on arms control and military involvement in humanitarian activities and a *Parameters* article on Provincial Reconstruction Teams.

Lieutenant Colonel Susan J. Neuhaus (PhD) joined the Australian Regular Army as an undergraduate medical officer and has served in Cambodia as Regimental Medical Officer, Force Communications Unit as part of the United Nations Transitional Authority Cambodia, and in Bougainville as Officer Commanding, Combined Health Element. She is a graduate of Australian Command and Staff College (Reserve) and is currently Commanding Officer, 3rd Health Support Battalion. She works in civilian practice as a Consultant Surgeon and is Clinical Senior Lecturer in Surgery, University of Adelaide.

Raj Rana is an independent researcher and consultant to international organizations. His fieldwork over the last decade has included experience as a peacekeeper in Bosnia-Herzegovina (1993–1994) and eight years as a delegate with the International Committee of the Red Cross (ICRC) in Afghanistan, Chechnya, Darfur and Iraq. In 2003 he joined the ICRC headquarters, where he led projects to revise the organization's policy and guidance on civil–military relations, and enhancing operational responses to emerging complex emergencies and disasters. Raj holds Bachelor's and Master's degrees in Architecture from Carleton University in Ottawa, Canada and is currently a PhD candidate at King's College, London, United Kingdom.

Dr Sebastiaan J.H. Rietjens holds a PhD in civil–military cooperation during peace support operations. As an assistant professor at the Netherlands Defence Academy he is currently involved in research and education on civil–military cooperation and provincial reconstruction teams. As a reserve-officer of the Royal Netherlands Military Forces, Sebastiaan is involved in managing the deployment of Dutch civil–military officers to Afghanistan and Bosnia. He has various international publications on civil–military cooperation, cultural differences, performance assessment, and decision methodology.

Captain Owen A.J. Savage is an officer in the Canadian Forces and a graduate of the Canadian Land Forces Command and Staff College and the Canadian Land Forces Technical Staff Course. In 1999, he was a part of the Canadian CIMIC effort in Kosovo, responsible for project management. In 2006 Owen completed his MA in Human Security and Peacebuilding at Royal Roads University.

Bernhard G. Voget is a research assistant and PhD candidate at the Department of Agricultural Economics and Rural Development, Georg-August-University, Göttingen, Germany. His research focuses on post-conflict reconstruction and civil–military cooperation as well as on agriculture and rural areas in South Eastern Europe. Educated in Kiel and Göttingen, he holds a Master's degree in Agricultural Economics from the Faculty of Agriculture at Georg-August-University. Bernhard is a trained reserve officer and commander of a (non-active) German artillery battery. To gain better insight into the post-conflict reconstruction efforts of the German military, he served in KFOR's Multinational Brigade South West, Prizren, Kosovo in 2004. On a second mission to Kosovo from January to March 2006, he has compiled an evaluation study of the German Armed Forces' agricultural reconstruction projects in Kosovo for the Bundeswehr Operations Headquarters. He has authored and co-authored studies for the German parliament, the Bundeswehr as well as private companies. His recent publications include articles on agriculture-related topics and on CIMIC projects in Kosovo.

Foreword

Larry Minear

This is a book that will be welcomed by those who, whether from the vantage point of policy-makers, practitioners, evaluators, or members of the concerned international public, have witnessed the growing engagement of military forces in the humanitarian sector. It addresses issues that in the post-Cold War era have moved from periphery to center stage but have yet to be scrutinized for their impacts and wider meaning. The issues include the tensions between classical humanitarian principles and political–military decision-making, the comparative advantages of military and humanitarian actors in the humanitarian sphere, the importance of creating secure environments for humanitarian operations, the financial costs of military engagement in humanitarian chores, and the challenge of preserving the integrity of humanitarian space.

Such issues figure prominently in contemporary social science research in the international relations field, which in recent years has itself devoted more and more attention to them. The work of the Humanitarianism and War Project, an independent policy research initiative based in the United States first at Brown University and then at Tufts, provides a case in point. Many of its several dozen case studies of humanitarian action in various complex political emergencies conducted over the past decade and a half demonstrate the important and growing role of military actors in the humanitarian sphere. Those case studies most germane to the topic of this volume are recapped in this Foreword.[1] Yet this particular research group's experience is by no means anomalous: analysts elsewhere in the United States and around the world have encountered and examined various permutations of the same issues. A brief review of selected findings and unanswered questions from our studies of the Persian Gulf crisis of 1990ff., the Rwandan genocide, the break-up of the former Yugoslavia, the upheaval in Kosovo, and the war in Afghanistan helps provide context for the chapters in this volume.

The *Gulf Crisis* of 1990–1992 provided the first major example of military–civilian humanitarian action in the post-Cold War era. The crisis had two major humanitarian dimensions: the exodus of more than a million Palestinian and other third-country nationals from Iraq and Kuwait following Iraq's invasion of Kuwait in August 1990, and the flight of some 1.5 million Iraqis to the Turkish border and into Iran during the civil war in Iraq from March 1991 onwards. Troops making up the Allied Coalition played a particularly key role in the second set of events, with Operation Provide Comfort, led by the US military, offering essential immediate protection and assistance before turning over such activities to civilian agencies.

Viewing the Gulf crisis as the harbinger of things to come, our study identified two issues that have loomed large in subsequent conflicts. These are the costs and benefits of international military forces under bilateral or coalitional rather than multilateral management and the desirability of strengthening the coordination of humanitarian activities under a multilateral aegis and of insulating them more effectively from political factors. "Humanitarian activities in the Gulf bore a heavy burden as a result of UN-approved military force, implemented by the Allied Coalition," we concluded in an otherwise generally positive reading of the military–civilian interface in the Gulf crisis. "These first enforcement actions of the post-Cold War era made use of massive fire-power and sophisticated weaponry not mobilized hitherto. The United Nations, however, did not participate in any control, command, or monitoring capacities once it had taken the pivotal political decisions. The feasibility of mounting future operations under fully multilateral command and control needs to be explored. UN-related military actions, undertaken and carried out with due regard to humanitarian consequences, might prove both more accountable and more effective [than bilateral or coalitional initiatives]."[2]

The *Rwanda* crisis of 1994 mobilized a rich array of international military assets, some of them pressed into service during the genocide, but most of them enlisted only in time for mop-up operations following the bloodbath. The three major configurations were UN peacekeeping troops within the UN Assistance Mission for Rwanda (UNAMIR), bilateral military contingents such as the French troops in Operation Turquoise and the American troops in Operation Support Hope, and individual national military contingents from countries such as Canada, the Netherlands, Japan, Germany, New Zealand, Australia, Israel, and Ireland which entered into specific functional partnerships with individual UN agencies. Our review differentiated among three related but distinct tasks provided by military personnel: fostering a secure environment for civilian populations and humanitarian organizations, supporting the work of such agencies, and providing direct services to civilians in need.[3] We concluded that despite significant contributions in the humanitarian sector, international military forces performed *least* well at the *most* indispensable of these functions, that of fostering a secure environment, and were *least* available when *most* needed (in advance of and during the genocide).

The Rwanda experience produced almost as many unresolved questions as there were military actors. These included issues such as the restrictive terms of engagement under which most of the international troops were provided, the comparative advantages of military vis-à-vis civilian organizations, the costs of involving military assets, and the wide-ranging tensions between the cultures of military and humanitarian institutions. The interest of troops in engaging in civic action, or "hearts and minds" activities, was well documented but was found to be not without its problems, both in terms of the core competencies of the military and of the blurring of lines with professional humanitarian agencies. Such issues would recur and evolve in subsequent theaters during the decade, as would the evident disjuncture between the aid agencies' overriding need and expectation from the military – for the provision of a secure environment – and yet the military's reluctance or difficulty in providing such security.

The humanitarian challenges of the break-up of the former Yugoslavia and the role of the UN peacekeeping operation UNPROFOR highlighted the recurrence of issues earlier foreshadowed in the first Gulf War and played out in the Rwanda crisis. Documenting tensions between the political–military side of the UN and humanitarian activities that went well beyond any experienced in Iraq, our 1994 study described UN action as a house divided against itself and called for consideration of a new institutional capacity within the UN "to provide assistance and protection where enforcement under Chapter VII of the Charter results in economic sanctions or military intervention." "Functioning in such an environment," we concluded, "is proving too treacherous for most members of the UN's existing humanitarian system."[4] We also found that, as in the case of Rwanda, international military forces, despite being pressed into service with all-too-restrictive terms of engagement, received disproportionate and too uncritical attention from the international media. In the former Yugoslavia, humanitarian efforts themselves served as "substitutes for effective decisions by governments and the international community to end the warfare and unconscionable violence."[5]

In the Kosovo crisis of 1999, international military forces were once again front and center, with NATO itself leading "the first major bombing campaign intended to bring a halt to crimes against humanity being committed by a state within its own borders."[6] The contribution of NATO contingents to the welfare of Kosovars fleeing into Albania and Macedonia in March "played an important surge protection function at a time when humanitarian organizations themselves were overwhelmed." Yet the perceived neutrality of humanitarian assistance was undermined by the high-profile involvement of the military in the humanitarian sphere. We also flagged "the lack of available data from the military on the costs of their involvement and the lack of an accepted methodology for determining what costs should and should not be included in such calculations."[7] In Kosovo as in the earlier Balkans crisis, the military were explicitly given tasks in the humanitarian sphere, yet experienced difficulty in carrying them out effectively. In a comment that has clearly not been borne out by events subsequent to Kosovo, our research team viewed "the future role of the military in the humanitarian arena as exceptional rather than routine." We recommended that the military be granted "a recognized niche in the humanitarian architecture of the future but be activated only in rare instances."[8]

Over a period of years, humanitarian activities in *Afghanistan* have demonstrated an evolving and increasingly interactive set of relationships with international military forces. During the decade of Soviet military occupation beginning in 1979, most humanitarian assistance to Afghans in need was delivered by aid groups within parameters established by the US-led anti-Soviet coalition.[9] International assistance activities also evidenced a heavy political animus during the civil war years 1992–1996 as the Northern Alliance and Taliban wrestled with each other for territorial control. Following the attack on New York and Washington, DC on September 11, 2001, the US launched a war against al-Qaeda and promoted talks in December 2001 that laid the groundwork for an elected Afghan regime. Assistance over a quarter-century has thus been an integral element in a series of political-military strategies related successively to the Cold War, the civil war, the Taliban years, and the post-9/11 era.

Such is the context within which the concept of Provincial Reconstruction Teams (PRTs), the subject of discussion later in this volume, were designed and implemented, initially in 2002 by the United States and eventually enlisting the participation of other governments. Grouping together under a single roof a range of government agencies – in the case of the United States, the PRTs included officials with civilian and military, intelligence, assistance and agriculture functions – the PRTs were described by the Pentagon as engaged in "combat humanitarian work." In interviews conducted in Afghanistan in late 2002, we found humanitarian organizations troubled by that intentional blurring of lines between civilian and military, humanitarian and intelligence functions. "What's going on here," one NGO told us with a certain clairvoyance, is a distortion of humanitarian action that "could redefine humanitarian work globally."[10] The issues at the military–civilian interface raised by the Afghan experience include matters of policy and operations, humanitarian principles and space, and the accountability of military as well as humanitarian actors. Beyond their relevance to an increasingly fraught situation in Afghanistan, these issues are widely viewed as important to future humanitarian operations in other high-profile settings around the world.

This brief review of the military–civilian interface in recent crises – to those mentioned here could be added other complex emergencies such as Somalia, Cambodia, Haiti, Georgia, Darfur and, once again, Iraq, as well as "natural disasters" such as the 2004 Tsunami – brings us back to the importance of this volume for understanding and anticipating future directions in relations between military forces and the humanitarian enterprise. There is no substitute for developing a more in-depth sense of these issues, necessarily contextualized by the rough-and-tumble of ongoing efforts to provide humanitarian assistance and protection. A review of recent experience makes it difficult to claim that field-based data have had much influence on accelerating desirable changes in institutions, whether military or humanitarian. Indeed, the recurrence of a consistent set of critical but unresolved policy issues in successive conflicts suggests that the process of lessons-learning and institutional change is a lethargic and halting one. That said, the increasing role of the military in the humanitarian sphere lends fresh urgency to the lessons-learning process with a particular eye to improving the interactions at the military–civilian interface.

Notes

1 For a discussion of the humanitarian interface with the military across the range of case studies conducted by the Humanitarianism and War Project, see Larry Minear and Thomas G. Weiss, *Mercy under Fire: War and the Global Humanitarian Community* (Boulder, CO: Westview Press, 1995, 168–179, and Larry Minear, *The Humanitarian Enterprise: Dilemmas and Discoveries* (Bloomfield, CT: Kumarian Press, 2002), 100–118. The individual studies are available in their entirety at hwproject.tufts.edu

2 Larry Minear, UBP Chelliah, Jeff Crisp, John Mackinlay, and Thomas G. Weiss, *United Nations Coordination of the International Humanitarian Response to the Gulf Crisis 1990–1992*. Providence, RI: Watson Institute, 1992, 39.

3 Larry Minear and Philippe Guillot, *Soldiers to the Rescue: Humanitarian Lessons from Rwanda*. Paris: Organisation for Economic Co-operation and Development, 1996. [also available in French from the same publisher as *Soldats a la Rescousse*].

4 Larry Minear, Jeffrey Clark, Roberta Cohen, Dennis Gallagher, Iain Guest, and Thomas G. Weiss, *Humanitarian Action in the Former Yugoslavia: The U.N.'s Role 1991–1993*. Providence, RI: The Watson Institute, 1994, x. Among the ten challenges that humanitarian organizations faced was one termed "Determining the appropriate uses of the military" (83–92).

5 Ibid., ix.

6 Adam Roberts, in "NATO's 'Humanitarian War' Over Kosovo," in Larry Minear, Ted van Baarda, and Marc Sommers, *NATO and Humanitarian Action in the Kosovo Crisis*. Providence, RI: Watson Institute, 2000, 121–150.

7 Minear, van Baarda, and Sommers, op. cit., 102.

8 Ibid., 117.

9 See Antonio Donini, *The Policies of Mercy: UN Coordination in Afghanistan, Mozambique, and Rwanda*. Providence, RI: Watson Institute, 1996, 21–60.

10 Ian Smillie and Larry Minear, *The Charity of Nations: Humanitarian Action in a Calculating World*. Bloomfield, CT: Kumarian Press, 2004, 103.

Acknowledgements

During the course of my own research into the world of Civil–Military Coopera-tion, I was struck by two things: the variety of perspectives and practices that marked the field and the number of young(ish) graduate students working in this area. I am happy that this book sheds light on both these important aspects.

By its very nature, an edited book relies on lots of people; this one is no exception. First I must thank the contributors to this volume for their enthusi-asm, scholarship, and patience. At times a refined group, at times an angry mob, they spurred me on to the finish. If it were not for them, this book would not have been written. Special mention must go to Larry Minear who responded to my 'out of the blue' request to provide the foreword to this book. He gave that and more besides.

Even with all the hard work of the contributors, without the wise advice and assistance from Andrew and Katie at Routledge, this book would not be pub-lished.

As ever, my family, led with grace and love by my wife Denise, provided me with the support I needed (but probably did not deserve) as I put this book together. For that – and for them – I am infinitely grateful.

1 Introduction

Interrogating civil–military cooperation

Christopher Ankersen

In the Western imagination, soldiers and civilians are categorical opposites; traditionally, soldiers 'break things and kill people' while civilians, especially those engaged in humanitarian work, dedicate themselves to healing and building. It should not be surprising, then, that activities which are seen to rely on a high degree of interdependence between these camps are controversial. One observer goes so far as to describe the admixture of violence and humanitarianism as a 'moral paradox' (Slim 2001). In spite of the apparent paradoxical nature of this relationship, it is not a new one. Battlefields have never been solely populated by soldiers; civilians have long been, and continue to be, actors there, as supporters, victims, and as those responsible for helping to pick up the pieces (Slim 1997; Sorensen 2006).

Civil–military cooperation is a military label used to describe those occasions that see elements of armed forces engaging, and even collaborating, with civilian entities (such as local authorities or other government agencies, non-governmental organizations, or international/intergovernmental organizations). This collaboration usually takes place during some form of crisis situation, whether it be after a natural disaster, war, or, increasingly, during complex peace support or stability operations. It can take the form of abstract contingency planning or the high level coordination of resources and objectives, but can also manifest itself as aid delivery or reconstruction activity by military forces.

Civil–military cooperation is on the rise, and has been since the 1990s and the conception of modern 'peace support operations'. Its contemporary incarnation as a large-scale activity can be traced to 1991 with 'Operation Provide Comfort', the US-led mission to provide humanitarian assistance to the Kurds following the first Gulf War. Military support to and provision of humanitarian relief was also the focus of the United Nations Protection Force (UNPROFOR) in Bosnia in 1992 and gained notoriety during the US led, UN sanctioned mission to Somalia in 1993, known as 'Operation Restore Hope'.[1] Stuart Gordon believes the explosion in CIMIC activities is due to the combination of a number of changes:

> the political objectives underpinning interventions have become more ambitious, resulting in a greater degree of complexity in the institutional

responses of states.... The convergence of the human security and the traditional, narrowly defined state security agendas, the gradual importation of 'political economy' approaches to conflict analysis, state and international organisations' [*sic*] pursuit of multi-dimensional missions and policy 'coherence' between the various aspects of these interventions have each been significant factors in this evolution.

(Gordon 2006: 340)

Whatever its pedigree, 'military humanitarianism', including civil–military cooperation was catapulted onto the international scene most forcefully in Kosovo in 1999 and in Afghanistan, since 2001. These two operations brought into clearer focus the controversial – some might say divisive – nature of the activity.

The divisive nature of CIMIC is the product of several factors. For one thing, there is little consensus, even amongst military thinkers, over what CIMIC is or should be. Across NATO, for example, national approaches overwhelm any sense of Alliance consistency (Wentz 2002; Landon and Hayes 2003; Jakobsen 2005). Even within a single nation's armed forces, radically different understandings and practices can be found (Kennedy 1997). Accordingly, attempts to generalize about what is CIMIC is, and subsequently, to attempt to draw lessons from such a fictitious universal portrayal do not do credit to the broad spectrum of military–humanitarian interactions.

Second, American activities have, for the most part, been the focus of analysis. CIMIC within the armed forces of the United States are, following the preceding observation, contingent on its own particular national realities (such as an interpretation of national interest; the nature of conflicts in which CIMIC activities are carried out; military culture and organization). It is, therefore, worth noting that other militaries act differently, and indeed, can be perceived differently by humanitarians, the media, and the local population (see Delaney 2000/2001).

Third, much of what has been written on the subject has proceeded from a strictly normative viewpoint that can be seen as antagonistic to the very premise of military involvement in humanitarian affairs. This kind of analysis can be seen in reports by NGOs and development think tanks (see Barry and Jeffreys 2002) as well as in articles from security experts (see Byman 2001). While this literature can be informative, its value is limited by its quasi-ideological standpoint. Polemic arguments founded on a belief that all militaries are bad (due to their use of force) and all humanitarians are good (due to the nature of their moral motivations) cannot advance our understanding of real-world practices. As Pugh rightly points out, given the realities of the current situation, 'the main challenge is to maintain the military–humanitarian link, not to ban it' (1997, 192).

An important aim of this volume is to move past these narrow foci that have informed much of the work in the field of civil–military cooperation. Instead the chapters in this volume (which will be visited individually in detail below) demonstrate aspects of CIMIC that are often neglected. An unfortunate side-effect of this neglect is that key questions go unasked. This volume asks questions in three broad interrelated categories:

1   What is CIMIC? How is CIMIC carried out?
2   Why do militaries perform CIMIC?
3   What difference does CIMIC make?

What is CIMIC?

It is vital to interrogate how CIMIC is conceived by the armed forces that practice it and those who provide them with their political guidance. Is it seen as a 'core activity' or is it a sideline? What is it that commanders are hoping to achieve by carrying out such activities? Do mainstream, conventional units perform CIMIC operations, or are they considered the domain of specialist (even special), or reserve forces?

The answers to this line of inquiry are important because they give us a clue as to the ultimate effect of CIMIC activities and lead to our second question. If armed forces understand CIMIC to be a central part of their mission, then we might expect them to dedicate considerable resources (human, financial, and intellectual) into refining their approach. We might expect, therefore, the incorporation of best practices from the field of development and relief. We would be justified in evaluating the efficacy of CIMIC against such standards. If, on the other hand, CIMIC is merely a supplemental activity, undertaken for reasons other than mission accomplishment, then it would be no surprise to see little effort put into the development of workable policies, doctrines, and procedures. The question, then, is to ask if CIMIC is 'good development'. Does it meet the aim of bringing relief to a stricken population? Or is it merely a tactical expedient aimed at pacifying the locals? Is CIMIC an innovative strategy, one which might contribute to the greater goal of conflict termination, or maybe even the ever-elusive goal of 'peace', however that might be defined? Or is CIMIC such a compromise that it takes on what might be called 'houseboat' status: houseboats, being a combination of two dissimilar items, make poor boats *and* poor houses. Perhaps, in this sense, CIMIC constitutes poor military practice *and* poor development.

The answer to these questions cannot rely on a single subject of observation. Robert Kagan asserts that 'on major strategic and international questions today, Americans are from Mars and Europeans are from Venus: They agree on little and understand one another less and less' (2002, 1). Assuming he is correct, can we expect that the activities their militaries undertake will be identical? Or are armed forces, especially within NATO, so similar in function and orientation that their practices are fundamentally aligned? (Pugh 2000). Perhaps there are elements of CIMIC that are done differently, by different militaries, and if so, perhaps it is these differences that can shed light on what might be considered to be an effective military contribution to relief and development.

Why CIMIC?

In looking for the answer to this question, we are really aiming to identify the 'logic' that underpins civil–military cooperation (Lauritzen 2006). There are many contending answers, which can be broken down into two categories. The first category contains what might be termed political considerations,[2] while the second is concerned with operational matters; that is, issues related to the performance of the military mission.[3]

Political reasons

Some observers contend that militaries conduct CIMIC as a part of some 'hegemonic strategy', thus furthering the scope and extent of Western imperialism. In the absence of, or alongside, combat operations, Western armies carry out their hegemonic domination through 'other means'. Hugo Slim has labeled these ideas as 'geopolitical conspiracy theories', but this has not convinced some of its proponents to abandon it. Others, while eschewing an openly conspirational tone on the part of the military, point to a wider trend within the West. Robin Luckham (2005, 13) states 'there is some hubris in the idea that the international community (and in particular the major donors and international bodies) can assist the reconstruction of entire states and national societies after war and state collapse'. In her conceptualization military CIMIC can be seen to form a part of the 'evolution' of post-conflict development practices, 'from simply funding development policies and programmes; to influencing aid recipient countries' policy frameworks under stabilisation and structural adjustment programmes; to directly transforming political and administrative institutions under the rubric of good governance' (Luckham 2005, 14). CIMIC, then, might be seen as a pillar of a Washington Consensus. Michael Ignatieff (2003) agrees, but frames military forays into relief and development activities as a constituent part of a (relatively) benign global superstructure he calls 'Empire Lite'.

Substitution theory is a related (but less sinister) concept to hegemonic theory. After the end of the Cold War, there had been a lack of good old-fashioned warfighting for armies to get involved with, so they turned to the next best thing – peacekeeping. As these missions progressed, changing in name from peacekeeping, to peace support to stability and support operations, armies seized upon CIMIC as a good way to occupy their time without engaging in combat, something which was often difficult given national and international rules of engagement which constrained their ability to apply force (see Barry and Jeffreys 2002; Lauritzen et al. 2006).

The chief reason a military might need to 'find something to do' with its time and resources is the maintenance of its domestic legitimacy. Some armies maintain their *raison d'etre* merely by being on hand to 'fight and win the nation's wars'. Others, though, look for other roles. Because an army wants to look good at home, it might portray itself in a manner in keeping with what it perceives the public (and the politicians) want. 'CIMIC as photo opportunity' provides an opportunity to bolster, boost, or at least maintain funding and political support. To some extent, whether or not this has been an animating reason for CIMIC, it has worked, at least as far as putting the image of 'peacekeeper' rather than 'soldier' into the public consciousness of many Western countries.

Operational issues

If political reasons are set aside (as they occur at, or above, the strategic level), it is possible to concentrate on the reasons why a military commander might want to conduct CIMIC operations, at the tactical or operational level. From this perspective, divorced from the idea of grand 'meta-narratives' involving imperial ambition, several ideas are posited as the logic behind CIMIC.

One of the most straightforward reasons given for the military to deliver aid is force protection. Simply put, CIMIC is predicated on the notion that, all things being equal, people do not bite the hands that feed them. If a school is built or food aid distributed, it will be 'paid back' through better relations with the locals. These better relations will mean a reduction in the number of attacks from the population, and perhaps even 'tips' as to the time and location of upcoming ambushes (O'Neill 2004; Perito 2005). The empirical evidence to support the efficacy of this strategy is largely based on isolated anecdotes, but it does have a strong influence in terms of justifying CIMIC activity.

A slightly different, but equally 'military-centric' reason that has been forwarded for the militaries CIMIC activities is that it keeps the troops happy. Building a school beats pulling another shift as gate guard and it allows soldiers to feel as if they have 'made a difference'. Rather than conducting their umpteenth vehicle patrol, soldiers can participate in the construction of a school or a water well, fulfilling their human, and humanitarian, reaction to being surrounded by abject poverty. (Barry and Jeffreys 2002, 7).

These reasons appear rather narrow and, arguably, of uncertain value, given the time and resources spent on CIMIC activities by militaries in post-conflict situations. Looking more broadly, CIMIC is conceived of as a part of a larger effort to conduct Information Operations. This perspective sees CIMIC activities as part of a campaign – along with psychological operations and public/media affairs – that aims at helping commanders 'shape their environment' and fulfill their missions by harnessing a wide variety of approaches. In this sense, CIMIC is a conduit for information: it allows military forces to gather information from the population, but is also facilitates the spreading of information into the society. Militaries can tie messages to the CIMIC activities they conduct, either directly to those participating in them or to the wider community.[4]

What difference does CIMIC make?

With possible answers to the 'what' and the 'why' of CIMIC, it is possible to ask the final question in our study: What difference does CIMIC make? There are two dimensions to this interrogation. The first regards the impact of CIMIC on the targeted population. Our criteria for evaluating this impact can come from a host of sources, theoretical and practical, from fields such as development and management. Here the focus is on whether the military is capable of achieving meaningful results through its aid activities, and at what cost (Weiss 1999).

The second dimension concerns the impact of CIMIC on actors other than the populations who may benefit from CIMIC activities. Here the criteria are much cruder: does the military bring out the best in other agencies involved in relief work? Is CIMIC truly a cooperative undertaking, as the name suggests, or does it reduce the overall effectiveness of the international community's development attempts in some way? Many practitioners and observers are convinced that military participation in the humanitarian space is always and everywhere a grave mistake (Gordon 2004). However, this is not a consensus position and, therefore, there is room for exploration (see Harris 2006). This volume aims to contribute to that debate.

Outline of the book

The book is broken into three parts. Part I (Chapters 2–5) contains theoretical studies which aim to explain how CIMIC works, either by examining it as a partnership or by interrogating its objective. Part II (Chapters 6–8) are case studies of particular nations. They look at how particular militaries have approached CIMIC and examine the thinking behind the doctrine. Furthermore, they evaluate that national practice, suggesting ways in which it could be improved. Part III (Chapters 9–10) is comprised of studies that extend our understanding of CIMIC beyond the conventional 'military-NGO partnership' perspective.

Andy Knight's second chapter places CIMIC in the context of human security. In this sense, CIMIC is a bridge between the humanitarian community's ability to dispel 'freedom from want' and the military community's ability to dispel 'freedom from fear'. Knight states that since the nature of interventions changed over the course of the 1990s, eventually becoming founded upon a '"new" norm in international relations – "the responsibility to protect" (R2P)'. This, in turn, 'lent credence to the fledging but growing norm of "human security"'. CIMIC is indeed an instrumental practice, one which aims to make the military commander's job easier. But, it is possible to see that militaries can 'engage in humanitarian work as well'. This can advance and improve Human Security, but there are limits. While some 'blurring' between military and humanitarian actives can be acceptable, when CIMIC activities occur next to, and concurrent with, traditional, active defence activities, problems arise. Indeed, human security gains are easily wiped out by offensive action and its effects.

Yann Braem, in the third chapter, sets out to 'to analyse the territorial stakes of military–humanitarian interactions, following a geopolitical analytical framework'. He interrogates CIMIC as a practice which binds militaries and NGOs together within – and as a product of – geography. Often, Braem states, geography is the only commonality between CIMIC actors. Furthermore, risk, especially in places like Afghanistan, is not distributed equally; rather it varies by geography. This variation, in turn, leads to variations in CIMIC styles and approaches.

In the fourth chapter, Cedric de Coning suggests a theoretical model, based on Complex System Theory, which can explain the lack of coordination and cooperation that are hallmarks of contemporary CIMIC. He states that 'despite a growing awareness that the security, socio-economic, political and reconciliation dimensions of peacebuilding systems are interlinked, the agencies that carry out peacebuilding programmes are finding it extremely difficult to meaningfully integrate these different dimensions into coherent country or regional conflict system strategies'. De Coning situates CIMIC within the context of peacebuilding and produces models that focuses on themes of coherence and interdependence. These themes, he believes, are the keys to success for CIMIC. Clearly, there is a lot to be improved on, as de Coning notes, 'there is still a considerable disparity between acknowledged best practice and operational reality'. CIMIC, like other peacebuilding practices, is conducted almost at random, with little connection to country or regional development strategies. Competition, rather than true cooperation, rules the day, creating a patchwork of programmes, rather than a integrated approach. De Coning suggests that separating management (in the 'control' sense of the word) from coordination (in the 'information sharing' sense of the word) might help reduce the corrosive and counter-product effect that competition has caused. Each actor should take responsibility for its own programmes and the resultant outcomes, and continually monitor their impact on the surrounding environment, including that which effects other CIMIC actors.

In the fifth chapter, S.J.H. Rietjens proposes to explain the way in which *both* parties in a CIMIC relationship (a military unit and a humanitarian agency or NGO) determine whether or not partnership is the right option for them. In fact, the model goes beyond explanation 'to develop a model that will support the co-operation between the military and the civilian actors in a peace support operation at a local level in response to a complex emergency'. Rietjens believes that both parties should go through a series of steps, each involving decisions which require them to reflect on their ultimate objective, as well as the best strategy for reaching that objective. He shares de Coning's view that continual evaluation of the outcomes (in this case, the quality and utility of the CIMIC partnership) is critical.

Owen Savage's sixth chapter interrogates the notion that CIMIC is peacebuilding, focussing on the Canadian Provincial Reconstruction Team's (PRT) performance in Afghanistan. Is CIMIC really about building peace, or has it more to do with achieving purely military objectives? Savage examines the necessary components of peacebuilding and evaluates the PRT against them, concentrating on the PRTs structure and its operations, as well as its impact on the environment within which it found itself. Ultimately, he finds that what holds the Canadian PRT back is its 'lack of a framework or clear strategic vision for operations'.

The objective of Voget's seventh chapter is 'to explain the German concept of CIMIC and the underlying theoretical approach, and to add empirical clarity about how the Bundeswehr executes CIMIC in practice'. It is an attempt to focus on a single country's understanding and experience, but not just any country. Germany's reluctant re-entry into the world of military operations abroad has been closely observed and this chapter provides an inside look at how it has dealt with a range of operations, which for most of its recent history, were conceived solely domestically. Voget concludes, perhaps surprising, that for the Bundeswehr, 'CIMIC is not "development-minded", but rather has an instrumental value for the Armed Forces'. Building on this foundation, Voget traces the limitations and implications of CIMIC thus imagined. Echoing de Coning, Voget finds that the coherence of the larger humanitarian and development effort is put in jeopardy as militaries conduct CIMIC according to their own perceptions and needs, rather than in accordance with the plans and strategies used by civilian agencies and NGOs.

Turning attention to the American understanding of CIMIC in the eighth chapter, Michael McNerney places the recent resurgence of CIMIC in the context of the post-9/11 world. Based on the unique set of conditions extant in Afghanistan, American decision-makers had to balance focused 'direct action' with broad-based emergency relief. As McNerney puts it, 'for both strategic and moral reasons, the United States could not ignore (or worse, exacerbate) the plight of millions of civilians during the conduct of a military operation. In this context, military and humanitarian activities could not be separate or sequential.' Accordingly, CIMIC has evolved in the US armed forces doctrine, if not always in practice, from a peripheral activity, carried out solely by specialists, to a more 'conventionally' understood line of operation, one which needs to be mainstreamed and integrated into the commander's overall plan. McNerney traces the evolution of CIMIC doctrine and practice in the American context and notes an acceleration of that evolution within Afghanistan, as the nature of that conflict changed over time. Paradoxically, McNerney claims that the U.S. got CIMIC correct in the campaign to unseat the Taliban, but has done less well in the counter-insurgency that followed.

Susan Neuhaus's ninth chapter focuses on the specialized field of medical CIMIC. Just as regular military units have entered the unfamiliarly territory of engaging with humanitarian actors and local populations, so too has the military medical community. Neuhaus demonstrates that despite the differences between combat and medical support units, many of the same concerns arise when dealing with CIMIC; issues such as the ethics of mixing military and humanitarian objectives and the lack of coherent doctrine to guide practice. Neuhaus reminds us that, even though doctors may appear to be impartial (guided by their Hippocratic Oath and the Geneva Conventions) 'military healthcare providers cannot, by definition, be neutral because they form part of a system that imposes its national or coalition values on another country. Therefore health provision by the military must strike a balance between a pragmatic and a principled response.'

Raj Rana's tenth and final chapter asks whether CIMIC is at a crossroads or a dead-end. He believes that CIMIC reached a pivotal moment in Kosovo, where NATO's simultaneous and expansive activities in the fields of combat and humanitarian relief, marked a watershed. Afghanistan, though, is a step beyond, perhaps one that goes too far. Rana, a former delegate of the International Committee of the Red Cross (ICRC) examines 'the ICRC's view of the civil–military relationship in contemporary humanitarian environments' highlighting the 'recent reconsideration of the [its] civil–military relations strategy'. He begins by tracing the development of how armed forces came to see themselves entering the 'humanitarian space'. Speaking to members of the humanitarian community, he states that, like it or not, the soldiers are here to stay. What is important is for actors, like the ICRC, who value their non-military status, and who depend on impartiality and neutrality for their legitimacy and their protection, to understand CIMIC so that they may gauge the level to which they might engage with it. Caught in a world where humanitarianism is being co-opted in the rush to integrate politics, security, and relief, Rana believes actors such as the ICRC must not falter in the promotion of their guiding principles.

Notes

1 For a chronology of American involvement in such missions, see DiPrizio 2002. For a more comprehensive treatment (in terms of geographic scope and timeline), see Wheeler 2000.
2 Here I use Harold Lasswell's definition of politics: 'Who gets what, when and how' taken from the title of this 1936 book (Lasswell 1990 [1936]).
3 The 'Why CIMIC' section of this chapter draws on material from Ankersen 2004 and Ankersen 2002.
4 See Ankersen 2006 for a more comprehensive discussion of the link between intelligence and CIMIC.

Bibliography

Ankersen, C.P. 2002. 'Was it Good For You? Why Militaries Engage in Civil–Military Cooperation', Institute for Research on Public Policy Paper. Ottawa: Institute for Research on Public Policy.

Ankersen, C.P. 2004. 'Coordination, Cooperation, or Something Else? A framework for Assessing Power Relations in Civil–Military Interactions', in *Challenge and Change for the Military: New Missions, Old Problems*. Douglas L. Bland, David Last, Franklin Pinch and Alan Okros, eds. Montreal and Kingston: McGill Queen's University Press: 80–100.

Ankersen, C.P. 2006. 'Peacekeeping Intelligence and Civil Society: Is CIMIC the missing link?', in *Peacekeeping Intelligence: New Players, Extended Boundaries*. London: Routledge: 160–175.

Barry, J. and Jeffreys, A. 2002. *A Bridge Too Far: Aid Agencies and the Military in Humanitarian Response*. Humanitarian Practice Network Paper No. 37. London: Overseas Development Institute.

Byman, D.L. 2001. 'Uncertain Partners: NGOs and the Military', *Survival* 43(2): 97–114.

Delaney, D.E. 2000/2001. 'CIMIC Operations During Operation Kinetic', *Canadian Military Journal* (Winter): pp. 29–34.

DiPrizio, R.C. 2002. *Armed Humanitarians: U.S. Interventions from Northern Iraq to Kosovo.* Baltimore: Johns Hopkins University Press.

Gordon, S. 2004. 'Military–Humanitarian Relationships and the Invasion of Iraq (2003): Reforging Certainties?', *Journal of Humanitarian Assistance* (July). www.jha.ac.uk; accessed 19 September 2005.

Gordon, S. 2006. 'Exploring the Civil–Military Interface and its Impact on European Strategic and Operational Personalities: "Civilianisation" and Limiting Military Roles in Stabilisation Operations?', *European Security* (15.3): pp. 339–361.

Harris, G. 2006. 'The military as a resource for peace-building: time for reconsideration?', *Conflict, Security, and Development.* 6.2 (June).

Ignatieff, M. 2003. *Empire Lite: Nation-Building in Bosnia, Kosovo, and Afghanistan.* London: Penguin.

Jakobsen, P.V. 2005. 'PRTs in Afghanistan: Successful but not sufficient', Danish Institute of International Studies Report 2005: 6.

Kagan, R. 2002. 'Power and Weakness', *Policy Review* (June). www.policyreview.org/JUN02/kagan.html; accessed 3 September 2002.

Kennedy, K.M. 1997. 'The Relationship Between the Military and Humanitarian Organisations in Operation Restore Hope', in *Learning from Somalia: the Lessons of Armed Humanitarian Intervention*, W. Clarke and J. Herbst, eds. Oxford: Westview Press, 99–117.

Landon, J.J. and Hayes, R.E. 2003. *National Approaches to Civil–Military Coordination in Peace and Humanitarian Assistance Operations.* Washington, DC: Evidence Based Research, Inc.

Lasswell, H. 1990 [1936]. Politics: Who gets What, When and How. New York: Peter Smith Publishers.

Lauritzen, E.K. and Olesen, G., with Straud, A. 2006. 'The Role Assignment of External Armed Forces in Societal Reconstruction', Working Paper. Oslo: Chr Michelsen Institute/Peace Research Institute, Oslo. www.cmi.no/afghanistan/?id=278&Civilian–Military-Relations; accessed 25 May 2006.

Luckham, R. 2005. 'The International Community and State Reconstruction in War-Torn Societies', in *After Intervention: Public Security Management in Post-Conflict Societies From Intervention to Sustainable Local Ownership*, Anja H. Ebnother and Philip Fluri, eds. Geneva: Centre for the Democratic Control of Armed Forces (DCAF), 12–47.

O'Neill, M. 2004. 'Winning Hearts and Minds', *Canadian Forces Feature Story.* www.forces.gc.ca/site/Feature_Story/2004/jan04/21_f_e.asp; accessed 12 May 2005.

Perito, R. 2005. 'Hearts and Minds Model?', *Armed Forces Journal* (December). www.armedforcesjournal.com/2005/12/1231940/; accessed 12 May 2006.

Pugh, M. 1997. 'From Mission Cringe to Mission Creep? Concluding Remarks', in *UN, Peace, and Force.* London: Frank Cass.

Pugh, M. 2000. 'Civil–military Relations in the Kosovo Crisis: An Emerging Hegemony?', *Security Dialogue* 31(2): 229–242.

Slim 1997. 'The Stretcher and the Drum: Civil–military Relations in Peace Support Operations', in *Beyond the Emergency*, J. Ginifer, ed. London: Frank Cass, 123–140.

Slim, H. 2001. 'Violence and Humanitarianism: Moral Paradox and the Protection of Civilians', *Security Dialogue* 32(3): 325–339.

Sorensen, B.R. 2006. 'Violence and humanitarian assistance: Reflections on an intricate relationship', *Journal of Humanitarian Assistance.* www.jha.ac.uk/articles/a194; accessed 10 October 2006.

Weiss, T. 1999. *Military–Civilian Interactions: Intervening in Humanitarian Crises.* Oxford: Rowman and Littlefield.

Wentz, L. 2002. *Lessons From Kosovo: The KFOR Experience.* Washington, DC: Department of Defense.

Wheeler, N.J. 2000. *Saving Strangers: Humanitarian Intervention in International Society.* Oxford: Oxford University Press.

Williams, M.C. 1998. *Civil–military Relations and Peacekeeping.* IISS Adelphi Paper No. 321. Oxford: Oxford University Press.

Part I
Theoretical approaches

2 Civil–military cooperation and human security

Andy Knight[1]

Introduction

Since the end of the Cold War, violent intra-state conflicts have overshadowed traditional wars between states. Some military analysts within the United States now refer to these modern day conflicts as "fourth generation" wars. According to these analysts, Fourth Generation wars are an indication of "the greatest dialectically qualitative change in the conduct of war since the Peace of Westphalia that ended the Thirty Years War in 1648."

These wars have four distinct characteristics: (1) the loss of the state's monopoly on war and on the first loyalty of its citizens; (2) the rise of non-state entities that command people's primary loyalty and that have the ability to wage war. These entities may be gangs, clans, religious groups, races and ethnic groups, tribes, business enterprises, ideological actors and terrorist organizations – the variety is almost limitless; (3) a return to a world of cultures, not, merely of states, in conflict; and (4) the manifestation of both developments – the decline of the state and the rise of alternate, often cultural, primary loyalties – not only "out there," but in North America itself.[2]

Many of the post Cold War conflicts have produced complex humanitarian emergencies (CHEs) that require the cooperation of military and civilian agencies for their resolution. CIMIC (civil–military cooperation) has become the shorthand for such cooperation. Apart from contributing to multidimensional peace support operations, CIMIC has been tried in other complex emergency situations stemming from natural disasters as well.

The purpose of this chapter is to expand on Christopher Ankersen's introduction by elaborating on the concept of CIMIC and on its link to a minimalist and maximalist (Min–Max) notion of human security. Throughout the chapter, the focus is decidedly on Canadian CIMIC operations for three reasons. First, Canada has been one of the global leaders in cultivating military–civilian relationships to deal with CHEs and other crises. Second, the Canadian government is a leading proponent of the human security norm and has tried explicitly to make that norm integral to its foreign and defence policy. Third, Canadian praxis in theatres of conflict and post-conflict situations – its experimentation with 3D strategies (defence, diplomacy, development) and its attempt to make the emerging

Responsibility to Protect (R2P) norm more robust at the international level – offers an interesting laboratory for testing out the claim of a linkage between CIMIC and human security. But first, let's begin by addressing the questions: what exactly is CIMIC, and what is its relationship to human security?

CIMIC and the link to human security

The answer to the first question may vary depending on whether it is being provided by someone in the military or by someone in the civilian sector. A military official would probably maintain that CIMIC represents the military's support to civilian authorities, civilian populations, international and regional intergovernmental organizations (IGOs), and international and local non-governmental organizations (NGOs) to ensure the attainment of some specific *military* goal, during conflict and post conflict situations.[17] Clearly, according to this position, CIMIC's immediate and long term purpose is to help create and sustain conditions within a theatre of operations that are designed to support the achievement of a military force's objectives.

The immediate and long term goals of the military element in CIMIC are, of course, different from those of traditional military operations. Instead of war fighting to defeat an enemy, military personnel attached to CIMIC are tasked, first and foremost, with protecting the local population and individuals working with civilian humanitarian agencies in conflict and post conflict settings. From the military's standpoint, this can involve the utilization of intelligence, surveillance, target acquisition, and reconnaissance (ISTAR) tools, communications personnel, psychological operations (PsyOps), and civilian police, when needed. For CIMIC, it is important to achieve military success with as little costs as possible in civilian lives and with as little damage to the target country's infrastructure. The optimal way of achieving this is for the military arm of CIMIC to engage in active cooperation with international and local civilian counterparts and to establish goodwill, trust and credibility with local civilian authorities and various local groups in the target state, while at the same time gathering information that will be useful to the military mission. As shall be shown later on in this chapter, attaining those goals is not an easy task.

For many in the civilian sector, CIMIC's preoccupation with achieving some military goal is problematic. Furthermore, they are wary of the military's new penchant to expand the scope of its activities to include humanitarian tasks in what is now being called "multidimensional peace support operations."[3] For these civilian groups, CIMIC represents nothing more than a necessary evil, an unhealthy compromise, and potentially problematic scenarios that could lead to undermining humanitarian activity. In their opinion, collaboration and cooperation with the military is less than ideal and could, in fact, blur the lines between coercive and humanitarian missions. However, given the complexities of current conflict and post-conflict situations, civilian groups have little choice but to accept the presence of the military because getting humanitarian assistance to local populations requires the kind of security that only the military can offer. The military is therefore seen as a necessary, but not always welcomed, partner that paves the way by providing a semblance of security – a protected corridor through which humanitarian assistance can get through to the local population unimpeded. As such, CIMIC, for these individuals, represent an uneasy partnership between a specific unit of the military and civilian humanitarian groups.

Of course, CIMIC is much more complicated than either of the above two positions allow. As Michael Pugh reminds us, CIMIC "can be represented in several dimensions: relations between external military forces and internal civilian authorities/society; between internal regular/irregular forces and external civilian agencies; and between the external military and civilian components of interventions."[5]

The need for CIMIC can be traced to the geopolitical changes that occurred immediately after the Cold War ended. While a number of proxy wars were brought to an end with the culmination of Cold War tensions between the then two superpowers, the United States and the Soviet Union, the phenomenon of weak states and failed or failing states meant a proliferation of internal armed conflicts that placed large numbers of civilians at risk. With the state's monopoly over the means of violence lost, in several instances, rebel groups and irregular forces took advantage of the situation to create conditions of human insecurity. Unlike traditional conflicts in which soldiers on opposing sides battled for supremacy, and in which civilians sometimes got caught in the crossfire, in post-Cold War intra-state conflicts innocent civilians became deliberate targets in many cases. Children were recruited as soldiers or to be part of rebel militia.[6] In some cases, these intra-state conflicts led to genocide, massacres, ethnic cleansing and other egregious forms of human rights abuse, the temporary or permanent displacement of large numbers of people, the systematic rape of women, and complex humanitarian crises. The international community could not stand idly by and allow this situation to continue.

In the early 1990s, this concern led to calls for outside intervention to protect innocent people living within countries torn apart by violence and to put a halt to the spill-over effects of such conflicts. The Report of the International Commission on Intervention and State Sovereignty put it this way:

> In an interdependent world, in which security depends on a framework of stable sovereign entities, the existence of fragile states, failing states, states who through weakness or ill-will harbour those dangerous to others, or states that can only maintain internal order by means of gross human rights violations, can constitute a risk to people everywhere.[7]

Underpinning those calls for intervention was a "new" norm in international relations – "the responsibility to protect" (R2P) norm which lent credence to the fledging but growing norm of "human security." This chapter argues that the development of CIMIC, at least the Canadian version, is an attempt to add robustness to both the R2P and human security norms.

Evolution of the human security norm

The concept of human security was proposed and popularized in the first half of the 1990s, at a time when there was much optimism about the transition from the old world order of the Cold War to a "new world order." There was also much talk, at that time, of a peace dividend in which security, defined as both "freedom from want" as well as "freedom from fear," would be enhanced.[8] This people-centered concept, human security, pushed vigorously onto the international stage in the early 1990s by the United Nations Development Programme (UNDP) and by Canada's foreign minister at the time, Lloyd Axworthy, provided an alternative to the Westphalian norm of state security.

This paradigm shift away from the traditional state-centric conceptualization of security rested on the realization that some states were unable or unwilling to protect their citizens from harm. In fact, some states have been charged with being directly responsible for the insecurity felt by their citizens and therefore cannot be trusted to provide security for those living under their jurisdiction. Furthermore, in many of the intra-state conflicts, "the antagonists were frequently gangs and/or private militias rather than standing national armies."[9] The solution to this problem, offered by individuals like Axworthy, was to "put people first" in matters of security, i.e. moving the security referent away from the state to the individual.[10] It also meant using traditional and non-traditional tools and strategies to address this problem.

Genesis of the human security concept

While the term "human security" may be of relatively recent origin, the ideas that underpin it are far from new. For more than a century – at least since the founding of the International Committee of the Red Cross in the 1860s – a doctrine based on the security of people has been gathering momentum. Core elements of this doctrine were formalized in the 1940s with the UN Charter, the Universal Declaration of Human Rights (UDHR), the four Geneva Conventions and the two additional Protocols on international humanitarian law in armed conflict, and the Convention on the Prevention and Punishment of the Crime of Genocide; in the 1960s with the twin Covenants on civil, political and social rights and economic and cultural rights; and in the late 1990s with the adoption of the Rome Statute that established the International Criminal Court (ICC).

In 1993 a United Nations Development Programme (UNDP) Report listed "New concepts of human security" as one of five pillars of "a people-centered world order" which "must stress the security of people, not only of nations." According to that report, "The concept of security must change from an exclusive stress on national security to a much greater stress on people's security, from security through armaments to security through human development, from territorial security to food, employment and environmental security."[11] However, the term "human security" is most commonly associated with the 1994 UNDP Human Development Report, which had as one of its explicit goals the attempt to capture the post-Cold War "peace dividend" and redirect those resources towards the development agenda. The human security definition advanced in that report was extremely ambitious. Human security was defined as the summation of seven distinct dimensions of security: economic, food, health, environmental, personal, community and political.[12] By focusing on people and highlighting non-traditional threats, the UNDP report made an important contribution to expanding post-Cold War thinking about security.

The very breadth of the UNDP approach to human security (i.e. freedom from fear and freedom from want), however, made it unwieldy as a policy instrument.[13] With such a large laundry list of threats, policy makers would have to devise multiple, diverse and, at times, incompatible sets of policy solutions to resolve them.[14] There was also a criticism that the 1994 UNDP Report, in emphasizing the threats associated with underdevelopment, largely ignored the continuing human insecurity resulting from violent conflict. It was evident that, even using the UNDP's own criteria, human insecurity peaked during war, and particularly during intra-state conflicts.[15] So although attempts were made during the preparatory stages of the 1995 Copenhagen Summit on Social Development to make the UNDP concept of human security a mainstream one, those efforts were rejected and the concept seemed to fizzle, at least temporarily.

However, with the outbreak of clan violence in Somalia (1992–93), internecine slaughter in Bosnia (1992–95), genocide in Rwanda (1994), and attempts at ethnic cleansing in Kosovo (1997–99), preoccupation with human security reemerged. This time, practice led theory. In the case of Somalia it was clear that brute force was not going to bring an end to the violent clashes between armed clans. The US military was forced to withdraw from that country on 31 March 1994 after eighteen US military personnel were killed and some of the dead were ignominiously paraded through the streets of Mogadishu the previous October. By 1995, the United Nations (UN) also withdrew its peacekeepers from Somalia, raising grave concerns about human insecurity in that country.[16] The failure of the international community, as represented by the UN, to prevent the massacre of thousands of civilians in Srebrenica again revived the notion of the need for human security.

But it was the genocide in Rwanda and the resultant humanitarian catastrophe (with over 800,000 Tutsi and moderate Hutus dead) that brought human security from the back burner to the front of the international community's agenda. The UN's inaction was heavily criticized and many countries made pledges that something like this should never again happen. Lloyd Axworthy, in an autobiography account, recalls that what happened in Rwanda "led me inexorably to my decision to support military intervention in Kosovo ... to stop what had become a massive case of ethnic cleansing of the majority of the Muslim population."[17] In fact, it was the Canadian government, with Lloyd Axworthy's leadership as foreign minister that led the way in making the human security norm operational.[18]

The Canadian government played a leading role in operationalizing human security with: the Ottawa Process – an initiative to ban antipersonnel landmines (instruments that inflict human suffering even after wars are over),[19] with the Report on the International Commission on Intervention and State Sovereignty and the elevation of the resulting norm of "responsibility to protect" (R2P), and with its contribution to the establishment of the ICC – a legal mechanism for holding individuals accountable for war crimes and crimes against humanity.[20] Each of those cases represents an attempt to introduce measures that are practical, powerful applications of the concept of human security.

In essence, therefore, human security has come to mean protecting people from both violent and non-violent threats. It is a state of being that can be characterized as freedom from pervasive threats to people's rights, their safety, and even their lives. Rather than focusing exclusively on the security of a territorial state, human security represents a paradigm shift that requires a refocusing on the security of the citizens within the state. It entails taking practical, preventive measures to reduce or eliminate the vulnerability of human beings and "taking remedial action when prevention fails."[21]

The Min–Max conceptual scale of human security

The evolution of the human security norm is best depicted as a notion placed on a minimum-maximum (Min–Max) sliding scale. The 1994 UNDP definition states that human security is the provision of safety to people from "chronic threats and protection from sudden hurtful disruptions in the patterns of daily life." This can be interpreted as a fairly narrow concept. But the Report also went on to elaborate on the various components of what would constitute "threats" to human beings, and in doing so it revealed a much broader conception of human security.[22]

Confirming that broad conception of human security, UN Secretary-General Kofi Annan called on the world community, at the United Nations Millennium Summit, to advance the twin goals of "freedom from want" and "freedom from fear." As a contribution to the further advancement of this effort, the Commission on Human Security (CHS) was established on the initiative of the Government of Japan. It was co-chaired by Sadako Ogata, former UN High Commissioner for Refugees and Amartya Sen, Nobel Laureate and Master of Trinity College, Cambridge, and had three distinct goals:

1   to promote public understanding, engagement and support of human security and its underlying imperatives;
2   to develop the concept of human security as an operational tool for policy formulation and implementation; and
3   to propose a concrete program of action to address critical and pervasive threats to human security.[23]

CIMIC can be considered an operational tool that can advance human security.

The definition of human security used in the 2003 CHS report demonstrates the breadth of the human security agenda, according to this body. For the members of the CHS, human security meant the protection of people's vital freedoms.[24] This included protecting people from critical and pervasive threats and situations and creating systems that would give people the building blocks of not only of survival, but also of dignity and livelihood. To accomplish this, the Commission offered two general strategies: protection and empowerment. "Protection shields people from dangers. Empowerment enables people to develop their potential and become full participants in decision-making."[25] As will be shown later, the Canadian CIMIC, by its actions, has striven to meet the Min–Max human security objectives of protection and empowerment.

Some academics agree with the broad formulation of the human security concept. For instance, Caroline Thomas posits that "The concept of human security involves a fundamental departure from an orthodox" international relations security analysis. She argues that human security goes far beyond the notions of "security of the individual." In her words:

> human security describes a condition of existence in which basic material needs are met, and in which human dignity, including meaningful participation in the life of the community can be realized. Human security is oriented towards an active and substantive notion of democracy, one that ensures opportunity of all for participation in decisions that affect their lives. Therefore, it is engaged directly with discussions of democracy at all levels, from the local to the global. Such human security is indivisible; it cannot be pursued by or for one group at the expense of another.[26]

The poor state of human security in Africa is blamed, for example, on the failure of some governments to adhere to the principles of democracy, failure to respect human rights and failure to implement good political, economic and corporate governance.[27]

The broad concept of human security was also adopted by the International Commission on Intervention and State Sovereignty (ICISS). According to that Commission's Report, "Human security means the security of people – their physical safety, their economic and social well-being, respect for their dignity and worth as human beings, and the protection of their human rights and fundamental freedoms."[28] And, the Canadian government initially subscribed to the Max end of the scale with respect to the human security concept and praxis. In fact the Canadian government adopted human security as a central part of its foreign policy in the mid to late 1990s. Its notion of human security was "premised on the need to enhance and promote human rights, to strengthen humanitarian law, to prevent conflicts, and to foster democracy and good governance."[29] Later, however, the Canadian government would proffer a conception of human security that was both broad and narrow.

Lloyd Axworthy best depicts that Min–Max position when he stated that human security

> is much more than the absence of military threat. It includes security against economic privation, an acceptable quality of life and a guarantee of fundamental human rights. This concept of human security recognizes the complexity of the human environment and accepts that the forces influencing human security are interrelated and mutually reinforcing. At a

minimum, human security requires that basic needs are met, but it also acknowledges that sustained economic development, human rights and fundamental freedoms, the rule of law, good governance, sustainable development and social equity are as important to global peace as arms control and disarmament.[30]

Thus for the Canadian government, the scope of the human security concept was both narrow and broad. However, in practice, the Canadian government more recently seems to have chosen to focus its Human Security Agenda on the personal (physical) security dimension (the Minimum end of the scale), in part to make it more distinct from the concept of human development (the Maximum end of the scale) and to permit a sharper concentration on issues that seem to cry out for immediate international attention. Yet, while the Canadian government took the lead in developing the human security concept as "freedom from fear (violence)" it also saw that maximalist position as a complement to the concept of "freedom-from-want." In part, advancing the narrower definition may have been a sincere recognition of the difficulty of translating the UNDP's broad notion of human security into actual concrete policies that would protect individuals.

This is not to imply that Canada abandoned the maximalist notion of human security. One can argue that policy makers in Canada (and elsewhere) quickly came to the realization that the advancement of human rights and human development can best be achieved when people are first protected from violent threats to their lives.[31] Without the guarantee of physical protection from violent conflict, the chances of meeting broader human needs will be, at best, slim.

According to the *Human Security Report* 2005 most proponents of human security agree that its primary goal ought to be first and foremost the protection of individuals. However, according to this report, consensus has tended to "break down over what threats individuals should be protected from."[32] Proponents of the "narrower" concept of human security, which underpins that particular *Human Security Report*, focus on dealing first and foremost with violent threats to individuals, while at the same time recognizing that these threats can be linked to poverty, lack of state capacity and various forms of socio-economic and political inequity. It is this recognition of the Min–Max element of human security that allows states and the international community to develop a range of policies to address the whole gamut of what is now considered "human security." The introduction of CIMIC can be seen as an attempt to develop a flexible policy instrument in support of this Min–Max scale on which the concept of human security rests.

CIMIC: the early beginnings

Like "human security," the notion of civilian and military cooperation is not completely new. It was part of the Allied armies' strategy during the Second World War. But, as Sean Pollick puts it: "cooperation with civilians was oriented primarily towards preventing them from interfering with, or becoming victims of the Allied armies."[33] This type of military–civilian relationship was top-down, with the military being on top. First generation UN peacekeepers did not have to contend with military–civilian cooperation. These early UN peace-keepers were interpositional forces that stood between two warring factions (mostly governments) and kept the peace long enough for them to get to the bargaining table. There was very little interaction with the population whom these peacekeepers were protecting.

However, since the end of the Cold War, the situation has changed significantly, as the nature of war was transformed. Intrastate conflicts have produced complex humanitarian emergencies that require the presence and assistance of both military and civilian organizations. In the past couple of decades, specific CIMIC military units have been formally recognized to facilitate military–civilian cooperation in those instances. Again, Canada has taken a lead in this.

The idea of CIMIC from a Canadian military's perspective boils down to "the resources and the arrangements that support the relationship between commanders and non-military agencies in areas where the Canadian Forces elements are, or will be operating, in order to assist in the pursuit of a military objective."[34] From the Canadian military perspective, CIMIC is about "winning the hearts and minds of the people" of a target community in which the military has an operation. These missions are usually complex in that they involve providing basic security while at the same time trying to deal with humanitarian issues. The ultimate objective of the military in such scenarios is to make the security/humanitarian mission as seamless as possible for the commander to do his/her job.

The early beginnings of Canadian CIMIC operations can best be described as ad hoc and as a "secondary duty" with military personnel in charge of such operations having little or no specific formal training in civil–military relations.[35] The first Canadian CIMIC cell was introduced in 1997 and since then we have witnessed a systematization of Canadian CIMIC operations. Now, each division of the Canadian Armed Forces has a CIMIC cell – using under Information operations or PsyOps. Basic CIMIC training in Canada was initially conducted at the Pearson Peacekeeping Centre, formerly located in Cornwallis, Nova Scotia, and later offered at the Canadian Forces Base (CFB) at Kingston, Ontario. Individuals recruited for CIMIC operations are generally over thirty years of age with lots of experience and excellent people and communication skills.

CIMIC Detachments meet on a regular basis for training exercises in communications, report writing, conflict management, conflict resolution, negotiations, cross-cultural communications, project management, dealing with contracts, construction and renovation, and improvement of basic time management skills. They also get background training on how to deal with local and international non-governmental organizations that are providing humanitarian assistance in conflict or post-conflict situations. Recently, a CIMIC Directorate was created in Edmonton, Alberta to oversee the preparation and deployment of CIMIC personnel to overseas missions, and there are prospects for the creation of new CIMIC teams in other regions of the country.[36]

Source: Department of National Defence, 2006.

The Canadian CIMIC personnel who are sent off to support peace operations abroad have counterparts in Canada – G9 Liaison officers. These officers provide assistance to civilian authorities in Canada during times of high emergency (e.g. major floods, ice storms, and forest fires). Just like the CIMIC personnel who work in emergency situations in far away lands, the G9 Liaison officers are also cognisant of the need to maintain close relations between the military and civilian, federal, provincial, municipal and non-governmental bodies that may be needed to provide assistance to people during times of crisis.[37]

The Canadian Forces utilizes primarily Army Reservists for CIMIC tasks. As Captain Mark Giles put it, this concept has worked well primarily "because Reservists bring a wealth of civilian experience to the table."[38] The ROTO 11 CIMIC team in Bosnia included a public works manager, a civilian police officer, telecommunications specialists, and a financial planner, who were all Reservists from Canada. Their civilian credentials allowed them to work closely with local authorities and NGOs operating in Bosnia to provide assistance in several infrastructure projects.

At a tactical level, Canadian CIMIC operations (whether at home or overseas), are concerned with three core functions that are all in support of the Min end of the human security scale. These functions are: (1) Civil–Military liaison and assessments; (2) support of the force; (3) support of the civilian environment.[39]

In the case of the first core function, military commanders attached to CIMIC are made aware of any local activities that could influence the military mission in a peace support operation. These commanders are advised of their responsibilities towards the civilian population. This function also entails making continuous assessments of the local civil environment and the local needs to see where the CIMIC unit can be of most help. It also requires the military to work towards establishing goodwill, trust and credibility with local authorities and building good working relations with all international civilian humanitarian groups that are working in the target country.

The second core function involves drumming up maximum civilian support for the timely entrance of the military into the target area, the conduct of operations and the eventual orderly withdrawal of the military once the primary task of security has been accomplished. At the same time, the CIMIC unit would try to reduce, to the extent possible, any attempts at civilian interference in operational matters related to the security function of the military (e.g. force protection), especially when working in a high threat environment, realizing that this could of course cause some tensions between the local civilian population and the intruding military force. This is a clear reminder that Canadian CIMIC units have to be mindful of the primary importance of the military mission, even though what it is doing is in support of human security.

The third core function relies on the ability of the CIMIC unit to obtain sufficient financial and other resources that would facilitate the proper execution of the CIMIC operation and bring some normalcy back to the target population. According to some CIMIC personnel attached to the Canadian military in Afghanistan, this function is especially tough because of the difficulty in securing funding. Most of the official development assistance (ODA) funding for Canadian CIMIC operations comes from CIDA. Anyone who has tried to obtain funding from CIDA would know that the process of doing so is not an easy one. Many in the Canadian CIMIC units have complained about the large amount of excessive paperwork that must be completed before CIDA dispenses with funds for humanitarian assistance work.

Canadian CIMIC in action

In spite of the funding challenges, Canadian CIMIC personnel have made important contributions in support of the Min–Max concept of human security. Canadian troops have successfully delivered over 1.8 million dollars worth of assistance on behalf of the Canadian International Development Agency (CIDA) between 1996 and 2000.[40] When one examines the nature of some of these projects, one realizes fairly quickly that Canadian CIMIC personnel and CIDA funding support a very broad interpretation of human security. Some of the projects include: street sign improvements; the building of veterinarian clinics; a new roof for a building that house the Red Cross; electrical wiring for reconstructed homes; re-establishing water supply to villages; sewer improvements and assistance to help a community acquire their own fire truck; actually working with local fire-fighters to fight fires; assisting with local and regional governments with economic development; and working with locals to establish a number of social projects in education, public health and sports.

The Kosovo experience offers some examples of Canadian CIMIC at work.

In 1999, The Canadian CIMIC cell of one PPCLI Battle Group in Kosovo iden-tified a specific need of the local community to decontaminate wells in Glogo-vac. The CIMIC unit searched out the most appropriate NGO to assist with this task and then obtained funding to accomplish it. CIMIC members found that the International Committee of the Red Cross (ICRC) was willing to do the job. Then they contacted CIDA for funds to complete the task. This example illus-trates that CIMIC, in practice, acts most times as facilitator, enabler and coordi-nator of human security-type projects.

In Rwanda, a Canadian CIMIC unit worked closely with a lead civilian agency and the United Nations Development Program (UNDP) to coordinate the delivery of close to 200 tons of humanitarian relief supplies by CC-130 to Rwandan refugees.[41] In March 2004, Canadian Forces CIMIC deployed ten personnel to Haiti. Their role was to provide a link between the NGOs operating in that country and the military. Since local and international NGO personnel were taking an enormous risk working in the hostile Haitian environment, the Canadian military brought the issue of security to the negotiating table. While the Canadian military forces provided security, the CIMIC unit utilized its resources and money to assist local groups and NGOs with their humanitarian projects. The Canadian embassy provided $50,000 to CIMIC to be used for aid. With this money, CIMIC personnel were able to establish conditions in which NGOs could continue to deliver their relief aid and assistance to the local population.

CIMIC also performed community impact projects such as: building tanks for clean drinking water; building desks for schools; and basic garbage clean up. According the Captain Jason Watt, this particular CIMIC deployment turned out to be a very effective one and NGOs cooperated well with the unit. This cooper-ation may in part be due to the fact that NGOs were operating in conditions of high security risk. In order to perform their tasks, they needed the protection of the military. It seems that the higher the security risk the greater the likelihood of cooperation from NGOs with the military, and CIMIC units help to facilitate that cooperation.[42]

Between May and July of 2004, Canadian CIMIC personnel completed the reconstruction of the main police station in Chahar Asiab that had laid in ruins for many years due to the civil conflict in Afghanistan. In this particular case, the CIMIC officers worked closely with the local Governor, Shir Mohammed, and Chief of Police in Kabul in identifying the need to reestablish one of the symbols of societal order. Once the project was chosen, the Canadian CIMIC organization connected the Canadian Forces (CF) with local contractors and authorities. The CF provided the needed funding for the reconstruction of the police station and in a short space of time CIMIC's collaboration with civilian authorities and com-panies paid off as another small step was taken to bring a semblance of order and security to that region of Afghanistan.[43] You should note that between 2003–2005, Canadian CIMIC teams completed 344 projects in Afghanistan and 204 were either planned or on-going at the time this paper was written.[44]

Also in Afghanistan, as the members of the 3rd Battalion, The Royal Cana-dian Regiment Battalion Group (3 RCR Bn Gp) prepared to rotate home after six months in-theatre, they took part in a medical civil–military cooperation (CIMIC) project that provided an ambulance for a local clinic – the Chardehi Poly Medical Clinic.[45] In March 2006, a Canadian CIMIC unit worked closely with the Task Force Kabul Force Protection Company to erect a much needed middle school – the Garzagah School – in Kabul. It involved working with the local community to rebuild a building that had been left in ruins because of the many years of civil war in Afghanistan. Since the school building was not large enough for the 4,000 or so students, the Canadian CIMIC team added a number of modular tents on the property "to provide an environment in which the children can focus on learning, protected from the elements and shielded from the destruction that lies outside."[46] Captain David Myles notes that the most frequent request of the Canadian CIMIC by the village elders, local mullahs and mayors in Afghanistan has been for schools to be repaired so that children could have a place to go to become educated.[47]

In February 2006, a Canadian CIMIC team attached to Operation ATHENA visited the Allahudin Orphanage to deliver much-needed blankets, pillows, clothing, toys and school supplies that were donated by generous Canadians. Operations ATHENA is Canada's contribution to the International Security and Assistance Force (ISAF) whose primary mission is to help maintain security in Kabul and its surrounding areas so that the process of reconstruction can continue in Afghanistan. The delivery of humanitarian aid to the orphanage was considered an important way to build trust with the Afghan people and thus make it easier for them to accept the presence of an external military presence. Captain Mark Gough puts it this way:

> Distributing toys and clothes might seem like a small gesture, but it means a great deal to the young Afghan orphans who receive these items. It also goes a long way in building bridges between the Canadian military and the Afghan community in which we live and work.[48]

The few illustrations above indicate that Canada's CIMIC units are engaged in putting flesh on the bones of the Min–Max concept of human security. These units, because they are attached to the military, cannot help but be concerned with protecting people in troubled areas, first and foremost, from physical harm (freedom from fear). This task is viewed by Canadian CIMIC personnel as vital and necessary in order for them to be able to engage in helping to meet those people's basic material needs in a way that would bring dignity and worth back to those individuals (freedom from want). In this sense, CIMIC, at least the Canadian version, is about implementing the Min–Max concept of human security.

Conclusion

CIMIC is short hand for civil–military cooperation. Such cooperation is needed desperately to address the complex humanitarian emergencies that stem from post-Cold War conflicts. These, primarily intra-state conflicts tend to put people living in the theatre of conflict at great risk and usually create major humanitarian crises. Military intervention may be needed in the short term to address the level of insecurity and bring some order and security to a hostile environment. But the military alone cannot properly address this situation of human insecurity. This is why large numbers of IGOs and NGOs have become involved in the CHEs that stem from these conflicts. The military is thus faced with having to work along-side a variety of civil actors.

This civil–military cooperation is not easy. As shown above, Canadian CIMIC units go beyond the military's mission of providing security to target populations. They engage in humanitarian work as well, thus blurring the lines between military and humanitarian work. Canadian CIMIC units are indeed con-tributing, through praxis, to realizing the Min–Max goals of human security. But in doing so, CIMIC units sometimes find themselves at odds with civilian humanitarian groups and with the civilian local population. As we have noticed recently in Afghanistan, while Canadian CIMIC personnel are trying to win the hearts and minds of the local people, the rest of the Canadian military is involved in a coercive anti-terrorism/anti-Taliban exercise that threatens the lives of local Afghan civilians. When this happens, unfortunately all of the good work done by CIMIC units in the area of human security becomes undone by coercive acts that actually create human insecurity.

Notes

1 Dr. W. Andy Knight is Professor of International Relations at the University of Alberta, Edmonton, Canada. The author wishes to thank Amanda Chisholm for her research assistance and for conducting personal interviews with Canadian military personnel attached to CIMIC in Afghanistan. The following individuals provided useful first hand information or important primary documents about the Canadian CIMIC operations in Afghanistan, Bosnia and Kosovo: Sgt. Matthew Kirkpatrick, Captain David Myles, Captain Jason Watt, Lauryn Oates, Captain Peter Avis and Eric Cameron of Canadian Department of National Defence, Public Affairs.

2 William S. Lind, "Strategic Defence Initiative," The American Conservative (November 22, 2004). Online, available at: www.defense-and-society.org/lind/lind_strategic_defense.htm, accessed on January 20, 2007.

3 Major A. Demers, "To Help or not to help – CIMIC and Project Management," *The Bulletin*, The Army Lessons Learned Centre, Canada, vol. 11, no. 1 (February 2005), p. 2.

4 Meinrad Studer, "The ICRC and Civil–Military relations in armed conflict," *IRRC*, vol. 83, no. 842 (June 2001), p. 367.

5 Michael Pugh, "Civil–Military Relations in Peace Support Operations: hegemony or emancipation?" Seminar on Aid and Politics, London (1 February 2001. Online, available at: www.odi.org.uk/hpg/confpapers/pugh.pdf, accessed on January 17, 2007.

6 www.waraffectedchildren.gc.ca/menu-en.asp, accessed on December 20, 2006.

7 International Commission on Intervention and State Sovereignty (ICISS), *The Responsibility to Protect*, Report of the International Commission on Intervention and State Sovereignty (Ottawa: International Development Research Centre, December 2001), p.5.

8 For a good discussion of the debates about the use and abuse of the human security concept, see Sandra J. MacLean, David Black and Timothy M. Shaw (eds), *A Decade of Human Security: Global Governance and New Multilateralisms* (Hampshire: Ashgate Publishing Ltd., 2006).

9 Sandra J. MacLean, David Black and Timothy M. Shaw (eds), *A Decade of Human Security*, p. 4 and Ian Smillie and Larry Minear, *The Charity of Nations: Humanitarian Action in a Calculating World* (Bloomfield, CT: Kumarian, 2004).

10 Lloyd Axworthy, "Human Security and Global Governance: Putting People First," *Global Governance*, vol. 7, no. 1 (2001), 19–23.

11 United Nations Development Programme, *Human Development Report 1993.* Online, available at: hdr.undp.org/reports/global/1993/en/, accessed on December 5, 2005, 2.

12 United Nations Development Programme (UNDP), *Human Development Report 1994* (New York: UNDP, 1994).

13 See DFAIT, "Human Security: Safety for People in a Changing World," Department of Foreign Affairs and International Trade Canada, Ottawa, April 1999, p. 3, and Tom Keating, "The Promise and Pitfalls of Human Security," paper presented at the Canadian Political Science Association Annual Meeting, Quebec City (2000). Also see Roland Paris, "Human Security: Paradigm Shift or Hot Air?" *International Security*, vol. 26, no. 2 (2001), 87–102, and Yuen Foong Khong, "Human Security: A Shotgun Approach to Alleviating Human Misery?" *Global Governance*, vol. 7, no. 3 (2001), 231–6.

14 Heather Owens and Barbara Arneil, "The Human Security Paradigm Shift: A New Lens on Canadian Foreign Policy? Report of the University of British Columbia Symposium on Human Security," in Majid Tehranian (ed.), *Worlds Apart: Human Security and Global Governance* (London: I.B. Tauris, 1999), 2.

15 If one takes a look at the 25 countries that sit at the bottom of the 1998 Human Development Index, it is evident that more than 50 per cent of them were suffering the direct or indirect effects of violent conflict. United Nations Development Programme, *Human Development Report 1998* (New York: UNDP, 1998).

16 W. Andy Knight and Kassu Gebremariam, "UN Intervention and Peacebuilding in Somalia: Constraints and Possibilities," in W. Andy Knight (ed.), *Adapting the United Nations to a Post Modern World: Lessons Learned* (Houndmills: Palgrave/Macmillan Press/St. Martin's Press, 2001), 77–94.

17 See Lloyd Axworthy, *Navigating a New World: Canada's Global Future* (Toronto: Alfred A. Knopf Canada, 2003), 162.

18 On this point see Fen Osler Hampson, Norman Hillmer and Maureen Appel Molot (eds), *Canada Among Nations: The Axworthy Legacy* (Don Mills, Ontario: Oxford University Press, 2001).

19 Andrew A. Latham, "Theorizing the Landmine Campaign: Ethics, Global Cultural Scripts, and the Laws of War," in Rosalind Irwin (ed.), *Ethics and Security in Canadian Foreign Policy* (Vancouver and Toronto: UBC Press, 2001), 160–78.

20 See www.dfait-maeci.gc.ca/foreign_policy/icc/canada_icc-en.asp#movement, accessed on January 30, 2007.

21 Canadian Ministry of Foreign Affairs, "Human Security: Safety for People in a Changing World," www.humansecurity.gc.ca/safety_changingworld-en.asp, accessed on September 24, 2006.

22 Walter Dorn, "Human Security: An Overview," (Ottawa: Pearson Peacekeeping Centre and National Defence, Canada, Royal Military College, 2001). Online, available at: www.rmc.ca/academic/gradrech/dorn24_e.html#e2, accessed on December 1, 2006.

23 See www.humansecurity-chs.org/about/Establishment.html, accessed on November 7, 2006.

24 See *Final Report of the Commission on Human Security*, 2003. Online, available at: www.humansecurity-chs.org/finalreport/index.html, accessed on November 5, 2006, 2–4.

25 See the UN Commission on Human Security, "Outline of the Report of the Commission on Human Security." Online, available at: www.humansecurity-chs.org/finalreport/Outlines/outline.pdf, accessed on August 29, 2006.

26 Thomas, Caroline, "Global Governance and Human Security," in R. Wilkinson and S. Hughes (eds), *Global Governance: Critical Perspectives* (London: Routledge, 2002), 114–15.

27 Mpho Mashaba, "African Human Security Initiative and its role in NEPAD: Carving a niche for the Medi. Online, available at: www.africanreview.org/docs/papers/work-shopnepad.pdf, accessed on January 19, 2007.

28 International Commission on Intervention and State Sovereignty (ICISS), *The Responsibility to Protect*, p. 15.

29 W. Andy Knight, "Soft Power, Moral Suasion, and Establishing the International Criminal Court: Canadian Contributions," in Rosalind Irwin (ed.), *Ethics and Security in Canadian Foreign Policy* (Vancouver and Toronto: UBC Press, 2001), 130.

30 Lloyd Axworthy, "Canada and Human Security: The Need for Leadership," *International Journal*, vol. 5, no. 2 (Spring 1997), 184.

31 Foreign Affairs and International Trade Canada, Human Security. Online, available at: www.humansecurity.gc.ca/menu-en.asp, accessed on January 10, 2007.

32 Andrew Mack, Director of the Human Security Centre, released the report in October 2005. See www.humansecurityreport.info/component/option,com_frontpage/Itemid, 1/ accessed on December 5, 2006.

33 Sean Pollick, "Civil Military Cooperation," *Canadian Military Journal* (Autumn 2000), p. 58.

34 M.K. Jeffery, "Lessons Learned in Civil–Military Cooperation (CIMIC)" *Dispatches* vol. 5 no. 3 (February 1999).

35 LCol. G.G. McLean, G9 *Briefing Note Civil Military Co-Operation (CIMIC)*, www.army.dnd.ca (September 2003), accessed on December 12, 2006.

36 For more information see Department of National Defence, "LFWA CIMIC Detachment." Online, available at: www.army.forces.gc.ca/lfwa_hq/LFWA_CIMIC.htm, accessed on January 1, 2007.

37 www.army.forces.gc.ca/lf/english/6_1_1.asp?FlashEnabled=0&id=362, accessed on January 20, 2007.

38 Capt. Mark Giles, "Army Reservists deliver CIMIC expertise in Bosnia." Online, available at: www.forces.gc.ca/site/Feature_Story/2003/feb03/13_f_e.asp, accessed on January 12, 2007.

39 Major A. Demers, "To Help or not to help – CIMIC and Project Management," pp. 2–3.

40 Stacey Douglas, "Towards a Comprehensive Canadian CIMIC Doctrine: Interagency Cooperation and the Influence of Allies in the Balkans," *Canadian Military Journal* (November 12, 2002).

41 M.K. Jeffery, "Lessons Learned in Civil–Military Cooperation."

42 Interview with Captain Jason Watt.

43 Department of National Defence, "Canadian CIMIC Completes Renovation of Chahar Asiab Police Station.". Online, available at: www.forces.gc.ca/site/Feature_Story/2004/jul04/16_f_e.asp, accessed on January 30, 2007.

44 Interviews with Canadian CIMIC personnel, February 2007.

45 See full story at www.forces.gc.ca/site/Feature_Story/2004/feb04/25_f_e.asp, accessed on January 12, 2007.

46 Private Jaimee Penney and Warrant Officer Jim Kolar, "Canadian soldiers give hope to Kabul students," Department of National Defence, Canada. Online, available at: www.forces.gc.ca/site/Feature_Story/2005/04/tents_f_e.asp, accessed on January 12, 2007.

47 Interview with Captain David Myles.

48 Capt Mark Gough, "Canadians help local orphanage," Department of National Defence. Online, available at: www.forces.gc.ca/site/Feature_Story/2005/03/cimic_f_e.asp, accessed on January 12, 2007.

3 Managing territories with rival brothers

The geopolitical stakes of military–humanitarian relations

Yann Braem

Recent military operations have demonstrated the importance of the deployment of both humanitarian and military actors. It can be gratifying for politicians, military decision-makers, and ordinary citizens to see images of one's soldiers helping humanitarian actors in the alleviation of humanity's suffering, in places like Africa, the Balkans, and South West Asia. From afar, Western interventions seem subject to the deployment of "military–humanitarian packages", but the development of military–humanitarian linkages cannot only be treated solely as a media phenomenon. Academic literature has witnessed great reflection about this topic, examining its political economy (Weiss 1999a), its sociology (Miller 1999; Byman 2001) and its institutional architectures (Minear *et al.* 1999; Wheeler and Harmer 2006). Now, since humanitarian and military actions are a geographically situated set of actions,[1] these interactions would benefit from a geopolitical analysis. After all, war is above all an issue of power over geographical space. "Geography is of use in making war, first",[2] and humanitarian action seems to be of an increasing importance for armed forces in their diverse missions. This chapter will then analyse the territorial stakes of military–humanitarian interactions, following a geopolitical analytical framework.

Geopolitics, as it has been described by Yves Lacoste (2001), is a methodology that analyses rivalries in territories, in their spatial aspects, interconnecting social science and physical/human geography. The two main instruments used to make geopolitical analysis are differentiation in the levels of spatial analysis and the study of geopolitical representations. The study of a territorialised phenomenon aims to integrate the diverse levels as they appear – the scales of the district, the city, the province, the country and continents – and the interactions with other phenomenon, at these diverse levels, with a multi-scale mapping process. This kind of analysis is intended to examine actors' territorial strategies, and, thus, has to consider representations appearing at different levels. Representations are ideas, beliefs – right or wrong – that organise the real in the perception of actors and shape the discourse. That said, a geopolitical analysis of humanitarian-military relations would have to determine the stakes of each actor and the levels of the interactions between them, in order to figure out the various logics that lie behind them.

Afghanistan and Kosovo have been chosen as case studies because of the wide spectrum of military actions undergone there, but also because they represent a historical sequence in terms of civil–military conceptual development capacities. Of course, the nature of the interventions differs. NATO's Kosovo intervention has been described as the first "humanitarian war", while operations in Afghanistan are the consequence of an aggression on US homeland. In both cases, however, many humanitarian actions[3] and military missions have been performed hand-in-hand; evidence, perhaps, of the link between the two spheres of activity growing stronger. An analysis of the geopolitical function of military–humanitarian linkages illustrates how they contribute to a wide array of strategies for territorial management.[4] But these linkages also have to be analysed considering a broader perspective, and integrated into a global geopolitical analytical framework, where humanitarianism seems to be increasingly instrumentalised. The remaining interrogation, then, has to focus on whether the humanitarian system encourages and participates in this trend.

Humanitarian action at war and refugee containment in the Kosovo crisis

Kosovo was a "humanitarian war", but not only in the terms we used to understand it. Of course, one can argue that saving Kosovar Albanian lives by the use of force (air power in this case) is a humanitarian action in nature, in accordance with criteria adopted in 2000 by the International Commission on Intervention and State Sovereignty.[5] Before the bombing campaign (24th March to 11th June 1999), NATO placed a special emphasis on monitoring the humanitarian situation on the ground, hand-in-hand with OSCE Kosovo Verification Mission, and justified the war by the humanitarian imperative,[6] even if the reasons for entering in war with Serbia were various.[7]

Soon after the beginning of air strikes, a strong flow of refugees spilled outside Kosovo, mainly in Macedonia and Albania.[8] Refugees wanted to flee the bombings but were also expelled by Serbian military and paramilitary forces that aimed to regionalise the conflict, increase difficulties for NATO forces and expel the Albanian population, which offered support to the Kosovo Liberation Army (KLA or UCK in Albanian), according to classical insurgency theory. Therefore, refugee flow represented a considerable threat to the success of NATO member-states operating in the area as southern neighbouring countries represented key partners in the bombing campaign.[9] In Macedonia, the situation was dramatic, with internal tensions potentially leading to a clash between Slavs and Albanians. And in Albania, the weight of refugees arriving two short years after state collapse represented a concrete threat to regional stability. Furthermore, refugee flow undermined Alliance cohesion: some governments and publics asked whether it was preferable to stop the bombings, first to focus on providing help to these victims, and secondly as it seemed to have accelerated refugee flows. In this context of ethnic war, the centre of gravity of the political crisis occurring in Kosovo revolved historically around the question of the population.[10] Civilians represented targets or resources for belligerents, before they were used as a weapon by Serbian forces to defeat NATO, as refugee flow could potentially lead to a regional destabilisation.

Furthermore, this scenario had not been expected by UN humanitarian agencies: "UNHCR did not anticipate the size and speed of the exodus, nor could it reasonably be expected to do so" (UNHCR 2000: 6). Civilian agencies were thus unable to provide help, letting Albania and Macedonia face the problem, where degraded domestic logistical capacities justified NATO deployment for humanitarian purposes. From this perspective, we can view the humanitarian-military deployment in Albania and Macedonia as a direct response to a civil–military threat (civilians pushed out by Serbian forces in order to produce a political-military effect). Successive decisions were taken from the beginning of the flow, less than one week after the first bombings, in order to mobilise NATO capacities in the humanitarian sector,[11] institutionalised through a civil–military agreement between Sadako Ogata (United Nations High Commissioner for Refugees) and Javier Solana (Secretary-General of NATO) on the 14 April 1999. Civil–Military task-forces oriented armed forces towards the improvement of logistical capacities[12] and the construction of refugee camps, while civilian agencies were tasked to run the refugee camps and assist Kosovo Albanians hosted in families (Minear *et al.* 1999). NATO support consisted in enabling the delivery of humanitarian goods to refugee-receiving regions, and resettling them from areas where they were potentially representing a danger, and this constituted key human and political challenges.[13] From this perspective, military work in logistics and the construction of refugee-reception capacities,[14] represented political-military stakes, offering an opportunity to contain threats to regional instability inside the Yugoslav borders.

Provincial Reconstruction Teams (PRT) and "field" state building in Afghanistan

Another example of territorial management based on the military–humanitarian linkage can be cited with PRTs in Afghanistan. PRTs are civil–military units, composed of a limited number of soldiers (50 to 300 soldiers) in charge of security, and few civilians: diplomats and development agencies officers (USAID, DfID, GTZ, CIDA, etc. depending on the "nationality" of the PRT). Development officers and donors represented in PRTs can fund and support NGOs and local administrations to implement development projects. These units are fully multinational: composed of several nations, and but also integrate an Afghan Ministry of Interior (MoI) officer. Following Peter Vigo Jakobsen (2005), we could stress that PRTs are different from traditional CIMIC because their mission is to support the Afghan Government (the centre) in the provinces (the periphery), while traditional CIMIC work has to support the force commander.

The idea of setting up PRTs has first emerged in the US armed forces, when, after one year of presence in Afghanistan, they noticed that Kabul authorities had no effective control over their provinces. They justified this architecture based on the difficulties experienced by civilian reconstruction agencies in southern provinces, where degraded security prevented them from working. From this perspective, PRTs had to support the extension of central government's authority by protecting civilians and allowing them to work in every part of the country, which was considered as the first step in addressing Afghanistan's political fragmentation. This fragmentation can be described following three main geopolitical trends. First, it is the product of remnant political-military groups led by warlords, who still control the reality of power on the ground, pursuing their own autonomous goals, while having more or less integrated governing structures.[15] Second, fragmentation is also the product of the remaining Taleban, Hezb-e Islami and al-Qaeda forces, who have retained important capabilities to prevent international organisations and the Afghan government from gaining or maintaining effective control in many provinces (especially those areas near the Afghan–Pakistani border). And third, as a result of so many years of destruction, the country faces many difficulties with its networks of transport and communication, which has the effect of leaving even those local representatives who are loyal to the central government barely any capacity to take orders or to circulate, except within their own provinces. Given these challenges, international presence and help was deemed to be required in the provinces.

Addressing all of these challenges could have meant the deployment of tens of thousands of troops. However the international community was engaged in Afghanistan following a "light footprint" approach, for both civilians and armed forces. PRTs and their mobile units have had to gain ground in their area of operations from their initial location in urban centres, extending progressively the Afghan government presence through the support to reconstruction. In the international community's view, showing "peace dividends" to local population, in the form of quick impact projects, reconstruction work and an increased governmental presence are the only way to legitimise the Afghan administration – and marginalise spoilers and terrorists. The Afghan Ministry of Interior officer affiliated to most PRTs is, then, an important figure in the unit. He enjoys a "chairman-like" position on every subject concerning government policy in the provinces, modern communication tools to link directly with its hierarchy, and an important displacement capacity in the provinces, as he is embedded in the PRT structure. Dispersed throughout Afghan territory, these little units have their security assured by different means: the acceptance of local population and leaders, supposing a great deal of negotiations at the micro-level, in addition to the use of aerial support[16] and extraction capacities, in case of important threats.

However, this general presentation does not account for the extreme geographical flexibility of the PRT concept. There is no generalised or unified application of the PRT, insofar as their efficiency is seen as the direct result of their adaptation to ground realities. No formal PRT guidelines exist, at least at the level of composition, structure, or day-to-day operations.[17] Moreover, PRTs existed under two different mandates (Coalition Forces and ISAF) until NATO assumed control over the entire territory at the end of 2006, and are still staffed by a variety of nations, each developing its own conception of the mechanism. We can conclude from these points that the civil–military power-sharing is anything but precise. The fact that civilian actors are embedded in military units (except in the case of the German structure), and that PRTs are due to respect National Development Priorities defined by the Afghan government, does not translate into civil–military equilibrium, even where civilian elements are supposed to take the lead on civil issues. The "black box" of the decision process has not yet been opened, and its content could change following events, changes in the security situation or negotiations with local leaders. Letting a soldier (even a local one) chair the work of civil national agencies could in fact undermine the so-called democratic control over armed forces and demilitarisation of Afghan policy. This position could easily lead to a security-oriented development process, which is quite different from socio-economic development following human development indicators. As examples, in Northern Provinces, the Mazar-e Sharif PRT has decided to focus on Security Sector Reform, and has done it well with its partners (UNAMA, local security commission with warlords and local representatives, donors and NGOs). In Great Paktiya (Provinces of Paktika, Paktiya and Khost), the Gardez PRT in close collaboration with government representatives and UNAMA, has negotiated the local population's participation in the 2004 electoral process with tribal leaders. It was among the first time that UNAMA and government representatives were seen in such extremely remote and dangerous regions. A mix of deterrence (representatives were air-supported), political interest (possibility to participate to the election process) and economic retribution (cooption of leaders, design of development projects following needs identified by the community leaders) has led to an important participation.

Yet across Afghanistan, PRT deployment lacks a strategic approach, letting micro-strategies address local challenges, leading to short term objectives and eventually lack of coordination (GAO 2004). Primary evaluations are therefore mixed. The geographical flexibility of the PRT model is presented as a strength, a tool "to buy time" (Jakobsen 2005) and show that occidental nations have the will to address Afghan problems. But in sensitive areas, or when PRTs focus on much more problematic issues, such as opium economy, things could get more complicated.

This brings us to our third point: the way NATO has taken responsibility over PRTs in Afghanistan still raises numerous questions. The Alliance was first in charge of Kabul and its surroundings, before Germany took control over the Kunduz PRT (Northern Afghanistan) in December 2003. From this date, the NATO area of responsibility (AOR) has been continuously extended north (2004), then west (2005) and finally to southern and eastern Afghanistan (2006). This extension has faced the reluctance of many member-states to engage troops in volatile (especially south-eastern provinces) or to very remote areas (such as Bâmyiân), following security and topographic parameters.

The geographically variable security situation in particular has demonstrated how lukewarm NATO member-state engagement proved to be in Afghanistan.

On the one hand, expansion in the most dangerous provinces of Afghanistan had been a very sensitive issue, particularly because relations between the reconstruction work of PRTs and anti-terrorist campaign was not clear, but also because of the risks of such a deployment. For the NATO countries assuming responsibility for southern Afghanistan (Canada and Netherlands), public opinion and parliaments worry about the risks run by their soldiers, showing quite weak public support for the new mission. On the other hand, PRTs in northern and western areas represented an opportunity to show support for anti-terrorist goals without being involved in a mission which could be seen as too risky. From this perspective, PRTs represented the advantage of contributing to the stabilisation of Afghanistan, being easily presented as a military–humanitarian mission, without assuming too much risk for the soldiers.[18]

As a final point, we could say that if the PRT mission is to address the political fragmentation of Afghanistan, the diversity of contributing nations of ISAF have demonstrated an ambiguity in becoming decisively involved in this difficult situation. Few nations seem ready to really invest in this project, whereas anti-government groups have shown a renewed vitality. This lack of cohesion could pose a concrete threat to the success of the operation, as shown by national caveats and reluctance from member-states to put additional troops on the ground. Furthermore, degraded security in southern provinces could rend the PRT approach ineffective. First, contacts with civil populations and civil organisations are crucial to the achievement of the mission, but are, at the same time, difficult to organise when suicide-bombers or improvised explosive devices represent a daily threat. Second, a more aggressive ISAF in southern Afghanistan, where Canadian, British and Dutch contingents face determined and significant resistance, could be tempted to use development work as a tool to gain population's sympathy, restringing development objectives to counter-insurgency tactics.

Information sharing and geography

In the two cases considered briefly in this chapter, it is clear that, as in the majority of peace and/or stability operations, military action takes place as part of multidimensional interventions, which aim to rebuild states, assure economic development and improve the local population's livelihood. The nature of contemporary peacekeeping make armed forces get deeply interwoven into peace policies, taking an active part in it, and soldiers become local actors themselves.[19] We have here to remember that military end-states in peace operations are conditioned by the success of the larger political process, blurring the distinction between "pure" military tasks and politics, complicating the notion of military action itself. We can also make reference to the notion of "*strategic peacekeeping*",[20] which underlines that military action relies less on the consent of the parties than in traditional peacekeeping, focuses on supporting the diplomatic process, mixing political and military pressure, extending the ability to use force, responding to multidimensional stakes, and requiring improved civil–

military relations. Peacekeepers have then to provide security – that is, attempt to manage the local production of violence – but, at the same time, have to moderate their own use of force, in order to facilitate a peace process.[21] In addition, they have to link their own objectives with civilian agencies present on the territory, with whom they have to be coordinated. The challenges raised by multidimensional peacekeeping or statebuilding affect the linkage between the aid community and armed forces for two geographically related reasons.

The first reason is that both types of actors are present on the same territory, having complementary missions to achieve. Generally speaking, armed forces focus on gaining control over the concerned territories, while aid agencies attempt to supply the population and rebuild the country under a military protective umbrella. On many occasions, armed forces and relief agencies have to enter into contact. The military mandate can task soldiers to protect humanitarian actors or secure access for the provision of relief (such as the establishment of safe areas or humanitarian corridors). This supposes discussions around, and agreements on, the definition of the spaces concerned. Furthermore, in case of strict military control over a territory, humanitarian actors have a direct interest in informing commanders of their activities, in order, for example, to be able to pass through check points, as in Kosovo in 1999–2000. In those cases, civil–military interactions rely heavily on information sharing and the definition of each actor's geographic strategy. This has been the mission of Civil–Military Operation Center (CMOC), the focal point where civilians and military can meet. CMOCs are points of convergence,[22] places where processes can be shared between diverse participants to the mission (civilians and military), allowing the exchange of information and services (Eurogroup Institute 2002: 43). But they are also physical places where civilians and military can meet, during security or coordination meetings. The definition of such meeting spaces is of critical importance, as the settling of both military and civilian headquarters has to be decided in accordance to geographical constraints, especially in large countries where road networks are weak. Ideally, this would suppose to define a "neutral" meeting place, so that humanitarian actors do not see it as a threat to their impartiality. From this point of view, meeting in military compounds is experienced diversely by different humanitarian actors. If in Kosovo,[23] it was not seen as a direct threat except in case of local violence, this issue turned to be much more problematic in Afghanistan, where aid agencies were targetted by terrorist groups, and perceived geographical proximity with ISAF or Coalition Troops as a direct threat.

The second reason why multidimensional peacekeeping concerns the military–humanitarian linkage is that both types of actors have to connect their respective agendas under a common political direction, particularly with the emerging integrated peace missions model. Military and relief activities constitute tools of critical importance for some issues, beyond their simple own duties. The example of minority refugees return in Kosovo is quite illustrative. As minority enclaves were protected by KFOR (and also civilian police) and supplied by relief agencies, the return process used both actors' specific skills complementarily: the armed forces performed security assessments and carried out protection measures, while relief agencies – very often NGOs contracted by UNHCR or USAID – tried to provide economic opportunities for returnees and their neighbours.[24] This process was supported by UNHCR and required a multi-sector and multi-level approach: at the regional level (e.g. negotiation between Serbian and Kosovar governments over the identification of potential returnees), the "national" or country level (e.g. identification of enclaves to be sustained by returns) and the local level (e.g. ground assessments and the physical relocation process). In this context, the link between political, military and relief agencies is vital, and sometimes there exists no official chain of command between them, due, in part, to subcontracting.[25] International organisations, NGOs financed by them and armed forces have found it necessary to exchange liaison officers, organise coordination meetings and try to improve the interactions at operational and tactical levels, the strategic one being more complex.[26] From a geographic perspective, it also requires that all planning use the same territorial references; in essence, everyone must be reading from the same map.

This last point has been the focus of a great deal of work, beginning in Kosovo and spreading to crisis management operations in general. In this regard, much of the information that circulates between civilian agencies and armed forces is geographical in nature. This supposes that territory is divided and understood the same way. The generalisation of Geographic Information Systems (GIS) computerised tools, following their first shared use during the Kosovo war, allows this unification of territorial representation, through the design of shared maps. Any improvement in information sharing, which would allow for the emergence of combined agenda, would have to first define the geographical space where these agendas would be implemented. This was the aim of the Afghanistan Information Management Service (AIMS) and, before it, the Humanitarian Community Information Centre (HCIC) in Kosovo. These mapping centres have the capacity to "combine data sets across functional areas to provide an integrated view of the operational environment and hence a basis for cooperation" (Dziedzic and Wood 2000). Geographical Information Systems, in this case can be described as a "civil–military interoperability" assets, and the model has been extended to many crisis management operations after Kosovo through the model of "Humanitarian Information Centres" supported by UNOCHA.[27]

These linkages between military forces and humanitarian actors have progressively emerged as tools to reinforce civil–military complementarities and integration. The United Nations system in particular has been one of the main contributor to this change, as stated in the Brahimi Report. Nevertheless, the emerging integration model reaffirms the distinction between humanitarian actors and armed forces, but tries to coordinate them on a case by case basis,[28] as described in the diverse Civil–Military Relations Guidelines drawn up by UNOCHA's Military and Civilian Defence Liaison Unit.[29] In the overall institutional architecture of the missions however, Resident or Humanitarian Coordinators are increasingly Deputy Special Representatives of the Secretary General, reporting directly to the political branch of Peace Operations, as it has been experienced in Afghanistan (Griffin 2003).

Relief and the military occupation of territories

More generally, and outside any consideration of inter-agency coordination, the link between relief and military action is considered as essential to the achievement of military mission for contingents deployed abroad. In CIMIC doctrines, relief activities performed by armed forces represent effective assets to enter into contact with local populations and improve the image of the intervening forces. This aspect of military relief efforts is worth highlighting, given the fact that, by their very nature, deployments take place inside foreign societies. Recalling aspects of colonial military endeavours, it can be seen that "hearts and minds" strategy is not new when exploring external operations. French colonial troops, for instance, used to deploy units on the ground to perform basic relief and civil administration duties; the Arab Offices of the first French colonial period in Algeria serve as examples, as have French Marine troops in post-colonial Africa. Relief activities, in colonial missions as in contemporary peace operations, give military missions the opportunity to manage relations with local actors, under the pretext of building schools, distributing medicines or providing free medical aid. Moreover, it is considered in military circles that armed forces have a direct interest in the improvement of the local population's livelihood, as harsh living conditions can lead to social protest and demonstrations, political extremism, and criminality.[30] Of course, numerous changes have occurred between colonial and contemporary operations. Most importantly, colonial philosophy does not appear to be the same as that which underpins peace missions like Kosovo's.[31] Nevertheless, the territorial argument is the same: militaries must perform relief activities in order to maintain their ability to control territory[32] and to minimise the potential for violence emanating from the local society by showing the positive aspects of military presence, *in addition to* the use of force. As a side-benefit, relief activities provide soldiers an opportunity to look at the way people live, think and react to their presence, thereby providing some degree of "environmental intelligence".[33] Such insight enables a military force to take the opportunity to change it, through a combination of quick impact projects, discussion and classical "heart and minds" operations (such as information campaigns and psychological operations).

CIMIC troops are usually specially equipped and trained to perform this kind of mission. With the aid of translators they possess an ability to manage civilian projects and negotiate with local stakeholders. This goes far beyond the technical skills required of construction. By themselves, logistical units could not be expected to be able to lead a project involving the rehabilitation of a school, not because they lack the technical knowledge, but because they lack the necessary socio-political understanding. Relief activities allow CIMIC teams to identify community leaders, establish working relations and discuss with them the main problems faced by communities. In this way, a given military Area of

Responsibility is analysed and managed considering the existent local networks and dispersed nodes of political power. The information gathered in the course of such CIMIC projects complements traditional intelligence, and this is important when rules, procedures or linguistic barriers do not allow soldiers to exchange with locals, or when, as is the case for ISAF troops in Afghanistan, the military deployment is not dense.[34] Individual projects represent focal points where interactions with locals, especially those in positions of authority, can occur most productively.

As we can see, then, the geographical characteristics of military presence over a territory have strong implications on the way local population and peacekeepers interact. Massive deployment does not imply the same relations with a local population as a light presence, nor when it is dispersed or concentrated, high or low profile. Many local actors see peacekeepers only when they arrive in villages, stay some hours and go away in a rush of 4×4 or armoured vehicles. And yet, the lack of contacts between populations and soldiers is identified as a major source of frustration and misperceptions from the locals, as soldiers' misunderstanding of local culture has been defined in numerous publications as a major source of stress among peacekeepers. This issue of local/international interactions has been largely neglected (Pouligny 2005), even as it constitutes the central core of the mission, be it the search for a broad political legitimacy in state-building processes, or the attempt to manage local civil environment from a narrower military perspective. Military "relief" activities and CIMIC could appear as means of addressing this lacuna, a way of "filling in the blanks", as it were, especially since, increasingly, livelihood is considered a security issue. However, such a perspective would require an overall revolution in the philosophy underpinning intervention and, above all, in the way international actors go about trying to understand the local societies they wish to change.

Global geopolitics of military–humanitarian linkages

More generally, military–humanitarian linkages still raise a number of questions related to broader trends in international relations and global geopolitics. Recent years have witnessed a growing concentration of humanitarian donorship, while peace operations obey a new global geopolitical division of work. First, we notice that peace missions seem to divide labour between several actors. UN-led peacekeeping missions are constantly staffed by countries from Latin America, Africa or the Indian sub-continent, in regions where the strategic interests of powerful/rich countries are less evident. Conversely, it appears that "northern" countries are more involved in peace enforcement operations. The use of force parameter has become a line of division between "northern" and "southern" countries (Chesterman 2004). In strategic places, such as the Balkans and Afghanistan, NATO subcontracting appeared as a solution to a perceived lack of efficiency in UN-led peace operations.[35] At the same time, nevertheless, the United States seems to prefer "coalitions of the willing" in enforcement operations (as in Afghanistan or in Iraq), more than even a NATO framework. Furthermore, they situate their own military engagement during the "enforcement" phases rather than in "stabilisation process" (Cobbold 2003: 248–249), as the NATO take over in Afghan PRTs illustrates.

This geopolitical division of labour, which corresponds with the distribution of global military power, is secondly coupled with a world distribution of the overall humanitarian market. "A striking feature of any analysis of official humanitarian aid is how a small number of donor bodies dominates funding, and is thus able to exert a significant influence over the shape of the humanitarian system" (Macrae 2002: 11). Those donors choose "high profile" emergencies and select strategic regions, but they are also often integrated in Euro-Atlantic structures.[36] The bilateralisation of aid and the increase in earmarking practises coming from these countries reinforces the initial impression that northern peacekeepers are also financing humanitarian action in their own areas of intervention. Former Yugoslavia could be the "cas d'école", being the last decade's first recipient in terms of humanitarian funding, especially for ECHO,[37] and witnessing the most important peace soldiers' deployment in the history of peacekeeping (some 70,000 soldiers in 1999).[38]

At the national level, these northern countries that intervene in post-conflict situations and finance humanitarian aid have also developed procedures to connect armed forces, diplomacy and national relief agencies. National crisis management tools are thus increasingly integrated at the strategic level, but also on the ground, in their areas of operations. The United States has been among the first to adopt a number of measures that aim to coordinate all national agencies operating in post-conflict situations, from Clinton's Presidential Decision Directive 56 in 1997, to the creation of State Department's Office of the Co-ordinator for Reconstruction and Stabilisation in 2004. Great Britain's Post-Conflict Reconstruction Unit has been established also in 2004, with the support of Ministry of Defence, DfID, Foreign and Commonwealth Office and HM Treasury. It has had to be complemented in the field by the "civil–military humanitarian advisors" DfID has tried to create. Canada has, for its part, created the 3D (Defence, Development and Diplomacy) concept and many other NATO countries are shaping new institutional instruments linking aid agencies, defence administration and diplomacy, according to a widely shared view of a new security-development nexus.

Of course, inter-agency processes are not based on the same model everywhere. For example, the French inter-ministerial process is very weak and the link between relief activities and military operations is the result of low-level networking activity, rather than the consequence of an explicit inter-agency architecture. Every complex contingency operation is an occasion to reactivate ad-hoc emergency crisis cells, gathering NGOs, development agency representatives, Foreign Affairs and Ministry of Defence officers. But these relationships only last for the duration of the emergency, barely mobilise assets at strategic, operational and tactical levels, whereas stabilisation process require durable engagements (Gaïa 2001). The lack of military–civilian institutionalisation is bypassed by the personalisation of relations between military and relief agencies, in France as well as in the field (Braem 2004). This networking activity has the advantage of being flexible, but also lacks durability and remains volatile following the diverse situations. For example, Kosovo witnessed an important work between NGOs and armed forces on the theatre, while contacts in Afghanistan turned to be very poor. The difficult situation in Afghanistan was one factor (NGOs were afraid of being seen with soldiers), but was complicated by the fact that the military presence was not dense, and that there were few CIMIC units. Inter-agency coordination and processes in the US seem stronger than in France. Tactical and operational coordination between the Disaster Assistance Response Teams of USAID and Civil Affairs appears as an important tool to manage complementarities of military and relief activities.[39] Despite the fact that the strategic level suffers inconsistency, as recent experiences in Iraq and Afghanistan have shown (Flavin 2004), US military and civilian field officers are accustomed to coordinate themselves at the tactical and operational level. Significantly, US CENTCOM invited members from Interaction (one the largest worldwide group of NGOs), UNJLC and UNOCHA to come to Tampa to coordinate and exchange information during Operation Enduring Freedom. Now, the US military–humanitarian linkage and integrative model has been accused by some observers of manipulating humanitarian aid for security reasons, as the Pentagon increasingly finance a number of NGOs through its "humanitarian" office (ODHACA, Overseas Humanitarian, Disaster Assistance and Civic Aid).

Humanitarianism militarised?

Civil–military integration still raises numerous questions, notably about the nature of power sharing between civilian and military authorities, as illustrated by the PRT example. The content of the "black box" needs to be further examined, particularly regarding the definition of the decision process between civilians and military. "The institutionalisation of 'humanitarianism' in military doctrine, mandates, discourse and structures may be placing military establishments in a hegemonic position that determines the framework of future civil–military relations" (Pugh 2000: 238). As in the US, civil–military institutionalisation could lead to a growing tendency to consider humanitarian actors and NGOs as "force multipliers".[40] In the overall context of national mobilisation against terrorism,[41] this trend has been qualified a "militarisation of humanitarianism" by some observers (Makki 2004). Of course, this trend is generally seen as a direct threat to classical humanitarianism, as many consider that "humanitarian action is – and should remain – first and foremost civilian in character" (Minear 2002: 105). But the civilian nature of humanitarianism is not accepted by other actors (Stockton 2002) who consider that armed forces have the right to perform humanitarian actions, under specific conditions. Such debates demonstrate, at least, that humanitarianism is not defined the same way everywhere and by everybody.

While we will not enter this very important debate very deeply, as it is not our main focus, we would note some widely accepted principles of humanitarian action: impartiality, neutrality and independence. Impartiality and independence seem to be quite easy to define, through a needs-based approach, technical protocols for the designation of beneficiaries, or attention given to the funding process.[42] But neutrality appears a far more difficult issue; as revealed in interviews, humanitarian officers do not share the same definition. Some argue that they should not take funds from countries involved in humanitarian emergencies (as the US in Afghanistan, or France in Ivory Coast). Others say that it is not so much important and that the key issue is the local population perception. Now, "politicisation" of assistance is described by all humanitarian actors as the exact opposite of those humanitarian principles, and a growing number of humanitarian actors, both institutional and non-governmental,[43] claim that they want to maintain distance with the institutional sphere,[44] whereas they rely largely upon institutional funding. Above all, military action is considered in many interviews as one of the most exacerbated outputs of state political interest, and a real practical threat to the local perception of humanitarian agencies' neutrality.

But the definition of humanitarian principles is also a matter of power relations, insofar as the designation of a "real and sincere humanitarianism" will lead to include some organisations and exclude others. The growing tendency to adopt codes of conduct and accountability principles and practises follows the logic of a normative definition of humanitarianism. This has strong consequences in terms of resources coming from private and public donors,[45] and this normative definition represents practical economic stakes for NGOs. Additionally, divergences around the definition of accountability and codes of conduct partly follow national dividing lines, as the controversy around the Sphere Project has shown.[46] This was particularly due to national differences in the definition of humanitarianism.[47] From this perspective, perceptions of military–humanitarian interactions rely heavily on the diverse conceptions of relief activities, normative definitions pointing out relations with soldiers as acceptable or not. For example, coherence between humanitarian action and politics has been perceived in France as diverging from traditional French humanitarianism, but particularly representative of an "Anglo-Saxon" understanding. Conversely, the different ways nation-states conceive interactions, following diverse degrees of institutionalisation, could imply differences in the way NGOs will interact with soldiers. This acceptance could be voluntary, based on a traditional strong link between public and private sphere, as in the United States. It could also be the result of a set of constraints, as NGOs rely heavily on state donation.

Geography of relief and military–humanitarian relations

Locally, the normative definition of "good humanitarianism" represents other stakes. In Afghanistan particularly, donors have been accused of using humanitarianism as a label, to prevent funds from being controlled by the new Afghan state, because they did not trust the local administration's capacity.[48] Funds were thus provided directly to NGOs, considered neutral and impartial. This has not improved relations between humanitarian NGOs and the Afghan administration.

PRTs have worsened this situation, notably because of their ability to subcontract NGOs, to monitor their activities, and because of civic actions conducted by military units. But in their relation with relief actors, PRTs and the Coalition Joint Civil–Military Operation Task Force made several mistakes. First of all, NGO/Coalition relations debased when US Special Forces wore civilian clothes and weapons offering humanitarian aid in exchange of intelligence. Second, US forces made several contradictory announcements, claiming that PRTs would coordinate NGO activities in their Area of Responsibility, provoking hostility amongst the un-consulted NGOs. Third, while opening several PRTs and beginning to run them, many free medical care and civic actions were performed inside NGO-led hospitals, without notification of the NGOs concerned.[49] In the post-Taliban Afghanistan, NGOs and humanitarian actors were thus experiencing struggles concerning their autonomy, and felt uncomfortable with these constraints.

Humanitarian actors expressed mixed feelings about PRTs, some of them advocating against their deployment. Others supported the PRT deployment, with a mix of constraints and voluntary acceptance. On the one hand, motivations could be political: one French NGO representative in Kabul told me in 2003 that PRTs represented the sign of a strong US engagement in Afghanistan that was, for him, the only solution to the country's problems. On the other hand, some NGOs were compelled not to advocate against PRTs, because they wanted to apply for PRT funds, or wanted to avoid the risk of having US or British funds cut in retaliation.[50]

As a consequence, the few NGOs that were strongly advocating against the PRT principle had significant difficulties in trying to make a consensus emerge against PRTs at diverse levels. In provinces, the main argument against PRTs was that military units represented a risk for humanitarian actors, and were blurring the lines in local people's thinking. It was also claimed that if one NGO was seen collaborating with armed forces, it would endanger the others by association. In Kabul, attention was more paid to the definition of humanitarianism following Red Cross Code of Conduct, and arguments focused on principles, efficiency and coordination of both actors, in addition to the practical security aspect. Some humanitarian actors tried to convince NGOs not to accept funds from PRTs, in order to stop the growing involvement of military units in the reconstruction process and avert the threat that PRT subcontracting represented. But this meant running against financial interests of some NGOs and they failed to build a consensus around this issue. Of course, it was easier in areas where there were few NGOs, as in Bâmiyân for example. There, the number of NGOs was limited, and several of them refused the collaboration with armed forces, facilitating the emergence of widely shared positions. This position may have been strengthened because coalition soldiers were reported to have used humanitarian aid for intelligence gathering, giving relevance to the security threat to NGOs. However, in other areas, the number of agencies made the consensus very difficult to achieve, leaving PRTs an open space to develop their subcontracting practises.

More generally, if we consider military–humanitarian relations in terms of a power struggle related to the operational definition of humanitarianism, it has to be underlined that diverging points of views and practises appear between relief and military actors, but also, surprisingly, inside the humanitarian sphere. There exists a real contradiction between the claimed principles of neutrality/impartiality and realities on the ground. We have here to recognise that all territories do not represent the same stakes for all humanitarian actors, despite the fact that their focus is alleviation of individual suffering. Territories represent economic, affective or political stakes for organisations themselves. One important challenge for humanitarian actors in the competitive field of aid, where resources are limited, is to appear visible in the "big shows" of humanitarian and development actions, such as high profile peace operations led by great powers. Economic and media interests could be one of the main arguments to explain the explosion in the number of agencies over territories concerned by high profile peace missions, such as Kosovo[51] or Afghanistan, whereas other areas in the world, unknown from a mass-media perspective cruelly lack such help and suffer for being unknown. Of course, war-torn countries and populations need humanitarian agencies. But the multiplication of NGOs, in addition to the change in military–humanitarian power struggle it supposes, radically changes the sense of humanitarian presence. Massive arrival of NGOs, occurring soon after military deployments and bombing campaigns, shows on what side of the conflict NGOs are. In the case of Afghanistan, this was crystal clear: the massive arrival of NGOs, many of them knowing nothing of the crisis,[52] showed that they were participating to the US led occupation and reconstruction of the territory, even if they claimed the contrary. In this case, the concept of "militarisation of humanitarianism" does not have to be understood as if NGOs were the victims of this trend. Geographical analysis shows that humanitarian actors participate in their own instrumentalisation, as deployments in high profile peace missions are, for many NGOs, motivated by opportunities perhaps quite apart from humanitarianism.

Conclusion

Whether accepted or rejected, military–humanitarian linkage appears a central trend in today's peace operations, as it has been recognised many times in international literature. However, one striking feature of recent developments has been the use of humanitarian assets in enforcement operations, showing that relief functions can have multiple effects on the ground, as direct contributions for armed forces and crisis management. From this point of view, Kosovo and Afghanistan could show the relevance of a shift from traditional "military humanitarianism", described as a "mechanical task, rather than a strategic effort characterised by uncertainty and changing tactics on the ground" (Weiss, 1999a: 196). Military–humanitarian linkages are increasing, though, as pre-requisites before intervention, in an effort to address root causes of armed conflict (Abiew 2003: 36), insofar as they provide territorial management tools. If "coordination by command" (Weiss 1999b: 118) appears difficult to achieve, quite sensitive, and perhaps not desirable, we can witness that the conjunction of organisational interests can lead to practical cooperation on the field, for better or for worse.

Notes

1   Humanitarian action's international dimension does not attribute to it any theoretical extra-territoriality, in comparison with policy analysis and its changes.

(Dauvin, Siméant & CAHIER 2002: 373)

Le caractère international de l'action humanitaire ne lui confère aucune extraterritorialité théorique par rapport à l'analyse de l'action publique et de ses mutations.

(Author's translation)

2 Title of a book written by Yves Lacoste: *La Géographie, ça sert d'abord à faire la guerre.* (Lacoste 1985) (author's translation).
3 We will use without distinction the words "relief" and "humanitarian" to refer to activities owing to provide help to populations in need.
4 We conceive in this case geopolitical analysis as a complement to public policy or institution-centred analysis.
5 On this debate, see Roberts 1999; ICISS 2001; Holzgreffe and Keohane 2003.
6 OSCE was monitoring troops movements and human rights abuses, with NATO support in security (Quick Reaction Force in Macedonia) and air surveillance (Ghebali 1999). In this context, the Racak massacre (15 January 1999) demonstrated the failure of the diplomatic process and further justified the beginning of air strikes.
7 These included the desire not to repeat a situation akin to that of Srebrenica in Bosnia; not to witness a spill over of the conflict in the region and to contain refugee flows inside the Balkans (Bellamy 2002).
8 There were 980,000 refugees outside Kosovo following UNHCR surveys at the end of the bombings: 444,200 in Albania, 247,400 in Macedonia, the rest of the refugees being hosted in third countries or in Montenegro.
9 Allied Rapid Reaction Corps was positioned in Macedonia, serving as Quick Reaction Force, and Albania had opened its airspace to NATO planes bombing Serbian forces in Kosovo.
10 Inter-ethnic hatred increased between the two main communities in the context of a economic, identity and political representation crisis, leading to ethnic cleansing strategies to achieve the control of the territory. See Roux 1999 and Malcolm 1998.
11 SHAPE agreed on 4 April 1999 to lead Operation Allied Harbour and orient the Allied Rapid Reaction Corps in Macedonia towards a humanitarian mission (construction of reception capacities and refugee camps).
12 The Tirana–Kukes road and the Tirana Airport were rehabilitated by NATO troops. The Euro-Atlantic Disaster Response Coordination Centre was activated in late March 1999 to coordinate civilian and military air traffic, in order to increase efficiency in air management while the overall flow reached an unprecedented level in the region.
13 In northern Albania (Kukes and Tropoje), refugees were threatened by trans-border shelling and their sheer numbers overwhelmed roads and the capacity of camps established to receive them. Furthermore, humanitarian agencies in this region were subject to predation by local criminal groups. A number of refugees were, in this case, resettled in southern and central Albania, in camps built by NATO forces. In Macedonia, their number was perceived as a threat by the government, possibly reversing the demographic equilibrium between Slavs and Albanians and were suspected to spread ideas of insurgency throughout local ethnic Albanian population.

Some 96,000 of these Kosovar Albanian refugees were temporarily placed in western countries (Braem 2004).

14 Even if "only" one-third of refugees were housed in NATO-built camps (UNHCR 2000: VI).

15 See USIP 2003, Chesterman 2002, and, for warlordism in Afghanistan, Giustozzi 2003.

16 Afghans have been impressed by the destruction capacity of Coalition air power, and PRTs occasionally demonstrate that they have air support, in order to achieve deterrence (interviews with military officers serving in Coalition Forces, Kabul 2003 and Paris 2005).

17 UNAMA consultation process conducted during the summer of 2003 is hardly relevant to account for the great flexibility of the model, and can not be taken as a guideline.

18 The German PRT's location have been chosen in a relatively quiet place (Kunduz) mainly because, according to interviews (Kabul 2003 and Geneva 2004), because of the areas border proximity, and thus possibility for extraction. The German government did not want to expose its soldiers to risk, as it has been made clear when German contingent retreated inside its compound during a demonstration in June 2004 (Jakobsen 2005: 25–26).

19 The emergence of the "Political Advisor" (POLAD) function in peace missions testifies that military commanders have to be aware of the political environment they are engaged in, but also that they have to make provisions about the consequences of their actions on this environment (Lange 1999).

20 See Dandeker and Gow, in Callaghan and Schonborn 2004, 19–20.

21 Peace missions involve much more complex issues regarding violence production than is the case under a more traditional definition of military operations, such as warfighting, which relies on the definition of an enemy and its destruction. This shift represents an important philosophical and practical dilemma. See Hills 2001 and Berdal 2001.

22 This corresponds to CIMCoord in UN civilian terminology. See UNOCHA Military and Civil Defence Unit's website at: ochaonline.un.org/webpage.asp?SiteID=237

23 Personal observation in Mitrovica area during surveys in 2001–2002.

24 We have, of course, very much simplified this central and complex issue of Kosovo refugees return, that integrate a wide spectrum of strategies. See UNMIK Office for Return and Communities' *Manual for Sustainable Return*, Pristina, January 2003.

25 This proved difficult in Bosnia Herzegovina under UNPROFOR, IFOR and SFOR mandates, see Williams 1999.

26 It is a matter of intergovernmental relations, while it seems more simple at the theatre level. In Kosovo for example, relations between KFOR and UNMIK have been enhanced by

> (1) the effort by KFOR and UNMIK to routinised processes for coordination of military support to civil authorities; (2) cross-organizational acceptance of a unified five region geographic plan for operation organisation; and (3) the advent within UNMIK of a unified mission structure for all major civil components.
>
> (Cockell 2002)

27 See hwww.humanitarianinfo.org/.

28

> The emphasis on distinction should not be interpreted as a suggestion of non-coordination between humanitarian and military actors. The particular situation on the ground and the nature of the military operations in a given situation will play a determining factor on the type of coordination that may take place.
>
> (IASC 2004: 7)

29 See the "Guidelines on the Use of Military and Civil Defence Assets in Disaster Relief" adopted by the UNDHA, May 1994, followed, after the Kosovo crisis, by the

"Guidelines for the Use of Military and Civil Defence Assets in Complex Emergencies" adopted UNOCHA in 2003.

30 Interview with KFOR officials and CIMIC Officers, Kosovo 2001 and 2006.

31 Most notable is the fact that the types of violence used by the armed forces are not the same, changing radically the sense of the interaction. We might set apart the ideological argument (the potential link between colonial domination, neo-colonial humanitarianism, and domination of a Western model of liberal society) which is beyond the scope of this chapter. On this debate see Rufin 2001, Ignatieff 2003 and Paris 2004.

32 "Control" being conceived as the ability to perform the mission.

33 Environmental intelligence is not so much intelligence in the classical term (gathering information from closed sources), but rather the process of collecting feelings, perceptions, and other open information about local daily life.

34 At the end of 2004, ISAF and Enduring Freedom Forces represented 20,000 troops in Afghanistan, so three soldiers per 100 square kilometre and 0.7 for 1,000 inhabitants; when, in Kosovo, proportions were 164 soldier per 100 square kilometre and ten for 1,000 inhabitants.

35 NATO's progressive involvement in peace and state building operations began with support to UN missions in Bosnia (UNPROFOR) before a subcontracted role emerged (IFOR and SFOR) allowing NATO to shape for itself a political–military role (Leurdijk, in Weiss 1998: 49–66).

36 USA are the first donor, then ECHO, UK, Netherlands, Sweden, Switzerland, Germany, Norway, Japan and Canada (Macrae 2002). We can here underline that much of these countries, and also European member states, are NATO members.

37 Despite the fact that ECHO status forbid the use of its funding for crisis management. CF. Council Regulation (EC) No. 1257/96 (06/20/1996).

38 The number of soldiers for every 1,000 inhabitants were 15 for IFOR, 22 for KFOR (at the beginning of itsmandate); 4 in UNITAF; 1 in MINUHA and 3 in UNAMSIL. Looked at from a geographical perspective, these numbers for 100 km^2 of territory was IFOR 117; KFOR 375; UNITAF 6; MINUHA 24; and UNAMSIL 24 (Comparison made by the *Institut Français de Relations Internationales – IFRI*).

39 See Field Manual 41–10 or Joint Doctrine for Civil–Military Operations.

40 As Colin Powell said in 2003, supported by official positions of USAID administrator Andrew Natsios in favour of NGO's support of US foreign policy.

41 On the advocacy plan, US relief agencies are said not to take part in public debates as they used to, showing that 9/11 has not been without consequences on humanitarianism (Minear 2002: 101; Macrae 2002: 16).

42 Avoidance of earmarking, and for NGOs, donor diversification in order to avoid dependency upon one donor.

43 Interviews in 2001–2005 with diverse international organisations such as UNHCR, UNOCHA or ECHO, and with NGOs in France, the US, Afghanistan or Kosovo.

44 Even if the traditional difference between state and non-state categories have been seriously questioned by social sciences studies, from a sociological point of view (Dauvin and Siméant 2004: 9–33) or following political economy analysis (Weiss and Gordenker in Weiss 1998: 30–45).

45 NGOs have to define "good" and "bad" behaviours in order to regulate humanitarian practises, which has the consequence of legitimating these same organisations in the eyes of private donors.

46 At least has it been perceived so through a national prism, with divergences at the margin (Interviews with French NGOs leadership).

47 In France, humanitarianism is though as a set of practises, but also as a commitment close to political engagement, well represented by *French Doctors* philosophy. It leads, in some important NGOs, to an ambiguous perception of professionalisation, largely imposed by donor will, and seen as a threat to advocacy, while US and British

NGOs rather consider professionalisation as a tool for better advocacy (Dauvin, Siméant and Cahier 2002).

48 See the debate between Alexander Costy, Nicholas Leader and Mohammed Aneef Atmar and Paul O'Brien in Donini, Niland, Wersmester 2004: 143–203.

49 Personal observation in Mazar-e Sharif (2003) and interviews with PRTs, NGOs and UNAMA officers.

50 Interview with International NGOs Program Officers in Kabul and Mazar-e Shariff, 2003.

51 The number of NGOs in Kosovo increased dramatically from 40 agencies before the conflict up to 300 a few weeks after KFOR entry and UNMIK arrival.

52 This is a central issue. How is it possible to perform neutral, independent and impartial humanitarian activity when field workers know nothing about the local context? How is it possible to define the "good beneficiary", when local cultural codes, socio-economic realities are unknown and political context extremely complex?

Bibliography

Abiew, F.K. 2003. "NGO-Military Relations In Peace Operations", In *International Peacekeeping*, 10.1: 24–39.

Bellamy, A.J. 2002. *Kosovo and International Society*. New York: Palgrave Macmillan.

Berdal, M. 2001. "Lessons Not Learned: The Use of Force in 'Peace Operations' in the 1990s", *International Peacekeeping*, 7.4: 55–74.

Braem, Y. 2004. "Les Relations Armées – ONG, Des Relations De Pouvoir? Caractéristiques Et Enjeux De La Coopération Civilo-Militaire Française: Le Cas Du Kosovo", Paris: Les Documents Du C2SD. www.C2sd.Sga.Defense.Gouv.Fr/Html/Recherche/FTP/BRAEM_Relations_Armees_Ong_Kosovo_Fevrier2004.Pdf.

Byman, D. 2001. "Uncertain Partners: Ngos and the Military", *Survival*. 43.2 (Summer): 97–114.

Callaghan, J. and Schonborn, M. 2004. *Warriors in Peacekeeping. Points of Tension in Complex Cultural Encounters*. Georges Marshall ECSS, Munster: LIT Verlag.

Chesterman, S. 2002. "Walking Softly in Afghanistan", *Survival*, 44.3: 37–45.

Chesterman, S. 2004. *The Use of Force in UN Peace Operations*, New York: United Nations Peacekeeping Best Practice Unit.

Cobbold, R. 2003. "Opérations de Stabilisation: Faire La Guerre, Maintenir La Paix", *Annuaire Français de Relations Internationales*, Bruxelles: Bruylant: 241–253.

Cockell, J.G. 2002. "Civil–Military Responses to Security Challenges in Peace Opearations: Ten Lessons from Kosovo", *Global Governance*, 8: 483–502.

Dauvin, P. and Simeant, J. 2004. *ONG Et Humanitaire*, Paris: L'Harmattan.

Dauvin, P., Simeant, J. and Cahier, C. 2002. *Le Travail Humanitaire. Les Acteurs des ONG, du Siège au Terrain*, Paris: Presses De Sciences Po.

Donini, A., Niland, N., and Wersmester, K. 2004. *Nation-Building Unraveled: Aid, Peace and Justice in Afghanistan*. Bloomfield: Kumarian Press.

Dziedzic M.J. and Wood W.B. 2000. "Kosovo Brief: Information Management Offers New Opportunity For Cooperation Between Civilian And Military Entities", United States Institute for Peace. www.usip.org/virtualdiplomacy/publications/reports/-Dziedzic-Wood.html.

Eurogroup Institute. 2002. "La Coopération Civilo-Militaire Dans Le Cadre Des Actions De Sortie De Crise Et La Problématique Des Financements Internationaux", *Rapport A La Délégation Aux Affaires Stratégiques*, Paris: Ministère De La Défense.

Flavin, W. 2004. "Civil–Military Operations: Afghanistan", Carlisle: US Army War College.

Gaïa, R. 2001. "Les Actions Civilo-Militaires De L'urgence Développement: Quels Outils Pour La France?" *Rapport D'information À l'Assemblée Nationale* No. 3167, Paris.

General Assembly Of United Nations. 2000. *Report of the Panel on United Nations Peace Operations*, A/55/305–S/2000/809.

Giustozzi, A. 2003. "Respectable Warlords? The Politics of State-Building in Post-Taleban Afghanistan", Crisis States Program Working Paper No. 33, London School Of Economics. www.crisisstates.com/download/wp/wp33.pdf.

Griffin, M. 2003. "The Helmet and the Hoe: Linkages between United Nations Development Assistance and Conflict Management", *Global Governance* 9: 199–217.

Hills, A. 2001. "The Inherent Limits of Military Forces in Policing Peace Operations", *International Peacekeeping*, 8.3 (Autumn): 79–98.

ICISS. 2001. *The Responsibility to Protect: Report of the International Commission on Intervention and State Sovereignty*, Ottawa: International Development Research Centre.

Ignatieff, M. 2003. *Empire Lite: Nation Building in Bosnia, Kosovo and Afghanistan*, London: Vintage.

Inter-Agency Standing Committee. 2004. "Civil–Military Relationship in Complex Emergencies." An IASC Reference Paper. 28 June.

Jakobsen, P.V. 2005. "PRTs In Afghanistan: Successful but not Sufficient", DISS Report 2005: 6. www.diis.dk/graphics/publications/reports2005/pvj_prts_afghanistan.pdf.

Keohane, R. and Holzgrefe J.L. 2003. *Humanitarian Intervention: Ethical, Legal and Political Dilemmas*, Cambridge: Cambridge University Press.

Lacoste, Y. 1985. *La Géographie, Ça Sert D'abord A Faire La Guerre*, Paris: La Découverte.

Lacoste, Y. 2001. "Rivalries for Territory", in Levy, J. *From Geopolitics to Global Politics. A French Connection*, London: Franck Cass: 120–158.

Lambeth, B. S. 2002. "Lessons from the War in Kosovo", *Joint Forces Quarterly* (Spring).

Lange, D.A. 1999. "The Role of the Political Advisor in Peacekeeping Operations", *Parameters*. (Spring): 92–109.

Macrae, J. 2002. "The New Humanitarianism: A Review of Trends in Global Humanitarian Action", HPG Report 11, London: ODI.

Makki, S. 2004. "Militarisation de L'humanitaire, Privatisation du Militaire", *Cahier d'Etudes Stratégiques*, Paris, CIRPES: 36–37.

Miller, L. 1999. "From Adversaries to Allies: Relief Workers' Attitudes toward the US Military", *Qualitative Sociology*, 22.3: 81–197.

Minear, L. 2002. *The Humanitarian Enterprise: Dilemmas and Discoveries*, Bloomfield: Kumarian Press.

Minear, L., Van Baarda T. and Sommers, M. 1999. "NATO and Humanitarian Action in The Kosovo Crisis", *Thomas J. Watson Jr. Institute For International Studies Occasional Paper* No. 36, Providence.

Paris, R. 2004. *At War's End. Building Peace after Civil Conflict*. Cambridge: Cambridge University Press.

Posen, B.R. 2000. "The War for Kosovo. Serbia's Political-Military Strategy", *International Security* No. 4.

Pouligny, B. 2006. *Peace Operations seen from Below. UN Missions and Local People*, London: Kumarian Press.

Pugh, M. 2000. "Civil–Military Relations in The Kosovo Crisis: An Emerging Hegemony", *Security Dialogue*, 31.2: 229–242.

Roberts, A. 1999. "NATO's 'Humanitarian War' Over Kosovo", *Survival*, 41.3: 102–123.

Roux, M. 1999. *Le Kosovo: Dix Clés Pour Comprendre*, Paris: La Découverte.

Rufin, J.C. 2001. *L'Empire et Les Nouveaux Barbares*, Paris: Latès.

Slim, H. 2004a. "Politicizing Humanitarian Action according to Need", Presentation to The 2nd International Meeting on Good Humanitarian Donorship, Ottawa, 21–22 October 2004.

Slim, H. 2004b. "With or Against? Humanitarian Agencies and Coalition Counter-Insurgency", Geneva: Centre For Humanitarian Dialogue.

Stockton, N. 2002. "Strategic Coordination in Afghanistan", Issue Paper Series, Kabul: Afghanistan Research and Evaluation Unit.

UNHCR 2000. The Kosovo Refugee Crisis. An Independent Evaluation of UNHCR's Emergency Preparedness and Response, Evaluation and Policy Analysis Unit.

US General Accounting Office. 2004. *Afghanistan Reconstruction*. www.gao.gov/highlights/D04403high.pdf.

USIP. 2003. "Unfinished Business in Afghanistan: Warlordism, Reconstruction, and Ethnic Harmony", USIP Special Report 105. www.usip.org/pubs/specialreports/sr105.html.

Weiss, T.G. 1998. *Beyond UN Subcontracting*, New York: San Martin's Press.

Weiss, T.G. 1999a. *Military–Civilian Interactions: Intervening in Humanitarian Crisis*, Oxford: Rowman and Littlefield.

Weiss, T.G. 1999b. "Learning from Military–Civilian Interactions in Peace Operations", *International Peacekeeping*, 6.2: 112–128.

Wheeler, V. and Harmer, A. 2006. "Resetting The Rules of Engagement: Trends and Issues in Military Humanitarian Relations", HPG Research Report, London: ODI.

Williams, M. 1999. "Civil–Military Relations and Peacekeeping", *Adelphi Paper* No. 321, Oxford: Oxford University Press.

4 Civil–military coordination and complex peacebuilding systems

Cedric de Coning

Research undertaken by Roy Licklider over the period 1945 to 1993 suggests that about half of all peace agreements fail in the first five-years after they have been signed (1995:690). There are many reasons why some peace processes are not sustainable.[1] Some relate to the motives of the belligerent parties while others are associated with shortcomings in the support provided by the international community. This chapter is focused on one of the aspects that contribute to the lack of sustainability in the latter context, namely the incoherent nature of the international response.

Despite a growing awareness that the security, socio-economic, political and reconciliation dimensions of peacebuilding systems are interlinked, the agencies that carry out peacebuilding programmes are finding it extremely difficult to meaningfully integrate these different dimensions into coherent country or regional conflict system strategies. Although approximately twenty peacebuilding operations have been undertaken over the last decade no generic model has yet emerged on which future peacebuilding systems can be based.

One reason why coherence has proven so elusive is the lack of a shared understanding of the role of coordination (van Brabant, 2001: 141). Some want to use coordination to bring more order among the different agencies in the system while others resist coordination because they associate it with losing control over their own independence (Strand, 2003: 263). Peacebuilding theory lacks a theoretical framework that explains the role of coordination in the system. This chapter will attempt to contribute to the development of such a theoretical framework by introducing a complex systems approach to coordination, including civil–military coordination, which is aimed at improving the coherence of peacebuilding systems without impacting on the independence of the participating agencies. For the purposes of this chapter this approach will be referred to as Peacebuilding Systems Theory (PST).

Peacebuilding

In the 1990s the approach to international conflict management, as developed in the context of Boutros Boutros Ghali's 1992 Agenda for Peace,[2] was to first try to prevent violent conflict (conflict prevention). If that failed the next step was to make peace by facilitating dialogue among the belligerent parties and to gather them around the negotiation table (peacemaking). If a cease-fire or peace agreement was reached that included a neutral third-party monitoring role, the UN or an organization authorized by the Security Council, would typically deploy a peace operation to monitor the cease-fire and to support the implementation of the peace agreement (peacekeeping). In some cases it was necessary, once all peaceful means have been exhausted, to use a degree of force to stabilize a situation (peace enforcement). Once the conflict zone has been stabilized, emergency humanitarian needs have been addressed and a peace process has been agreed upon, the international community shifted its focus to post-conflict reconstruction. This phase was focused on rebuilding and reconciliation with the aim of addressing the root causes of the violent conflict so as to prevent it from reoccurring again (peacebuilding) (de Coning, 2005).

As a result of the peacekeeping and peacebuilding challenges experienced in the 1990s, our approach to conflict management has become more complex in the beginning of the twenty-first century. There is now recognition that the different elements of conflict management introduced in the *Agenda for Peace* do not necessarily follow on one another in a linear or chronological progression. Instead, in practise, they overlap, are interlinked, mutually support each other and often take place simultaneously. A similar awareness has emerged in the development world. Humanitarian relief and development were regarded as two separate elements until the mid to late 1990s, but since then a new understanding of the interrelationship between relief and reconstruction have emerged and resulted in initiatives, such as the World Bank and UNHCR's so-called 4Rs approach (Repatriation, Reintegration, Rehabilitation and Reconstruction), to try to bridge these previously distinct fields of practise.[3]

Our understanding of the dynamics and linkages within the peace and security field on the one hand, and the humanitarian assistance and development field on the other, has thus undergone considerable change over the last decade. At the same time there is now a growing realization that there is a nexus, not only within, but also between development and security, and that we need to improve our understanding of how these previously separate paradigms are interrelated (Uvin, 2002: 5). In the context of these developments peacebuilding is increasingly seen as the collective framework under which these peace, security, humanitarian and development dimensions can be brought together under one common country strategy.[4]

In PST, peacebuilding is a complex system that provides for parallel, concurrent and interlinked short-, medium- and long-term programmes that work to prevent disputes from escalating, or avoid a relapse, into violent conflict by addressing both the immediate consequences and the root causes of a conflict system. The peacebuilding process starts when a cease-fire agreement or peace agreement, that calls upon the international community to support the peace process, enters into force. It typically progresses through three stages, namely a stabilization phase, a transitional phase, and a consolidation phase.[5] The peacebuilding process ends when a society has developed the capacity to manage and sustain its own peace process without external support. It requires a wide range of internal and external actors, including governments, civil society, the private sector and international agencies, to work together in a coherent and coordinated effort. These actors undertake a broad range of programmes that span the security, political, socio-economic and reconciliation dimensions. Collectively and cumulatively, these programmes address both the causes and consequences of the conflict system, and builds momentum over time that facilitates its transformation. In the short term the goal of peacebuilding systems are to assist the internal actors with stabilizing the peace process and preventing a relapse into conflict, but its ultimate aim is to support them in transforming the causes of the conflict and laying the foundations for social justice and sustainable peace and development.[6]

Civil–military coordination

One area within the larger security and development nexus that has attracted considerable attention since the 1990s is civil–military coordination. Although some form of civil–military interface has always accompanied war and military occupation, a distinct form of civil–military coordination has emerged since the mid-1990s in the peace operations context. This form of civil–military coordination first emerged during the operations in Somalia and Bosnia as an attempt to systematically manage the relationship between military forces and humanitarian agencies at the operational and tactical levels.

Since then it has developed into a recognized command function in NATO,[7] EU[8] and UN[9] peace operations. Contemporary civil–military coordination policies and doctrines provides for dedicated command and staff structures aimed at supporting this civil–military interface. In the UN humanitarian context,[10] coordination range from 'cooperation' to 'coexistence', where cooperation is viewed as the closest relationship that can exist between humanitarian and military actors, for instance during a response to a natural disaster. When they cooperate they agree to plan together, exchange information and organize themselves around an agreed division of tasks.

The other end of the coordination spectrum, referred to as 'coexistence', implies a minimum level of coordination necessary to exchange critical information. This level of coordination is the norm, from the perspective of the humanitarian agencies, when the military force is perceived to be a party to the conflict. Under such circumstances coordination is limited to deconflicting respective objectives via the exchange of information in critically important areas such as the security of the humanitarian agencies and local population, and the use of shared resources such as airports, ports, roads and communication infrastructure.

For the purposes of this chapter, civil–military coordination refers to the liaison and coordination processes and mechanisms that are established to facilitate relations between military forces and civilian agencies in a peacebuilding system.

Coherence

The need for, and benefits of, improved coherence is widely accepted today in the international multilateral governance context. Although there is a better understanding today of the fact that inconsistent policies entail a higher risk of duplication, inefficient spending, a lower quality of service, difficulty in meeting goals and, ultimately, of a reduced capacity for delivery,[11] there is still a considerable disparity between acknowledged best practice and operational reality. The lack of coherence between programmes in the humanitarian relief and development spheres and those in the peace and security spheres have been highlighted by various evaluation reports and studies,[12] and acknowledged in a number of UN reports.[13]

For example, the Joint *Utstein* Study of peacebuilding, that analyzed 336 peacebuilding projects implemented by Germany, the Netherlands, the United Kingdom and Norway over the last decade, has identified a lack of coherence at the strategic level, what it terms a 'strategic deficit', as the most significant obstacle to sustainable peacebuilding (Smith, 2003: 16). The *Utstein* study found that more than 55 per cent of the programmes it evaluated did not show any link to a larger country strategy.

These evaluation studies have consistently found that the peacebuilding operations undertaken to date have been less coherent than expected, and that this lack of coherence has undermined their ability to achieve their strategic objective, namely to assist societies emerging from conflict to lay the foundations for social justice and sustainable peace and development.

It is also important to recognize that while there is a drive towards greater coherence, there is also at the same time a recognition that coherence can never be fully achieved, because of the dynamic and non-linear nature of complex systems. However, even though coherence can never be fully achieved, it is possible to distinguish between systems where there is little coherence and ones where there is more coherence, and it is recognized that striving for coherence creates more efficiency in a system.

In PST, coherence is the effort to direct the wide range of programmes undertaken in the peace, security, socio-economic and reconciliation dimensions of a peacebuilding system towards a common objective.[14]

Factors that cause incoherence

There are many factors that frustrate coherence in the peacebuilding context, but two deserve particular attention. The first is the sheer number of international and local actors involved, and the second is the wide-ranging scope of activities undertaken by these actors. The interaction between the large number of actors and the interconnectedness among the multiple dimensions contribute to the complexity inherent in peacebuilding systems. To these we can still add an infinite number of complicating factors, including amongst others, the socio-cultural gaps between those undertaking peacebuilding programmes and the beneficiaries they are intended to assist, the lack of synchronization between the rate of delivery and the ability of the host community to absorb the assistance, and the inconsistencies and selectivity of the dominant neo-liberal international policy regime that serve to compound existing global inequalities (Pugh and Cooper, 2004: 197).

The information revolution has multiplied the number of actors involved in peacebuilding policy processes and operations. It has amplified the influence of the media, nurtured the development of a more educated and better informed public, and increased the number of institutions and agencies engaged in peace, security, relief and reconstruction actions.[15]

Among the many different actors involved in peacebuilding systems the donor countries deserve particular focus from a coordination perspective. A relatively small number of donor countries, approximately 12–20, are responsible for funding the majority of peacebuilding programmes.[16] Most of these donor countries are also prominent players in the peace and security dimension. There is an opportunity for greater coherence and coordination among the donor countries, perhaps more so than among any other grouping, as they have substantial influence on both the peace and security dimension and the relief and reconstruction dimensions of peacebuilding systems.[17] If they make use of this influence, they will considerably ease the burden on the programmes, agencies and the host countries that otherwise have to try to harmonize policies and programmes in the field.[18] Although the benefits of coordination for donors and their tax paying publics are obvious, and although their own rhetoric echo this conventional wisdom, there is a well documented discrepancy between their expressed willingness to coordinate and actual practice (Wood, 2003).

The second factor that inhibits coordination is closely related to the large number of actors, namely the multidimensional and multidisciplinary scope of the programmes that populate peacebuilding systems. In order for positive momentum to come about in a society emerging from conflict, every individual in that society must make thousands of micro-decisions about their own security, shelter, health, wellbeing, employment, education and future prospects. Peacebuilding systems have recognized the complex nature of society and attempt to mirror each of these facets with matching programmes that, when interlinked, are intended to have a system-wide impact on the peace process across the whole conflict spectrum.[19]

The reality is, however, that many of these disciplines have developed in separate paradigms over many years, and in this process some have developed a negative history of each other. As a result most programmes are planned and implemented in relative isolation by specialists from a particular discipline. Coherence is further hindered by inter-institutional rivalries, competition for resources, information hording and a lack of understanding of a clear and common purpose. The lack of coordination among this large number of actors, and the diverse scope of functions and disciplines they represent, hamper the ability of the internal and external actors in a post-conflict setting to achieve coherence.

Competing solutions

Two schools of thought have emerged over the last decade in response to the problems associated with coordination and coherence between the security and development dimensions. The first advocates that coordination can be achieved by introducing more order into the system, or what Donini (2002) refers to as coordination by command. It favours centralizing coordination in one agency or introducing some kind of integrated mission coordination process that will result in all the different dimensions feeding into one central coordination process.

The UN experimented, but abandoned, one such form of integration in Afghanistan. This attempt was known as the Strategic Framework Initiative (SFI) and came about as a result of an attempt to implement some of the recommendations of the Joint Evaluation of Emergency Assistance to Rwanda in 1995 (Eriksson, 1996). This was followed by the so-called 'integrated missions' concept that, in its most extreme form to date – in the UN Mission in Liberia (UNMIL) – resulted in the full integration of the humanitarian coordination function in the UN peace operation. The Resident Coordinator/Humanitarian Coordinator (RC/HC) function has been 'integrated' into UN peace operations in the past with success, most notably for instance in the so-called 'Doss-model' in Sierra Leone, but in Liberia the process has gone two steps further. Firstly, the humanitarian coordination support function normally provided by the Office for the Coordination of Humanitarian Affairs (OCHA) was also integrated into UNMIL, and secondly the Special Representative of the Secretary-General (SRSG) also assumed the Designated Official (DO) security role normally assigned to the RC/HC. Although the SRSG is meant to be the overall representative of the Secretary-General, and therefore of the UN system, in a country where there is a UN peace operation, in reality (s)he reports to the UN Security Council, through the Secretary-General and the Department of Peacekeeping Operations (DPKO). This implies that the SRSG represents the political and security constituency, not the development and humanitarian community. For many in the humanitarian and development community integration in UNMIL has gone too far in that the institutional arrangements resulted in the humanitarian imperative being de facto subsumed by the political-military (represented by DPKO in the UN context) management structure.[20]

Some have gone further to propose creating a new UN agency that would be responsible for peacebuilding (Paris, 2004), and others have introduced the same concept at national level, establishing a coordinating office where the responsibility for peacebuilding will lie.[21] Some have argued that the problem lies in the fact that the Security Council, that has a peace and security, not a development and humanitarian, mandate, lose interest in peacebuilding once the peacekeepers leave. The 2005 High-level Panel on Threats, Challenges and Change[22] proposed that a 'Peacebuilding Commission' be established at the United Nations to oversee peacebuilding initiatives, and this recommendation has since been adopted and implemented. A Peacebuilding Commission has been established in

2006 and it has started its work, supported by a Peacebuilding Support Office in the UN Secretariat.

The second school of thought has a minimalist approach to coordination, or what Donini (2002) refers to as coordination by consensus. They reject any notion of centralized coordination or integration, and some are even opposed to recognizing coordination as a distinct element of action. They emphasize the importance of independence in humanitarian action and oppose any initiatives that may result in this independence being compromised by integrating humanitarian action into political and security agendas, as the example of integration in UNMIL mentioned above suggest. Some in this school argue that the benefits of coordination are limited and that the time, energy and resources devoted to coordination unnecessarily increase the administrative costs of delivering assistance.[23] Although some in this school would support the lead agency concept, i.e. that a credible humanitarian agency like the UNHCR or UNICEF should take the lead in coordinating other agencies during an emergency, they reject coordination when it is initiated by those they associate with the security or political elements of a peace operation. In fact, some in the humanitarian relief school have even resisted coordination by the Resident Coordinator (RC), when the latter is from a developmental agency like the UN Development Programme (UNDP), on the grounds that the UNDP is not impartial because it has a mandate to advise the government of the day.[24]

Support for more control and integration comes mostly from those in the political and security community whilst the humanitarian and development community generally support the principles of independence and voluntary coordination. This is a further indication of how our different paradigms, organizational cultures and professional and academic disciplines complicate our ability to coordinate, or even to have a common understanding of the role of coordination.

This chapter introduces an alternative approach to coordination and coherence that aims to synthesize the two schools of thought that have dominated the coordination debate to date, namely Peacebuilding System Theory (PST). PST addresses the need for improved coherence, the condition that motivates the first school, and it suggests a way in which this can be achieved without requiring individual programmes and agencies to surrender their independence, the principle that motivates the second school.

Peacebuilding Systems Theory

Peacebuilding Systems Theory (PST) holds that peacebuilding systems are populated by a large number of diverse, but interdependent, programmes. These programmes form a complex system when their collective and cumulative efforts start to have an effect on the conflict system they intend to transform that none of the programmes could have achieved on their own. PST combines the insights of two theories and introduces two supporting rules.

The first theory is Interdependence Theory (IT) that provides the motivation for coordination in complex peacebuilding systems. The second is Complex Systems Theory (CST) that explains how complex systems are able to adapt, adjust, correlate and synchronize through a process called self-organization. PST makes use of CST to show how peacebuilding systems self-organize at two levels: at the level of the individual programmes that are the basic building blocks of the system, and at the level of the system itself. The two rules are first that the rate of delivery needs to be synchronized with the capacity of the host community to absorb assistance, and the second is the separation of coordination and management.

Interdependence Theory

PST recognizes that a peacebuilding system is a complex system that consists of a large number of independent programmes, with the common binding assumption that collectively and cumulatively they promote, support and sustain the objectives of the system, i.e. to lay the foundation for social justice and sustainable peace and development in a given country or regional conflict system. For instance, most contemporary peacekeeping operations are mandated to support a Disarmament, Demobilization and Reintegration (DDR) process. In support of this larger process, these peace operations will typically undertake various programmes aimed at supporting the national disarmament and demobilization process, with the assumption that other actors will prepare the ground for the reintegration part of the process. On the other hand, various development actors will start planning and undertaking reintegration programmes in support of the national DDR process. The various programmes engaged in the DD and R parts of the overall process are interdependent in that none of them would have any meaning if the others were not playing their roles in the overall process. However, in the peacebuilding systems context, it is important to understand that these roles cannot be equated to the roles performed by the parts of a machine, in that they are neither pre-determined, nor are they linear in progression. The DDR process differ in each case, and the roles of the different actors that normally participate in DDR processes differ in each case, and the outcomes of the DDR processes differ widely in each case. Each aspect of the DDR process, including the roles of the various actors, thus have to be developed by the actors engaged in the process. And the DDR process itself is only one part of a larger dynamic peace process, and a peacebuilding system.

In PST, the success of each individual programme is a factor of the contribution the programme makes to the achievement of the overall peacebuilding objective. If the peace process fails and the conflict resumes, the time and resources invested in each individual programme have been wasted, even if a particular programme has achieved some of its own objectives. An individual programme may have done some good, but if it has not contributed to the overall objective of sustaining the peace, it has failed to sustain that good. For instance, some may argue that even if a conflict resumes, an abandoned DDR process would at least have contributed to reducing the number of arms available in the conflict system, but the reality is that the belligerents will find ways of arming themselves again, and that this process may become an integral part of the political economy of the new conflict. Disarmament is thus not sustainable without successful Demobilization and Reintegration, and DDR is not sustainable if it is not embedded in a successful long-term peace process.

It is only if the combined and sustained collective effort of all the programmes proves successful in the long term that the investment made in each individual programme can be said to have been worthwhile. All the programmes in a peacebuilding system is thus interdependent, and this aspect of PST is called Interdependence Theory (IT).

IT holds that the rationale behind the decision to undertake each individual peacebuilding programme is to contribute to the achievement of the overarching peacebuilding goal. The success of each individual programme is thus linked to the success of the collective and cumulative effect of the overall undertaking (Smuts, 1926: 78). Once this interdependence is recognized by the agencies that implement programmes, they realize that it is in their best interest (thus rational choice) to pursue coherent strategies and to coordinate the implementation of their programmes with each other. Because if they do, it is much more likely that they will achieve the overall peacebuilding objective, and thus individual programme success, than if they don't. Contributing to the overall peacebuilding objective thus becomes an integral part of the individual programmes's goal, and the way in which it achieves such a linkage becomes an important part of its objectives.

IT argues that when this linkage between individual programme performance and the successful implementation of the overarching peacebuilding objective is recognized, coordination emerges as a crucial tool to achieve coherence between individual programme performance and the larger goal it pursues. If the link between the individual programme and the overall goal is broken, the programme loses its reason for being. IT transforms coordination from being perceived as an action that threatens independence to a process that ensures coherence. In PST coordination is the process that ensures that an individual programme is connected to the larger system of which it is a part and without which it has no meaning and cannot succeed.

Complex Systems Theory

PST builds on the inherent capacity of complex systems to self-organize. Although any complex system will self-organize, various factors can influence this process, and it is thus possible to hinder or help the self-organization process. To encourage, support and facilitate self-organization, PST supports and enhances synchronization at the level of the individual programmes as well as at the systemic level. Enhancements suggested in the latter include, (a) the need for a clearly articulated overall strategic vision as well as a process for monitoring, adjusting and providing feedback on the progress achieved at the overall systemic level, and (b) a range of interlinked mechanisms at all levels to facilitate operational coordination, including civil–military coordination, and in the former (c) policies and processes aimed at enabling each individual programme to coordinate with others in the system, so that they can become responsive to developments elsewhere in the peacebuilding system of which they are part, instead of being directed by, and serving, the needs of the institutions that implement and fund them.

To understand self-organization in complex systems it is necessary to recognize that complexity negates central control.[25] Complexity comes about as a result of the interaction between the components of the system and is thus manifested at the level of the system (Cilliers, 1998: 2). It would be impossible for any single entity to have sufficient knowledge of and control over this complex system because if it did it would have to be as complex as the system itself (Cilliers, 2002: 77–84). Instead complex systems rely on a process of self-organization for 'control', and this is an 'order' that emerges out of the cumulative decisions of each individual programme that make up the system.[26] Each individual programme, and in the peacebuilding context this will include groupings of programmes that have some form of collective decision-making function, like a peace operation, continuously make judgements about the effect its activities are having on the system, or part of the system, it is trying to influence. Based on the feedback they receive, these programmes are continuously adjusting their efforts. The cumulative effect of these programme level decisions organize the system as a whole.

A key feature of complex peacebuilding systems is that there is a relationship between the level of coherence in the system and the quality and flow of information in the system. Too little information will cause it to break-up and re-group into smaller systems that have sufficient information to exist. Too much information can also stress a system, but this is a different problem as it relates to the ability of the system to process information rather than the lack of sufficient information to bind it together.

For instance, one of the common motivations for coordination is to avoid duplication. However, when we study complex systems we realize that they maintain a degree of redundancy in order for them to remain flexible to changing needs of their environment. In other words, in a dynamic environment, robustness is not necessarily a function of efficiency and leanness, survival can also depend on the level of redundancy or duplication in the system, because in this way the system can respond to changes in the environment in multiple ways and by learning from them, it can determine which responses are the most effective, and then adjust itself accordingly. It would thus appear as if duplication, to a certain degree, can be a strength, but that when we go beyond that point it becomes a burden that adds to the inefficiency of a system. The point at which duplication becomes a negative force will continuously shift as the demands on the system changes. In a very dynamic environment more redundancy will result in better performance, while in a more stable environment less redundancy will be more efficient. Obtaining and processing information about these changing demands, and how the system is responding to them, is thus critical for the system to manage the degree of robustness it needs to maintain to achieve optimal efficiency.

Feedback, meaning conveying information about the outcome of any process or activity to its source (Capra, 1997: 57), plays a critical role in this process. In essence the flow of information needs to produce a feedback effect, i.e. it should convey data that will enable the various programmes to judge their performance against the performance of others and the system as a whole. They need to share best practices and alert each other to emerging problems, set-backs or delays.

Self-organization is thus a continuous process of adjustment, fuelled by the flow of information through the system. In PST an important function of coordination mechanisms and processes are that they should act as filters that can identify and process useful information and direct it rapidly to those areas where it is needed in the system. In PST improving the ability of the system to process greater volumes of information, at a higher speed and with superior quality of analysis, we will thus improve its ability to self-organize.

In practice, however, peacebuilding systems are burdened by institutional cultures and traditional management and command structures that discourage information flow. They block, hinder or distort the flow of information and thus starve the system from the information it requires to self-organize. This causes the system to break-up into smaller systems. If this tendency is not managed information silos emerge that operate, at best, isolated from each other, or at worst, against each other. All the evaluation studies[27] referred to earlier report the occurrence of this phenomenon to a greater or lesser degree in the peace-building systems they have evaluated, and one can thus conclude that this is a widespread and systemic problem in contemporary peacebuilding systems.

To counter this tendency the PST encourages the establishment of coordination mechanisms and processes at all levels in the system that are designed to create multiple linkages (connections) among the various agencies and their programmes, to ensure that the flow of information, and thus feedback, through the system is facilitated, supported and maintained. It does so in two ways, the first is by recognizing that the principal responsibility for coordination lies with each individual programme and the second is by establishing specific enabling coordination mechanisms at various levels and nodes in the system.

In PST coordination is the responsibility of each individual programme, and as a result coordination is distributed across the system. In PST each individual programme, as a routine part of its programme management process, shall strive to be connected to the other programmes in its sector (which has disciplinary, e.g. water and sanitation, and geographical implications) and to the peacebuild-ing system overall. To be connected in this context implies taking various steps to ensure that there is sufficient flow of information, and thus feedback, between the programme and the rest of the system, so that the programme can adjust itself to changes experienced elsewhere in the system on a continuous basis. This will enable it to continuously synchronize its short and medium-term objectives and activities with the overall progress achieved at various levels in the peacebuilding system. Naturally, some developments will be more relevant to an individual programme than others, and in general programmes will be more connected to others in its sector and its geographical area of operations. However, it needs to maintain the ability to be connected to the overall objectives of the system as well, as changes in the overall progress of the peacebuilding system, that may be influenced by developments far away (in a geographic and/or disciplinary context) from a given programme, may have important implications for its work.

Synchronization is thus the ongoing process whereby individual programmes voluntarily coordinate their plans and activities with each other and with the system as a whole.[28] For the synchronization process to work optimally, each programme must adjust its own actions in response to progress or setbacks experienced elsewhere in the system. As this process unfolds over time, the various programmes coordinate their plans, policies and operations with others in the same sectors, clusters and dimensions and the overall cumulative and collective effect results in improved coherence in the system.

In the peacebuilding context one does not have the luxury of time to allow the 'invisible hand' of the self-organization process to unfold entirely at its own pace. The effects of self-organization can be suppressed and inhibited, or it can be modulated and enhanced in many ways. The *Utstein* and other studies referred to above have found that in many cases the management processes and operating procedures that we have introduced in the past have obstructed and hampered coordination. It would thus make sense to develop mechanisms and processes that would speed-up the desired feed-back effect needed to enhance coherence in peacebuilding systems. This can be achieved by (a) creating coordination mechanisms and processes that encourage, facilitate and support the flow of information at various levels and nodes within the system, and (b) by identifying and removing or adjusting operating procedures that hinder or block the flow of information.

The objective is to encourage programmes to pursue coherence and synergy, where appropriate, in every phase of the project cycle (through combined assessments, integrated planning, joint operational coordination and cooperative monitoring and evaluation), to facilitate these processes by establishing coordination mechanisms where liaison and coordination can take place, and to ensure that there is an enabling environment where managerial practises, organizational rules and regulations and financial management systems encourage coordination and coherence.

The Civil–Military Coordination branch of the military component has been developed to be the link between the military component and the rest of the civilian agencies. It is thus a key node for the security and development interface. The military component is especially inclined to isolation because its baseline culture is designed to protect its command, control and communication systems from external threats. However, in the peace operations context it is vital that the security dimension is connected to the overall peacebuilding strategy and civil–military coordination thus becomes a critical node that needs to be connected with the rest of the system.

The importance of strategic coordination

The PST approach argues that an individual programme has no meaning if it is not coherent with the overall peacebuilding objective. The overall peacebuilding objective refers to the strategic direction of the peacebuilding system, taken as a whole, as produced by the cumulative and collective planning efforts of all the programmes and agencies in the system. An important assumption of the PST approach is that the strategic planning process has produced a set of clearly articulated and credible overall peacebuilding objectives, for instance in the form of a common country strategy, that individual programmes can use in their own planning processes.

As the *Utstein* study and other studies[29] referred to above have pointed out, the lack of a clearly articulated overall strategy is, in fact, a critical shortcoming in many past and contemporary peacebuilding systems. Without a clear country strategy individual programmes are unable to position, adjust and monitor the degree to which they may be making a contribution to the overall peacebuilding objective. Instead they are likely to continue to blindly work according to their own programme goals regardless of the pathological consequences this may have for their own programme or the larger peacebuilding objectives.

This problem can be observed between dimensions at the operational level where, for instance, the political component insists on pursuing a pre-determined election timetable without taking critical delays in some of the other dimensions into account. If the planning of the election was premised on the achievement of certain benchmarks in other dimensions, e.g. sufficient progress in the demobilization and reintegration of ex-combatants and the return of refugees and IDPs, so that they can be included in the voters roll, then it may follow that consideration should be given to adjusting the election timetable to accommodate these delays. The political component may continue to insist on the pre-determined election timetable because in their analysis the political capital needed to adjust it may not exist, or they may choose to use the timetable as a way of maintaining pressure on the parties and the momentum of the peace process. The point is that whatever the outcome may be, it should be a conscious strategy produced by an overall strategic planning and monitoring process that have discounted inputs from all the various dimensions of the system. The chosen course of action needs to be closely monitored to measure whether it is indeed having the desired effect because complex systems (CST) are non-linear and the outcome is never exactly the same as was intended at the outset (Gleick, 1987: 80).

Each programme, sector, component and dimension needs to be understood as interdependent and interlinked (IT) and therefore their various planning processes must seek coherence through synchronization with the other. For this reason, the process of developing and adjusting (through ongoing monitoring) a common country strategy, and continuously sharing this information (feedback) with all the dimensions, agencies and programmes in the system, acquires a critical role in the PST approach to peacebuilding.

Timing and sequencing

Closely linked to the strategic planning, coordination and feedback process is the ongoing need for operational coordination. Various operational coordination mechanisms have developed over the years within the various functional dimensions, with relatively good progress achieved to date in especially the Resident Coordinator/Humanitarian Coordinator (RC/HC) and civil–military coordination functions. Where the lack of coordination is most critical, however, is between the different dimensions. We need to improve our ability to synchronize the project cycles of the different dimensions, clusters, sectors, agencies and programmes to ensure that the combined effect on the society is positive, consistent and produced at a rate that can be absorbed by local institutions and the body politic.

The latter aspect – the ability of the local or internal actors to absorb the assistance provided by the external actors – is largely ignored in contemporary peacebuilding systems. The success of a programme tends to be measured in terms of the resources (inputs) and activities (outputs) that were expended to undertake it instead of evaluating the sustainable capacity (outcome) that was developed as a result of its work. The legacy of violent conflict typically results in the host society having a much lower capacity to absorb assistance than the international community anticipates. Despite this, peacebuilding systems are typically planned at the outset as intense three to four year interventions and the bulk of the money theoretically available for peacebuilding systems is made available in the early stages of the intervention. The result is considerable wastage in that large amounts are spent on programmes that the host society simply cannot absorb.

The pressure to attract and spend the funds potentially available for a peacebuilding system in the initial years is influenced by a perceived narrow window of opportunity, determined by the period that the international media attention remains focused on the post-conflict story. Not surprisingly this approach of focusing the international attention and support on the initial post-conflict period has not had much success with achieving sustainable peace. Its only long-term effect is donor fatigue on the side of the international community and prolonged instability, underdevelopment and continuous cycles of conflict on the side of the recipient societies.

The way to counter this effect is to synchronize the rate of delivery with the rate of absorption. The PST approach suggests that the synchronization of delivery with absorption should be one of the most important factors in the overall timing and sequencing of peacebuilding systems and the actual rate of absorption should be closely monitored. If the programmes and agencies, and their donors, recognize that the ultimate aim of the peacebuilding system is sustainable peace, then the overall strategy and the pace of its implementation have to reflect the optimal relationship between delivery and absorption.

Individual programmes need to be evaluated not only on their outputs but on the degree to which the beneficiaries have absorbed and benefited from them (outcome), and how this has contributed to the overall peacebuilding objective (impact).

Monitoring and evaluation

If donors and the agencies that implement peacebuilding programmes accept the logic of interdependence (IT), coherence would become an important norm in their programme management policies. But how does one encourage each programme to take responsibility for its own coordination? The PST approach suggest using the monitoring and evaluation system to encourage each programme to demonstrate how it is contributing to the overall strategic objective, and how it is synchronizing its activities with other programmes and the peacebuilding system as a whole. Monitoring and evaluation is not only crucial in that it provides the feedback the system needs to function, it is also a norm-creating,[30] in that it encourages programmes to demonstrate how they have used coordination to improve coherence with the larger system of which they are part.

This is not how most peacebuilding programmes are currently evaluated. Individual programmes are measured against their stated objectives, outputs and timeframes within the context of the policies of the agency that undertakes the programme and donor requirements. The assumption is that the programme would have been designed to be compatible with the overarching strategic goals, but as the *Utstein* study quoted earlier pointed out, more than half of the programmes it studied showed no link to a country strategy. In most cases the original planning was done months before the programme was implemented and the institutional culture leaves little room, if any, for adjustments during the project cycle. In the peacebuilding context, which is highly dynamic, programmes that are unable to continuously adjust to changes in their environment become dysfunctional and in many instances counter-productive.

In the current dominant programme management culture, changes to the plan are seen as a sign of failure. Failure on the side of the project management team to implement the plan as foreseen, or failure on the part of the planners to have foreseen all possible contingencies. Changing the programme plan requires much more political capital than just seeing it through as conceived. As a result the current dominant institutional culture discourages synchronization during the operational phase of the project cycle.

Introducing monitoring and evaluation mechanisms that take into account how an individual programme functions in the context of related programmes, its sector and the larger peace process will result in a fundamental shift in our management and coordination cultures. It will require programme managers and staff to recognize that success requires the ability to synchronize your efforts with those of others, and with the system as a whole. Synchronization with the overall system will need to become an organizational virtue, and new tools and methodologies will have to be developed to realize it. Individual and organizational behaviour that encourages programme synchronization will need to be encouraged and rewarded and behaviour that inhibits synchronization will have to be discouraged and sanctioned. Programme managers and others in policy and operational decision-making roles will need to be trained to understand the system of which they are part (the different components of the system and how they interact) and the environment (conflict dynamics, development processes, the political economy of war, etc.) within which they have to operate.

Common spaces

One of the key issues that becomes evident when the notion of evaluation and monitoring is raised is the lack of a 'common language' amongst the professionals in the different peacebuilding dimensions, and especially between the military, political and development actors. 'Strategic objectives' imply longer-term goals to most civilians, while to most military officers it would refer to the level at which the objectives were set. The need for a clear 'exit strategy' is important to the military while civilians, in general, are more comfortable with a longer-term process approach that may imply several phases, each with its own goals and objectives, e.g. the three phases in PST, namely the stabilization, transitional and consolidation phases. The time horizons of the various dimension and programmes are not aligned. As most military units are deployed for six months at a time, such units are naturally more focussed on short-term results. Military headquarters are normally staffed for a slightly longer period, in most cases a year. What all military units and staff officers have in common is that they want to leave the mission with a clear sense of what they achieved in the period that we were deployed. Most civilian agencies have a longer-term approach and an awareness that their initiatives need to be sustainable to be successful. One element of the overall strategic planning, ongoing monitoring and periodic evaluation processes are thus educating each other about our different institutional cultures and developing ways of sharing our information and perspectives. We need to create multi-disciplinary spaces that are able to combine inputs, collate and analyse information and form a common picture of the overall effect a given peacebuilding system is having on a conflict system.

Separating management and coordination

Lastly, but critically important in the PST approach is the need to maintain a firewall between the management or command function on the one hand and the coordination function on the other. The purpose of the firewall is to protect the independence of individual agencies and programmes. Decision-making takes place in the vertical management or command function, while the coordination function is used to exchange information horizontally and diagonally. Coordination can not endanger any agency or programme's independence because each individual agent retains full control over their own decision-making function. Coordination provides the decision-makers with information about what is happening elsewhere in the system, but the decision-making power to respond to that information remains fully in the hands of each individual programme and agency. For coordination to be palatable to defensive institutional cultures it has to be non-threatening. And for it to be non-threatening it has to be voluntary and free of any decision-making power over the participating agency.

There should thus be a separation between the management structures, including reporting lines, which are vertical and hierarchical, and the coordination function, which is about the flow of information horizontally or diagonally. Horizontal coordination does not imply that it is, or should be, limited to strata in the vertical axis. For coordination to be most effective it should not be boxed in to levels or dimensions related to the vertical hierarchical management axis. When coordination processes operate outside the constraints of the management hierarchy, the flow of information inside the hierarchy is enriched because it is continuously verified and compared with the information outside the hierarchy. Horizontal and diagonal coordination should pose no threat to the vertical management processes as all decisions are made within the vertical hierarchy behind the management or command firewall. The firewall concept between management and coordination is an important element of the PST approach because it addresses the basic fear most agencies have about coordination and integration, namely that it will impact on their independence and institutional sovereignty.

This implies that those who need to maintain their independence, but who will benefit from participating in system-wide coordination mechanisms, can do so freely and without fear that they will be absorbed or subsumed. This applies, of course, especially to those in the humanitarian community who work 'in' conflict, rather than 'on' conflict. All those that are engaged in peacebuilding work will fall in the latter category and would be interdependent (IT), but while those in the former category will need to understand what is happening in the peacebuilding context, they are not part of it. They are part of the conflict system, however, and in that context they do need to coordinate, in one way or another, to discount the impact of the peacebuilding system on their work and vice versa.

Military commanders use their civil–military coordination assets to manage civilian interference in what they perceive to be their core tasks. An important converse responsibility that civil–military coordination officers have is to advise their commanders not to extend their reach into the political, humanitarian and development dimensions. Where a commander may thus wish to exert some degree of 'control' over those other actors that happen to be in their area of operations,[31] the civil–military coordination officer needs to advise the commander on what the appropriate civil–military relationship between the military component and the various different categories of internal and external civilian actors are. The appropriate relationship will depend largely on the degree to which the military component is perceived to be a party to the conflict or not.[32]

Conclusion

This chapter started by pointing out that one of the reasons why coherence has proven elusive is because the agencies that undertake peacebuilding pro-grammes lack a shared understanding of the role of coordination. Some see coordination as a way to create order while others associate it with losing control over their own independence. It then set out to contribute to the development of a theoretical framework that would explain the role coordination can play in binding the different programmes and agencies into a coherent and integrated system.

Peacebuilding Systems Theory (PST) is aimed at improving the coherence of peacebuilding systems without impacting on the independence of the participating agencies. Interdependence Theory is one element of PST and it recognizes that a peacebuilding operation functions as a complex system made up of a large number of interdependent programmes undertaken by multiple agencies over time with the common binding assumption that they would collectively and cumulatively promote and support sustainable peace across all aspects of the host society.

At the core of this theory is the argument that programmes and agencies are interdependent in that no single programme can achieve the goal of the peacebuilding system – addressing the root causes of the conflict and laying the foundation for social justice and sustainable peace and development – on its own. The success of each individual programme, and the agencies that undertake it, is a factor of the contribution the programme makes to the achievement of the overall peacebuilding objective. It is only if the combined and sustained effort proves successful in the long term that the investment made in each individual programme can be said to have been worthwhile.

PST is based on a number of rules. Principle among them is the separation between management and coordination. Decision-making takes place in the management function, while the coordination function is used to exchange information. By keeping these two functions separate, coordination does not pose any threat to a programme's independence because each individual agent retains full control over their own decision-making function.

The PST approach emphasize the need to develop and maintain a set of clearly articulated overall peacebuilding objectives against which individual programmes can benchmark their own plans and progress. The process of developing and adjusting such a common country strategy, and continuously sharing this information with all the programmes and agencies in the system, is a critical element in the optimal functioning of the system because this strategic-level coordination generates the feedback that individual programmes need to adjust their own programmes to progress and setbacks elsewhere in the system.

Operational coordination is achieved through a synchronization system in which each individual programme takes responsibility for its own coordination, but the overall self-organization process is modulated and enhanced through various mechanisms and processes that facilitate linkages and connections among critical nodes in the system. The process is supported by monitoring and evaluation systems that not only provides feedback on individual and overall progress, but also encourages programmes and agencies to participate in the synchronization process by requiring them to report on the steps they took to synchronize their plans and operations with others in their sectors and the overall objectives. The evaluation process becomes a normative process by encouraging and rewarding behaviour that enables coherence, and by discouraging and sanctioning behaviour that inhibits coordination.

Another crucial PST rule is the peacebuilding system's ability to monitor the effect it is having on its environment. The project cycles of the different programmes and agencies need to be synchronized to ensure that their combined and cumulative effect on the society is positive, consistent and delivered at a rate that can be absorbed. If the ultimate aim of the peacebuilding operation is sustainable peace then the overall strategy and the pace of its implementation have to reflect the optimal relationship between delivery and absorption.

Civil–Military Coordination has a critically important role to play as part of the larger coordination process at all levels: strategic, operational and tactical. It has to link the security dimension and military component with the rest of the system and ensure that the information generated within the military component is shared with the rest of the system and vice-versa. It also has to assist with maintaining the separation of management and coordination, thereby promoting the independence and flexibility of both the military and other components, and it has to participate in the system-wide monitoring and evaluation processes so that it can contribute to and benefit from the information generated through this feedback process.

The chapter argues that a complex systems (CST) approach will be more flexible and responsive to the dynamic needs of a post-conflict environment than a model dominated by a single bureaucratic agency that assumes overall responsibility for peacebuilding systems through a centralized coordination function.

The PST approach has the potential to assist multilateral institutions, states, donors and peacebuilding agencies, including the military component, to develop a common theoretical understanding of the need for coherence, and the role coordination can play in binding the different programmes and agencies into a coherent peacebuilding system.

Notes

1 For a quantitative analysis of the factors that have influenced the outcome of peacebuilding operations since 1944, see Doyle and Sambanis, 2000.
2 The peacebuilding concept was first introduced in *An Agenda for Peace: Preventive Diplomacy, Peacemaking and Peace-keeping* that was released by then UN Secretary-General, Boutros Boutros Ghali in 1992.
3 In 1997, the UN High Commissioner for Refugees (UNHCR) and the World Bank jointly launched the Brookings process to involve all partners in coordinating and jointly programming activities in a country. Its success has been limited but the so-called 4R's terminology developed in the process is still widely in use. Final Report of the Commission on Human Security, Chapter 4, p. 58 (www.humansecurity-chs.org/).
4 See for instance the 2005, *In Larger Freedom: Towards Security, Development and Human Rights for All*, Report of the Secretary-General of the United Nations (www.un.org/largerfreedom), and the 2006, *Delivering as One*, Report of the Secretary-General's High-Level Panel on System-wide Coherence, United Nations, New York (www.un.org/events/panel).
5 There are a number of different interpretations of these phases, but most convey the

same essential progression. See for instance the Association of the US Army and Centre for Strategic and International Studies (CSIS), *Post-Conflict Reconstruction: Task Framework*, Washington, DC, 2002, in which they identify three stages, namely: the initial response, transformation and fostering sustainability.

6 This definition was initially developed by the author and Senzo Ngubane in *Peacebuilding in Southern Africa*, an ACCORD (www.accord.org.za) report commissioned by JICA in 2004, and was further elaborated by the author in *A Post-Conflict Reconstruction Policy Framework for Africa*, a draft policy framework facilitated by ACCORD for NEPAD (www.nepad.org) in May 2005.

7 The NATO definition of Civil–Military Cooperation (CIMIC) is the co-ordination and co-operation, in support of the mission, between the NATO Commander and civil populations, including national and local authorities, as well as international, national and non-governmental organizations and agencies (NATO, 2000: 1).

8 The EU definition of Civil–Military Cooperation (CIMIC) is the co-ordination and co-operation, in support of the mission, between military components of EU-led Crisis Management Operations and civil role-players (external to the EU), including national population and local authorities, as well as international, national and non-governmental organizations and agencies (EU, 2002: 9).

9 The UN Department of Peacekeeping Operations (DPKO) definitions of civil–military coordination is: 'UN Civil–Military Coordination is the system of inter-action, involving exchange of information, negotiation, de-confliction, mutual support, and planning at all levels, between military elements and humanitarian organizations, development organizations and the local civilian population to achieve UN objectives' (UN, 2002).

10 The UN humanitarian community has its own definition for humanitarian civil–military coordination (UN-CMCoord), namely: 'the essential dialogue and interaction between civilian and military actors in humanitarian emergencies that is necessary to protect and promote humanitarian principles, avoid competition, minimise inconsistency, and when appropriate pursue common goals. Basic strategies range from coexistence to co-operation. Co-ordination is a shared responsibility facilitated by liaison and common training' (IASC, 2004). See the June 2004 IASC Reference Paper on 'Civil–Military Relationships in Complex Emergencies', and the March 2003 'Guidelines on the Use of Military and Civil Defence Assets to Support United Nations Humanitarian Activities in Complex Emergencies.'

11 See 'Building Policy Coherence', OECD, www.oecd.org/puma/strat/coherence.htm.

12 Among others: Dahrendorf, 2003; Porter, 2002; Sommers, 2000; Stockton, 2002; Donini, 2002; Reindorp and Wiles, 2001; and Duffield, Lautze and Jones, 1998.

13 UN reports, op. cit., footnote 4.

14 With apologies to the definition of coherence on p. 4 of the Henry Dunant Center for Humanitarian Dialogue's February 2003 report: *Politics and Humanitarianism: Coherence in Crisis?*: 'Coherence came to mean: the effort, notably by the UN and some donors, to ensure that all international aid and interventions in a particular crisis are directed towards a common objective.'

15 OECD, op. cit., footnote 11.

16 Refer, for instance, to the members of the Organization for Economic Cooperation and Development (www.OECD.org).

17 See Chesterman 2002, for a discussion on the refusal of some of the largest donors to have their money pooled into a trust fund for Afghanistan.

18 There are various promising developments in this direction, e.g. the February 2003 *Rome Declaration on Harmonisation* signed by 28 developing countries and 49 donor organizations. The four main principles highlighted in the Declaration are: recipient countries co-ordinate development assistance, donors align their aid with recipient countries' priorities and systems, donors streamline aid delivery and donors adopts policies, procedures and incentives that foster harmonization.

19 This does not necessarily come about through a concerted effort by one agency. In fact, this development is a good example of self-regulation in complex systems. No one agency has identified the need, or decided that all peacebuilding systems should address all these dimensions, but various systems has responded to their needs over time and through this process a diverse range of programme responses have emerged that address individual needs across a wide spectrum. This does not exclude the possibility that specific needs in any given situation may be neglected. And where they are, a complex peacebuilding system, perhaps through co-ordination processes, should identify such a need and try to facilitate a response.

20 For a detailed analysis of the Integrated Missions concept see the 'Report on Integrated Missions: Practical Perspectives and Recommendations', Independent Study for the Expanded ECHA Core Group, King's College and the Norwegian Institute for International Affairs (NUPI), May 2005.

21 In 2004 the United Kingdom established a cross Government and multi-disciplinary Post Conflict Reconstruction Unit (PCRU) and in 2005 the US State Department established an Office of the Coordinator of Stabilization and Reconstruction.

22 UN reports, op. cit., footnote 4.

23 See Stockton 2002 and the argument he makes that co-ordination is in effect a levy on the scarce resources allocated to beneficiaries.

24 Note the case studies on co-ordination in Sierra Leone and Rwanda in Sommers 2000.

25 See Donini, 2002, where he argues that the objectives and organizational cultures of the development, humanitarian and peacekeeping communities are essentially irreconcilable within a single centralised structure.

26 In complexity theory this process is referred to as *autopoiesis*, see Maturana and Varela, 1980 and Luhmann, 1995.

27 The evaluation studies listed in footnote 12.

28 This process is similar to what Poincaré and Prigogine refer to as correlation. See Prigogine, 1996, pp. 121–125.

29 Smith, 2003 and the evaluation studies listed in footnote 12.

30 See Chapter 3 'Promoting Norms' in Axelrod, 1997.

31 Military commanders tend to confuse 'area of operations' and 'area of responsibility', in that they assume to have responsibility for all activities taking place in the area of operations allocated to them, and as a result often feel the duty to co-ordinate others in their area of operations. In reality they typically have a mandate that limits their responsibility to ensuring a safe and secure environment, and they should thus co-ordinate with others as equal partners in the spirit of interdependence (see IT in the body of the paper).

32 Refer to the UN humanitarian civil–military co-ordination policies listed in footnote 10.

Bibliography

Axelrod, R. (1997) *The Complexity of Cooperation*, Princeton: Princeton University Press.

Capra, F. (1997) *The Web of Life*, New York: Anchor Books.

Cilliers, P. (1998) *Complexity and Postmodernism: Understanding Complex Systems*, London: Routledge.

Cilliers, P. (2002) 'Why We Cannot Know Complex Things Completely', *Emergence*, 4 (1/2), 77–84.

Chesterman, S. (2002) *Tiptoeing Through Afghanistan: The Future of UN State-Building*, New York: International Peace Academy.

Dahrendorf, N. (2003) *A Review of Peace Operations: A Case for Change*, London: King's College.

de Coning, C.H. (2006) 'Peace and Peacekeeping Diplomacy', in Geeraerts, G. and Pauwels, N. (eds), *Dimensions of Peace and Security: A Reader*, Brussels: P.I.E-Peter Lang.

de Coning, C.H. (2007) 'Civil–Military Coordination and UN Peacebuilding Operations', in Langholtz, H. Kondoch, B. and Wells, A. (eds), *International Peacekeeping: The Yearbook of International Peace Operations*, Vol. 11, Brussels: Koninklijke Brill N.V.

Donini, A. (2002) *The Policies of Mercy: UN Coordination in Afghanistan, Mozambique and Rwanda*, Occasional Paper #22, Thomas J. Watson Jr. Institute for International Studies, Providence: Brown University

Doyle, M.W. and Sambanis, N. (2000) *International Peacebuilding: A Theoretical and Quantitative Analysis*, Washington, DC: World Bank

EU. (2002) *Civil–Military Co-operation (CIMIC) Concept for EU-Led Crisis Management Operations*, ESDP/PESD COSDP 67, Brussels: European Union.

Duffield, M., Lautze S. and Jones, B. (1998) *Strategic Humanitarian Coordination in the Great Lakes Region 1996–1997*, New York: United Nations Office for the Coordination of Humanitarian Affairs (OCHA).

Eriksson, J. *et al.* (1996) *The International Response to Conflict and Genocide: Lessons from the Rwanda Experience – Synthesis Report, Joint Evaluation of Emergency Assistance to Rwanda*, Copenhagen: DANIDA.

Gleick, J. (1987) *Chaos: Making a New Science*, New York: Penguin.

IASC (2004) *Civil–Military Relations in Complex Emergencies*, June 2004, UN Inter-Agency Standing Committee (IASC), New York: United Nations.

Licklider, R. (1995) 'The Consequences of Negotiated Settlements in Civil Wars 1945–93', *American Political Science Review*, Vol. 89, No. 3: 681–690.

Luhmann, N. (1995) *Social Systems*, Stanford: Stanford University Press.

Maturana, H. and Varela, F. (1980), *Autopoiesis and Cognition*, Dordrecht: D. Reidel.

NATO (2000) *NATO Military Policy on Civil–Military Co-operation (CIMIC)*, CIMICWG 001–00, WP(MC411), Brussels: NATO.

Paris, R. (2004) *At War's End: Building Peace After Civil Conflict*, Cambridge: Cambridge University Press.

Porter, T. (2002) *An External Review of the CAP*, New York: United Nations Office for the Coordination of Humanitarian Affairs (OCHA).

Prigogine, I. (1996) *The End of Certainty: Time, Chaos and the New Laws of Nature*, New York: The Free Press.

Pugh, M. and Cooper, N. (2004) *War Economies in a Regional Context*, London: Lynne Rienner.

Reindorp, N. and Wiles, P. (2001) *Humanitarian Coordination: Lessons from Recent Field Experience*, A study commissioned by the Office for the Coordination of Humanitarian Affairs (OCHA), London: Overseas Development Institute (ODI).

Smith, D. (2003) *Towards a Strategic Framework for Peacebuilding: the Synthesis Report of the Joint Utstein Study on Peacebuilding*, Oslo: PRIO.

Smuts, J.C. (1926) *Holism and Evolution*, 1987 edition, Cape Town: N&S Press.

Sommers, M. (2000) *The Dynamics of Coordination*, Thomas J. Watson Jr. Institute of International Affairs, Occasional Paper #40, Providence: Brown University.

Stockton, N. (2002) *Strategic Coordination in Afghanistan*, Kabul: Afghanistan Research and Evaluation Unit (AREU).

Strand, A. (2003), *Who's helping Who? NGO Coordination of Humanitarian Assistance*, Doctoral Dissertation, Department of Politics, York: University of York.

UN DPKO. (2002) *Civil–Military Coordination Policy*, New York: UN Department of Peacekeeping Operations (DPKO).

Uvin, P. (2002) 'The Development/Peacebuilding Nexus: a Typology and History of Changing Paradigms', *Journal of Peacebuilding and Development*, Vol. 1, No. 1: 5–24.

Van Brabant, K. (2001) 'Understanding, Promoting and Evaluating Coordination: an Outline Framework', in Gordon, D.S and Toase, F.H. (eds), *Aspects of Peacekeeping*, London: Frank Cass.

Wood, B. (2003) *Development Dimensions of Conflict Prevention and Peace-building*, New York: UN Development Programme (UNDP).

5 A management perspective on co-operation between military and civilian actors in Afghanistan

Sebastiaan J.H. Rietjens

Introduction

The international community has no universally agreed multilateral or interdisciplinary concept of response to complex emergencies[1] (Mackinlay, 1996). Despite the plethora of 'lessons learned', procedures change as the community crosses each new threshold of operational experience. Civil agencies, including human rights groups and diplomatic offices, now constitute the major response element. They often identify the early symptoms of a complex emergency and apply a variety of conflict prevention and peace maintenance strategies. Normally they attempt resolution some time before the situation attracts the attention of the international media and some form of wider political, emergency or military response. However, once the situation degenerates and human rights violations increase beyond the immediate capacity of the deployed agencies and Non Governmental Organisations (NGOs)[2] to resolve, and the situation escalates into a full-scale conflict-related disaster, a wider composite response may be required.

Attempts at such wider composite responses are made by the UN. In *An Agenda for Peace* of June 1992, the then Secretary-General Boutros Boutros-Ghali noted that the UN and its security arm have emerged as 'a central instrument for the prevention and resolution of conflicts and for the preservation of peace'. Based on this Agenda, the UN, authorized by the Security Council, has in recent years initiated many peace support operations in response to complex emergencies. UNPROFOR (United Nations Protection Force) in former Yugoslavia, UNOSOM (United Nations Operations in Somalia) and UNMIH (United Nations Mission in Haiti) are good examples. Next to these UN operations, operations are carried out under the auspices of NATO or a 'coalition of the willing' (e.g. International Security Assistance Force (ISAF) in Afghanistan and Stabilisation Force Iraq (SFIR)).

These peace support operations take place in environments served by multiple civilian institutions and humanitarian organizations and a challenging array of issues that are not at all 'military' in nature. This has increased the need to manage the civil–military interface, particularly that between the military and the humanitarian organizations. This process of management is frequently described as civil–military co-operation (CIMIC) (Gordon, 2001).

In most peace support operations, the approach to CIMIC has been essentially improvisational and pragmatic (Currey, 2003; Gourlay, 2000). As such it has evolved over time in response to specific needs on the ground. The logic of structured co-operation should lead to efficiency gains and greater respect for the comparative advantages of civilian and military actors. A promising way forward is to experiment with improved models for co-operation between the military and the civilian actors (Gourlay, 2000).

Previous research paid little attention to the development of models to structure the co-operation between military and civilian actors. At the global and regional levels Baarda (2001) modelled which forms of co-operation could be fruitful without entailing too many risks for humanitarian independence and impartiality. However, as many responsibilities are delegated to local level co-operation becomes most obvious at this level. The objective of this research is to develop a model that will support the co-operation between the military and the civilian actors in a peace support operation at a local level in response to a complex emergency. For involved actors and their leaders this support expresses itself in the development of checklists, an increased understanding of (potential) conflicts in the process of co-operation and elements for procedures to increase the performance of the co-operation. It offers academic researchers a framework for future empirical studies that can confirm or disconfirm the legitimacy of the model.

The paper is outlined as follows. First the research methodology is presented. Based on theories on co-operative arrangements and CIMIC the subsequent section develops an initial model. Next, the model is reviewed in seven partnerships of the International Security Assistance Force (ISAF) and civilian actors in Kabul in 2003. The last section finally draws conclusions.

Research methodology

To meet the formulated objective, the first step was to do an extensive literature review on CIMIC. Most literature focused on just a few aspects of civil–military co-operation. Duffey (2000) primarily dealt with cultural differences in peace support operations, Forman and Parhad (1997) emphasized on the resources and Eriksson (1999) focused on trust, different time perspectives, co-ordination and on the exchange of intelligence and information between the military and the NGOs.

Bollen and Beeres (2002) state that 'by no means does civil–military co-operation constitute an exception with regard to other inter-organizational alliances. However as a result of structural fundamental differences between the military and their civilian counterparts alliances are bound to be fragile. Taken on their own, interdependencies generate too few safeguards to shield the collaborators from hidden agendas, self-interest or from their partners' opportunistic behaviour (Bollen and Beeres, 2002). Inter-organizational alliances, mostly referred to as co-operative arrangements, have been studied in great detail (e.g. Hoffmann and Schlosser, 2001; Das and Teng, 1997; Faulkner, 1995;

Yoshino and Rangan, 1995; Gulati, 1998). Literature on co-operative arrangements can offer a lot to CIMIC and applying theories on co-operative arrangements to CIMIC can improve the co-operation between civilian and military actors.

The next step of this research was therefore to review a number of theories from literature on co-operative arrangements to establish to what extent these could offer useful elements to explain the performance of CIMIC. To identify these elements three fields of research had been reviewed. At first, theories on strategic alliances are studied, as these are the main form of co-operative arrangements. Some researchers even argue that virtually all kinds of co-operative arrangements should be called strategic alliances (Lorange and Roos, 1992).

Since theories on strategic alliances mainly focus on bilateral relations between business organizations and many different actors are present in a peace support operation (e.g. NGOs, military, local authorities and the population), using only theories on strategic alliances was too limited. Many researchers state that their theories on strategic alliances are also valid in case of multiple actors, but to ensure validity for multi-actor co-operation, theories on networks have been reviewed. Third, theories on strategic alliances and networks usually focus on private actors. In a peace support operation both private actors (e.g. NGOs) and public actors (e.g. military, international organizations and local authorities) interact with each other. Theories on public–private partnerships have therefore also been reviewed.

Based on the literature reviews on CIMIC and on co-operative arrangements, an initial model was developed. Next, a case study protocol was developed to apply the initial model in practice.

To review the initial model in practice multiple case study research was carried out. Seven partnerships between ISAF and civilian actors were reviewed. To increase validity both methodological and data source triangulation were employed. At first a general literature study was done. To get detailed information on the partnerships 13 semi-structured interviews were held with key persons of ISAF and the civilian actors. Key persons of ISAF were based in the CIMIC Coordination Centre (CCC) and the J9 branch of the HQ. These included liaison officers, personnel of the planning and operations branch and personnel of the project team.

Based on the interviews with military key persons, civilian partners were identified and their key persons contacted and interviewed. In addition many documentary sources were consulted. These sources consisted of situation reports, personal diaries of involved persons, detailed project information, notes of the meetings, internal memoranda, memory books, evaluation reports and scores of photos.

Initial model

Based on Mohr (1982), research models are classified into 'variance' models and 'process' models. The fundamental objective of a variance model is to search for causal relationships between potential predictors (independent variables) and outcomes (dependent variables), to generalize knowledge by predicting patterns of phenomena across situations (Lei, 1994). The methods of a variance model are concerned with identifying predictors and outcomes, testing the empirical association between the two, inferring a causal relationship (If X, then Y, If more X, then more Y) at a statistical confidence level.

In contrast with a variance model, a process model assumes the precursor to be insufficient to 'cause' the outcome, but necessary for it to occur. The outcomes are not conceived as variables that can take on a range of values (i.e. varying degrees of a single dimension), but rather as discrete or discontinuous phenomena (i.e. having a qualitatively different 'change of state'). The role of time in a process model is dynamic. It focuses on sequences of events over time in order to explain how and why particular outcomes are reached.

Mohr (1982) states that variance and process models can 'peacefully coexist', but that distinctions between them should not be blurred in an attempt to gain the advantages of both within a single theoretical approach. In this research a process approach is used. This is because by its structure, a variance model assumes that a certain outcome will invariably occur when necessary and sufficient conditions are present. It assumes a real, uni-directional cause-effect relationship. This assumption is as yet too stringent for CIMIC in a peace support operation. Secondly, the role of time in CIMIC cannot be assumed static, since a peace support operation is not stable, orderly and cannot be characterized by knowable, constant relationships. A process model is thus the most appropriate way to model CIMIC in a peace support operation.

The input of the model is the revelation of a complex emergency. In response to this, a political decision-making process at international and national level is initiated. If this results in a mandate, which provides a legal basis for the deployment and actions, military contingents of different nations are deployed to the host nation of the complex emergency. Parallel to the deployment of military forces, humanitarian organizations attempt to provide assistance (e.g. humanitarian aid, protection of minorities, refugees and displaced persons, medical care and reconstruction) in the complex emergency, based on their own charter and mission. Having arrived in the host nation all actors operate in the same operational environment. Then they have the choice to work separately or to co-operate, which is the starting point of the process model.

In the development of the model, at first the phases in the development of the partnership are discussed. Many researchers argue that the development of a partnership is similar to a relationship between people: first two people meet, then they fall in love, next they get engaged and finally they grow old together or sometimes divorce (Kanter, 1994). Although no partnership travels the same path, a successful partnership generally unfolds in several overlapping phases (Das and Teng, 1997): the formation phase, the operation phase and the evolution phase. These phases are adopted in the model.

In order to make the model operational, the three main phases are divided into six steps. In the formation phase three steps are identified, based on the theories on co-operative arrangements. At first the decision whether or not to co-operate is to be made by each of the actors (Yoshino and Rangan, 1995). If an actor concludes that co-operation is a promising way forward, the second step consists of the selection of an appropriate partner (Geringer, 1991). Having selected a partner, the third step is to design the partnership (Lewis, 1990). This step should result in a detailed implementation plan, describing inter alia the rights and duties of each partner. Based on this implementation plan, the partnership is to be operated. Step four consists of the implementation of the partnership. In this step the actual performance of the partnership is to be made.

The third phase of the model is the evolution of the partnership. In theories on co-operative arrangements the evolution phase distinguishes between termination and modification of the partnership (e.g. Kanter, 1994). However, since military forces should not be involved in the crisis for a long term (NATO, 2000), the partnership has to be terminated after completing the implementation plan. If both partners want to continue the relationship, a new implementation plan should be developed. As Whitman (2000) questions, *'What happens if the military leaves?'* step five of the model consists of the transfer of tasks and responsibilities. The final step of the model is to evaluate the partnership. This results in the final output of the model, which is the performance of the partnership for each of the participating actors. Figure 1 presents the initial model. In the presentation a distinction is made between inputs and outcomes, which are indicated with a circle and processes, which are indicated with a square.

Empirical review

To apply the initial model to daily practice, seven partnerships between ISAF and civilian actors have been studied in detail. These partnerships took place in two subsequent rotations of ISAF led by the German–Netherlands Corps (ISAF III: February 2003 – August 2003) and NATO (ISAF IV: August 2003 – January 2004). The following partnerships were studied:

1 Information sharing and co-ordination of activities with the Agency Coordinating Body for Afghan Relief (ACBAR).
2 Various activities (e.g. co-ordination of activities, driver training, protection) with United Nation's Assistance Mission in Afghanistan (UNAMA).
3 Various medical activities (e.g. joint checking of patients, delivery of medical supplies) with the German NGO Die Johanniter.
4 Various activities (e.g. back to school programme, demining of warehouse location) with United Nation's Children Fund (UNICEF).
5 Information sharing and co-ordination of activities with the Afghan NGOs Coordination Bureau (ANCB).
6 The reconstruction of a local school in Zemma with the Ministry of Education (MoE) and a local contractor.
7 Refurbishment of a sub fire-station in Pol-e-Charki with the Ministry of Interior (MoI) and a local contractor.

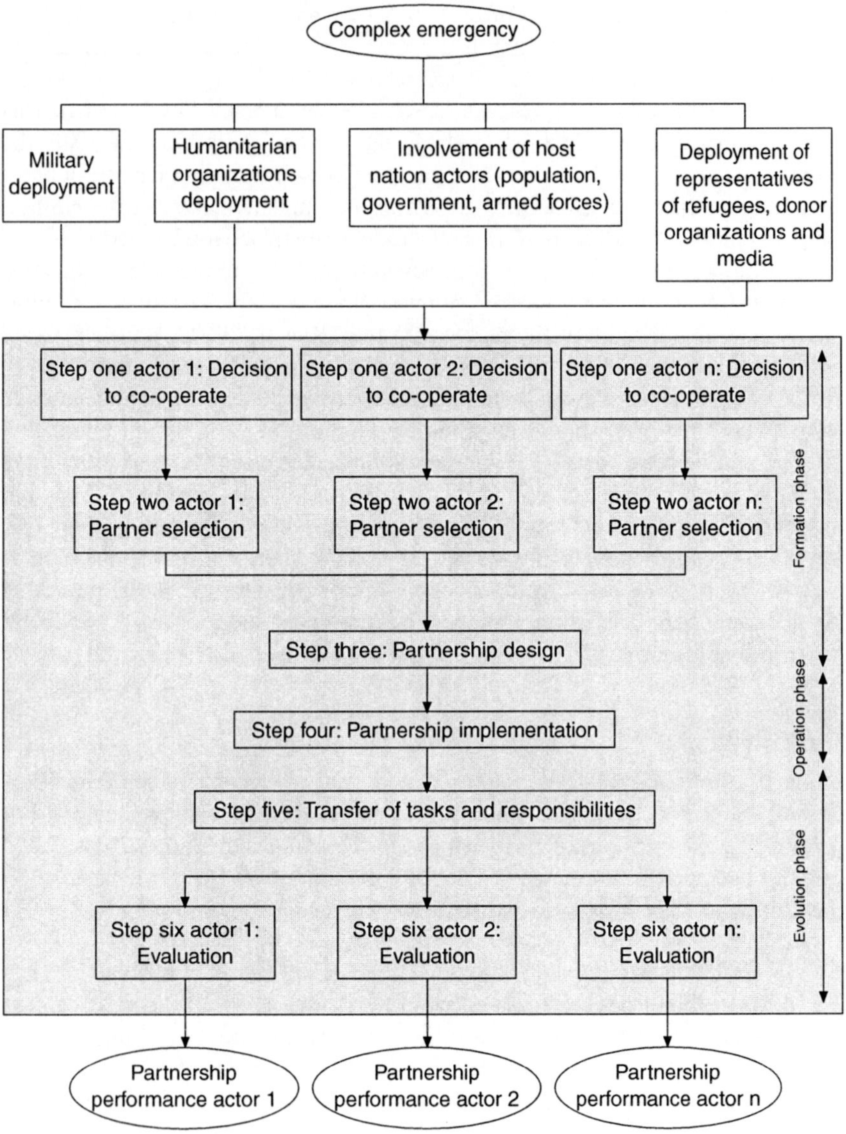

Figure 1 Initial model.

The results of the case studies are elaborated on in the sections below. Each section deals with one step of the co-operation process.

Step 1: Decision to co-operate

Decision to co-operate ISAF

To analyse the external environment and thus to increase situational awareness ISAF had tactical support teams (TSTs) at its disposal. Each team consisted of four to six men or women and to divide the Area of Responsibility (AoR) of ISAF each TST was assigned to a police district. The main task of the TSTs was to make civil estimates. By interviewing the local population and authorities the TSTs tried to get answers on the ethnic distribution, built up of the area, education, health, shelter, water, power supply (electricity), food situation as well as refugees and IDPs. Next, information on the local situation was gathered through the Afghanistan Information Management Service (AIMS) and through several IOs and NGOs

To structure the information the TSTs and the staff of CCC constantly made assessments of the local situation, by using the ARRC CIMIC Tracking and Reporting System (ARRC, 2003). This system made use of a traffic light (green, yellow, red) to indicate the status of a functional area in a police district. Two main problems occurred in the use of this system. At first, the functional areas, on which assessments were made, were not at all consistent. In the overall assessment of the CCC during ISAF IV six functional areas were used: water, power, health, housing and shelter, education and food and nutrition. In a presentation of the CCC of ISAF IV five different functional area were used: civil administration, humanitarian affairs, civil infrastructure, economy and commerce and cultural affairs. While during ISAF III and IV the CCC, as well as many of the TSTs, presented their assessments in the following functional areas: food, health, power, shelter and water.

Second, if was often unclear which measures to use to indicate the colour of the traffic light. No objective measures were used, which resulted in subjective and arbitrary judgement of the assessments. In this colouring process regularly 'Western' standards were used, meaning that sympathy for the local population sometimes played a decisive role.

To get an overview of the civilian actors, which were operating in the AoR, ISAF had several means at its disposal. At tactical (local) level personnel of the TSTs frequently met with representatives of IOs and NGOs during their activities in the police districts. In the weekly CIMIC co-ordination meetings of the CCC, each TST presented its activities to the other teams. These meetings were open to the public and were, although not frequent, visited by IOs and NGOs. Next, two to three liaison officers were added to the staff of the CCC to come and stay in contact with the representatives of the civilian organizations.

However, it was not until August 2003 that the first CIMIC liaison plan was written. The objective of this plan was to assess the civilian actors in the AoR of

ISAF in a structured way. Although during ISAF I, II, III frequently contact was made with civilian actors, it was often ad-hoc and no permanent liaison relationships were set into place. This resulted in a constant lack of situational awareness regarding which civilian actors were operating on what areas. This is illustrated by the fact that the CIMIC liaison officers of ISAF IV were handed over only three contacts by their predecessors of ISAF III.

To fulfil the CIMIC mission ISAF had, in addition to the capacity in the TSTs and the liaison capacity, a German CIMIC platoon and several minor CIMIC assets of the troop contributing nations (TCNs) at its disposal. Within means and capabilities units of Kabul Multinational Brigade (KMNB) could also be employed in this framework. This led to the following internal strengths of ISAF with respect to the CIMIC mission:

- Short reaction times.
- Accessibility of all areas by military transport.
- Diversity of means and knowledge (i.e. transport, manpower, machines, technical knowledge and security).
- Large assessment capacity in TSTs.

To co-ordinate all the CIMIC activities the CCC had approximately 20 persons at its disposal, including inter alia two to three liaison officers, a security officer, information managers and a project-team. This project-team consisted of a legal advisor and a varying number of one to three engineers or architects and its main task was to initiate and monitor projects.

The main problem of the CCC was its inability to direct and command the CIMIC assets of ISAF, including most of the TSTs. Of the 19 TSTs, which operated during ISAF IV, eight were directed by the CCC, seven were commanded by KMNB and four were under national command. This division of command made it very difficult for the CCC to co-ordinate all the CIMIC assets and it led to a situation in which many of the TSTs had their own approach towards CIMIC.

A factor, which intensified the lack of a common approach, were the finances. Most TCNs did provide their national TSTs with a budget. TSTs with large budgets were able to carry out many assistance activities compared to TSTs, which only had small ones. As most of the TSTs were assigned to a police district, this created great inequality between the areas in Kabul. This could eventually influence the local attitude towards ISAF in a negative way.

A lack of training of both CIMIC personnel at HQ-level and at TST-level was frequently indicated as another internal weakness of ISAF. Only a limited number of people had participated in a NATO-training course. This again contributed to the multiple approaches towards CIMIC within ISAF. It also intensified the feeling of many persons *to do good* rather than to do the right things.

Based on these internal and external characteristics there were several motives for ISAF to co-operate with the civilian actors. It was frequently said that the main reason for co-operation simply was because it was included in the CIMIC mission. Other motives, which were raised, are:

- Civilian actors could provide and facilitate contacts of ISAF with representatives of the local population.
- To legitimize the deployment of ISAF, co-operation with civilian actors and the visibility of it was highly valued by politicians. An example is the so-called Lighthouse project. To underline the lead-nationship of Germany and the Netherlands during ISAF III a special project was selected, which should act as a beacon. After a thorough selection the refurbishment of a maternity clinic (i.e. Darulaman Clinic) was chosen as the Lighthouse project, despite the fact that both the CCC and UNAMA were not in favour of this project. This was for obvious reasons as the lack of experienced and trained personnel to operate the clinic, the lack of medical machines and supplies.
- Civilian actors (e.g. ACBAR, ANCB, UNAMA) could provide ISAF with knowledge of and expertise on the local situation, customs and humanitarian assistance.
- Co-operation with Afghan authorities was essential since tasks and responsibilities were often to be transferred to them after finishing assistance activities. Involving the Afghan authorities in the co-operation process was thus of great importance.
- Co-operation with local construction companies would increase the local capacity and thereby stimulate the local economy.
- Since ISAF and the civilian actors were operating in the same areas, prevention of duplication of effort was considered very important. Doing this would decrease the waste of scarce resources.
- Employment of ISAF personnel: As ISAF faced few injuries and wanted to keep the medical staff in good shape, several medical activities were performed in co-operation with Die Johanniter. This increased the morale of the military.

In assistance activities, from which the local population directly benefited, ISAF used several checklists to determine whether or not to initiate co-operation. These usually consisted of:

- Military criteria (e.g. will the project support the Commander's mission?; will the project stimulate the flow of information required to support current/future military operations?).
- Feasibility criteria (are all necessary skills and manpower available?; what is the duration of the project?).
- Concerns (e.g. will the project require future force maintenance?).

If an assistance activity complied to several of these criteria (it was unclear which conditions were necessary to comply with and which were only desirable) ISAF often took the initiative to initiate the activity. The approach of ISAF III was to pursue co-operation with humanitarian organizations, which could fulfil (part of) the activities. If no organization was found to participate, the project was tendered through the project-team of the CCC. During ISAF IV the main approach was to directly tender the project to local constructors. However, this enhanced the direct involvement of and increased the dependency on ISAF troops.

Based on its supply, ISAF also took the initiative to support humanitarian organizations. As ISAF faced few injuries, to keep the doctors in practice, they wanted to perform medical activities. Die Johanniter was approached to jointly treat local patients.

In their partnership UNAMA strongly urged ISAF not to get heavily engaged in the winterization programme. It was argued that the Ministry of Rural Reha-bilitation and Development (MRRD) would act responsible and pro-active. ISAF took these concerns seriously and only provided support with respect to security. In other cases (e.g. back to school programme of UNICEF) humanitar-ian organizations took the initiative and approached ISAF to request support in fulfilling the needs of the local population.

In addition to the activities from which the local population directly bene-fited, civil–military co-operation took place regarding the co-ordination of assis-tance activities, information sharing and fulfilling each other's direct needs (e.g. training by ISAF personnel to personnel of a humanitarian organization or vice versa, protection by ISAF). ISAF used for these activities, although not explic-itly, the same criteria as in the checklists.

Having decided to co-operate, ISAF normally did not set any particular targets or objectives. However, in its concept of operation at operational level ISAF had formulated objectives. These consisted of (1) CIMIC end state, (2) CIMIC mission, (3) CIMIC centres of gravity and (4) CIMIC priorities (see Box 1).

In the CIMIC centres of gravity, the general NATO CIMIC objectives (i.e. liaison, support to the civil environment and support to the force) are clearly rec-ognizable. Of these objectives, force protection was often the main driver. However, perceiving this as *winning the hearts and minds* of the local popu-lation is too simplistic. According to involved ISAF personnel it should be regarded as influencing the perception of the local population. This basically involves influencing certain persons or groups in the AoR of ISAF, who are or might become a serious threat to the overall mission. This therefore, does not necessarily imply assistance to the local population. For example, during ISAF III a detailed plan was made to develop a recreation area, just north of Kabul. It was believed that through this development, people could experience the advan-tages of the more safe and secure environment, which was provided by ISAF. Since most people could remember the former recreation area, this would posi-tively influence the attitude towards ISAF. While, certain police districts faced far more serious problems (e.g. lack of sufficient medical facilities), ISAF con-centrated part of its assets on the recreation area.

The CIMIC priorities in the concept of operations were derived from the National Development Framework as established by the ATA. However, it is unclear why exactly these priorities were selected and why the content differs from the 12 priority areas used by the National Development Framework. In addition, the CIMIC priorities were not completely corresponding with the functional areas that were used in the assessments of ISAF. In summary, this made it difficult to determine the status of a priority.

Decision to co-operate civil actors

It was estimated that approximately 650 humanitarian organizations were present in Kabul during the deployments of ISAF III and IV. These organizations varied from small local organizations (e.g. World in Need) to key players in the assistance community as ICRC, Care and the UN agencies. Some international organizations, like UNICEF, had the possession of many materials

---

Box 1 Objectives of ISAF

CIMIC end state
The CIMIC end state will be reached when the Afghan Transitional Authority (ATA) or official government authorities, supported by UNAMA and other IOs/GO/NGOs, are able to function effectively without COMISAF's support, and regional stability is restored.

CIMIC mission
To conduct CIMIC activities in order to assist ISAF in strengthening the overall security situation in Kabul and surroundings (ISAF's AoR), by assisting/supporting the civil bodies in the improvement of quality of life for the population. Thus promoting the overall stabilization process in Afghanistan and increasing the authority of the TA necessary to conduct the constitutional Loya Jirga in Dec 2003.

CIMIC centres of gravity
- Close and robust liaison to all key civil actors in the AoR.
- Support the process of economic and nation recovery in close co-ordination with UNAMA.
- Close liaison with CJCMOTF (i.e. Combined Joint Civil Military Operations Task Force, which is part of Operation Enduring Freedom (OEF)).
- Force protection.

CIMIC priorities
- Water.
- Health.
- Education.
- Support to returnees.
- Support to policy and security.
- Development of emergency service.

---

and goods, had large financial means and had a large staff capacity. Others, like Die Johanniter, had a small staff and did not have many means and capabilities. Many of the international NGOs present in Afghanistan had been working in the country for more than one decade either through implementing programmes directly, or contracting work out to local partners. However, unlike ISAF most of the organizations were focused on one functional area (e.g. UN-Habitat focused on housing and shelter problems, Die Johanniter and ICRC focused on medical problems).

To co-ordinate and to manage the efforts of the assistance community, several organizations and structures were active in Kabul. First, UNAMA was tasked to fulfil the UN's obligations in Afghanistan, as outlined by the Bonn Agreement and to manage UN humanitarian activities in co-ordination with the Afghan authorities.

Second, to facilitate substantive interaction between government, donors, UN agencies and NGOs, Consultative Groups (CG) were established. Each CG focused on one of the 12 national programme areas highlighted in the National Development Framework (e.g. refugee and IDP return, education, health and nutrition) and was chaired by a different Afghan ministry.

In addition to UNAMA and the CGs organizations like ACBAR and ANCB functioned as co-ordinating bodies for the humanitarian organizations. ACBAR mainly intended to co-ordinate the activities of international organizations, while ANCB only focused on Afghan organizations. The strengths of bodies like ANCB and ACBAR were their extensive network of humanitarian organizations, their knowledge and expertise on development issues and knowledge of local situation and customs. However, through their function as co-ordination bodies, both ANCB and ACBAR were not able to task its member organizations.

Due to the great variety of humanitarian organizations it is difficult to generalize. With regard to co-operation with ISAF, at an operational level the larger organizations generally regarded the humanitarian principles as strict guidelines. However, rather than blocking any form of interaction, most of these organizations valued information sharing and co-ordination with ISAF.

With regard to information sharing, in particular in the earlier stages of the military operation, the assistance community did not have sufficient capacity to assess the local needs and the security situation. As a result they frequently made use of the information, which was gathered by the TSTs of ISAF. In later stages the capacity of the assistance community increased, inter alia through AIMS. The aim of this project was to build information management capacity in government and deliver information management services to organizations across Afghanistan. Unlike the CGs and ISAF, AIMS clustered its information in 15 different functional areas.

For humanitarian organizations, the aim of co-ordination was mainly to prevent duplication of humanitarian effort and to avoid *doing harm* to the local population by the CIMIC activities of ISAF. For example the distributions of goods to the local population by ISAF troops were considered a severe threat to the *Cash for Work Programmes* of UNAMA and several NGOs. It could happen that in one area people were employed by UNAMA and the NGOs to carry out works, while in the same area other people were freely given clothes, food or other goods.

At tactical level many people tended to be more pragmatic on the humanitarian principles and several opportunities were identified with respect to co-operation with ISAF:

- Direct or indirect security provided by ISAF troops. Examples included the mine clearance, extra patrolling, and direct protection of individuals.
- Manpower, transport capacity and technical knowledge within ISAF. Several humanitarian organizations (e.g. UNICEF) made use of the transport capacity of ISAF, while several others made use of the manpower and technical knowledge of ISAF (e.g. drivers of UNAMA were trained by ISAF).
- Goods and materials, which were donated to ISAF troops. Many countries donated goods through their contingents of ISAF. To distribute these to the local population the knowledge, expertise and distribution channels of humanitarian organizations was frequently used.
- Financial means within ISAF. Through national governments, the European commission and private donors in the TCN ISAF had financial means at its disposal.

Relatively few Afghan organizations were active in the area of Greater Kabul. Since the international assistance community had a large presence, these organizations focused more on areas outside Kabul. However, it was sometimes difficult to make a difference between an Afghan NGO and a contractor. To avoid paying tax several local contractors claimed to be an NGO. In addition to these local contractors, non-Afghan companies, particularly Turkish, Iranian, Chinese and Pakistani were operating in the area of Kabul. Fierce competition took place between these companies to get reconstruction contracts.

Although the humanitarian organizations did not set objectives or targets on the level of a partnership, conditions for co-operation were often formulated. These conditions were normally derived from the Oslo Guidelines (United Nations, 1994) or the code of conduct of the ICRC (ICRC, 1994). In most cases this implied that all assistance activities were to be carried out according to the humanitarian principles. It also included conditions on the use of force protection by ISAF troops and wearing military dress.

Step 2: Partner selection

Partner selection ISAF

Based on the overview of civilian actors, ISAF undertook several actions in its search for appropriate organizations to co-operate with. Most of these actions involved both formal and informal talks with the staff of the CCC, personnel of the TSTs and personnel of the J9 HQ with representatives of humanitarian organizations.

Next, the existing co-ordination structures, like ACBAR, ANCB and the CGs, proved to be good places to meet with both international (i.e. ACBAR) and national (i.e. ANCB) NGOs. Before August 2003 the liaison officers of ISAF were not allowed at the meetings of ACBAR. This was primarily because some organizations were fiercely against any association with ISAF. However, through mediation of the Area Co-ordinator of UNAMA and because the female liaison officer of the CCC of ISAF IV could get very well with the director of ACBAR, ISAF was finally allowed at the meetings. Both ACBAR and ANCB and several of the larger organizations (e.g. UNAMA) were used to verify humanitarian organizations on inter alia reliability and professionalism.

To determine whether a humanitarian organization was an appropriate partner, some staff members of the CCC used as the main criterion: *personnel of the organizations should not be creeps or criminals*. This might be a little oversimplified, but it shows that very little attention was paid to explicit partner selection. Implicitly the following criteria were used to select an appropriate partner:

- Compatible strategies and objectives: having compatible strategies and objectives was regarded as very important by ISAF. Since ISAF operated under UN-mandate it supported UNAMA and the other UN-agencies. Moreover, the location of the assistance activities played an important role. A prospective partner should also be operating in the police district of Kabul in which the activities would take place;
- Complementary resources: The resources of humanitarian organizations (e.g. knowledge and expertise) were to be complementary to ISAF's resources.
- Network of the partner organization: Organizations like ACBAR, ANCB and UNAMA did have many contacts with other humanitarian organizations. Co-operation with these organizations was preferred since it provided easy access to these other organizations.
- Personal fit; Personnel of ISAF very much liked the emergency officers of UNICEF and World in Need. One field officer of UNAMA was former military, which also strengthened the personal fit. Moreover, gender played an important role in the personal fit. The female liaison officer of the CCC was very well trusted by the director of ACBAR and by the representatives of several small women organizations.
- Compatibility of cultures; both the director of ACBAR and the liaison officer of the CCC were Dutch, just like the representatives of Zuid Oost Azië Vluchtelingenzorg (ZOA) and the chief of the CCC. Language and similar cultural backgrounds clearly facilitated the co-operation.
- Nationality: Afghan organizations were preferred as partners to increase the local coping capacity. Next, co-operation with Afghan organizations was likely to empower local leadership. For example, supporting a local organi-

zation in the distribution of goods increased the trust of the local population in this particular organization, thereby contributing to the overall trust in the development process of Afghanistan.

To tender construction activities ISAF used several criteria to select an appropriate company. Based on reputation and earlier experience, the CCC had a list of approximately 25 preferred suppliers. These companies were known through small construction activities on and around the compounds of ISAF, through earlier involvement in projects and through contacts with IOs and NGOs. In addition there was a transparent black list of unreliable contractors.

To start new construction activities five to six of these approved companies were invited to attend a meeting at the construction site. Often one or two new companies were also invited to join the bidding process. At the site the contractors were given the construction drawings by an engineer of the CCC and were allowed to make a bid on the construction works. The engineer of the CCC then decided, which contractor was selected. The main criteria to do this were time, quality and costs. However, the project-team of the CCC used several additional criteria: trust, level of English and local capacity (Afghan companies were preferred to foreign ones).

Partner selection civil actors

Despite some military who believed that only ISAF determined whether they were *doing business* or not, humanitarian organizations also used several partner selection criteria. In relation to the tasks, which were to be carried out, complementary resources (e.g. security, transport capacity) and compatible strategies and objectives were frequently raised. With respect to the latter, the fact that ISAF was UN-mandated made co-operation considerably easier. Second, contrary to the units of OEF, which had to carry out direct combat activities, ISAF troops were only tasked to create a safe and secure environment. This positively influenced the attitude of many humanitarian organizations towards ISAF. However, activities of ISAF with the aim of force protection were hardly compatible with the objectives of the humanitarian organizations.

Additional criteria, which were used by the representatives of the humanitarian organizations were:

- Compatibility of cultures: As the emergency officer of Unicef said 'Unicef did not have a Finnish officer and therefore we did not co-operate with the Finnish contingent of ISAF'.
- Personal fit: This was perceived as the most important partner-related criterion by the respondents.
- Humanitarian principles: The activities of many humanitarian organizations were only to be carried out according to the humanitarian principles.
- Force protection: Personnel of ISAF in general and the CCC in particular did not use a high degree of force protection.

- Added value: Co-operation with ISAF could increase the scope (i.e. the functional areas on which co-operation takes place) and the scale (i.e. the number of activities on one particular functional area) of the humanitarian organization.

Step 3: Partnership design

In the partnerships between ISAF and humanitarian organizations normally oral or so-called gentleman's agreements were made. Based on trust these agreements included the definition of rights and duties (e.g. ISAF was not allowed to carry weapons on the premises of many humanitarian organizations) and details of the implementation (e.g. planning). These agreements also dealt with the activities of each actor in the partnership, for example which actor would share its information on what times. In particular during ISAF III, the absence of a written contract was not felt as a problem.

Both interviewees of humanitarian organizations and ISAF raised several drawbacks by the prospect of having a written contract. In general the situation was normally too uncertain to rely on a contract. Second, the military could not guarantee to be involved in humanitarian activities for a specified period. If the situation changed they could have been forced to focus on activities other than the partnership's. Finally, the risk of legal claims was raised as an important drawback.

During ISAF IV the lack of formal arrangements was seen as a problem. In the partnership with ANCB the intention of the CCC was to make a contract through a Memorandum of Understanding (MoU). However, although the NATO CIMIC doctrine supports the settlement of institutional arrangements, due to unknown reasons HQ J9 blocked the MoU with ANCB.

In the partnership with UNAMA, it was agreed that ISAF would provide rapid emergency response support in case of a major natural disaster. However, due to an imminent rotation of ISAF, its representatives were not willing to sign an MoU with UNAMA at that moment. It was said that 'the willingness to assist in case of emergency however exists'. In subsequent rotations of ISAF no follow-up was given to the making of such an MoU.

Interviewees raised that, although an MoU does not have any judicial status, it can increase clarity and transparency of the partnership. This is done through (1) agreement on clear and realistic objectives, (2) keeping and protecting core competencies, (3) definition of rights and duties and (4) implementation plan.

In addition to these advantages of having an MoU, one of the CIMIC liaison officers of ISAF IV made an interesting point. She argued that through formalizing a relationship (e.g. MoU, Letter of Intent or Terms of Reference) the continuity, or rather the lack of it, could be addressed. Since most military units rotate once every four or six months and also personnel of humanitarian organizations come and go, it is very difficult to build a sustainable relationship between a military force and a humanitarian organization. Drawing up an MoU could facilitate the transfer from one rotation or person to another. The partnership would thus become less person-bonded and *ad hoc*. This would diminish the spoiling of scarce resources and the waste of effort. It was not uncommon that organizations presented itself to each other dozens of times, simply because they were unaware of former co-operation activities or attempts to it.

With respect to local constructors ISAF made use of detailed contracts. These included inter alia the terms of the contract, a description of the project, price and payment, taxes and duties, inspections and supervision.

Regarding the beneficiaries of the assistance activities ISAF sometimes made arrangements with the Afghan authorities, which were to be responsible after completion of the activities.

In addition to the involvement of the Afghan authorities, many humanitarian organizations regarded the direct involvement of the local population in the design phase as very beneficial. So-called grass-root contracts could enumerate the expectations, roles, rights and responsibilities of local communities. They could positively contribute to the participation of women and other vulnerable segments of the population. And communities would have better faith in the transitional administration and greater confidence in the country's future. Moreover, involving a major or other leading person in the assistance activities would strengthen his or her position. In return he or she would probably be more willing to do something in return.

With respect to assistance activities in which no IO or NGO participated, ISAF normally contacted the local beneficiaries and its leaders. Consultation of these persons did not lead to written contracts before the implementation started, but arrangements were entirely based on trust. Due to the Afghan culture, people did not value written contracts, but trusted each other by word.

Step 4: Partnership implementation

The actors were involved in the actual implementation of the assistance activities in several ways. The first cluster of activities was co-ordination between ISAF and the humanitarian organizations. Through co-ordination assistance activities were synchronized and duplication of effort was prevented (e.g. the construction of multiple sub fire-stations in a small region). It also gave humanitarian organizations the opportunity to prevent ISAF's CIMIC activities from *doing harm* to the local population. ISAF valued in particular co-ordination with main organizations like the UN-agencies (e.g. UNAMA, UNICEF, UNHCR), the co-ordinating bodies (e.g. ACBAR, ANCB) and large IOs (e.g. IOM) and NGOs (e.g. AIMS).

The second cluster of activities regarded information sharing. ISAF had a large capacity at its disposal to gather information. This was, in particular in the earlier stages of the operation, of great use to the assistance community. Information, which ISAF shared, included assessments of the local situation, maps of Kabul, information on OEF and security information. Many humanitarian organizations freely shared their information with ISAF regarding development issues, local customs and manners.

Third, activities to support each other's direct needs were frequently observed. Both ISAF and the humanitarian organizations supported each other's needs, thereby indirectly addressing the needs of the local population. ISAF's support to humanitarian organizations consisted of security-related support (e.g. demining the location of a warehouse of UNICEF and planning the evacuation of civilian staff in case of an emergency through the *Emergency Planning Group*). The support, which was not directly related to security included inter alia a training for 45 drivers of different organizations (e.g. UNHCR, IOM, Care International). Humanitarian organizations did also frequently support ISAF in its direct needs. Delegates of ICRC provided training for the TSTs on the Law of Armed Conflict. UNAMA facilitated the acceptation of ISAF to ACBAR's co-ordination board, while ANCB mediated between ISAF and Afghan NGOs.

The fourth and last cluster of activities concerned support to address the needs of the local population. Both ISAF and the humanitarian organizations supported each other in directly addressing the needs of the local population. In the back to school programmes, ISAF supported UNICEF with transport capacity. In co-operation with AGEF, demobilized soldiers were provided with practice and contacts with different contractors. As part of the number of unskilled labourers usually hired by the contractor, these soldiers were trained at construction sites supervised by ISAF.

In directly addressing the needs of the local population, ISAF initiated many reconstruction activities itself. These activities, the so-called 'projects', were initiated by the TSTs or the CCC and normally carried out through local contractors. During the execution of the projects the TSTs and the project-team regularly monitored the activities of the local constructors. The projects included inter alia the reconstruction of medical clinics, fire stations, schools, kindergartens and irrigation works. Often no humanitarian organization was involved in these activities, because they regarded other activities as more beneficial (i.e. different priority setting) or because they were not approached by ISAF. Figure 2 shows the total number of projects, which were carried out from January 2002 until July 2003.

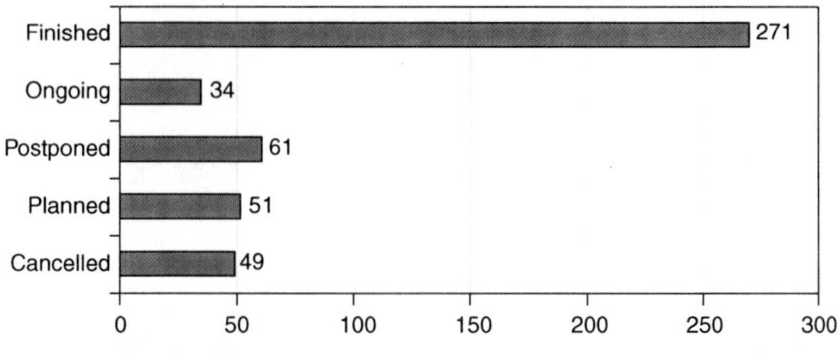

Figure 2 Total number of projects.

The numbers in Figure 2, however, have to be taken with care. Due to the lack of direction, which the staff of the CCC could provide, many projects were initiated through the TSTs. During ISAF IV it turned out that many more projects had been carried out, but were not reported to the CCC.

Apart from contracting out activities, ISAF itself had limited implementing capacity. This consisted of means and resources of the TCNs, which were commanded through the KMNB or the nations itself. The most obvious of these resources was the German CIMIC platoon. This unit was directly involved in several construction activities (e.g. Darulaman clinic, police stations). Many humanitarian organizations regarded the German CIMIC platoon as a competitor of both themselves and the local constructors. In any case this unit was not increasing the local coping capacity. In addition, it was often argued that the German CIMIC platoon applied western methods and standards in their construction activities and it was blamed from lacking sufficient knowledge on development issues and the local situation and customs.

Step 5: Transfer of tasks and responsibilities

In activities regarding co-ordination, information sharing and support to each other's direct needs (cluster 1–3), the transfer of tasks and responsibilities was not regarded as an important issue. However, in most assistance activities, in which the local population directly benefited, the transfer was seen as an important step in the co-operation process.

The largest share of these activities consisted of the projects in which ISAF contracted activities to local constructors. Having finished these activities many of the constructions had large requirements in order to become and remain fully operational. Medical clinics needed employees, some of which had to be highly educated and trained. Since there was a great lack of educated people, there was a severe risk that these people were removed from one area to another, thereby creating a gap in the former. Clinics furthermore needed appropriate machines to work with, medical supplies to treat patients and funds for maintenance. Similarly constructions like fire stations, schools, police stations and kindergartens had several requirements to be fully operational.

In general ISAF did not pay attention to these issues. In the partnership design, often no arrangements were made regarding the operation of the construction. This resulted inter alia in schools, which had an insufficient number of teachers and a lack of education material. Several months after completion these schools were not used as such, but served purposes like shelter for families.

In other projects explicit attention was paid to the function of the construction. In the partnership design of the Pol-e-Charki sub fire-station clear arrangements were made with the MoI regarding the transfer of tasks and responsibilities. However, despite the upfront agreements the MoI did not provide water, electricity and telephone connections. The sub fire-station could therefore not function as such. In addition the chief of Pol-e-Charki Sub Fire-Station had complained about the contractor's works. Boilers were broken, toilet and water taps leaked and paint flaked off. Approximately three months after the initial handover the problems were still not addressed. ISAF then decided to start a second project through competitive bidding to address these problems. This project took an extra two months.

In the partnerships in which ISAF and humanitarian organizations jointly addressed the needs of the local population (e.g. back to school programme with UNICEF, medical treatment with Die Johanniter, distribution of water with JICA) the transfer of tasks and responsibilities was regarded as very important, but few problems arose. This was often due to the rather simple nature of activities. However, several respondents stressed that if the local population is more heavily involved in the co-operation process, a quick transfer of tasks and responsibilities is essential in order to achieve a sustainable situation.

To deal with the problems of transfer, respondents stressed that Afghan ministries and the direct beneficiaries were to be involved in an earlier stage (i.e. partnership design). In its meetings with liaison officers of ISAF, the representative of the Afghan Ministry of Reconstruction (MoR) also urged for such early involvement. However, as was seen in the construction of the Pol-e-Charki sub-fire-station, these statements have to be taken with care. As one of the liaison officers raised, *'Various ministers I met could only talk about the lack of money and donors and never talked about their own responsibility'*.

In accordance with the measure of early involvement, it was raised that the construction of inter alia new schools or medical clinics should keep pace with the building of local capacity. If one or the other is far ahead, scarce resources are wasted. It is thus of great importance to assist Afghan ministries in building local capacity (e.g. training of teachers) and opposing corruption.

Third, including humanitarian organizations in an early stage could address the problems in the transfer of tasks and responsibilities. Since these organizations are often in the area for a longer time guaranteeing the sustainability of assistance activities is also in their interests.

Apart from a humanitarian perspective, failing to transfer tasks and responsibilities could also negatively influence the mission of ISAF. If the local population observed or perceived that the assistance activities did not contribute to the development of the area, their attitude towards ISAF troops could change in a negative way. Belligerent groups or leaders could use this changed attitude to hinder the troops.

Step 6: Evaluation

In partnerships in which ISAF co-operated with a humanitarian organization very few evaluations were held. The ones, which were held, often consisted of internal meetings or chats. Most military and civilian respondents did stress the importance of an evaluation to get feedback on the performance. The emergency officers of UNICEF stressed the importance of joint evaluations by military and civilian actors, which could then preferably be co-ordinated by UNAMA. The activities, which ISAF contracted to local constructors, did contain small evaluations (ISAF, 2003). After the completion of the object an engineer of the project team of ISAF carried out this evaluation. However, these evaluations primarily focused on technical aspects (Bergenstjerna, 2003), while many other aspects (e.g. what did the partnership contribute to the extent of force protection?) were overlooked.

Assessing the performance of the partnerships leads to the following findings (Rietjens *et al.*, 2005).

Most of the activities, which ISAF contracted to a local constructor, contributed little to the military mission. Belligerent groups or key leaders were seldom taken into account; many activities did not directly contribute to a safe and secure environment; and through the activities situational awareness was often not increased. Most assistance activities were for the benefit of the community, thereby generally reaching a large number of direct and indirect beneficiaries. However, as the military operation started already in January 2002 and the activities took place in the course of 2003, the impact on the perception of the local population towards ISAF was not large.

With respect to the support of the civil environment, many of these activities did fill a gap and addressed the needs of the local population. Since most of the activities were contracted to local contractors, local capacity did largely increase. However, the sustainability of the projects was inadequate. Many facilities could not properly function, since they lacked either teachers and educational material (i.e. schools) or medical supplies and funds for maintenance (i.e. clinics). Late in 2003 staff of ISAF visited several facilities, which were built under supervision of ISAF. It turned out that approximately 40 per cent of these facilities did not function any more.

Despite this rather negative performance of most projects, they were often perceived as successful by ISAF. Some staff members of ISAF III and IV did criticize the projects, but during their stay in Kabul they were either not aware of this or were not able to act.

The partnerships with humanitarian organizations contributed to a small extent to the military mission of ISAF. Some organizations (e.g. UNAMA and ANCB) provided ISAF with increased situational awareness, but none deliberately included belligerent groups or key leaders or contributed to a safe and secure environment.

These partnerships did greatly differ with regard to the total number of people, which were reached. With relatively little effort the delivery of materials in the back to school programme with UNICEF included approximately 160 schools, thereby reaching nearly 13,000 teachers and 230,000 students. To the contrary the medical activities in co-operation with Die Johanniter did only reach a very limited number of people.

All the partnerships with humanitarian organizations did support the civil environment through information sharing, co-ordination and the support to the direct needs of the humanitarian organizations. As ISAF faced few injuries, to keep its doctors in shape, it wanted to perform medical activities. Die Johanniter was approached to jointly treat local patients. Although these medical activities were based on the supply of ISAF, it did increase the scale of that organization, thereby contributing to its mission. An increase of both scale and scope was also the case in the partnerships with UNAMA and UNICEF. Except the partnerships in which ISAF co-operated with Afghan organizations (e.g. ANCB, World in Need) few contributed to increasing the local capacity. However, all were sustainable.

Despite the differences in the performance, all investigated partnerships with humanitarian organizations were regarded as successful by both ISAF and the humanitarian organizations. This is in accordance with the 'altruistic self-interest principle' of Seiple (1996), who views civil–military co-operation as a pragmatic strategy whenever partners consider themselves interdependent to reach their objectives (Rietjens *et al.*, 2005). Civilian actors and their military counterparts will look favourable upon co-operation as long as they expect co-operation to serve their best interest.

With regard to the costs of the partnerships, most were relatively low. In most construction activities local contractors were hired and local personnel was employed. Information sharing and co-ordination are seen as low cost activities, with usually high benefits (e.g. duplication of effort). The activities, in which large capacity of ISAF was involved (e.g. German CIMIC platoon), were regarded as very expensive as they substituted local contractors and personnel. In this respect Siegel (2002) stresses the fact that the yearly price of a US soldier in Afghanistan, when both direct and indirect expenses are included, is approximately US\$215,000 while humanitarians usually cost a tenth of this.

Conclusions

The objective of this research was to develop a model that will support the co-operation between the military and the civilian actors in a peace support operation at a local level in response to a complex emergency. The model as it was presented seems to be appropriate. Based on literature on CIMIC and on co-operative arrangements it describes and explains the co-operation process between military and civilian actors at local level. It is concluded that civil–military partnerships go through six successive steps. First, each actor decides whether or not co-operation should be pursued. Next, an appropriate partner is searched for. The third step contains the agreements, which are made upfront. These include for example clear and realistic objectives, an implementation plan and the definition of rights and duties. In the fourth step the partnership is implemented and the actual activities are carried out. After completion of the activities step five deals with the transfer of tasks and responsibilities. The final step determines the performance of the partnership through an evaluation.

Applying the model to the co-operation between ISAF and civilian actors in Kabul, Afghanistan, leads to the following major conclusions:

- The external analysis of most actors was done in an unstructured way, resulting in great duplication of effort and the waste of scarce resources.

- The functional areas on which ISAF made assessments (i.e. food, water, health, power, shelter) did not correspond with the CIMIC priorities (i.e. water, health, education, support to returnees, support to policy and security, development of emergency service). This resulted in a mismatch between the supplied and the requested information and made it difficult to determine the status of a priority.
- The functional areas of ISAF differed from the areas on which the assistance community assessed the area of Kabul, thereby making it unnecessarily difficult to compare and exchange information.
- As no partnerships between ISAF and civilian organizations were formalized they all remained *ad hoc* and person-bonded. This led to the waste of many scarce resources.
- Local capacity was to a large extent used to fulfil many of the assistance activities, thereby stimulating the Afghan economy.
- Most activities carried out or supported by ISAF units did contribute little to the objective of force protection.
- Many activities proved not to be sustainable. After completion, many facilities were not able to function properly as inter alia materials, trained employees and funds for maintenance were not arranged. A main reason for the lack of sustainability is the absence of upfront arrangements. Even clear upfront arrangements do not guarantee a smooth transition as is proven in the sub-fire-station in Pol-e-Charki. However, completely lacking these arrangements and only trusting enthusiastic persons will definitely decrease the chances of successful transition.
- There is a great difference between the perceived and real performance. While almost all activities were perceived as highly successful, objectively assessing them often shows a rather negative outcome.
- Due to a lack of common (NATO) training, different personal capabilities, different budgets and a lack of direction there was no common approach to CIMIC within ISAF.

To use the developed model as a framework for future civil–military partnerships it is important to apply it to different operational settings CIMIC. Future research should include the provincial reconstruction teams (PRTs), which are currently operating in many provinces in Afghanistan and which are a good example of an integrated civil–military approach. Second, this case study focused on a complex emergency rather than a natural disaster. Recent events such as the tsunami in South East Asia and the earthquake in Pakistan show the relevance of upfront thinking on an effective response. It is important to investigate whether the model can also be applied to cases of natural disasters. Finally, large international commercial companies have become active in the response to a complex emergency. As these organizations, especially private military firms, can substitute for military organizations in several activities, it is important to determine whether the model remains valid if activities are outsourced.

The application of the model in these settings increases insight in the

differences and similarities of actors' approaches towards CIMIC and contributes to an improved understanding of the successes and failures of this
special form of co-operation.

Notes

1 A complex emergency is characterized as a humanitarian disaster that is due to a political or ethnical conflict and that causes massive population movements, a shortage of
food and health care and in which political authority and public services have deteriorated or completely collapsed (Natsios, 1996; Last, 1997; Allen, 1999).
2 The NGO sector is extremely divers and includes thousands of different organizations
– differentiated by size, maturity, expertise, quality and mission – which makes it difficult to generalize about them.

Bibliography

Allied Rapid Reaction Corps (ARRC) (2003). *CIMIC Tracking & Reporting System.*
NATO Unclassified.

Baarda, T.A. van (2001). 'A legal Perspective of Cooperation between Military and
Humanitarian Organisations in Peace Support Operations.' In: *International Peacekeeping*, Vol. 8, No. 1, pp. 99–116.

Bergenstjerna A. (2003). *Final Report Pol-e-Charki Sub Fire Station*, ISAF, Kabul.

Bollen, M.T.I. and R. Beeres (2002). 'On the Conditions for CIMIC during Humanitarian
Operations.' In: Bollen, M.T.I., R.V. Janssens, H.F.M. Kirkels and J.L.M. Soeters, eds.
NL Arms: Civil–Military Cooperation: A marriage of Reason. Breda: Royal Nether-
lands Military Academy, pp. 19–30. In Dutch.

Currey, C.J. (2003). *A new model for Military/Nongovernmental Relations in Post-
Conflict Operations.* Carlisle: U.S. Army War College.

Das, T.K. and B. Teng (1997). 'Sustaining strategic alliances: Options and guidelines.'
In: Journal of General Management, Vol. 22, No. 4, 1997, pp. 49–64.

Duffey, T. (2000). 'Cultural Issues in Contemporary Peacekeeping.' In: *International
Peacekeeping*, Vol. 7, No. 1, pp. 142–168.

Eriksson, P. (1999). 'Civil–Military Co-ordination in Peace support operations – an impossible necessity?' In: *The Cornwallis IV: Analysis of civil–military interactions.* Nova
Scotia: The Lester B. Person Canadian International Peacekeeping Training Centre.

Faulkner, D. (1995). *International strategic alliances: Co-operating to compete.* London:
McGraw-Hill Book Company.

Forman, S. and Parhad, R. (1997). 'Paying for essentials: Resources for humanitarian
assistance.' Paper prepared for meeting at Pocantico Conference Center of the Rocke-
feller Brothers Fund. New York.

Geringer, J.M. (1991). 'Strategic determinants of partner selection criteria in international
Joint Ventures.' In: Journal of Business Studies, Vol. 22, No. 1, pp. 41–62.

Gourlay, C. (2000). 'Partners Apart: Managing Civil–Military Co-operation in Humanitarian Interventions.' In: *Disarmament forum*, Vol. No. 3, 2000, pp. 33–44.

Gulati, R. (1998). 'Alliances and networks.' In: *Strategic Management Journal*. Vol. 19,
no. 4, pp. 293–317.

Hoffmann, W.H. and R. Schlosser (2001). 'Success factors of strategic alliances in small
and medium-sized enterprises – An empirical survey.' In: *Long Range Planning*. Vol.
34, No. 3, pp. 357–381.

International Red Cross and Red Crescent Movement (1994). *Code of conduct.* Geneva: International Red Cross and Red Crescent Movement.

ISAF (2003). *Final report*, ISAF, Kabul.

Kanter, R.M. (1994). 'Collaborative advantage: the art of alliances.' In: Harvard Business Review, Vol. 72, No. 4, pp. 96–108.

Last, D.M. (1997). *Theory, doctrine and practice of conflict de-escalation in peacekeeping operations.* Toronto: Canadian Peacekeeping Press.

Lei, L. (1994). *User Participation and the success of ISD: An integrated model of user-specialist relationships.* PhD-thesis. Rotterdam: Erasmus University.

Lewis, L.D. (1990). *Partnerships for profit.* New York: The Free Press.

Lorange, P. and J. Roos (1992). *Strategic alliances; formation, implementation and evolution.* Massachusetts: Blackwell Publishers.

Mackinlay, J. (1996). *A guide to peace support operations.* Providence: The Thomas J. Watson Jr. Institute, Brown University.

Mohr, L.B. (1982). *Explaining Organizational Behavior: The Limits and possibilities of Theory and Research.* San Francisco: Jossey-Bass Publishers.

NATO (2000). *NATO civil military co-operation (CIMIC) doctrine.* AJP-09, NATO Unclassified.

Rietjens, S.J.H., M.T.I. Bollen and J.T. Voordijk (2005). *Assessing civil–military cooperation in peace support operations.* In: *Euroma Conference 2005: Operations and Global Competitiveness.* Budapest.

Seiple C. (1996). *The US Military/NGO Relationship in humanitarian interventions.* Carlisle Barracks: Peacekeeping Institute Centre for Strategic Leadership, U.S. Army War College.

Siegel, A. (2002). 'Civil–Military Marriage Counseling: Can this Union Be Saved?' In: *Special Warfare.* December 2002, p. 30.

United Nations (1994). *Guidelines on the use of military and civil defence assets in disaster relief.* Geneva: United Nations.

Whitman, J. (2000). 'A cautionary note on humanitarian intervention.' In: The Journal of Humanitarian Assistance. Document Posted 3 June 2000.

Yoshino, M.Y. and U.S. Rangan (1995). *Strategic alliances; an entrepreneurial approach to globalization.* Boston: Harvard Business School Press.

Part II

Cases

6 Yes, but is it peacebuilding?

Evaluating civil–military cooperation in Afghanistan

Owen A.J. Savage

In August 2005, Canada joined ten other countries in fielding a Provincial Reconstruction Team (PRT) in Afghanistan. Based in Kandahar city, the Canadian PRT brings together military personnel, civilian police, diplomats and development professionals with the collective goal of stabilizing Kandahar province by reinforcing the authority of the Afghan government. In meeting this goal, the PRT claims to employ a holistic and integrated approach in a range of areas, namely "security and stabilization, humanitarian relief, institution building [and] economic development" (Graham, 2005). This description, as will be shown below, corresponds with accepted definitions of peacebuilding and implies that the PRT is not only meant to be bringing stability, to Kandahar, but further, to be bringing peace.

This chapter will evaluate the effectiveness of the Canadian PRT as a vehicle of peacebuilding. It commences with a brief examination of the evolving relationship between security and development activities in conflict and post conflict settings. It then traces the development of PRTs, beginning with a brief history of recent events in Afghanistan and the development of a perceived need for PRTs. Finally, it will examine the issue of whether, and if so, to what extent, the Canadian PRT is merging security and development operations within a new integrated peacebuilding tool.

The need to build peace

The threat of failed or failing states

Since 1990, the world has witnessed increased threats to national and human security, often through the spectre of failed or failing states. In nations such as Sierra Leone, Afghanistan and now arguably Iraq, governments "can neither govern themselves effectively nor provide for their citizens" (Snow, 2003, p. 118). These nations typically experience:

> generalized violence [affecting] the society as a whole, social turmoil, disruption of social and political relationships and socio-economic livelihoods, fragility and breakdown of State Institutions and physical destruction and generalized insecurity.
>
> (Rodicio, 2005, para. 9)

Further, these states appear to be becoming home to both domestic and international terrorist organizations, which have gained a space to operate within the chaos created by a lack of governmental structures (Rotberg, 2002).

In states that lack an indigenous capacity to reorient themselves towards peace, a simple separation of combatants is insufficient to the long-term establishment and maintenance of peace. Equally, in countries with a low GDP and other indicators of need, as in Afghanistan, it has been recognized that there is often a "complex interplay between failed development strategies, the impact of globalization, the expansion of global criminal networks and civil wars" which has fuelled the emergence of violent conflict (Tschirgi, 2003, p. 7). The implication was expressed in a 2005 Report of the Secretary General to the UN General Assembly as follows:

> In the twenty-first century, all States and their collective institutions must advance the cause of larger freedom – by ensuring freedom from want, freedom from fear and freedom to live in dignity. In an increasingly interconnected world, progress in the areas of development, security and human rights must go hand in hand. There will be no development without security and no security without development. And both development and security also depend on respect from human rights and the rule of law.
>
> (UN, 2005, p. 55)

In short, in modern failed or failing states, there is a need, among other things, for security and development activities to be integrated if the society is to move towards a long term, sustainable peace and to avoid descending into the type of chaos from which international terrorist organizations now appear to be finding a base for operations.

The concept of peacebuilding

Recognizing the emerging relationship between security and development in societies in conflict, in 1992, the then-Secretary General of the UN, Boutros Boutros-Ghali, provided the first formal policy discussion of the linkage between development and security[1] in *An Agenda for Peace* (Boutros-Ghali, 1992). Merging concepts drawn from security and development operations, Boutros-Ghali introduced the concept of peacebuilding, which involved "actions to identify and support structures which tend to strengthen and solidify peace in order to avoid a relapse into conflict" (Boutros-Ghali, 1992). For Boutros-Ghali, peacebuilding could be contrasted with other tools to address violent conflict such as peacemaking, actions to bring "hostile parties" to an agreement, and peacekeeping, the deployment of an international military force whose primary goal is to prevent conflict by separating belligerents (Boutros-Ghali, 1992). For Boutros-Ghali, peacebuilding was meant to mend failed states, by not only ending violence in the manner of peacekeeping, but further, by creating societal tools designed to prevent a relapse into conflict.

Since 1992, there has been extensive literature development on peacebuilding. Whereas Boutros-Ghali had focused on peacebuilding as a process that followed peacemaking and peacekeeping activities and which was primary designed as a method of preventing a relapse into violent conflict,[2] commentators such as Keating and Knight have broadened the concept to include post and pre-conflict activities[3] (Keating and Knight, 2005). The idea that peacebuilding has post- and pre-conflict components has helped reinforce and move understandings of peacebuilding from simple discussions of measures aimed at ending disputes to addressing the complex issues surrounding failed and failing states. This broader approach sees peacebuilding as a process with an end state of generating long term, self-sustaining peace.

Peace, as it will be used throughout this paper, refers to what Galtung (1964) described as positive peace. More than simply the absence of violence, which Galtung refers to as negative peace, positive peace is "the presence of social justice through equal opportunity, a fair distribution of power and resources, equal protection and impartial enforcement of law" (Galtung, 1964, p. 2). Following this definition, peacebuilding is the process by which a society moves beyond negative peace, or imposed stability, towards positive peace, as evidenced by effective social structures and institutions.

Kenneth Bush, who refers to peacebuilding as an "impact" or "outcome" rather than a set of activities, argues that

> the process entails both short- and long-term objectives, for example, short-term humanitarian operations and longer-term developmental, political, economic, and social objectives. Peacebuilding is therefore a twofold process of deconstructing the structures of violence, and constructing the structures of peace.
>
> (Bush, 2005, p. 25)

Notably in order to reach these states Bush argues unique types of operations are required, specifically, there

> are two interrelated but separate sets of activities that must be undertaken simultaneously. Any intervention that includes one without the other is guaranteed not to have a net positive peacebuilding impact.
>
> (Bush, 2005, p. 25)

Simply put, in order to be successful and create peace, Bush suggests that security and development activities must be undertaken simultaneously and in an interrelated manner.

In achieving the goal of long-term peace that goes beyond merely ending an immediate manifestation of a conflict, commentators have suggested that peacebuilding must look beyond symptoms, which have drawn the majority of international attention in the past, and go deeper to target the ailment[4] (Keating and Knight, 2005). This entails identifying and targeting "peacebuilding gaps:

regional or international political, economic, social, and security initiatives requiring attention to sustain peace"[5] (CPR Network, 2004). It is understood that this should be reflected in visible and tangible increases in the political, social, cultural, economic and environmental security for individuals and communities (Keating and Knight, 2005).

For commentators such as Keating and Knight and the Conflict Prevention and Post Conflict Reconstruction Network, the achievement of long-term peace is dependent upon changing deep-seated root cause behaviours, such as the proliferation of severe social inequality, and upon the existence of alternative solutions, such as the development of stable social structures. As is discussed below, in order to achieve these outcomes commentators suggest operations must have three characteristics: they must be multifaceted, multi-partnered and involve harmonized actions (Thomson, 2005).[6]

Key characteristics of peacebuilding

Multifaceted

The issues surrounding shifting societal behaviour and structures are complex and multidimensional. As a result, solutions to address them must be sophisticated and multifaceted. Multifaceted refers to the various activities and programs that are necessary for effective peacebuilding, including de-mining, Security Sector Reform (SSR), Disarmament, Demobilization and Reintegration (DDR), assistance in monitoring and supervising electoral processes, the promotion of formal and informal participation in the political process, capacity-building for human rights and reconciliation, and public sector service development and reform. It is understood that there is no one set of programmes that will address the needs of every situation but rather that needs assessments specific to the unique culture and history of the target nation are an essential aspect of peacebuilding (Bush, 2005). Through these assessments, multiple tools and instruments, considered essential if the society is to generate the capacity to develop an independent peace, are identified and are designed to meet short-, medium- and long-term goals.

A multi-programmatic approach may greatly increase the complexity of programming and require organizations to utilize scarce resources on mutual coordination and information exchange rather than programming itself. Nonetheless, the approach is considered essential to counteracting the overlapping factors that reinforce the enticement of violence over peaceful solutions. The goal is to broadly and extensively engage various actors over time in activities designed to create peace.

Multi-partnered

In order to meet the goal of being multifaceted it is necessary to draw on an array of expertise and experience. The term multi-partnered refers to the collaboration of various international and external organizations with local actors in peacebuilding activities. In most cases, it is understood that essential local partners include the government and, local social groups and representatives from the local populace Pugh includes this in his definition of peacebuilding, which he considers

> a process of social, political and economic adjustment to, and underpinning of, conditions of relative peace in which the participants, especially those who have been disempowered and immersed by violence, can begin to prioritize future goals beyond immediate survival. Survivors not only need a stake in achieving these adjustment goals but need ultimate direction over the means to achieve them.
>
> (Pugh, 2000b, para. 5)

A multi-partnered approach entails identifying and targeting stakeholders inclusively, with special emphasis on those individuals most likely to contribute to or detract from peace efforts. Activities are then coordinated and undertaken in a collaborative manner with the various players, with a special emphasis upon ensuring that local actors (including vulnerable populations) have input in the process.

Although gathering input from multiple partners may increase the cost of programming, ensuring that operations are multi-partnered is considered important for three reasons. First, local input is essential in the development of programmes, as the specific socio-political culture of a specific environment is unique and is not always apparent to external actors. Second, input is required to increase "buy-in" and sustained involvement from local populace, thereby increasing the likelihood of a successful handover of programming to the community from external actors. In addition, as suggested above by Pugh (2000b), the inclusion of local actors increases the democratic nature of programming, by ensuring those impacted have a voice.

Harmonized

While various national, international and non-governmental organizations may undertake operations aimed at creating peace in conflict- and post-conflict societies, commentators suggest that to effectively and efficiently address root causes, peacebuilding endeavours must be undertaken in a harmonized manner. As stated by the British Department of Foreign Development (DfD), "development, diplomatic and defence professionals *must work together* to achieve common aims" (*Fighting Poverty*, 2005, p. 26). (Emphasis added)

The underlying assumption is that, by working together on various fronts, peacebuilding actors will reinforce and build upon each other's actions in time and space, thereby creating a peacebuilding synergy. As described by Keating:

> Peacebuilding, ... involves a number of diverse instruments and players, and much like an orchestra, the instruments must be finely tuned and the

players, and must work in the concert in order to produce anything resembling a coherent approach at postconflict reconciliation and sustainable peace.

(Keating and Knight, 2005, p. XXXII)

In short, by integrating operations it is hoped that peacebuilding actors will encourage efficiency, reduce duplication and generate mutually reinforcing patterns of peaceful conflict resolution. This is seen when organizations have synchronized programmes and evaluation and are using joint planning to tackle issues. The counter argument, or concern with this approach, is the potential loss of impact by each component due to homogenization of policies and processes.

Problems in organizing peacebuilding

With limited exceptions, (see for example, Hendrikson *et al.*, 2005 and Ankersen, 2003) there has been a dearth of literature examining how the above characteristics take shape on the ground, or, put another way, are "operationalized". Accordingly, in practice, peacebuilding operations have developed in response to specific crises and without formal guidelines and frameworks. Similarly, in large part, understandings of the relationship between conflict and development in failed states have evolved with operations rather than preceding and informing them (Keating and Knight, 2005).

A review of operations and the limited literature which does exist suggests that there have been two stages of development in attempts to merge security and development operations: first, a form of *ad hoc* cooperation between military and civilian bodies evolved; second, a form of coordinated response to conflict, particularly through the introduction of Civil Military Cooperation (CIMIC), developed. While these endeavours have built upon each other, as will be further discussed below, commentators suggest that they have failed to achieve a consistent level of integration (Duffield, 2001).

Ad hoc

In the face of humanitarian crises, the nature of activity by military personnel serving in conflict zones has expanded into activities that may be described as reconstruction and development. For example, as discussed by Ratner, peacekeeping soldiers with the United Nations Transitional Authority Cambodia (UNTAC) were tasked with ensuring the security of Cambodian civilians and UNTAC personnel; however, eventually, they also became involved in "what amounted to civic assistance programs" such as de-mining, providing medical assistance and infrastructural reconstruction (Ratner, 1995, p. 171). Commentators such as Fetherston point to this and other examples as evidence that the military has consistently been engaged in a form of peacebuilding while on traditionally "peacekeeping" missions:

First, peace building is an activity targeted specifically at rebuilding eco-nomic and/or political infrastructure. So ... [whether] peacekeepers sit on village roofs in Lebanon to deter shelling from destroying houses, rebuild bridges in Bosnia [or] provide security for farmers in Cyprus ... they are engaging in ... peacebuilding. Second, [it] is activity targeted specifically at reconciliation and restoring severed interactions. When peacekeepers in Cyprus organised village meetings between Greek and Turkish Cypriots attempting to rebuild trust and create an atmosphere in which the villagers felt safe enough to leave their homes, they were engaging in peace building. ... Third, [it] is the provision of humanitarian aid. When peacekeepers deliver relief supplies in Bosnia or Somalia they are engaging in peace-building.

(Fetherston, 1994, pp. 137–138)

Although informal and low-key, this suggests that peacebuilding has historically and routinely been an aspect of peacekeeping.

For the most part, the expansion of the military into traditionally "civilian" spheres was the result of a perceived need that the military became uniquely placed to fill, for example, because it alone had personnel on hand at a specific time or because it possessed the necessary resources to accomplish a defined task. As the military began to share an operational footprint with civilian bodies, ad hoc coordination resulted.

For example, in Kosovo, the rapid departure of the Serbian military created a gap between security and development aspects of the peace support operation. As a result, very few personnel, apart from military, were on the ground, which led to coordination between military and civilian governmental bodies. One result was that the Canadian Battle Group maintained and ran various develop-mental projects on behalf of CIDA and DfID. For the most part, these projects involved military members utilizing CIDA and DFID funds to hire local con-tractors to undertake reconstruction efforts. Military oversight of projects occurred until CIDA and DfID were able to establish their own field representa-tives. Projects included infrastructure reconstruction and development through local contracts (Delaney, 2000).

In this and other cases, it appears that both military and civilian parties per-ceived a benefit from short-term ad hoc coordination. For example, the Kosovo example described above was considered a win-win situation, as the CF pro-vided reliable, accountable, free and available labour to CIDA and DfID, while being seen performing the development tasks provided an excellent public rela-tions opportunity and in roads with the Kosovars for the CF (Delaney, 2000). In addition, both parties appear to have concluded that, most importantly, coordination ensured that the infrastructure needed to rebuild the society was provided sooner than would otherwise have occurred and locals were provided work that not only stimulated the economy but gave people purpose and focus.

While ad hoc coordination resulted in moderate success, in terms of the achievement of limited goals, missions, in which this type of coordination occurred, were often characterized by friction, discord and unnecessary overlap. This resulted in the majority of actors being unwilling to develop the relationship beyond the ad hoc basis. In large part, this appears to have been due to the "highly distinctive organizational cultures" and "time horizons" of military and civilian organizations (Byman, 2001, p. 99). The military was often sceptical of the capabilities and use of non-governmental organizations,[7] considering them to be a hindrance or liability rather than a partner in the field. While civilian organizations, had little trust in the military and often questioned its motives and commitment to the creation of peace (The International Council on Human Rights Policy, 2002). In addition, both civilian and military partners raised concern that civilian organizations were better placed to undertake many peace-building activities.

Further, given that most civilian agencies, particularly non-governmental organizations rely on the appearance of impartiality and neutrality as a means of security, they have been reluctant or unwilling to be seen as part of the military and hence, become "guilty" by association (Cuny, 1991, p. 76). Pugh (1998) argues that development activities should be left to civilian organizations because they are best placed to fulfil them and because doing the other associates development with military, thereby placing civilian workers in the field at risk. In addition, referring to the military and humanitarian, in his 1999 Nobel Prize acceptance speech, Médecin sans Frontière President stated: "[w]e are not the same, we cannot be seen to be the same, and we cannot be made to be the same (Orbinski, 1999, para. 12).

The perceived need for a more stable form of coordination appears to have arisen as a result of events such as the 1994 genocide in Rwanda and the crises in Haiti, in which civilian and military bodies on the ground were unable to react in an effective manner to the crises.[8] The perceived challenge was to coordinate various military and civilian elements within peace support operations in order to ensure efficiency, promote complimentarily and to prevent duplication. Notably, by the late 1990s, the number of bodies to coordinate had grown to include various military bodies, civilian governmental actors such as diplomats, development agencies and police bodies, and increasingly, non governmental organizations, often subcontracted by nations, the UN and regional organizations, to provide aid and developmental assistance (Weiss, 1999). The lack of confidence in the ad hoc approach led many organizations to examine the potential for and seek a more formalized approach to coordination.

Coordination

An early response to the need for more efficient and effective coordination was the introduction of Civil Military Cooperation (CIMIC) within military and civilian organizations. CIMIC is a set of concepts and guidelines that is designed to foster effective communication and coordinated activity between military and civilian bodies.[9] For example, NATO defines CIMIC as "the co-ordination and co-operation, in support of the mission, between the NATO Commander and civil actors, including national population and local authorities, as well as international, national and non-governmental organizations and agencies" (NATO, 2003, pp. 1–1).

In addition, CIMIC bodies have been formed by various organizations. The Military and Civil Defence Unit (MCDU) was established within the UN Office for the Coordination of Humanitarian Affairs (OCHA) by a decision of the Inter-Agency Standing Committee (IASC) in 1995 with a mission "to ensure the most efficient use of military and civil defence assets in support of humanitarian operations" (OCHA, n.d., para. 1). Similarly, bodies such as the International Committee of the Red Cross (ICRC), have adopted policies of assigning one or more people as responsible for liaison with the military command in the field and others, at headquarters, with the supreme military command concerned (Studer, 2001).

As the potential for a formal structure to coordination was examined, the relationship between the military and civilian organizations vacillated. Studer (2001) describes the relationship of the ICRC with the military as one that has oscillated between three policies: Isolationism, Proselytism and Ecumenism. These three positions can be used to categorize the philosophy and interaction of most NGOs with the military. Isolationism refers to the avoidance of any contact with the military at the operational level; proselytism is the attempt to rally all humanitarian agencies around the principles of neutrality, impartiality and independence; and ecumenism refers to a level of tolerance that seeks a complimentary relationship (Studer, 2001). However, "changing attitudes due to repeated interaction in recent years have softened much of the relief-agencies suspicion of the military, improving the overall prospects for cooperation" (Byman 2001, p. 98).

Identifying a need to decontaminate wells in Glogovac, a CF CIMIC Officer coordinated with the International Committee for the Red Cross (ICRC) and CIDA to, respectively, develop and fund a decontamination project (Delaney, 2000). This example, taken from the experience of the Canadian Battle group in Kosovo, illustrates a successful coordinated experience, based upon the action of CIMIC. Nonetheless, it may be noted that coordination has been limited to conflicts in which a relatively low level of security risk to personnel is present. Further, it has been argued, that when success has been achieved, it has been more the result of "the extraordinary efforts of ... personnel in the field" than widespread patterns of effective communication and coordination (Oslo, 2002, para. 5).

In a recent article, Ankersen (2005) suggests that there are two main causes for the barriers that have undermined the implementation of CIMIC policies and guidelines: culture and values. Culture in this context includes the dominant structures it creates within an organization: specifically, the military is considered to be predominately hierarchical and accustomed to the following of orders while civilian organizations are typically organized "horizontally" with a large sense of independence for individual members (Ankersen, 2005, p. 77). Differences in values primarily relate to the value given to "time, efficiency, impartiality and neutrality and the use of force" (Ankersen, 2005, p. 78). Although Ankersen's observations relate primary to military relationships with NGOs, they appear to also be applicable to the relationship between military and other governmental bodies.[10] These differences will be more pronounced in some relationships than others; for example differences are likely more pronounced between the military and a grass roots NGO vice a bureaucratic governmental aid agency. Nonetheless, they create a barrier in both cases that hinders harmonization.

Summary

As a result of documents such as *An Agenda for Peace*, it is generally accepted that "peacebuilding" is necessary if societies embroiled in violent conflict, and particularly failed states, are to achieve long term peace. Commentators suggest that effective peacebuilding addresses the root causes of a conflict through operations that are multifaceted, multi-partnered, and achieve a level of harmonization between security and development activities and between military and civilian actors. To date, while there has been limited success with the two aforementioned factors, (Thomson, 2005) military and civilian harmonization has remained an elusive goal, in large part due to animosity between actors borne of differences in culture and values.[11] Nonetheless, commentators suggest that harmonization is key if effective strategies are to be developed to address the challenges within failed states.

Afghanistan and the PRT

The remainder of this paper examines how the Canadian PRT, during its first six months of operation, has been responding to the challenges of Afghanistan. It seeks to develop a clearer understanding of what the PRT looks like on the ground, with a view to Canada's foreign policy goal of responding to failed states through peacebuilding. The question it asks is whether the PRT is simply a tool of "negative peace" and stability, or whether it has also become a tool of "positive peace" by creating stability while also building the structures of peace.

Afghanistan is an archetype of a failed state. Due to its unique history and circumstances, the international community has developed the Provincial Reconstruction Team in order to allow development and security activities to be undertaken in the highly volatile and insecure environment. As will be discussed below, in some cases, PRTS have begun to merge security and development as envisaged in peacebuilding while in others, PRTs have remained primary military tools whose goal is simply stability.

The emergence of PRTs in Afghanistan

The primary purpose of PRTs is strategic, namely to provide the US military and central government presence among key locations, including Afghanistan's four primary ethnic groups, the former Taliban headquarters, and the base of the country's most difficult warlord, Ishmael Khan (Perito, 2005, p. 2). Nonetheless, the development of PRTs began with the idea that small US-led coalition elements in Operation Enduring Freedom could expand the "effects of ISAF" beyond Kabul in order to expand and accelerate reconstruction (Dziedzic and Seidl, 2005).[12] PRTs were considered a method of addressing the causes of "Afghanistan's instability: terrorism, warlords, unemployment, and grinding poverty" (Perito, 2005, p. 2).

To this end, the PRT concept "was not narrowly conceived in terms of winning hearts and minds for local force protection, but – in the style of UK special forces (SAS) troops in the Dhofar Campaign in the Oman in the 1970s – as a way for a small military unit to improve conditions in local communities, recognizing that the use of force would not address the root grievances driving the conflict and could in fact exacerbate the situation" (Hendrickson *et al.*, 2005, p. 15). An open question remained whether the PRTs would in fact address the root causes creating these manifestations, in the manner of peacebuilding, or focus solely on stability and counter-insurgency.

In its broadest sense a PRT is a joint operations group of civilian and military elements consisting of 50 to 150 personnel. According to NATO documents, the key objective of the PRTs is reconstruction in the broadest sense and more specifically to:

1 Support the GOA in the development of a more stable and secure environment.
2 Assist in extending the authority of the GOA.
3 Support where appropriate the SSR initiatives.
4 Facilitate the reconstruction effort and reinforce national development priorities.
5 Enable unity of effort amongst civil actors.
6 Demonstrate the International Community's commitment to Afghanistan's future.

While key aspects of all PRTs appear to be performing stability operations, security sector reform, and the rebuilding of infrastructure (i.e. wells, schools and roads), the specific mission and emphasis given to these tasks varies depending upon the provincial location and national objectives of a PRT.

The initial plan and structure for PRTs was provided by the US government and by early 2003 there were US-led PRTs in Bamian, Kondoz, Mazar-e-Sharif, Kandahar, and Herat. The US Embassy in Kabul provided a set of parameters and principles that established "three primary objectives for the PRT program: extend the authority of the Afghan central government, improve security, and promote reconstruction" (Perito, 2005, p. 2). However, during the early years, the Coalition was largely focused on combat operations. Accordingly, with limited input from the Afghan government, individual PRTs generally developed operating structures and practices in an independent manner (Hendrickson *et al.*, 2005).

PRT structure

Although all PRTS were originally US-led and formed part of the Operation Enduring Freedom, it was decided early on that PRTs would more appropriately be a part of ISAF. Accordingly, on 13 October 2003, the United Nations Security Council passed Resolution 1510 which allowed ISAF to expand its role to support the Government of Afghanistan beyond Kabul. In response, ISAF established nine PRTs in locations including Mazar-e-Sharif (UK), Meymana (UK), Feyzabad (Germany) and Baghlan (Netherlands).[13] While, of the 22 PRTs in Afghanistan, 13 remain under the OEF, it is eventually planned that all PRTs within Afghanistan will be under ISAF control.[14]

The PRT Executive Steering Committee (ESC), chaired by the Afghan Ministry of Interior, now manages all PRTs with support from members from UNAMA, OEF, ISAF, NATO and lead PRT nations. The committee is also supported by the PRT Working Group (WG) which provides operational direction to the PRTs. Nonetheless, given the independent development and two command structures (OEF and ISAF), the Executive Steering Committee's ability to influence PRTs is limited as the teams are allowed significant latitude in "interpreting" directions and directions are generally considered to lose potency as they are passed down the command structures (Interview, 2005).

In general PRTs have followed the structure and organization of the first US PRT. However, given the PRTs have also been evolving and changing, in reflection of "a number of factors including the large number of countries involved in PRTs, the presence of two separate military operations and commands in Afghanistan, and different approaches to civil–military activities", (Hendrickson, 2005, p. 15) since 2003, PRTs have "developed distinct personalities" (Perito, 2005, p. 3). For the purposes of this chapter the two dominant and most relevant PRTs are the American and British model.

American

Generally, American PRTs are led by an Army Lieutenant Colonel and are composed of up to 100 American military and civilian personnel. These typically include representatives from the Department of State, the Agency for International Development (USAID), and the Department of Agriculture (USDA). It is also common for PRTs to have a representative from the Afghan Ministry of the Interior (MOI) and a number of local interpreters (Perito, 2005). Component parts report to the military commander.

To date, US PRTs have focused on governance, security, and reconstruction. However, "U.S. commanders [have] viewed promoting the authority of the central government as the primary mission", which has translated into direct support for the respective provincial governor (Perito, 2005, p. 6). Security and reconstruction are reflected as force protection, and quick impact development projects to "win hearts and minds", run and financed primarily by the military and focused on direct reconstruction efforts (Jakobsen, 2005). The US administration considers PRTs to be a key "non-kinetic" aspect of US counter insurgency operations in Afghanistan.[15]

The American PRT has been the most highly criticized model for various reasons, including the initial tendency of US PRT personnel to operate out of uniform and in unmarked vehicles (this has since stopped), and an inclination to use some of its initial aid conditionally as a method of securing military or campaign objectives (Interview, 2005). Other criticism has been levied for the PRTs' "ambiguous political identity" and "quick-impact" projects (Sedra, 2004).

In light of these criticisms, it appears that early US PRTs were not conducting operations in line with the concept of peacebuilding. However, it may be noted that US PRTs have been shifting their focus and concepts in the past year. For example, in Kalat, the local PRT has begun operating a trade school as well as creating partnerships between soldiers, who have civilian training in specific areas, and local government workers. In one pairing, a member of the National Guard who works as an accountant will be partnered with and tutor a government employee of the treasury (Interview, 2006).

British

Like the US model, UK PRTs are led by a military commander, but have a joint leadership structure. PRTs are composed of a majority of military forces with representatives from various civilian bodies including the Department for International Development (DfID), the Foreign Commonwealth Office (FCO), and may include representatives from counterpart American or other coalition country organizations. Unlike in the US model, constituent parts "report to superiors within their own institutional structure" rather than to the military commander (McHugh and Gostelow, 2004, p. 25).

The UK has been operating in the north of Afghanistan where security is considered to be less of an issue than in the south and east of the country. The UK PRTs' efforts have centred on security sector reform, support to institution building and the promotion of economic development (Sedra, 2005). The PRTs have focused on interaction with local populations and appear to have committed to long-term reconstruction projects (Sedra, 2005).

Generally, the UK model has been praised for its "more precise 'concept of operations'" as compared with other models and for the concrete achievements by PRTs such as that at Mazar-e-Sharif, which are considered to have contributed to stability, police and army training, and DDR (Friborg, 2004). In addition, through constant, visible interaction, the Mazar-e-Sharif PRT is considered to have established effective relationships with local populations, creating linkages for other organizations such as UNAMA and in certain cases, intervening to mediate and diffuse tension between local commanders (McHugh and Gostelow, 2004). Nonetheless, it may be noted that the latter praise has been tempered by the criticism that an inability to prevent incidents from occurring in the first place exists (McHugh and Gostelow, 2004). Due to the mixed nature of these reviews it is difficult to determine if the UK PRT is a vehicle of peacebuilding. However, it would appear to be operating in a manner conducive to peacebuilding.

Evaluations to date of the PRTs

To date, due to the relative youth of PRTs and "the lack of a comprehensive empirical review of (their) mandates, activities and impact", there is very little evidence to support either "positive" or "negative" assessments of PRTs (Kings, 2005, p 10). Of the literature that does exist, PRTs have received mixed reviews, particularly with regard to their potential and actual accomplishments in the realm of peacebuilding.[16] However, it is important to note that the majority of criticism is from NGOs who do not generally perceive Operation Enduring Freedom favourably.

With regards to being multifaceted, concerns have been raised as whether the military partners within PRTs have the necessary skills to conduct civilian peacebuilding and humanitarian work. Specifically, many NGOs and non-government humanitarian agencies argue that, given the lack of necessary skills, the military should only be employed in peacebuilding and humanitarian capacities when there is a lack of other professionals capable of performing necessary tasks (Pugh, 1998). However, this perception may be flawed as the PRTs wish to fill this shortfall by partnering with other organizations in order to undertake multifaceted programming. While there seems to have been some success in Mazar-e-Sharif, it is argued that US led PRTs have failed to involve appropriate partners, given that their focus has been on winning the "hearts and minds" of strategic allies rather than focusing upon long term reconstruction efforts (McHugh and Gostelow, 2005, p. 14).

Commentators suggest that the level of harmonization between the different partner organizations within PRTs has varied greatly between the different national models of PRTs. US PRTs appear to achieve a moderate level of harmonization at an operational level. However, given that non-military elements are generally considered to act towards military rather than their own independent goals, the level of harmonization in programming and the establishment of goals is limited (McHugh and Gostelow, 2005).

Conversely, the British PRT is generally considered to have achieved a moderate level of harmonization at both an operational and planning level between the Department of International Development (DfID), Foreign and Commonwealth Office and the Ministry of Defence (MoD).[17] "The tri-partite DFID-FCO-MoD management arrangement allows the PRT's military activities to be better harmonized with the developmental and political situation in the area of operation" (Kings, 2005, p. 24). Specifically, Friborg (2004) suggests that the UK PRT in Mazar-e-Sharif has demonstrated how a small task tailored organization can improve the security situation in a region through patrols, assistance in the DDR, police training, and ANA deployment. A key aspect of the harmonization appears to be integration of the 3Ds, and the "strong working relationship between the FCO, MOD and DFID representatives who jointly make policy" (Kings, 2005, p. 31).

Conclusion

In order to achieve long-term peace in Afghanistan there is a need to integrate security and development efforts. Building upon this need PRTs were developed, among other things, to begin the process of peacebuilding. To date, PRTs share characteristics such as military and civilian government member-ship, however, they differ in two key aspects: who sets the priorities and the emphasis placed on peacebuilding vice other goals. Commentators have sug-gested that the UK has fielded the most effective peacebuilding model to date given its integration of security and development. Further, the UK model is praised for "not engaging in assistance projects in sectors where other actors are better equipped to work and [for] limiting its involvement in assistance to areas which support its core stabilization focus, particularly the security sector" (Hen-drickson *et al.*, 2005, p. 24).

Meeting the criteria

Against the context set out above, Canada decided to field a PRT by taking over the US-led PRT, operating as part of OEF, within Kandahar Province. This placed Canada at a crossroads: would Canada follow the US lead and aim to use the PRT as a tool of Operation Enduring Freedom and more generally, the "war on terror" such that its emphasis would be strongly on security and stability? Or alternatively, would it remake the PRT building on the UK model and focus on peacebuilding? As discussed below, the answer appears to lie in recent policy statements.

Canada's approach to failed states

The attack on the World Trade Center in 2001 has challenged previous approaches to foreign policy in North America. A failed state once considered of marginal international relevance became home to a terrorist organization from which deadly attacks on US soil occurred. As a result of these attacks, not only did the US call upon its allies to assist it in "rooting out terrorism" but Canada was faced the possibility of similar attacks, creating two reasons to take action.

In other countries, the potential for domestic attacks arising from failed states has resulted in a military led response. Notably, the US launched the "war on terror", invading Afghanistan and then Iraq[18] in a bid to find and root out the source of terrorist attacks on US soil. Despite the approach taken by other coun-tries, the Canadian International Policy Statement, released in 2005 has been clear that Canada's approach to failed states remains focused upon strengthening the indigenous ability of a society to orient itself toward peace and in maximiz-ing and prioritizing human security:

> Our strategy to address the multiple challenges posed by failed and fragile states is focused, first and foremost, on prevention, through development

strategies, support for human rights and democracy, diplomacy to prevent conflict, and contributions to build human security.

(GOC, 2005d, p. 9)

When read in conjunction with CIDA's definition of peacebuilding, set out below, the International Policy Statement may be interpreted as advocating peacebuilding as the primary method of addressing the security challenges posed by failed states.

> The overarching goal of peacebuilding is to enhance the indigenous capacity of a society to manage conflict without violence. *Ultimately, peacebuilding aims at building human security, a concept which includes democratic governance, human rights, rule of law, sustainable development, equitable access to resources, and environmental security.*
>
> (CIDA, n.d.) (Emphasis added)

The cornerstone of the strategy is the "3D approach" which involves "undertaking Defence efforts to strengthen security and stability, pursuing Diplomacy to enhance prospects for nation-building and reconstruction, and making certain that Development contributions are brought to bear in a coordinated and effective way" (GOC, 2005e, foreword). The goal of this "whole of government approach" is not only that defence, diplomatic and development activities, undertaken respectively by the military, Foreign Affairs and CIDA occur, but that they occur with some level of integration. In the words of former Foreign Minister Pierre Pettigrew, defence, diplomacy and development are to be "harnessed together in a single coherent framework" (Pettigrew, 2005, para. 2). Or, as stated in the International Policy Statement itself with regard to failed states:

> The Government of Canada believes that an integrated "3D" approach, combining diplomacy, defence and development, is the best strategy for supporting states that suffer from a broad range of interconnected problems. In short, our official aid programs and our broader international policies must operate in tandem. This requires government departments to work more closely together – from planning through to execution – so that contributions as disparate as police force training, civil engineering and private sector development combine into one, comprehensive approach to capacity building.
>
> (GOC, 2005e, p. 20)

Specifically, within the context of failed or failing states, foreign policy documents envisage that aid programs will provide special funding which will be coordinated "in a whole-of-Government manner involving Foreign Affairs Canada, the Department of National Defence, CIDA, and other relevant agencies" (GOC, 2005c, p. 24).

Even before the issuance of the International Policy Statement, initiatives within the Canadian government sought to develop operational models for the 3D approach. For example, the Canadian Peacebuilding Initiative brought together FAC and CIDA with the dual goal of:

> [assisting] countries in conflict in their efforts towards peace and stability, and [promoting] Canadian peacebuilding capacity and Canadian participation in international peacebuilding initiatives. *These objectives are interactive and interdependent.*
>
> (CIDA, n.d.) (Emphasis added)

In order to achieve these goals, the Initiative aims to address issues surrounding conflict prevention and resolution, as well as post-conflict activities, largely by focusing upon socio-economic and political efforts and emphasizing local ownership of conflict resolution (CIDA, n.d.).

Nonetheless, the weak link in integration appeared to be the harmonization of civilian approaches to peacebuilding with those undertaken by the Canadian Forces. Specifically, while FAC and CIDA embarked upon the Canadian Peacebuilding Initiative, DND pursued a different operational philosophy and programmatic approach to peacebuilding through the doctrine of Fourth Generation of Warfare (4GW)[19] and the Three Block War.[20]

The response to Afghanistan

Against this background, Canadian foreign planners faced the challenge of responding to the vacuum of governmental structures in Afghanistan after the fall of the Taliban. Initially focused upon the development of government in Kabul, by 2003, deteriorating security outside of the capital had highlighted the need for Canada and its allies to support the spread of the government into areas such as Kandahar province. The operational challenge lay in the high risk posed to both international and domestic civilians in these areas. As noted above, the question was whether Canada, through the PRT, would pursue the goal of an integrated peacebuilding operation or pursue a primarily military response following the lead of the United States.

Initially, the PRT appeared to be conceived as a primarily military endeavour and was described as being lead by the military element due to the high security threat (Faldwell, 2005). Therefore, although the PRT was composed of an element from CIDA, it was initially described by CIDA as a separate body, which would provide the stability in the region necessary for CIDA and other civilian professionals to pursue their own separate development agenda (Hingorami, 2005).[21]

As the PRT has developed, no one mandate has been articulated by government officials and it appears to have been characterized in moderately different terms by the different elements that comprise it. For example, while in the official background document to Canada's activities in Afghanistan, the PRT is placed under the heading of defence activities (GOC, 2005f), the RCMP describes it as part of the Canada's "3D approach ... in international peacekeeping peace support activities" (RCMP, 2005, para. 5). The official backgrounder to the PRT states, "Canada's objective is to help Afghanistan become a stable, democratic and self-sustaining state" and that the PRT "will engage with Afghan officials and members of civil society as well as with international military and civilian organizations" (GOC, 2005g, para. 1). Accordingly, while it maintains a focus upon security and stability, official statements suggest that the PRT is seeking to make tangible the goal of an integrated peacebuilding tool, at least at the governmental level, envisaged by the International Policy Statement.[22]

Before Canada embarked on this mission, various preparatory steps were undertaken including an evaluation in Afghanistan by DND and FAC personnel to assess the value and potential of PRTs. On their return a conference was held by the Peace Operations Working Group of the Canadian Peacebuilding Coordinating Committee to examine issues surrounding PRTs and was distributed to the various government bodies (Peace Operations Working Group, 2003). Based on these assessments, Canada deployed a PRT to Kandahar as described below. The conclusion drawn appears to have been that Canada should follow the UK lead in fielding a PRT focused on peacebuilding rather than the mere achievement of stability (Interview, 2006). This decision appeared to be based upon the goal of the International Policy Statement that Canada employ a peacebuilding approach to the challenges of failed states. Notably, in retrospect, the Canadian Government has described the PRT as an innovative application of the Policy Statement (GOC, 2005h).

The Canadian PRT

Overview

Following a primarily UK model, the Canadian PRT is led by a military officer and consists of defence, diplomatic and development elements, namely, the Canadian Forces (CF) and Royal Canadian Mounted Police (RCMP), Foreign Affairs Canada (FAC), and the Canadian International Development Agency (CIDA). In addition, the PRT contains representatives of the United States Agency for International Development (USAID) and the British Department of International Development (DfID).[23] The numbers of personnel from each organization are listed in the below table.[24] There are also a number of locals who work with the PRT including a Minister of Interior representative, interpreters, security personnel and general labourers.

Organization	CF	CIDA	FAC	RCMP	USAID	DfID
Personnel	150	1	2	2	1	1

While defence elements currently outnumber civilian members, officials state that personnel numbers will become more balanced as security in the Kandahar region increases (Faldwell, 2005).

The PRT's Area Of Responsibility (AOR) is the entire Kandahar Province, an area of approximately 47,676 km^2, which lies in the South of the country along the border with Pakistan and has a population of over 2.5 million. The focus of the PRT's operations during its first six months was the provincial capital, Kandahar City, which lies in the middle of the province and is home to approximately two million inhabitants.[25] Activities were focused in the capital in order for the PRT to become fully established on the ground and to enable the PRT to provide support to the upcoming elections. Since early 2006, the PRT has begun to increase operations outside the capital and is expected to continue to expand throughout the province in the coming year.

Objectives

Although originally part of the Operation Enduring Freedom, it was planned from its commencement that the Canadian PRT would become part of ISAF (Alexander, 2005). As a result, while Canada has not established public objectives for the PRT, it appears to have adopted by default the following six key objectives that NATO has established for ISAF PRTs:

1   Support the GOA in the development of a more stable and secure environment.
2   Assist in extending the authority of the GOA.
3   Support where appropriate the SSR initiatives.
4   Facilitate the reconstruction effort and reinforce national development priorities.
5   Enable unity of effort amongst civil actors.
6   Demonstrate the International Community's commitment to Afghanistan's future.

In summarizing the PRT's approach to these goals, the PRT has been described as a "large embedded training team" (Interview, 2006), whose core responsibilities are to conduct stability operations and to conduct GOA support activities, primarily in the area of Security Sector Reform (SSR). However, as is discussed below, these objectives are reflected differently in the operations and goals of the various elements of the PRT.

Operations

Security elements: the Canadian forces and RCMP

The CF primarily describes its role as security sector reform and stability operations. It aims to provide security sector reform by supporting the ANP, through the provision of para-military training (consistent with training provided to the RCMP), patrolling with the ANP and reinforcing local police as first responders to critical security incidents. In addition, it supports other governmental departments within the PRT by providing transportation, security and logistical support. During the first six-month deployment, the commander also had a $1 million fund to spend in support of the CF's mandate. Notably, this mandate was broadly interpreted and the funds have been used to build several ANP substations, repair and purchase equipment and are earmarked for the future construction of offices for the Secretariat of the Provincial Development Committee. In addition the Canadian PRT pays for the employment of security personnel for the PRT's Camp Nathan Smith who are nationally trained as police officers and work as employees of the Ministry of the Interior.

The other security partner, the RCMP, describes its primary role as "[assisting] in building the capacity of local Afghan police forces" (RCMP, 2006, para. 7). More specifically, the first goal is, to establish relationships with the ANP and act as focal point of contact between the PRT and local police, and second, to advise, mentor, monitor and train local Afghan police forces[26] (Interview, 2006). The RCMP's PRT website suggests that specific activities for the latter include making recommendations on police Standard Operating Procedures, assisting in the planning of the deployment of the police force, advising on logistical support, command and control, relationships between local police and the population, advising and conducting police training, and, finally, supporting Afghan police ownership in reconstruction efforts.

Civilian elements: FAC and CIDA.

FAC and CIDA, in the context of security sector reform, have a primary focus of rebuilding the civilian elements of government. The focus of the FAC is governance through activities such as providing support to democratic development through operations that emphasize the electoral process, the development of governance institutions, and the promotion and protection of human rights (Interview, 2006). While it was originally envisaged that FAC would focus on governmental reform, such as reform of the judiciary, due to the limited development of the GOA to date, the FAC has primarily acted as an advisor to the PRT and to the Canadian embassy in Kabul with regard to measures by which Canadian engagement in Afghanistan may be better coordinated. In addition, it has acted in an advisory capacity to the Afghan government by advising the Provincial Governor on various issues, including, judicial reform and women's rights.

The one organization within the PRT with a development mandate, CIDA describes its focus as longer-term sustainable projects focused at a national level with some flexibility for short-term, high impact projects[27] (CIDA, n.d.). Given its primarily long-term goals, to date, the specific operations undertaken by CIDA on the ground have been limited. Nonetheless, it has recently received approval for the Security Sector Initiatives Programme (SSIP), a multi-year $10 M project, by which it plans to create the conditions for long-term development projects. One of the initiatives within the programme is Confidence in Government, an initiative aimed at developing trust between the villages and their elected leaders. Through SSIP, it is planned that small to mid-size grants will be awarded through the newly elected Provincial Council to help build local capacity for self-government.

Interpretations

Each of the PRT's elements have expressed the mission of the PRT and operationalized the above ISAF goals with respect to their individual roles differently. For the most part, these individualized missions reflect the unique skills and expertise of the PRT's elements and the corresponding emerging elements within the Government of Afghanistan to which they have targeted their operations. A unifying aspect of all departmental publications to date is the understanding that the pillars of the PRT's mission correspond to the first three NATO goals and their focus upon GOA Support, Stability, and Security Sector Reform (SSR). However, the commitment of the various departments to the 3D approach, and the harmonization of the PRT, appears limited as there was little pre-deployment coordination or collective training and there is no central command or headquarters in Canada that oversees the PRT's activities.

Operationalization

At the time of writing, the PRT as a whole had conducted over 1,100 missions in pursuit of the above-described objectives (Interview, 2006). These missions included:

1   Kandahar City Mounted Presence Patrols.
2   Personnel Escort missions.
3   Foot Presence Patrols.
4   Afghan National Police Substation Tours.
5   Missions to Governors' Compound.
6   Route Designation missions.
7   Civil Military Cooperation missions.
8   Information Operations Patrols.
9   Village Medical Outreach Patrols.
10 Afghan National Police Regional Training Centre Patrols.
11 Field Support Teams missions.
12 Quick Reaction Force (QRF) Rollouts; and
13 Improvise Explosive Device (IED) Emergency Response (CF Presentation, 2005).

Where possible, missions were multi-purpose, in that they included a primary mission and where possible a secondary or tertiary mission. For example, an Afghan National Police Substation Tour, by the RCMP, could incorporate a Civil Military Cooperation mission, and include representation by FAC in order to collect information.

In terms of the involvement of personnel and resources, a focus has been meeting with Shuras[28] in an attempt to visibly integrate PRT members within the local community and to communicate the goals of the PRT and receive input into these goals. Another focus has been presence patrols, which are conducted on both foot and by vehicles in a non-intrusive manner similar to a police officer walking the "beat" or "patrolling" in North America. Through these two endeavours, it is believed that the PRT "gets to know" the community and the community "gets to know" the PRT (Interview, 2006). Patrols appear to have been particularly successful during the September 2005 elections, at which time the PRT conducted over 50 patrols in Kandahar City within three days, contributing to relative stability in what had otherwise been predicted to be a volatile period (Interview, 2006). Nonetheless, concern within the PRT also exists that the PRT's use of Shuras, participation, has prioritized and reinforced the rule of one social mechanism, namely the elder male dominated Shuras, potentially limiting the growth of other social groupings.

Despite a current emphasis on security operations like patrols, there is general consensus among PRT members that "institutional development", such as the implementation, as part of SSIP, of the Provincial Development Committee, will eventually begin to occupy the majority of the PRT's future tasks (Interviews, 2006). Further, while the most visible achievements of the PRT to date have been in the area of stabilization, it is understood that these and other activities have in part been aimed at laying a foundation for the achievement of medium- and long-term security sector reform and development (Interviews, 2006).

Evaluation

Objectives

The six NATO objectives, which the PRT appears to have adopted, point more directly to PRT activities than to specific outcomes internal to the Afghan government and society. As such, following Bush's approach to peacebuilding, namely, that it is determined by outcomes, little can be concluded as to whether or not the Canadian PRT is conducting peacebuilding.

Further, it may be noted that the NATO objectives are sufficiently general that they may lead to any number of outcomes, some of which may be classified as peacebuilding, while others might constitute conflict propagation, or, "winning a war" by alternative means. For example, "supporting the GOA" may encourage the establishment of a sustainable peace; however, if the government persecutes Muslims who convert to Christianity, it is unlikely to create freedom from fear and therefore does not meet the criteria of human security and therefore, peacebuilding.[29] In addition, simply building a well as a reconstruction effort does not necessarily equate to peacebuilding, as the mere existence of the well may exacerbate existing tensions within a village if the well is located within an area dominated by one particular ethnic group.

In this regard, it is notable that the United States, who have adopted very similar objectives, has classified PRTs as non-kinetic[30] tools of its general counter insurgency operations, and more generally, its "war on terror" in Afghanistan. Given the generality of the NATO objectives, they also appear equally suited to an operation with a peacekeeping or peace support mandate. For example, the mandate in Kosovo contained similar aspects, namely, to create "an immediate end of violence in Kosovo; the complete withdrawal of Serb forces; the unconditional and safe return of all the refugees; and the stationing in Kosovo of an international military presence" (Baril, 1999, speaking notes for Chief of Defence Staff for Appearance at the Business Council on National Issues. Toronto, Ontario, 14 April).

Given the above, it appears that limited implications may be drawn from the wording of the NATO objectives with regard to the PRT's ability to or accomplishment of peacebuilding. Accordingly, whether or not the Canadian PRT is a tool of peacebuilding appears to depend more upon the manner in which it has interpreted and met each of the stated NATO objectives, as discussed below, rather than in the wording of the objectives themselves.

Operations

NATO objectives 1–3: Stability, GOA support and SSR

In interpreting and addressing the first three NATO objectives, the Canadian PRT has focused on security activities, including stability operations, such as training for the Afghan National Police. During these operations, a goal of the PRT has been to ensure that the GOA is visibly presented to the public as the primary "player" (Interview, 2006). It is believed that this will encourage the public legitimacy of the GOA as opposed to alternative bodies such as tribal leaders who are vying for public support. At the time of writing, a primary operation had also been presence patrols, and particularly those conducted in support of the September 2005 elections (Interview, 2006).

On one hand, operations like the patrols may be considered peacebuilding in that they have encouraged the process of democratic development, with the outcome being a successfully elected Wolesi Jirga (Lower Chamber of Parliament). On the other hand, the PRT's contributions to the election appear to have largely involved the CF acting in a stabilization capacity rather than involving additional PRT partners in security sector reform and development, as has been the case in many previous peacekeeping missions, most notably Bosnia (Schreiber, 2002). Accordingly, it appears not to have had the significant depth or breadth that characterizes an operation focused upon peacebuilding rather than one which merely accomplishes certain activities related to it.

A second key operational goal has been support for the development and reform of the Afghan National Police and the Afghan National Highway Patrol. Correspondingly, a focus of the PRT's RCMP elements has been the establishment of a strong working relationship with the Afghan National Police, through which resource and training needs are communicated to the PRT and efforts are made to address them. In addition, the RCMP as well as other elements of the PRT engage in daily communication with the Ministry of Interior (MoI) representative,[31] the government bureaucrat responsible for police activity in the province.

A limitation of the police reform programme is that it primarily involves only the RCMP and the Afghan National Police, with little input from other potential key participants such as women's and community groups and other PRT members. However, it may be noted that the RCMP will be increasing the input of other actors in and outside of the PRT in the types of activities and training that it undertakes with local police forces (Interview, 2006). As a result, the police reform program to date appears to be the first steps in multistage, long-term development process and as such, appears to represent a first step in peacebuilding.

NATO objective 4: Reconstruction

With regard to the fourth NATO objective, contracts have been let for various infrastructure reconstruction, including the construction of Afghan Police Sub-stations around the city, the enhancement of Kandahar University (Generators, Computers, Library IT), the creation of radio transmitted public service announcements, and the provision of a dump truck for the local hospital. Nonetheless, these measures are focused on short-term goals and although consistent with unpublished campaign plans, they have been ad hoc in that they are not being undertaken within a systematic view to developing the necessary infrastructure to support long-term societal rebuilding in Kandahar. As such, they lack key characteristics of peacebuilding such as a holistic plan to synchronize efforts and coordinate medium- and long-term development.

At the same time, it may be noted that CIDA has developed the Security Sector Initiative Programme (SSIP), which aims at creating the conditions for long-term development by addressing sources of insecurity (CIDA, n.d.). The proposal includes four elements: knowledge development, local programming, field level operations and a Provincial Development Committee, and includes all elements of the PRT: FAC, working to bring the GOA onside and in ensuring discussions are fair and equitable; CIDA, identifying the areas and projects for discussion; and, DND, providing security. (PRT, 2005). With the approval of SSIP, it appears that a long term, integrative plan may be established for development activities. Nonetheless, to date, it appears that the ad hoc, informal manner in which various efforts have been undertaken has fallen short of the NATO goal of more broad based reconstruction and has not constituted the multi-partnered, multifaceted nor harmonized activity, which characterizes peacebuilding.

NATO objective 5: Civilian unity

With regard to the fifth criteria, the PRT has had moderate success, at the field or tactical level, in bringing together actors from allied government organizations namely, FAC, CIDA, DFID, and USAID. However, there are additional civilian actors with whom the PRT can and might interact, including NGOs, International Organizations and civilian Afghans.

With regard to NGOs and International Organizations, it may be noted that, although it was never the aim to incorporate these organizations into the PRT, the fifth NATO goal was to enable a "unity of effort" among PRT elements and other civilian actors operating in Kandahar. However, to date success in this regard appears to have been limited for two reasons. First, for the most part, communications between the PRT and these bodies occur on an ad hoc, random, rather than formalized basis. For example, although since a more reliable relationship has been formed with the World Food Programme and the PRT 2005, the first contact between the two groups occurred through a chance encounter at a social function (Interview, 2006). Further, while the PRT meets with UNAMA on a weekly basis and sits on the Disbandment of Illegal Armed Groups (DIAG) committee, meetings with these groups primarily result only in a sharing information rather than the coordination of activities and operations as envisaged by the fifth NATO objective. The PRT's interaction with NGOs has been even more limited; an apparent result of an unwillingness on the latter's part to be associated with the PRT (Interview, 2006).

Second, when formal communication occur at strategic levels, for example, through the PRT Working Group, communications are often characterized and dominated by antagonism and miscommunication between military elements and NGOs. The former, who have limited control over their mandate, are only interested in discussing "practical matters", while the latter, often single issue, specialized NGOs, refrain from effective communications out of a feeling that they have "better things to do" than discussing non-policy issues (Interview, 2006). Various factors appear to account for this situation, including an initial policy decision on the part of the PRT not to prioritize the establishment of working relationships with NGO and International Organizations, the high risk security situation throughout Kandahar, which limits NGO and International Organization activity in the area, and the decision by large NGOs like OXFAM, who are working throughout the country, to adopt the policy of refusing to work with PRTs (Interview, 2006).

In recognition of the need for qualified NGOs and International Organizations to become actors in Kandahar if long-term peacebuilding is to occur, FAC has suggested that the PRT, in cooperation with governmental departments in Ottawa, begin to develop a plan to facilitate and encourage the eventual return to the region of NGOs, International Organizations, development agencies, and other entities (Berry, 2005). In the meantime, it is suggest that the PRT examine ways of facilitating the involvement of NGOs for short-term projects (Government of Canada, 2005g). Nonetheless, at the time of writing, it seems likely that organizational and operational differences between the majority of PRT members and NGOs and International Organizations will limit the establishment of effective working relationships through which this might be achieved. Accordingly, without significant change, it appears that this limits the PRT's ability to achieve the fifth NATO goal of unity among civilian actors.

An additional challenge in unifying civilian actors arises as a result of the limited government apparatus with which the PRT may interact. The PRT has often found itself being forced to channel a wide range of activities through the one government representative in a region, such as a police chief, who may lack appropriate experience and authority (Interview, 2006). Further, given the lack of new leaders within the Provincial Council and other Afghan government bodies, the PRT has often entered into increased communications with tribal leaders who are not part of the government and may not share its views (Interview, 2006). This tendency to engage potentially inappropriate actors may undermine the PRT's ability to achieve civilian integration as described in the fifth NATO objective, and more generally, its ability to engage multiple appropriate actors as required in peacebuilding.

NATO objective 6: Demonstration of international commitment

Finally, with regard to the sixth NATO objective, the PRT's simple presence appears to have in some ways demonstrated a commitment by the international community to assist in the reconstruction of Afghanistan. Nonetheless, given Afghanistan's history and the continued influence from anti-Western elements of the society, Afghans have, to date, appeared unconvinced that the simple presence of the PRT indicates a commitment by the international community to Afghanistan's long-term future (Interview, 2006). Accordingly, in many cases, Afghans have appeared cautious to committing to and engaging in long- and medium-term projects proposed by the PRT (Interview, 2006). In other cases, it appears that Afghans have actively engaged in efforts to undermine the ability of the PRT to operate in Kandahar, as was recently witnessed by the axe attack on Captain Trevor Greene (*Axe Attack*, 2006).

One recommendation to demonstrate the PRT's commitment that may encourage faith from the local populace is additional "little projects" to demonstrate that there will be "follow through" by the international community, in addition to an overall increase in the scope and mandate of the PRT (Interview, 2006). Whether or not this recommendation finds voice with policy planners, it appears that, to date, the inherent limits on the PRT in personnel and resources have meant that it has not been able to lay the groundwork for wide scale peacebuilding activities. Further, these limits have meant that the international community's commitment to the region has appeared more minimal than described in formal policy documents and generally hoped by Afghan leaders and the populace.

Summary

To date, the efforts of the PRT have been focused upon meeting the first three NATO objectives. Through presence patrols, it is supporting the development of a more stable and secure environment in the Kandahar region, and through SSR initiatives, it is assisting in the development of a more highly trained and effective ANP. The presentation of the GOA as the leader in activities appears to be building the latter's public legitimacy, and hence ability to re-establish the ability of the Afghan government to govern the country.

However, while moderate success has been achieved with regard to the first three goals, the PRT has been less effective in addressing the remaining NATO goals. The adoption of the SSIP plan may allow for more effective development efforts in the future and hence allow the PRT to more effectively meet the fourth NATO goal. Nonetheless, barriers to the development of effective relationships with International Organizations and NGOs and inherent limits on PRT resources and personnel suggest that it will continue to struggle to achieve the effective level of civilian unity and demonstrate an international commitment suggested by NATO goals 5 and 6.

The manner in which the PRT has operationalized the NATO objectives, and specifically, its focus upon Objectives 1–3, suggests that its work may only be considered to be laying groundwork for peacebuilding. Further, the PRT's stability operations and efforts to extend the authority of the GOA are similar to those conducted in the majority of past peace support operations. For example, in Bosnia, the operationalization of the SFOR mandate of providing security and stability by the 3rd Battalion Princess Patricia's Canadian Light Infantry Battle Group included the "creation of both a unified strategy and the development of a real team atmosphere within the [International Community]" aimed at political and economical reform (Schreiber, 2002, p. 16). Accordingly, at most, the PRT's efforts are consistent with the first stages of peacebuilding and the deconstruction of conflict. Further, the PRT has fallen short in development efforts. While plans are being developed to rectify this weakness, the lack of strategy for reconstruction and a limited unity of effort with civilian actors prevent it from being able to build the structures of peace.

Factors encouraging and hindering peacebuilding

While the PRT's work to date suggests that it is not a tool of peacebuilding, an underlying assumption of this research is that Canadian foreign policy makers intended that peacebuilding would be its goal. This assumption is based on the above-discussed descriptions given by policy makers and Canada's International Policy Statement of Canada's preferred manner of addressing the problem of failed states. Accordingly, the following section examines those aspects of the PRT that are moving it towards, and those which have hindered it from fulfilling a peacebuilding mandate.

Structure

Encouraging factors

As peacekeeping and peace support operations have evolved from the Suez in 1956 through the Balkans in the 1990s, so too has aspects of peacebuilding. As a result the military has begun to take on activities, such as reconstruction and support for governance initiatives, often leading the military and other organizations in sharing an operational footprint on the ground. The dependency on coordination centres like CIMIC or ad hoc relationships to work with other agencies has often resulted in a stovepipe approach, whereby information has only passed vertically within organizations rather than laterally between them. This often led to the duplication of effort, resulting in inefficient use of resources and time.

This stovepipe approach appears to have been avoided in the PRT through the structural integration of CIDA, FAC, DFID, USAID, RCMP and the CF. This integration also allows the PRT to undertake security and development concurrently rather than sequentially, which has been one of the principal difficulties in the operationalization of peacebuilding. For example, rather than the CF working with the ANP during initial stability operations, and then working with the RCMP once regional stability has been reached and "peace" is established, the CF and RCMP are working in conjunction, building and reinforcing one another's projects and goals. This has not only prevented redundancy but has also created synergy both within the PRT and the ANP.

However, this structure is not reflected within Canada; although the stovepipes have been eliminated in theatre, they still exist in Ottawa. This was seen in the inability of Departments to identify key personnel, primarily from CIDA and FAC, prior to elements being deployed, with the result that the PRT was prevented from partaking in joint training prior to deployment and its elements, were left to amalgamate and meld as a team in theatre (Interview, 2006). This added to the stress and steep learning curve already being experienced by personnel and suggested that while the PRT structure lends itself to creating synergy, it does not guarantee it.

Hindrances

The current PRT is composed of elements from the military and four civilian organizations and is considered to be a "team". Nonetheless, it seems clear that, to date, the PRT has a strong military emphasis. There are two possible reasons for this. First, a military colonel leads the PRT. Although, the intent, as given by the Chief of Defence Staff, was that the military would "lead (the PRT) from behind", in that the commander was not there to force his will and vision upon the PRT but rather to bring it together as a cohesive and functioning unit, the military appears to set priorities indirectly.

Second, CF personnel within the PRT highly outnumber non-CF personnel. Specifically, as compared with approximately 150 CF, non-military personnel are as follows: one person from CIDA, one from DFID, from USAID, two from FAC and two RCMP Officers. The result is a total of seven non-military personnel or less than 5 per cent of the PRT. At face value, these numbers are misleading in that the role of the military is to, as well as acting as a "team" member, provide general, logistical support to the PRT. Accordingly, even in an optimal peacebuilding team, military would outnumber civilian members. Nonetheless, the current representation from non-military organizations is far below what is necessary to undertake a moderate level of operations, and far below what might be considered an appropriate balance in order to achieve multifunctional, harmonized PRT operations.

One result of the military emphasis is that the majority of missions undertaken by the PRT are security based. These operations are very similar in nature to those undertaken by modern peacekeeping. For example, as discussed above, there is little difference between the Kandahar operations and CF operations in Kosovo in 1999, during which time the Princess Patricia's Canadian Light Infantry Battle Group performed presence patrols, met with local leaders and managed development projects. Although the argument can be made that the context itself differentiates this Kandahar mission, in that the PRT is on the side of the Afghan government rather than trying to be a neutral force, nonetheless, the outcome remains the same: the PRT is primarily performing security, stabilization operations and police training, potentially at the expense of other operational focuses.

A second result arises from the fact that Afghanistan has been embroiled in conflict for 30 years. Given this history, there is a tendency for local leaders to have a combined religious, political and military character, with an emphasis upon strength and legitimacy based in military power. Into this context, the military presentation and focus of the PRT has reinforced the understanding among Afghans that the PRT is a primarily military endeavour. As a result the PRT Commander is automatically deferred to in Shuras and local leaders appear to direct all concerns towards the commander. While attempts have been made to mitigate this effect by encouraging inclusive participation of all PRT elements at Shuras, the result has unavoidably been a reinforcement of the military based aspect of the PRT, undermining a coequal emphasis upon its other goals and upon the equal participation of military and non-military members.

Operations

Encouraging factors

As discussed above, the lack of an overall mandate for the Canadian PRT and extremely broad direction given to the various elements has allowed for these elements to interpret their role broadly. In the case of the current Canadian PRT, this has allowed for greater latitude in the implementation of stability operations and security by the military. For example, it has allowed the Commander to spend contingency funds on ANP substations rather than traditional security activates. This flexibility has been key to the integration of the PRT's operations, in that it has allowed other elements of the PRT to channel resources into areas that may be outside their normal purview and thus, allowed the PRT as a unit, to focus its energies on the most relevant root causes of ongoing conflict in the region, such as the lack of an effective police force.

In terms of attempts to involve multiple relevant partners, the Canadian PRT has sought local guidance and partnerships since its initial arrival in Kandahar. For example, in its arrangements for security in their camp, the Canadian PRT has created an arrangement with the MoI whereby personnel who were nationally trained as police are paid by the PRT to provide camp security. Although a fairly simple arrangement, it is notable that many other PRTs do not practice this, either conducting their own security, relying on personnel hired from outside the country or on local, non-government trained, private security, the latter of which is a violation of Afghan law. The security force is, thereby, working on behalf of the MoI and gaining valuable experience, which will eventually be transferred to the Afghan National Police.

In terms of its attempts to initiative multifaceted operations, on one hand, the incorporation of CIDA, FAC, RCMP, CF, DfID, and USAID into the PRT has, to a limited extent, automatically ensured that PRT operations are multifaceted. Nonetheless, as can be seen by the nature of its missions and operations to date, the PRT has been primarily focused on stability operations and has initially been dominated by the CF and RCMP.[32] It is understood that as CIDA and FAC become established in Kandahar and begin to implement their strategies and initiatives, the PRT will become increasingly multifaceted.

In terms of attempts towards harmonization, it is notable that, while the three apparent foci of the Canadian PRT, Stability Operations, Security Sector Reform and support to the GOA, could easily be divided between the military, RCMP, FAC and CIDA separately, instead there has been an attempt to tackle them in a united effort. The integration and blending of the missions is a natural fit to the structure of the PRT and it appears that the Lines of Operations of the different organizations overlap both in time and space creating synergy. Accordingly, while effective harmonization has been hampered due to the late arrival of key personnel into theatre and a lack of collective pre-theatre training, it appears that effective working relationships are forming between PRT participants, enabling the PRT to move towards an integrated approach to operations.

Hindrances

At an operational level, three sources of limitation on the ability of the PRT to undertake effective peacebuilding are discussed below: the economy of force, the lack of experience of PRT personnel and the lack of a coordinating body.

Economy of Force. The term "economy of force" has been used to describe the international community's approach to Afghanistan and its goal that minimal resources be expended on projects with maximum effect. For example, UNAMA is designed to have a "light footprint" and PRTs are described as a "stop gap" at best (Interview, 2006). There are two main reasons for this approach to Afghanistan: one, the large international, and specifically American, commitment to Iraq has resulted in limited contributions to the country; and, two, policy makers have focused international contributions on counterinsurgency activities which do not typically require a large number of personnel on the ground (Interview, 2006).

The "economy of force" approach to Afghanistan and limits in terms of personnel and resources has meant that the potential accomplishments of bodies such as the PRTs are limited. In terms of acting as an effective peacebuilding body, this has meant that the PRT is unable to undertake the type of large-scale projects that appear necessary to reconstruct Afghan society, such as large-scale educational programmes. Further, the limitations suggest that the PRT may start projects it is unable to accomplish, or that it may appear ineffectual when it does succeed due to limited nature of its accomplishments or the fact that such accomplishments may be spread too thinly across the province.

Experience within PRT. Given that peacebuilding is aimed at empowering a populace in order to create internal change, it is necessary that peace builders have a firm understanding of the politics and society and the nature of the conflict (Interview, 2006). However, in terms of sources of learning related to modern day Afghanistan, while certain understandings of society existed at a tactical level, there are only limited academic sources in Canada on Afghanistan, especially the Pashtun dominated south. Further, there is little "deep policy thinking", which is of fundamental strategic importance to a body such as the PRT and particularly to its policy planners (Interview, 2006). As a result, it appears that in some cases, instead of operations aimed at peacebuilding, misunderstandings of the context has led to the PRT being used as a leverage tool for individual members of the community, ultimately resulting in their individual, rather than community, benefit (Interview, 2006). In response to this type of development, it appears that PRT personnel have in some cases responded by falling back onto model activities from past peace support operations rather than personalizing operations towards the society, as required by peacebuilding (Interview, 2006).

Coordination Centre. Despite the need for synchronization of information and resources in order to achieve a level of harmonization among PRT elements, coordination of this nature is limited within the PRT. One reason appears to be that there is nobody responsible for the coordination of operations, or as it has been termed, an "Effects Integration Committee" (Interview, 2006). Notably, although CIMIC is well positioned to take on the role of a coordinating body within the PRT, as it already coordinates all elements of the PRT and is trained in matters pertaining to both development and security, it has kept its focus external. As a result, it appears that, to date, other members of the CF have taken on a coordinating role, leading them to describe their role as "enablers", whose main job is to "support the people putting the support in" (Interview, 2006). This has led to resources being taken away from other CF activities, and may also have led inadvertently to further military emphasis within the PRT.

Environment

Encouraging factors

As mentioned above, while the structure of the PRT appears to encourage synergistic activities, cooperation and the resulting synergistic programming may be more a requirement of the security situation in Kandahar rather than a free structural choice by PRT elements. Specifically, the insecure environment has forced the PRT's elements to work together, for example, in coordinating their movement, and as a result, to discover that more can be accomplished as a "team". The result appears to be an increasing integration of operations such as the incorporation of all 3Ds in SSIP. Further, the security situation may have encouraged groups to overcome traditional antagonisms and may have facilitated a stronger mutual understanding and appreciation of the relative contribution of the various civilian and military partners in the PRT. This was seen throughout the researcher's interviews with personnel, in which, although there were differences of opinion and attitudes, there was general agreement that the mission of the PRT could not be accomplished without the inclusion of all the organizations.

Hindrances

Key aspects of the PRT's operating environment which limit its ability to develop into an effective peacebuilding tool are: one, the constant threat to which members of the PRT are exposed, which has resulted in limits on movement and access to the Kandahar region; two, the larger military environment in which the PRT is operating and three, the quasi-militarized, hierarchical and tribal nature of Afghan society.

Security. It is interesting that one of the contributing factors to the creation of the PRT is also one that is preventing it from bridging the gap between security and development as a peacebuilding tool. It is hoped that the high impact this situation will lessen as security increases in the region. Nonetheless, at the present time, protection of the PRT consumes a significant number of resources and therefore undermines its ability to focus on peacebuilding activities.

Military Environment. Although the PRT is not waging war, the PRT's close proximity to KAF and its predominantly military image given the nature of its equipment and primarily uniformed personnel has led Afghanis and members of the international community to question whether it is independent of its military neighbours. It appears that "Afghans have little understanding of PRTs and do not see what they add, apart from intelligence gathering" (Interview, 2006). Accordingly, there appears to be lack of trust for members of the PRT, which undermines its ability to undertake peacebuilding.

Afghan Society. A history of invasion and war, lack of access to independent sources of information and a general lack of education appear to have led to a high level of suspicion of outsiders and vulnerability to propaganda within Afghan society. For example, one subject spoke of fellow Afghans who believed that the US was conducting suicide bombings in order to have a reason to stay (Interview, 2006), while another stated the internationally imposed restraints on education was the heart of the problem: the "enemy" wants to "prevent the populace from learning as they will stop listening" (Interview, 2006). From the point of view of the PRT, this has created, at minimum, suspicion and hesitancy among local Afghanis to collaborate with PRT elements on peacebuilding projects. In extreme cases, it has caused trepidation, as radical elements of Afghan society that are ideologically opposed to the PRT target it and those who associate with, limiting its ability to operate and undermining peacebuilding projects.

Conclusions

> It is the people that must be supported, it is always the people – they defeated the Russians. Their support will make us successful. Let us bring peace, not with bullets...
>
> (Interview, 2006)

Findings

Since 1992, the concept of peacebuilding has evolved in order to respond to the changing and often more challenging nature of intra-state conflict, and to developing understandings of the relationship between security and development in the creation and sustainment of violent conflict. Originally, the concept developed as a response to traditional approaches to peacekeeping and evolved into a form of ad hoc military–civilian interaction in relatively benign environments, such as Kosovo.

However, as the complexities and the proliferation of failing states and inter-state conflict has increased, so too has the apparent disparity between security and development operations in the field. Incongruity between military and civilian organizations often has led to an atmosphere of apprehension and operational isolation. Further, friction caused by the overlap of mandates and operational footprints appears to have become detrimental to peacebuilding in several cases. Accordingly, a movement towards a more formal form of coordination through CIMIC has occurred. Nonetheless, while to some CIMIC represents a step forward in military and civilian communication and in some cases, coordination, at a strategic level little has been done to implement the coordination and develop effective relationships between military and civilian actors in the field.

The end of Taliban rule in Afghanistan, the need for peacebuilding that it created and the high level of insecurity in areas such as Kandahar created an environment in which a new form of security and development merger was required. While civilian development organizations were and remain necessary if the country is to move towards a self-sustaining peace, the environment made the region inaccessible to most government and non-governmental development organizations, operating without some form of military protection.

One policy response in Canada has been the creation of the Kandahar PRT, which brings together Canadian security and development governmental actors. In its first six months, the Canadian PRT built upon the successes and failures of past PRTs fielded by the United States and other NATO allies, particularly the United Kingdom, by adopting an operational structure that brings together aspects of development and security in a context that allows full dialogue between its constituent military and civilian elements. To date, the PRT has focused its operations on security and stability activities, often led by its military components. Nonetheless, the collaborative operational structure, which it has adopted, has simultaneously been laying a groundwork for further future peacebuilding activities in four ways. One, it allows for experts in development, in CIDA and other related governmental and non-governmental organizations, to have early access into otherwise inaccessible areas. Two, it allows the military to incorporate peacebuilding into stability operations. Three, by integrating operations, the transition from military dominance to a civilian dominance within the PRTs dovetailed, both increasing the likelihood of success and potentially shortening the peacebuilding process. Finally, the current structure allows civilian and military organizations to learn from each others' experiences in a manner that may reinforce each organization's individual ability to contribute to the creation of a sustainable peace in Afghanistan.

Nonetheless, a key weakness in the current PRT in terms of its ability to be a vehicle of peacebuilding is the lack of a framework or clear strategic vision for operations. Currently the Canadian PRT is relying on the personalities in theatre and their experience to make both procedural and operational. There is no parallel organization, either in Ottawa or Kabul, to act as an operational or strategic coordinating body. Further, the military contribution to the PRT in personnel numbers and resources seriously outweighs the contribution of other partners, leading to the PRT having a military emphasis and risking the PRT developing an episodic character and strategy as the CF rotates its personnel every six months. Finally the current approach appears to undermine the contribution of the FAC and CIDA, particularly as there is no personnel depth with either organization such that when a member leaves theatre there is no ongoing representation.

The PRT is a relatively new endeavour and has been evolving since its conception. Although moderately successful in meeting the goals of stability, to date the PRT has not become a vehicle of peacebuilding, the suggested method of addressing the challenge of failed states as articulated in Canadian foreign policy documents. The PRT's ability to become a vehicle of peacebuilding is dependent on it remaining separate from the dominant US PRTs and NATO military activities, having strong leadership from the various components within in the PRT and "3D" guidance at the strategic and operational level and being provided with sufficient resources and personnel to undertake long term sustainable peacebuilding projects.

Notes

1 Galtung (1976) discusses the concept in *Three Approaches to Peace: peacekeeping, peacemaking and peacebuilding*, however, no formal policy discussions occur until the presentation of *An Agenda for Peace*.
2 See: *An Agenda for Peace* and the 1995 Supplement.
3 Knight and Keating argue it applies to the "broad spectrum of conflict", they borrow

the terms "operational" and "structural" from the Carnegie Commission on the Prevention of Deadly Conflict to differentiate between the two respectively (operational peacebuilding referring to post-conflict and structural peacebuilding referring to pre-conflict).

4 The Conflict Prevention and Post Conflict Reconstruction Network (CPR) refer to "proximate" and "root causes" that may be contrasted with "manifestations". Defined as the "structural or underlying causes of conflict" the CPR suggests that examples are human rights abuse, lack of good governance, lack of social and economical development and unequal access to resources.

5 The way to identify these "gaps" is by asking the question: "Will/did the activity foster or support sustainable structures and processes which strengthen the prospects for peaceful coexistence and decrease the likelihood of the outbreak, reoccurrence, or continuation of violent conflict?" (Keating and Knight, 2005, p. 42).

6 See also United Nations General Assembly Resolution A/RES/60/180 The Peacebuilding Commission

7 Animosity has been pronounced with humanitarian organizations but has also included other non-governmental bodies aimed at development work.

8 The need for more effective communication was witnessed in the ongoing crises in Haiti.

> In Operation Uphold Democracy, humanitarian activity and support to NGOs was not a primary focus of the military forces deployed, but was more of a supporting effort.... The lack of operational planning among agencies led to problems throughout the mission ... Clearly, to coordinate effectively, the military and humanitarian communities had to plan together.
>
> (Benton and Ware, 2006, p. 17)

9 Publications and learned practices have sprung up in both sets of organizations, as have learned practices.

10 Ankersen (2005) does caution that these differences are generalised and that the differences may not be as large as they seem, arguing that the military does have a role in peacebuilding and can work along side NGOs.

11 As a result, a core recommendation of the United Nations Panel on Reforming UN Peacekeeping was the creation of a separate UN body, the Peacebuilding Commission. This may help integrate and bring about "collaboration among political, military, humanitarian and development actors" (UN, 2005) and thereby helping to avoid possible tragedies similar to Rwanda. As will be seen below, an additional innovation in Canada has been the emergence of the PRT.

12 First named Joint Regional Teams, the bodies were later named Provincial Reconstruction Teams at the request of the ATA. Commentators suggest that it is unfortunate that "reconstruction" was included in the title as actual reconstruction of any significance continues to play a "relatively minor role" in PRT activities (Stapleton, 2003, p. 2).

13 PRTs are divided between two areas: Regional Area Coordinators (RAC) North, located in Kunduz with five PRTs reporting to them; and RAC West, located in Heart with four PRTs reporting to them. A Forward Support Base (FSB), in turn, supports each these. It is planned that these structure and operations be expanded to the south and includes a PRT and FSB in each of the four regions.

14 Note: "Only the military elements of PRTs are integrated in the ISAF chain of command" (www.afnorth.nato.int/ISAF/).

15 Non-kinetic operations in this context refer to civil affairs, information operations and other non-lethal forms of engaging combating insurgency.

16 One of the greatest difficulties in discussing the issue of PRTs is that they have distinct characteristics depending on the lead country and its national caveats, the location and which military operation it falls under.

17 These are the UK's 3Ds (Development, Diplomacy and Defence)
18 Not a failed state on invasion, though arguably now fitting into this category
19 4GW "involves operations against non-state combatants or remnants of armies in a battle space where there are no definable battlefields or front lines, where deadly threats emerge suddenly and disappear just as quickly and where combatants mingle freely with non-combatants" Lieutenant-General Marc Caron Chief of the Land Staff, *We all need to be thinking soldiers*, www.army.forces.gc.ca/lf/English/6_1_1.asp?id=642, September 2005.
20 Coined by General Charles Krulak, the 31st Commandant of the United States Marine Corps. Although a core component of these doctrines is that, in response to complex security situations, soldiers will conduct peacebuilding alongside civilian actors, there appears to have been little attempt within either the DND or FAC and CIDA to integrate concepts of and approaches to 4GW into initiative such as the Canadian Peace-building Initiative.
21 Yannick Hingorami (webcast.international.gc.ca/cpc/Afghanistan/prt.mov
22 Equally, it is a manifestation of the *The Responsibility to Protect* (R2P). R2P was a Report produced by the International Commission on Intervention and State Sovereignty and as a concept argues "the right of humanitarian intervention" (www.iciss.ca/report-en.asp).
23 Although the Kandahar PRT was originally led by the US, when Canada took over they did not adopt the US model. They did, however, incorporate the already in-situ representatives of DFID and USAID.
24 Numbers are from the initial six months
25 Kandahar is the second largest city in Afghanistan, with an approximate population of 1.5 to 2 million.
26 The RCMP work in close cooperation with Germany who is the lead nation for police reform.
27 PRT Mission statement:

The Canadian PRT will conduct interdepartmental operations to assist the Government of Afghanistan in extending its authority in order to facilitate the development of a stable, secure environment in the province of Kandahar. CIDA's role in support of the mission: To create the conditions for long-term development by promoting security and stability in Kandahar Province.

28 Shuras are any group of elders at any level of Afghan culture.
29 See: *Afghan Christian asks for asylum*. (2006, March 27) BBC News. Retrieved from news.bbc.co.uk/2/hi/south_asia/4851244.stm
30 "[A]ctivities that can be employed to engage the minds and resolve of the population – to avoid acts of violence and their consequences among host populations" (Center for Strategic and International Studies, 2005, para 2).
31 In fact he has an office collocated with the PRT.
32 The reasons for this are discussed in detail in the following section and are more attributable to the environment than the PRT.

Bibliography

Alexander, C. (2005) Canada's Role in Kandahar – Provincial Reconstruction Team (PRT) Retrieved 26 April, 2006 from www.dfait-maeci.gc.ca/cip-pic/library/transcriptprt-en.asp.

Ankersen, C. P. (2005) "Praxis versus Policy." Keating, T. and Knight W. A. (eds), *Building Sustainable Peace* (pp. 71–92). Edmonton, Canada: the University of Edmonton Alberta Press.

Axe attack was an ambush, Canadian military says (2006, March 5) Retrieved May 5, 2006 from CBC News.

Berry, G. (2005) *Foreign Affairs Recommendations.*

Boutros-Ghali, B. (1992) *An Agenda for Peace.* A/47/277 – S/24111. United Nations.

Boutros-Ghali, B. (1995) *Supplement to An Agenda for Peace.* A/50/60 – S/1995/1 United Nations.

Bush, K. (2005) "Commodification, Compartmentalization, Militarization of Peacebuilding." Keating, T. and Knight W. A. (eds), *Building Sustainable Peace* (pp. 23–46). Edmonton, Canada: the University of Edmonton Alberta Press.

Byman, D. L. (2001) "Uncertain Partners: NGOs and the Military." *Survival*, vol. 43, no. 2, 97–114. London, UK: The International Institute for Strategic Studies.

Canadian International Development Agency (n.d.) Retrieved April 24, 2006, from www.acdi-cida.gc.ca/peace.

Center for Strategic and International Studies (2005) *The Future of the U.S. Military and Irregular Warfare.* Retrieved April 30, 2006 from www.csis.org/component/option, com_csis_events/task,view/id,779/.

Cetin, H. (2004) Afghanistan at the Crossroads of History. [Electronic Version] *Turkish Policy Quarterly*, Vol. 3, No. 2.

The Conflict Prevention and Post Conflict Reconstruction Network (2005) *Early Warning and Early Response Handbook.* [Electronic Version] Retrieved April 24, 2006, from cpr.web.cern.ch/cpr/Library/tools/EW-HandbookFinalEn_v2.3.pdf.

Cottey, A. and Forster, A. (2004) Reshaping Defence: New Roles for Military Cooperation and Assistance, *Adelphi Paper No. 321.* Oxford, UK: Oxford University Press.

Cuny, F. C. (1991) "Dilemmas of Military Involvement in Humanitarian Relief." Gordenker, L. and Weiss, T. G. (eds), *Soldiers, Peacekeepers and Disasters.* Houndsmill, Basingstoke, Hampshire, UK: Macmillan Academic and Professional.

Dahrendorf, N. (2003). *A Review of Peace Operations: A Case for Change.* [Electronic Version] London, UK: King's College London.

Delaney, D. E. (2000) CIMIC Operations during Operation Kinetic [Electronic version]. *Canadian Military Journal*, Vol. 1, No. 4, 29–34.

Department National Defence (2005) *Kandahar PRT Info Brief to CTC Gagetown.*

DFID (2000) *Annual Report of the Chief of the Defence Staff 1999–2000.* [Electronic version] Ottawa, Canada: Department of National Defence.

DFID (2005) *Fighting poverty to build a safer world: A strategy for security and development.* London, UK: Department for International Development.

Duffield, M. (2001) *Global Governance and the New Wars: The Merging of Development and Security.* London, UK: Zed Books.

Dziedzic, M. J. and Seidl, M. K. (2005) "Provincial Reconstruction Teams and Military Relations with International and Nongovernmental Organizations in Afghanistan." *United States Institute for Peace Special Report*, 147. Retrieved April 24, 2006, from www.usip.org/pubs/specialreports/sr147.

Faldwell, L. (2005) Canada's Role in Kandahar – Provincial Reconstruction Team (PRT) Retrieved 26 April, 2006 from www.dfait-maeci.gc.ca/cip-pic/library/transcriptprt-en.asp.

Fetherstone, A. B. (1994) *Towards a Theory of United Nations Peacekeeping.* New York: St. Martin's Press.

Friborg, A. T. (2004) *Afghanistan: Lessons Learned from a Post-War Situation.* Copenhagen, Denmark: Danish Institute for International Studies.

Gallagher, D., Moussalli. M. and Bosco, D. (1997) *Civilian and Military Means of Providing and Supporting Humanitarian Assistance during Conflict: a Comparative Analysis.* Washington, DC: Refugee Policy Group.

Galtung, J. (1964) An Editorial. *Journal for Peace Research.* Vol. 1, No. 1, 1–4.

Glaser, B. G. and Strauss, A. L. (1967) *The Discovery of Grounded Theory: Strategies for Qualitative Research.* Chicago, US: Aldine Publishing Company.

Government of Canada (2005a) Commerce. [Electronic Version] *Canada's International Policy Statement: A Role of Pride and Influence in the World.* Ottawa, Canada: Government of Canada.

Government of Canada (2005b) Defence [Electronic Version] *Canada's International Policy Statement: A Role of Pride and Influence in the World.* Ottawa, Canada: Government of Canada.

Government of Canada (2005c) Development. [Electronic Version] *Canada's International Policy Statement: A Role of Pride and Influence in the World.* Ottawa, Canada: Government of Canada.

Government of Canada (2005d) Diplomacy. [Electronic Version] *Canada's International Policy Statement: A Role of Pride and Influence in the World.* Ottawa, Canada: Government of Canada.

Government of Canada (2005e) Overview [Electronic Version] *Canada's International Policy Statement: A Role of Pride and Influence in the World.* Ottawa, Canada: Government of Canada.

Government of Canada (2005f) *Protecting Canadians Rebuilding Afghanistan, Canada-Afghanistan Relations.* Retrieved April 28, 2006, from www.canada-afghanistan.gc.ca/background-en.asp.

Government of Canada (2005g) *Protecting Canadians Rebuilding Afghanistan, Canada's Provincial Reconstruction Team.* Retrieved April 28, 2006, from www.canada-afghanistan.gc.ca/prov_reconstruction-en.asp.

Government of Canada (2005h) *Protecting Canadians Rebuilding Afghanistan, Canada in Afghanistan: The International Policy Statement in Action.* Retrieved April 28, 2006, from www.canada-afghanistan.gc.ca/background-en.asp.

Graham, B. (2005) "The Canadian Forces Mission in Afghanistan: Canadian Policy and Values in Action," Speech Delivered to The Canadian Club of Ottawa, September 29.

Grinnell, R. M. and Unrau, Y. A. (2005) *Social Work Research and Evaluation Quantitative and Qualitative Approaches*, 7th Edition. Oxford, UK: Oxford University Press.

Hendrickson, D., Bhatia, M., Knight, M. and Taylor, A. (2005) *A Review of DFID Involvement in Provincial Reconstruction Teams (PRTs) in Afghanistan.* London, UK: King's College London.

Hingorani, Y. (2005) Canada's Role in Kandahar – Provincial Reconstruction Team (PRT) Retrieved 26 April, 2006 from www.dfait-maeci.gc.ca/cip-pic/library/-transcriptprt-en.asp.

International Council on Human Rights Policy (2002) *Human Rights Crises: NGO Responses to Military Interventions.* Versiox, Switzerland: International Council on Human Rights Policy.

ISAF Provincial Reconstruction Teams (PRTs) (2005) Retrieved April 24, 2006, from www.afnorth.nato.int/ISAF/Backgrounders/BackPRT.htm.

Jakobsen, P. V. (2005) "PRTs in Afghanistan: Successful but not Sufficient," Danish Institute of International Studies Report.

Keating, T. and Knight W. A. (eds) (2005) *Building Sustainable Peace.* Edmonton, Canada: the University of Edmonton Alberta Press.

McDonnell, G. P. (2005) *Bagram Provincial Reconstruction Team (PRT).*

McHugh, G. and Gostelow, L. (2004) *Provincial Reconstruction Teams and Humanitarian-Military Relations in Afghanistan*, London, UK: Save the Children.

Macrae, J. (1998) "The Death of Humanitarianism? An Anatomy of the Attack." *Disasters*, Vol. 22, No. 4, 309–317.

NATO Civil–Military Co-operation (CIMIC) Doctrine (2003) Retrieved April 24, 2006, from www.nato.int/ims/docu/AJP-9.pdf.

Oakley, R. B. and Hammes, T. X. (2005) "Securing Afghanistan: Entering a Make-or-Break Phase." *Strategic Forum*, No. 205.

Orbinski, J. (1999) *The Nobel Lecture.* Retrieved April 24, 2006, from www.msf.ca/nobel/speech.htm.

Oslo Guidelines (2002) Retrieved April 24, 2006, from www.reliefweb.int/mcdls/mcdu/oslo_guidelines/oslo_guidelines.html.

Office for the Coordination of Humanitarian Affairs Civil Military Coordination Section (n.d.). Retrieved April 24, 2006 from ochaonline.un.org/webpage.asp?SiteID=237.

Patton, M. Q. (1999) "Issues in Qualitative Research." *The Nature of Qualitative Inquiry.* London, UK: Sage Publications Ltd.

Peace Operations Working Group of the Canadian Peacebuilding Coordinating Committee (2003) *NGO/Government Dialogue on Provincial Reconstruction Teams (PRTs) in Afghanistan and the Militarization of Humanitarian Assistance.* Retrieved April 24, 2006, from action.web.ca/home/cpcc/en_resources.shtml?x=49860.

Peake, G., Gormley-Heanan, C. and Fitzduff, M. (2004) *Warlords to Peacelords: Local Leadership Capacity in Peace Processes.* [Electronic Version] University of Ulster, Ireland: INCORE.

Perito, R. M. (2005) "The U.S. Experience with Provincial Reconstruction Teams in Afghanistan: Lessons Identified." *United States Institute for Peace Special Report*, 152. Retrieved April 24, 2006, from www.usip.org/pubs/specialreports/sr152.

Pettigrew, P. (2005) Notes for an Address by The Honourable Pierre Pettigrew, Minister of Foreign Affairs, Speech to the House of Commons about the 2005 Federal Budget. Retrieved April 24, 2006 from www.parl.gc.ca/38/1/parlbus/chambus/house/debates/064_2005-02-24/han064_1150-E.htm#TOP.

Pugh, M. (1998) "Military Intervention and Humanitarian Action: Trends and Issues." *Disasters*, Vol. 22, No. 4, 339–351.

Pugh, M. (2000a) "Civil–Military Relations in the Kosovo Crisis: An Emerging Hegemony?" *Security Dialogue*, Vol. 31, No. 2, 229–242.

Pugh, M. (2000b) "Post-conflict Rehabilitation: social and civil dimensions." *The Journal of Humanitarian Assistance.* Retrieved April 28, 2006, from www.jha.ac/articles/a034.htm.

Pugh, M. (2001) "The Challenge of Civil–Military Relations in International Peace Operations." *Disasters*, Vol. 25, No. 4, 345–357.

Punch, K. F. (2005) *Introduction to Social Research Quantitative and Qualitative Approaches*, 2nd edition. London, UK: Sage Publications.

Ratner, S. R. (1995) *The New UN Peacekeeping: Building Peace in Lands of Conflict After the Cold War.* New York: St. Martin's Press.

Rodicio, A. G. (2005) *Addressing the Challenges of Peace-Building: The 2005 World Summit Decision to Establish a Peacebuilding Commission.* Retrieved April 27, 2006, from www.nd.edu/~krocinst/events/unaddressing.shtml.

Rotberg, R. (2002) "Failed States in a World of Terror." *Foreign Affairs*, Vol. 81, No. 4, 127–140.

Royal Canadian Mounted Police (2005) *Royal Canadian Mounted Police: Canadian Police Involvement in a Provincial Reconstruction Team (PRT) in Afghanistan.* Retrieved April 28, 2006 from www.rcmp-grc.gc.ca/peacekeeping/prt_e.htm.

Rubin, B. (2000) "The Political Economy of War and Peace in Afghanistan." [Electronic Version] *World Development*, Vol. 28, 1789–1803.

Schreiber, S. (2002) "Creating Compliance: Some Lessons in International Cooperation in a Peace Support Operation." [Electronic version]. *Canadian Military Journal*, Vol. 3, No. 4, Vol. 2, No. 11–22.

Sedra, M. (2004) "Nil-Military Relations in Afghanistan: The Provincial Reconstruction Team Debate." Discussion Paper 9. Vancouver: Asia Pacific Foundation of Canada.

Snow, D. M. (2003). *Cases in International Relations: Portraits of the Future*. Toronto, Canada: Longman.

Studer, M. (2001) "The ICRC and Civil–Military Relations in Armed Conflict." *International Review of the Red Cross*, Vol. 83, No. 842, 367–392.

Thomson, A. (2005) *General Assembly Informal Consultations of the Plenary on the Peacebuilding Commission: UK Statement on Behalf of the European Union*. Retrieved May 5, 2006 from www.reformtheun.org/index.php?module=uploads&func=download&fileId=1121&.

Tschirgi N. (2003) *Peacebuilding as the Link between Security and Development: is the Window of Opportunity Closing?* Retrieved April 28, 2006, from www.fes-globalization.org/publications/031212_01_New.pdf.

United Kingdom House of Commons Defence Committee – Fifth Report (2006) [Electronic Version].

United Nations (2004) *Report of the UNDG/ECHA Working Group on Transition Issues*. New York, USA: United Nations.

United Nations (2005) "Report of the Secretary General." *In Larger Freedom: Towards Development, Security and Human Rights for All*. Retrieved April 27, 2006, from www.un.org/largerfreedom/contents.htm.

Weiss, T. G. (1999) *Military–Civilian Interactions: Intervening in Humanitarian Crises*. Lanham, USA: Rowman & Littlefield.

Williams, M. C. (1998) Civil–Military Relations and Peacekeeping, Adelphi Paper No. 365. Oxford, UK: Oxford University Press.

7 Civil–military cooperation of the German armed forces

Theoretical approach and contemporary practice in Kosovo

Bernhard G. Voget[1]

Introduction

The Federal Republic of Germany, as an integral part of the international system of collective security, makes a number of contributions to military missions worldwide. By doing so, the country aims to meet its commitments to its allies and to assert its own elementary security interests. But the *threat of violence* and security risks, which the entire International Community (IC) has to face today, is characterized by a great variety of possible types of armed conflicts (Chesterman *et al.* 2005; Münkler 2004; Pradetto 2004; Enders 2003: 8; Ignatieff 2003; Forsteneichner 2002: 2ff.; PTLEF 2002; Huntington 1996). Furthermore, the term "security" has gained an extended meaning: it affects, besides aspects of foreign and defense policy, also economic, financial and development issues, social, cultural, humanitarian, constitutional, and ecological features (BMVg 2006; Study Group on Europe's Security Capabilities 2004; Diering 2004: 16; BMVg 2003: para. 36). Therefore, the Bundeswehr, as the German government's politico-military instrument, is adapting itself to this modified security environment within the frame of the objectives and interests of German foreign and security policy. Yet, inasmuch as missions abroad increasingly call for other than purely soldierly skills, the military is also tasked with development activities in crisis regions in so-called complex emergencies (BMVg 2003: para. 5ff.; Mey 2002: 3). Examples are the current situations in Kosovo, Afghanistan or Lebanon, where the Bundeswehr contributes its own forces in various Peace Support Operations (PSOs) and is thus an actor in crisis regions (BMVg 2006 and 2004a). In carrying out these tasks, set by the German government, the Bundeswehr, *inter alia*, enters the field of civil–military cooperation (CIMIC).

The objective of this chapter is to explain the German concept of CIMIC and the underlying theoretical approach, and to add empirical clarity about how the Bundeswehr executes CIMIC in practice. To this end, the text is organized in two major parts. The first section outlines the Armed Forces' theoretical framework of CIMIC and introduces its intellectual, historical, and political context as well as the organizational structures and procedural mechanisms. The second section then turns to the situation in Kosovo. It surveys a number of case-studies which reveal problems and inadequacies of German CIMIC projects, presents different explanations for the cause of these dysfunctions, and offers suggestions that could be followed to conduct post-conflict reconstruction and improve force protection at the same time.

The Bundeswehr's conceptual approach to civil–military cooperation

The German understanding of civil–military cooperation underwent considerable change over the course of the 1990s. Under the conditions of the Cold War, the German military discussed CIMIC from a host nation perspective. Then, CIMIC encompassed all procedures and aspects involving cooperation between national military agencies, friendly forces, and national or municipal agencies in case of national and collective defense (Maase 2005: 155; Vorhofer 2003: 754ff.; Berchthold and Leppig 1980). Subsequently, the changes experienced in the field of security policy initiated an adaptation process resulting in the elaboration of a completely novel CIMIC concept for and by the Bundeswehr (Echterling 2003b: 32) which "[...] is clearly beyond the traditional classification as a mere procedure as well as beyond the categorization as logistic challenge that is frequently used as well" (EinsFüKdoBw 2003: 5).

In this context, Hardegger stresses the complex meaning of the term CIMIC. On the one hand, he points to the necessity of unambiguous differentiation between CIMIC as the "[...] formalized doctrine and/or concept of a military or civil actor" (2003: 32), and CIMIC as "general cooperation between military and civil agencies" (Hardegger 2003: 32) on the other.

Recent CIMIC concepts developed by NATO, for instance, are first of all based on the experience made during out-of-area operations, with the Balkan missions playing a dominant role (Douglas 2002: 2ff.; Tarry 2002: 33). While previous approaches saw CIMIC as a secondary duty concentrating on humanitarian assistance to take care of the immediate needs of the civilian population, the operations in the Balkans have demonstrated over time that CIMIC can also be an important force multiplier for a commander in PSOs. It is not a new insight that military units will be both safer and more effective with the local population as an ally, not an adversary. Hence force protection as an outcome of CIMIC measures is based on "winning the hearts and minds". Furthermore, as today's military operations take place in complex environments where soldiers cannot rely on functioning civil institutions and/or intact infrastructure, the military has to address a variety of tasks that are not precisely "military" in nature (Longhurst 2004: 7).

Taking all these aspects into account, NATO has gradually discovered the need for a coherent and institutionalized CIMIC policy. The Alliance's current CIMIC approach is based on two main documents. One is the Military Council doctrine 411/1 (MC 411/1; NATO 2001)), which intents to launch a NATO military policy on CIMIC. The other one is the Allied Joint Publication 9 (AJP-9; NATO 2003), which provides the actual guiding principles and procedures for the implementation and execution of CIMIC.

According to MC 411/1, the extant NATO definition of CIMIC is as follows: "The co-ordination and cooperation, in support of the mission, between the NATO Commander and civil actors, including national population and local authorities, as well as international, national and non-governmental organizations and agencies" (NATO 2001). In this respect, NATO (2003) discriminates between three main functions of civil–military cooperation:

- "Civil–Military Liaison".
- "Support to the Civil Environment", and
- "Support to the Force".

In the first case, the intention is to create and strengthen connections between civil and military actors. The other two functions from one perspective imply the assignment of military funds to support the civil environment. However, from another perspective they imply the maintenance of the availability and utilization of civil means for the support of military protagonists (Rehse 2004: 33f.; Hardegger 2003: 41; Rollins 2001: 123ff.).

As will be described in the following paragraphs, Germany's CIMIC conceptualization partly pictures NATO doctrine. However, the modern civil–military cooperation approach of the Bundeswehr unites two fields in one concept; but there are distinctions between CIMIC at home and abroad.

Domestic CIMIC activities in Germany

Germany's current domestic CIMIC approach focuses on enhancing the cooperation of federal, state and municipal offices, and agencies with the military and its various units throughout the country (Echterling 2003b: 32). The development of joint counter-terrorism procedures, the formation of structures to effectively fight natural disasters, such as floods or forest fires, as well as to deal with catastrophes such as train accidents or plane crashes, are on the agenda. The common aim is to secure a smooth coordination of Bundeswehr operations with the measures of all competent authorities on the civilian side if circumstances should demand an engagement of Armed Forces. In such a case, military commanders and their staff need special input and experts' advice on the characteristics of the civilian situation whereas management personnel from the civil administration might have to adapt to military procedures and the unique corporate culture of the Armed Forces. This requires mutual understanding which can only develop over time as the various actors on either side get to know each other during joint trainings and emergency exercises (Rosenbauer and Kreis 2005: 45f.).

The new underlying structural concept mirrors the transformation of the Bundeswehr from a staff-intensive Cold War defense army to an efficient, modern intervention army. Especially the reserve force concept is of particular importance for the domestic CIMIC approach (Echterling 2004: 16ff.). As of 2007, special CIMIC headquarters (HQ) are deployed in the capitals of every German federal state and function as a point of contact for the state governments. These HQ also coordinate the activities of volunteering reserve officers on the municipal level, who have been offered honorary CIMIC posts implemented by the Armed Forces to function as contacts and be part of local networks. This subsidiary approach enables the Bundeswehr to appropriately respond to any requests for assistance by the civil administration on every hierarchical level be it local or regional. Because with its particular organization in a domestic CIMIC context the military can easily delegate their own representatives in any crisis management group or emergency task force. Accordingly, the specially trained CIMIC personnel and their relevant counterparts from other agencies and public bodies can get acquainted with each other on a semi-permanent basis, and before any joint action needs to take place (Rosenbauer and Kreis 2005: 45f.). However, the lead responsibility for domestic response is with the civil authorities, whereas military operations have a clear supporting nature. This is CIMIC on a local basis at home, and it aims at being prepared for any worst case scenario (Büsching 2005: 10).

The Bundeswehr's CIMIC activities abroad

When the Armed Forces were deployed to the Balkans as part of NATO Peace Support Operations, it became obvious that there was neither a state-of-the-art set of CIMIC guidelines nor any specific Bundeswehr unit capable of conducting CIMIC activities (Meyer 1998: 782ff.). It was only very slowly that comprehensible organizational structures and procedural mechanisms were developed on an official basis out of a multitude of different, hitherto rather uncoordinated CIMIC-actions and individual efforts (Millotat 2004: 9f.). Finally, the German Ministry of Defense (BMVg) came up with the following definition: CIMIC:

> comprises any plan, agreement, measure, force and asset regulating, easing or promoting the relations between military agencies/agencies of territorial defense administration and civil and/or military forces/authorities and the civil population. Such activities include cooperation with non-governmental organizations or international authorities, organizations and agencies.
>
> (BMVg 2001: 5)

With the issue of the new Defense Policy Guidelines, the new German CIMIC concept has also been incorporated into the catalogue of the Bundeswehr's tasks:

> As a contribution to the reconstruction of social order and infrastructure in crisis areas [relief services of the Bundeswehr] [...] may be conducted as individual operations. The procedures for the performance of such operations have to undergo further development in close cooperation with other governmental institutions and civil relief organizations.[2]
>
> (BMVg 2003: para. 83)

It is important to stress that all these measures primarily aim at supporting the underlying military mission by improving the acceptance of their own soldiers among the local population and key players in the area of responsibility (EinsFüK-doBw 2004: para. 202). CIMIC personnel functions as a hinge between the military and its surrounding civil environment (Braunstein *et al.* 2001: 37). To back this approach, CIMIC activities in a PSO are also to be presented to the public by active media employment aimed at explaining the internal and external goals of CIMIC, showing coherence and, finally, enhancing the image of the Forces as well. In this context, cooperation between CIMIC and psychological operations (PsyOps) units as well as between CIMIC and the respective press and information centre can be observed in various PSOs (Thürnau 2005b; Yrayzoz 2003; Stelzenmüller 2002: 74). By communicating certain CIMIC projects, the Bundeswehr attempts to positively influence the perceptions, attitudes and behavior of the local population toward the troop and to catch favorable media attention at home (Heinemann-Grüder *et al.* 2004: 68ff.; Meyer 2003: 119).

In essence, this means contributing to overall force protection by winning hearts and minds of the local populace. CIMIC as applied by the Bundeswehr, however, is first and foremost a military instrument (force multiplier). The actual positive outcomes of individual projects in support of the military mission rank second in terms of humanitarian aid, reconstruction of infrastructure or structural development unless there is an explicit political mandate for such undertakings (EinsFüKdoBw 2004: para. 209). "However, NATO action does inevitably contribute towards nation building" (Rollins 2001: 123). Since quite a number of purely military CIMIC operations and projects result in the improvement of the civil framework conditions for the operational forces, it also becomes clear that the superior principle is: The better the CIMIC work the better the protection of own forces. This is a decisive reason to implement or support projects in the military line (Georgi 2003: 100ff.). Of course, CIMIC is not "development-minded", but rather has an instrumental value for the Armed Forces. So a main question is what are the actual prerequisites and limitations of CIMIC? It should not be forgotten that improvement of the overall political and economic situation in a crisis region does have an impact on a military mission as well. The sustained increase of stability within a region or country hitherto shaken by conflict means that force reduction sooner or later will be possible. This aspect does gain importance given often tight budgetary restraints on a national basis. By assisting the local population to develop functioning economic and democratic structures, CIMIC teams and their projects can also support the political goal of cost-decreasing force reduction in a realistic timeframe. This can be seen as a political response to public opinion at home. After all, it is the electoral cycle in Western democracies which creates pressure for quick results in state-building and an exit timetable for military engagement.

Structures

In addition to the development of a CIMIC doctrine, the Bundeswehr has also built up regular CIMIC structures to be able to professionally take on both humanitarian and reconstruction activities in Crisis Response Operations (CROs).

On a national level, the so-called CIMIC Battalion 100 with six companies and a permanent staff of 118 soldiers, most of them staff officer, officer and non-commissioned officer (NCO) ranks came into existence in April 2003 (Dersch 2005). But facing the challenges of a rising number of out-of-area operations combined with budget constraints at home, the BMVg has recently developed plans to entirely restructure Germany's military sector (Lange 2005; Voll 2005). Central elements of this Transformation of the Armed Forces, as it is called, are multinational interoperability, jointness, flexibility and adaptability in order to be capable of conducting Network Centric Operations (ECOs) and Effects Based Operations (EBOs) in the future. The Bundeswehr is building a new set of force categories that are named response forces, stabilization forces and support forces. These try to gain a capability profile adapted to modern tasks: Command and control capabilities, intelligence collection and reconnaissance, mobility, operational effectiveness, support and sustainability, as well as survivability and protection are decisive for combating asymmetric and non-traditional threats such as the war against international terrorism, conflict prevention, crisis management, and the protection of emerging democracies (Schneiderhan 2005). In this context, the CIMIC Battalion 100 has been enlarged and renamed: As of 4 May 2006 Germany's new CIMIC Operations Centre functions as a reservoir of more than 300 permanent CIMIC staff, which can be deployed according to the individual CIMIC requirements of the Bundeswehr's different missions (Mertins 2006).

Besides these efforts, selected staffs and joint staffs also deal with CIMIC on a full or part time basis throughout the German Armed Forces. From the brigade level onwards, permanent S5/CIMIC personnel[3] is part of the regular staff structure today (Dersch 2005; Echterling 2003a). In theatre, genuine CIMIC personnel can be part of a CIMIC battalion or a CIMIC company (Kosovo). Soldiers wearing the CIMIC patch are members of so-called "Liaison and Observation Teams" (LOTs)[4] in Bosnia-Herzegovina, they fill vacant posts in KFOR's "Liaison and Monitoring Teams" (LMTs)[5] in Kosovo and they are included in the staff of Provincial Reconstruction Teams (PRTs)[6] in Afghanistan.

On the international level, Germany – along with the Czech Republic, Denmark, the Netherlands, Norway and Poland – has participated in the formation of CIMIC Group North Headquarters (CGN HQ) since 2001. CGN HQ is a NATO International Military Headquarters, "[...] functionally attached to Regional Headquarters Allied Forces North Europe (RHQ AFNORTH)" (NATO 2004a). Shortly after this new institution had properly started operations, NATO's Allied Command Transformation (ACT) and Allied Command Operations (ACO) stated their willingness to transform the CGN HQ into a Civil–Military Co-operation Centre of Excellence (CCOE) in order to tackle the changing operational environment of modern crisis response operations. Despite the fact that the CCOE is accredited as a NATO Centre of Excellence, its capacity and experience is also available to other international organizations like the European Union (EU), Non-Governmental Organizations (NGOs) or scientific institutions. Like the preceding CGN HQ, the CCOE conducts CIMIC courses and serves as a forum for CIMIC issues and consultations (CCOE 2006).

Human resources

The German Armed Forces have developed a two-pillar approach for their assignment of genuine CIMIC personnel. One pillar is made up of so-called all-rounders;[7] regular soldiers from the German-based CIMIC Operations Center, or other units who are trained to work on general tasks connected to CIMIC, for example managing a CIMIC Center. This entails an office as contact point for the local population in theater. All-rounders also give advice to the commander of an operation or work in the G5/J9 branches[8] of staffs and joint staffs (Echterling 2003b).

Functional specialists, who most often are from the reserve force, form the second pillar of the Bundeswehr's CIMIC staff concept. These individuals assess, design and conduct CIMIC projects with regard to humanitarian issues, civil infrastructure issues, civil life support or civil administration issues. Of course, a balance between regular military training and individual capability is required. The functional specialists have certain qualifications and professional experience which differ greatly from that of their full-time military counterparts. They include lawyers, architects, agronomists or civil servants who are assigned to a military mission, carrying arms but working in their particular field of expertise (Dersch 2005).

Areas of CIMIC responsibility

CIMIC, both at home and abroad, uses various manifestations to accomplish the aims, which are set out by political and/or military leaders. As outlined above, the three areas of CIMIC responsibility are coordination of civil–military relations, support of the civil environment and support of the force. Concentration of forces is variedly applied in one of these three areas according to the prevailing situation and guidelines. The following paragraphs will introduce these three CIMIC manifestations in detail.

Coordination of civil–military relations

This CIMIC field is aimed at creating closely woven relations within the scope of networking activities. The networking of the civil and military echelons of command serves to coordinate planned actions, and exert influence on the appropriate bodies as well as to give well-directed support wherever required. The civilian part includes not only local government institutions but also involves the relevant International Organizations (IOs) and/or NGOs that are present in the region (Georgi 2003: 101). The Bundeswehr acknowledges the importance of establishing liaison with aid agencies etc., in order to accelerate cooperation. In practice, this could result in the following situation according to Echterling

(2003b: 33): "[…] to avoid for example that the [Multinational Brigade South-West, Kosovo Force,] reduces patrolling activities precisely in an area where the other organizations are starting a resettlement project […]", representatives of the military and the NGOs will exchange information and coordinate their procedures to maintain a safe and secure environment for the refugee project.

Another aspect of the coordination of civil–military relations can be crucial if there is a major state of emergency at home, such as the explosion of a chemical plant in a densely populated area. Bringing the military and its local counterparts from the municipal administration together with representatives of the fire brigade or experts from community hospitals within the framework of a crisis management group is important to ensure a targeted composition of forces as well as a coordinated approach, both of which increase the probability of a successful operation. Hence, domestically, it is aimed to establish such networks on a semi-permanent basis with regular joint training, etc. to be prepared for a worst case scenario. However, internationally, due to the ad hoc nature of the deployments and a severe lack of institutional structure in most of the operational areas, such established liaison is usually difficult to come up with.

Support of the civil environment

Until recently, the Bundeswehr still defined this area of responsibility as follows: "The support of the civil environment includes the planning and coordination – as well as implementation, if required – of all necessary CIMIC actions that the responsible civil authorities/facilities/organizations are not in a position to perform in theatre" (EinsFüKdoBw 2003: 9; see also BMVg 2001: 5). However, the central procedure for the conduct of CIMIC has been altered. Nowadays, the Armed Forces differentiate between short-term CIMIC measures, so called quick impact projects (QIPs), which basically can be undertaken by every military unit during a PSO, and long term CIMIC projects, which can only be conducted by special CIMIC personnel (Maase 2005: 160ff.; EinsFüKdoBw 2004: 8ff.).

This approach can be illustrated with an example. Consider the commander of a battle group (BG) or task force (TF) in Kosovo. His intent may be to patrol a certain village on a regular basis. In order to gain the villagers' good will, he asks his S5 officer to talk to the mayor to find out whether or not there are any urgent needs. The S5 then has to categorize the reported shortcomings into two categories: Those which can be independently solved by the BG (e.g., a poor family needs blankets and some children need pencils), and those which require the expertise of special CIMIC personnel (e.g. the reconstruction of a school building). The battle group commander might decide that the support of the poor family and the children (short term CIMIC measures) can have a positive impact on the general acceptance of his soldiers in village in question. The S5 officer can carry out such a measure together with own staff and resources mobilized by the BG. Regarding the school renovation, a notification will be sent to the G5/J9-branch of the commanding entity, which will make an assessment and eventually order the CIMIC company to take care of such a project.

The different lines of action that "support of the civil environment" involves are determined by the "[...] process of moving from a focus on emergency life saving to creating the basis for a good life" (Siegel 1999: 2). Taking into account the various players and their different institutional backgrounds, Traub stresses: "This [...] process involves a delicate navigation from a phase of neo-colonial dominance to the full return of sovereignty, as well as from an essentially military operation to an essentially civilian one" (2004: 32). And Ignatieff emphasizes: "The essential paradox of nation-building is that temporary imperialism – empire lite – has become the necessary condition for democracy in countries torn apart by civil war" (2003: vii). Such a development is typical for many post-conflict situations:

- At the end of hostilities, there are usually many refugees and displaced persons who require basic services within the scope of immediate humanitarian emergency aid. There are hardly any civilian organizations that are ready with the essential resources and competence to deploy into a post-conflict environment and provide ad hoc emergency leadership at large. Also, the capacities of NGO's frequently do not meet the actual needs on location, so that only Armed Forces with their logistics and apparatus are able to actually improve the situation on a broader scale (Mockaitis 2004: 29; Braunstein *et al.* 2001: 42; Pugh 2000: 236ff.). Ideally, however, the military will only perform tasks that are not covered by civil relief organizations (Georgi 2003: 101).
- In the second phase, important facilities of the governmental and civil infrastructure require reconstruction so as to ensure their function. Essentials are e.g. power and water supply, the sewage system and traffic network, but also the establishment of a police service and installation of a school system. The housing situation of the population is of great importance especially when buildings destroyed by acts of war have to be reconstructed for protection in wintertime (Georgi 2003: 101). This again can be an opportunity for the military to improve its standing among the local population. Besides, NGOs often focus on specific projects but not on total area coverage (Traub 2004: 32). This is due to a characteristic feature of NGOs: Most often, their "independence" relies on the constant acquisition of funding to be able to cover all their expenses. It is highly probable that this economic dependence makes it more tempting for an NGO to realize only those projects which promise high media attention (Danish Refugee Council 2002; Merchet 2002). After all, "[t]he reality [...] is ferocious competition among donors, United Nations agencies and non-governmental organizations for a market share in money and misery" (Ignatieff 2003: 98).
- The third phase often comprises the support of structural development, i.e. by agricultural counseling or promotion of economic development taking into consideration what is specifically emphasized by Dobbins *et al.*: "[If] the stock of both human and physical capital (have) deteriorated substantially before the conflict, [...] post-conflict recovery [is] [...] much more difficult" (2003: 114).

With regard to funding for peacemaking, peacekeeping or peace-building as well as humanitarian tasks, the military has a comparative advantage over its civil competitors due to the fact that the Armed Forces assume labor costs and overhead themselves. Thus, any funds that are raised are laid out only for projects without deduction for operating expenses, etc. (Klingebiel und Roehder 2004: 22). Considering the German CIMIC activities, Echterling (2003b: 34) points out that no funds of departmental budget 14 (Federal Ministry of Defense) of the German federal budget are available for such projects. The projects are rather reconnoitered by CIMIC and checked for feasibility. Subsequently, CIMIC personnel endeavors to secure financial support from public or private donators (e.g. Federal Foreign Office (*Auswärtiges Amt*, AA), German Technical Cooperation (*Gesellschaft für Technische Zusammenarbeit*, GTZ), Federal Ministry for Economic Cooperation and Development (*Bundesministerium für wirtschaftliche Zusammenarbeit und Entwicklung*, BMZ), charitable foundations (Lions, Rotary etc.)) with CIMIC competing with the NGOs for financial support.[9] Project implementation can begin no earlier than the approval of the respective application and subsequent release of the funds by the Bundeswehr Operations Headquarters (*Einsatzführungskommando*, EinsFüKdoBw) in Potsdam-Geltow near Berlin. Then local firms in the operational area are invited to tender for the implementation of a project, with the best offer leading to awarding of a contract specifying the services to be rendered. At the same time, the local agencies are involved by means of cooperation contracts with the project-related local executive bodies.[10]

Support of the armed forces

The third CIMIC area of responsibility involves giving advice to military leaders who have to be informed on how a military action will affect the civil environment and/or what impact civilian measures might have on the troops. It is vital to know, where certain resources may be found and how they might be made available to the troops. Thus, this area of responsibility is primarily concerned with collection, analysis and assessment of information in accordance with the military principle "Situation – Assessment – Conclusion". The aim is to compile a complete picture of the military situation. As required, the CIMIC experts make their contacts available to other military elements for better coordination (BMVg 2001: 5; Echterling 2003b: 33ff.). In this way, theoretically, any impairing of the safety situation should already be prevented *ex ante*.

To illustrate this, consider the Internally Displaced Persons (IDPs) in Kosovo, such as Kosovo Serbs (KOS) who live in Kosovo Force (KFOR) field camps since their homes were destroyed during the March riots in 2004. In order to improve their situation, the United Nations Interim Administration Mission in Kosovo (UNMIK) and Kosovo's Provisional Institutions of Self Government (PISG) as well as local authorities joined in mutual efforts to rebuild the KOS's houses. As they refused to leave the field camps, stressing that their houses had not been rebuilt to the previous standard, the commander of a KFOR brigade wanted to know whether these claims are true or not. He asked his CIMIC experts to make an assessment of the reconstruction efforts. With such a report from functional CIMIC specialists, the commander then had a factual basis for future discussions with UNMIK, the PISG and local bodies as well as with the KOS themselves.

But CIMIC components can also support the Armed Forces in a different way. When a military contingent provides police-type services in order to establish basic security and maintain a secure environment in a province, conducting house searches and looking for illegal weapons etc. might be part of their job. In the course of such operations, all houses of a village might be searched during the night. This could cause disturbance especially among families with young children. Furthermore, troops might damage property, such as windows or doors in order to gain access to some buildings. To ease the situation, military commanders can use CIMIC personnel to undertake post-operation conciliation efforts. This could involve talking to all villagers, recording potential damages caused by the searching task force and assuring quick compensation for material loss.

CIMIC as part of Germany's state building initiatives

All things considered, "Nation-building has become the cure of choice for the epidemic of ethnic civil war and state failure that has convulsed the developing world since the end of the long imperial peace of the Cold War" (Ignatieff 2003: 93). Not astonishingly, in the context of the evolution of PSOs during the 1990s, almost everything which happened at the civil–military interface was referred to as civil–military cooperation of some sort (Hardegger 2003: 8). Nonetheless, Braunstein states: "The intention of the International Community to provide comprehensive assistance for the necessary rebuilding of government and society in former conflict regions has led to a new drive of conceptual considerations for crisis management and conflict prevention in many nations and organizations – not only in NATO" (2000: 48). These considerations also comprise the wide scope of CIMIC activities of the military especially since the practical experience gathered during various missions abroad has spurred the development of national CIMIC concepts (EinsFüKdoBw 2004: 102ff.; Pollick 2000: 57ff.). In the case of the Bundeswehr, this development was highlighted above. However, Hardegger concludes in retrospect: "[…] the term [CIMIC] has been made accessible to scientific analysis to a very limited degree only […]. For a long time, the term 'CIMIC' could not be backed by a standard definition accepted by the most important actors" (2003: 29).

This is due to two factors. On one hand, the military forces more and more claim for themselves the enlargement of their role to include aspects of statebuilding, thus exceeding their traditional security and protection function, and offering the option of comprehensive integrated crisis management to their government (NATO 1991: para. 31ff.). Armed Forces make use of their comparative advantages in the field of reconstruction (road construction, mine clearance, transport and communications capabilities, etc.) and thus also try to at least partially compensate for their relative loss of importance (due i.e. to cuts in defense budgets) suffered at the end of the East–West confrontation (Pugh 2000: 236). Von Bredow summarizes this process as follows: "The soldier, so to say, becomes an armed social worker in global mission" (1995: 21).

On the other hand, the formation of a "market for humanitarian aid" with a high number of potential "suppliers" inevitably results in the simultaneous presence of the military, sent to crisis regions on the grounds of security policy, and the representatives of humanitarian relief organizations acting there (Tarry 2002: 34ff.). The need for a coordinated approach increases with the points of contact that arise in such a scenario (Studer 2000: 9ff.). From the military's point of view, this is where CIMIC steps in.

With regard to the Bundeswehr, it has already been emphasized that in the course of a complex emergency, the Armed Forces not only care for the creation of a safe environment but can also provide humanitarian assistance, undertake economic reconstruction and build a public administration. The Bundeswehr began to engage in these undertakings despite the fact that its mandate still largely ignored the necessity of such measures at the time. To this day, many of the soldiers involved – whether they are on active duty or from the reserve – lack proper training or education in post-conflict reconstruction (Millotat 2004: 9f.; Braunstein et al. 2001: 42). Thus, servicemen responsible for implementing measures to rebuild conflict-ridden or war-torn countries are increasingly in search of guidelines that allow them to make use of standardized instruments, as opposed to trial-and-error project execution whenever they enter a new arena.

Against this background, the post-Cold War evolution of the German CIMIC concept can be classified as *andante* formation of a state-building doctrine of the military. It has been slowly leaving behind sole "support of the mission" and "force multiplication" aspects while increasingly incorporating development issues and true facets of post-conflict reconstruction, and thus going beyond prevailing NATO concepts (EinsFüKdoBw 2004: para. 202; Hardegger 2003: 39f.). The approach in its different stages, that is various internal working papers, analysis and finalized instructions and directives (cf. Maase 2005), reflects the endeavors over time which the Bundeswehr and its conceptual masterminds have made in order to adapt to altering domestic political constraints, international politics, lessons learned in PSOs and changing environments in the different theatres where German soldiers are involved.[11]

Nonetheless, this process does not show the agility which is needed to handle matters properly in the aftermath of domestic conflict. Furthermore, despite all avowals that have been made by politicians, a truly integrated approach, which aims at developing a national state-building doctrine involving all stakeholders from the various ministries and federal agencies as well as the academic world, the military and practitioners from NGOs etc., cannot be found in Germany today. Instead, the concert is many-voiced and there's no conductor for the dissonant symphony (cf. BMVg 2006 and 2004b; BMZ 2004; Bundesregierung 2004; EinsFüKdoBw 2004). A main reason for this appears to be to be the competition between CIMIC as tactical procedure for military operations to create force protection based on the commander's intent on one hand, and CIMIC as political contribution to overall state-building efforts based on the respective national interest on the other.

For the time being, it therefore seems reasonable to have a look in which way CIMIC is handled by the Bundeswehr in order to cast light on the German military's approach to state-building. In the following section, Kosovo is taken as an example.

Applied CIMIC: humanitarian assistance and state building in Kosovo[12]

Following the adoption of Resolution No. 1244 by the United Nations Security Council (UNSC),[13] the first German soldiers entered Kosovo on 11 June 1999 as part of "Operation Joint Guardian". At the time, it was the situation of some 750,000 Displaced Persons (DPs), which was most crucial and constituted one of the focal points of military activity (Auswärtiges Amt 2000: 34ff.). According to Braunstein *et al.* (2001: 41f.) the following measures were taken:

* Within the first month of the operation, a field kitchen prepared more than 600,000 warm meals for hungry people and distributed approximately 155 tons of food.
* Reconnaissance activities led to a detailed assessment of the overall situation in the municipalities of the German Area of Responsibility (AOR) with special emphasis being laid on the particular degree of destruction (village profiles).
* This was followed by efforts to perform a rough winterization of existing houses and accommodations.
* Unsheltered families were given building materials and more than 1,600 damaged houses were refurbished by soldiers.
* Soldiers distributed more than 1,000 tons of humanitarian aid.

For the newly formed German-led Multinational Brigade (MNB) South with its HQ in Prizren a whole CIMIC battalion soon concentrated on humanitarian issues – at times with over 100 personnel. After the rapid implementation of so-called CIMIC Centers or KFOR Offices, these became a cornerstone of German CIMIC efforts.[14] These centers functioned as contact point with the local population and thus exist in various towns throughout the German AOR. If the applicants qualified for help, they were given food and other humanitarian aid. The longer the initial conflict is over, however, the more time is spent helping applicants with problems regarding the public authorities, or assisting them in claiming pensions to which they might be entitled due to contributions made during their time as immigrants in Germany (Pütger 2002: 12).

Furthermore, KFOR units spontaneously stepped in where civil structures were dysfunctional due to the chaotic situation after the downfall of Serbian rule in mid-1999 (Millotat 2004: 9). For example, German soldiers:

- temporarily managed a prison;
- supplied fuel oil for the heat generators of various hospitals; and
- arbitrated between employers and employees when salaries were not paid in time, and even helped the former with military resources to pay in kind.

The German CIMIC battalion's focus changed substantially as of spring 2000, when the soldiers' main efforts were concentrated on the systematic reconstruction of destroyed villages.

> The German brigade has been quite aggressive in rebuilding homes for Albanian Kosovars, even lending the brigade's military resources to the project. They may, however, have been motivated as much by domestic political considerations within Germany as by concern for refugees. With one of the world's most generous asylum policies, Germany had allowed a large number of Albanian refugees to enter the country. With the war over, [the German government is encouraging] these refugees return home.
>
> (Mockaitis 2004: 19f.)

The formulation of a national strategy paper describing aims and guidelines for reconstruction efforts (Braunstein *et al.* 2001: 42) was the visible result of domestic political pressure caused by some 170,000 immigrants from Kosovo in Germany. Accordingly, not only private homes but also a large number of schools, hospitals, and other public facilities were rebuilt by German soldiers in Kosovo. Due to the attempt to quickly bring most of the refugees in Germany back to Kosovo, financial means for CIMIC projects in the initial phase were mainly provided in an unbureaucratic fashion by the German government.

"All the same, infrastructure cannot create a nation" (Ignatieff 2003: 104). So gradually, CIMIC personnel also started to plan structural development schemes. Millotat reports a number of "naïve-appearing projects" (2004: 9), such as supporting a wine factory. Despite the well-intentioned and expert dedication of quite a number of soldiers and functional specialists combined with the reasonable financial means invested in the project, the outcome was rather poor.[15]

In essence, the overall situation with regard to CIMIC in Kosovo was dominated by a severe lack of coordination of reconstruction efforts between HQ KFOR and its five MNBs. This led to "CIMIC at random" (Millotat 2003: 421), which reflects the competition between CIMIC as tactical procedure for military operations to create force protection based on the commander's intent on one hand, and CIMIC as political contribution to overall state-building efforts based on the respective national interest on the other. Confronted with this situation, KFOR's think-tanks tried to counter the development that the individual brigades more and more resembled heterogeneous little "kingdoms" instead of a homogeneous international intervention force. Therefore, the operational area of the Italians (MNB West) was merged with that of the Germans (MNB South) to create the new MNB Southwest (MNB-SW) headquartered in Prizren in November 2002. This measure was aimed at creating true multi-nationality and cooperation between troops with a different national background by overcoming old brigade borders and establishing new AORs (Millotat 2003: 423f.).

At the same time, the merger meant an extension of the German CIMIC unit's operating range, while the unit has continued to be a formation under the direct command of the brigade. With the situation gradually easing it was also decided to downsize the CIMIC battalion to a CIMIC company. Beside the unique national structures and command chains particularly with regard to financial aspects, the main difference between CIMIC teams from Austria, Turkey, Italy, and Spain operating in the respective AORs of their battle groups and the Prizren-based German CIMIC unit remains the presence of various functional specialists who enable the Germans to adopt a much broader focus:

- For example, the German CIMIC company has supported the founding of agricultural cooperatives as part of its effort to promote institution building in the private sector (Voget 2004b: 4).
- For several years, functional specialists have conducted seminars on cattle management or crop production for local farmers as an ongoing project.
- CIMIC personnel with a scientific economic and/or judicial background have functioned as consultants for local companies.

When the 9th German KFOR contingent took up service on 19 May 2004, the new joint Italian–German staff of MNB-SW soon began to revise the operational procedures and to introduce flexible plans for mobile operations. After the devastating experiences of 17 and 18 March 2004, when Kosovo was shaken by riots and civil unrest while KFOR almost completely lost control, the goal was that the brigade would never experience such a fiasco again (Messner 2004: 14ff.). For the German CIMIC company, however, there were no changes except for an occasional order to its own personnel available for brigade operations as described in the section on "Support of the Armed Forces".

The following examples illustrate what kind of CIMIC measures were taken in 2004.

- A humanitarian aid troop distributed more than 120 tons of various aid goods, such as firewood, warm clothes, sanitary products, basic furniture, and shoes, which were mainly financed and donated by "*Lachen helfen e.V.*", a private association founded and supported by German soldiers (Höft 2004: 7).
- With funding from the Stability Pact for South East Europe, the CIMIC company reconstructed 25 private houses for very poor families belonging to different ethnic groups, who were identified in an assessment process.
- The German Foreign Office financed two projects dubbed "Humanitarian Assistance" (€24,000) and "Winter Assistance" (€45,000). With this money, the CIMIC company was enabled to distribute food, fuel and other goods to meet urgent humanitarian needs among poor families and needy

individuals. A single aid package to assist survival in postwar confusion and during the winter was worth approximately €150.

- In addition, the winterization of dwellings providing shelter to needy humans who suffer from long-term unemployment and poverty could be realized.
- The construction of a school and a sports field (planning, project supervision and general organization undertaken by CIMIC functional specialists) in Skorobiste cost roughly €270,000. Of this, the municipal administration of Prizren contributed €170,000 (von Hoerschelmann 2004b: 2).
- With a similar co-financing approach, the reconstruction of an outpatient clinic in Velika Hocha was realized. This village is inhabited by Serbs. It has approximately 650 inhabitants living in 190 households. The village inhabitants accomplished the necessary work under the supervision of CIMIC personnel. Financial means of €5,000 were donated by the German section of The Order of St. John, and the municipality Orahovac added the same amount of money (von Hoerschelmann 2004d: 4).
- The CIMIC company planned the construction of a school in the municipality Guncat, worth €220,000. After securing the financing (45 percent raised by the municipal administration, 23 percent by the Federal Ministry for Economic Co-operation and Development (BMZ), 23 percent by the German Technical Co-operation Agency and 32 percent by the Baden-Wurttemberg foundation), the project was supervised by German soldiers while private companies from Kosovo did the necessary work (von Hoerschelmann 2004e: 4).
- One functional specialist dealt with training future school headmasters. After identifying gaps that had not been filled by other aid workers, an appropriate program was developed and tested in practice by the CIMIC soldier. His project was based on a close cooperation between the CIMIC company and the Kosovo Ministry of Education (KME). All IOs and NGOs working in the schooling sector were also involved. Some financing was made available by the GTZ, which meanwhile has taken over the program together with the KME.
- An agricultural team of the CIMIC unit provided a donation of mobile soil laboratories for Kosovo's Ministry of Agriculture, Forestry and Rural Development (MAFRD) (Thürnau 2005a).

In essence, the fifty all-rounders and functional specialists of MNB-SW's German CIMIC company managed a financial turn-over of roughly €1,000,000 of public funding and private donations during their deployment from May until December 2004. The fruitful cooperation with local administrative bodies in the AOR is without precedent. This enabled the unit to conduct a number of co-financed projects. For the first time since the KFOR operation had started, the German CIMIC company was able to persuade local officials to make substantial contributions on a larger scale. For Kosovo, this might indicate that "[...] the balance of will between local people and internationals is more even than the imbalance of their resources may suggest" (Ignatieff 2003: 119).

Problems observed

Taking into account the thoughts of Chesterman *et al.* (2005), Fukuyama (2004) and Ignatieff (2003) on how the international community engages in nation-building in the aftermath of state collapse or state failure, the military's contribution to overall efforts can be described as a core element of the overall initiatives. After all, most human interactions in the course of an international intervention occur between members of the Armed Forces and the local community. Therefore, the impressions people get of the foreign soldiers and their home countries determine either support or diminish the efforts of the international community. "However, construction is more difficult than destruction, and nationbuilding operations can be long, complex, and expensive" (Anderson 2004: 47). Critics argue, however, that many projects conducted by the Armed Forces display severe weaknesses and are by no means "best practice" (see for example Millotat 2005, 2004 and 2003; Klingebiel and Roehder 2004; Fritz-Vannahme 2003; or von Randow and Stelzenmüller 2000). Hence, an analysis of what goes wrong and why, might help to improve future missions.

Force Protection in terms of winning the hearts and minds remains the official top objective of German CIMIC activities. Serving the implementation of humanitarian aid or the development goals of the Federal Government is only a means to this end, and military leaders incorporate CIMIC elements into their conduct of operations with the primary purpose of improving the image of their troops among the local populace (Platzer 2005).

Even though German politicians and officials formally address the Bundeswehr's CIMIC projects as part of overall nation-building efforts, this is not consistent with current NATO doctrine (Hardegger 2003: 38ff., Rollins 2001: 122ff.). Such inconsistencies between national and Alliance concepts add to the complex discussion surrounding CIMIC – least among the Bundeswehr's own soldiers. Millotat (2004: 9) echoes this concern when he emphasizes that both military leadership and the corresponding decision-making process should be supported by proper post-conflict reconstruction guidelines for the German Armed Forces. He signals that the integration of such guidelines into all commands and instructions is overdue in order to effectively overcome conflict and achieve successful state building – also with the help of CIMIC measures. But at the same time, what Widder expresses is also true:

> Peace operations in particular are subject to intensive media coverage. Every action a soldier takes is broadcast into living rooms in almost real time, and political leaders must answer for those actions immediately. The pressure on the political leadership to act or to explain is particularly acute. This pressure frequently generates a tendency to want to control everything. This tendency often finds its expression in direct interference with the operational and tactical leadership on the ground [...].
>
> (2002: 6)

And this is the crux of the matter. Although individual projects are high-lighted once and again in the media, the current CIMIC concept as well as the concrete practical implementation of so-called post-conflict reconstruction of the Bundeswehr is not free of problems (Fritz-Vannahme 2003: 21). "Economic development is impossible, and humanitarian aid is a waste of time, so goes the theory, unless the country in question has effective governance: rule of law, fire walls against corruption, democracy and a free press" (Ignatieff 2003: 93). In short: erecting buildings, such as clinics, schools and orphanages, is one thing; creating strong and legitimate state institutions as well as civil society is another. Thus, current CIMIC activities cannot be considered a panacea. For example, in Kosovo some weak spots may be identified with respect to the military contribution to the reconstruction of the country.

Due to the specific nature of CIMIC activities, the Bundeswehr competes with international relief organizations also acting in the crisis region in the Balkans.[16] From time to time, this creates problems with respect to the allocation of tight budgetary sources for humanitarian projects and it can lead to waste in the form of parallel structures and duplicate effort (Klingebiel und Roehder 2004: 22f.; Hardegger 2003; von Randow und Stelzenmüller 2000: 12ff., Pollick 2000). Economically speaking, it results in avoidable inefficiencies. Although economists generally argue that competition in economic markets yields benefits to consumers, it must not be forgotten that in the case of post-conflict reconstruction, there is no level playing field. As mentioned above, the Bundeswehr has a comparative advantage over its civil competitors for funding due to the fact that the Armed Forces can assume labor costs and overheads (Klingebiel und Roehder 2004: 22f.).

And even though Byman states: "Engagement between the military and NGOs would speed response and increase efficiency during all phases of humanitarian crisis [...]" (2001: 108), the proper orchestration of NGOs in a crisis region in order to minimize unnecessary effort is rather utopian. Most of the NGOs come and go as they like and there is nothing such as real co-operation. As a result, quite a large amount of money was squandered in Kosovo, and even organized crime benefited from certain relief projects (Millotat 2003: 426).

Moreover, the necessity of measures implemented within the scope of CIMIC is not always comprehensible, with respect to neither political goals nor to the strategic, tactical and operative aims of the superior military command (Heinemann-Grüder *et al.* 2004: 68). Consider, for example, the CIMIC efforts to support a joint project between a well-known German construction-company and a local brick manufacturer in Kosovo. In order to help create jobs ("structural development") in Kosovo, the German soldiers conducted a foundation soil analysis on a Kosovar entrepreneur's property to identify a safe location where the German investor could install his heavy equipment for brick production. However, this does not necessarily fit into any of the aforementioned military tasks of CIMIC. If the Bundeswehr uses own personnel to assist and support a private company in Kosovo, it is thus creating a severe advantage over possible competitors. Although the project itself is possibly paying off for both companies involved and some jobs might be created, such an undertaking could also have negative impacts on the general military mission. Rival businesses might ask why they are not supported by a CIMIC unit and their discontentment could cause a hostile attitude toward the troops. In this respect, it is important to note that there is no scientific proof whether the German military really achieves force protection with its CIMIC measures.

Added to this, CIMIC projects frequently do not take into consideration economic interdependencies and socio-cultural specialties.[17] Instead, "[...] military personnel tend to treat most problems as logistical" (Mockaitis 2004: 28f.). But, as Siegel stresses, "[i]n most interventions, the state's (and society's) limited 'absorptive capacity' causes problems for the transition from war to peace" (2001: 12). Knack and Rahman (2004) elaborate on this issue in detail from a development aid perspective. In aggregate, there are certain constraints, such as an inefficient administration, a defective infrastructure or a lack of qualified personnel as well as weak performance incentives, asymmetric information, multiple objectives or difficulties in measuring outcome, etc., which define the absorption capacity of a region or a country in the sense that it is only able to disburse and absorb a certain amount of projects, international investments and foreign assistance (Svensson 2005: 1f.). But how does this look like in theater? The plan to help the reconstruction of Kosovo's railway system can serve as an example. It led to a project involving a CIMIC team and the GTZ in 2000. Five locomotives were brought to Kosovo. CIMIC functional specialists initially oversaw their maintenance and trained local staff to service the trains (Braunstein *et al.* 2001: 42; also: Reinhardt 2002: 215). In 2004, however, these engines were all non-functional due to frost damage, and no member of the 9th German KFOR contingent's CIMIC unit knew anything about the historical project. Presumably, the engines were handed over to Kosovo authorities, and these were not able or willing to ensure that the locomotives were serviced in the required manner. This case not only illustrates a lack of absorptive capacity but also inadequate project realization in terms of sustainability.

Another example points in the same direction: In 2002, a donation by the public foundation owned and funded by the German federal state Baden-Wurttemberg enabled the German CIMIC unit to renovate part of an old stable which belonged to the agricultural premises of a former Socially-Owned Enterprise (SOE). The front part of the stable was transformed into a classroom. This building then was labeled "Agricultural Information Centre" (AIC). It became a well-known place, where functional specialists or other instructors held training sessions with farmers and staff from the administration. The responsibility for maintaining the AIC as well as conducting future seminars and sessions was officially transferred to Kosovo's MAFRD in 2003. The Ministry, however, did not do anything due to a lack of budget and staff. Despite this development, the project itself was very much appreciated by local officials and politicians because there was no other agricultural school anywhere close (Voget 2004a: 5). Nonetheless, it was not possible to enlarge the original classroom and realize plans to create a pilot farm on the premises of the SOE in 2004. Although the CIMIC company could have invested more than €100,000, which had been partly donated by the German Foreign Office and partly by the Baden-Wurttemberg foundation, it was not possible to reach an agreement securing the projected investment with the Kosovo Trust Agency (KTA), an UNMIK office responsible for privatizing state owned property. As a consequence, the CIMIC company had to pass the money back to the donor institutions without being able to make any arrangements for an alternative utilization of the funding.

CIMIC projects often fail to take structures and projects already existing in the respective fields into account. When taking a closer look at Germany's CIMIC projects over time and the different missions, one can identify a lack of systematic effort to adapt individual projects to an environment under dynamic development and to coordinate them with the other stakeholders (IOs, GOs, NGOs, CIMIC elements of other nations contributing KFOR troops) to achieve gains in efficiency. Reflections of such possibilities most often take place during the conception phase of individual projects but are not carried on in a coordinated manner as the initial project ideas are put into practice. Especially the dialogue between all relevant layers of command and higher HQ could be improved. This is why Rollins points out the following: "Care should be taken not to confuse activities conducted as part of a theatre-level CIMIC plan and those carried out by national military contingents" (2001: 127). For example, without knowing of each other's operations, French and German KFOR CIMIC units tried to found agricultural cooperatives in the same area in spring and summer 2004. Only by accident did they finally meet and start to coordinate their activities on the working level. None of their superiors (J9/G5 officers etc.) had informed them about the ongoing projects of other KFOR units (von Hoerschelmann 2004a: 7 and 2004c: 3; Voget 2004a: 4).

Why do we observe such weaknesses and difficulties? The main reason has to do with human resources.

- The expert background of most personnel involved is very heterogeneous with respect to quality. Of course, this does have implications for the standards of project assessment and realization.
- Furthermore, despite the high amount of personnel with an academic education, many soldiers serving in German CIMIC units are not sufficiently proficient in English. Strong English language communication by non-commissioned officers and officers nonetheless constitutes a key element within the capability profile for international military missions.
- The high fluctuation of personnel as contingents change makes the implementation of mid-term or long-term projects by the military more difficult since actors take their knowledge and specific information with them when they leave the country after a tour of duty. Many workers with other organizations that are acting in a crisis region for a longer period complain that due to frequently changing points of contact with the military, useful cooperation is almost impossible.

- Focusing on team-work, the following can be said: Instead of trying to improve CIMIC undertakings altogether by discussion and exchange, many functional specialists tend to work in isolation. This inevitably results in uncontrollable risks to the project work. Hence, due to missing information, many CIMIC projects do not match standards and success criteria known from evaluations of development cooperation (cf. BMZ 1989).

- Perhaps in an effort to prevent others from interfering in their special area of expertise, quite a number of functional specialists serving in CIMIC units conduct their projects in a rather non-transparent manner. In most cases, their superiors – well-trained and experienced soldiers who are by no means familiar with economic, agricultural or architectural concepts and technical knowledge cannot evaluate the projects properly and therefore an uncontrolled growth of projects and activities in certain areas can occur. Economists classify most of these issues as problems of asymmetric information (cf. Akerlof 1970).

- The opposite of this situation is the interference by a military commander in the field of expertise of a CIMIC specialist, who is in theatre because of his or her specific knowledge. Such actions can have negative effects on the motivation of personnel and the general execution of CIMIC projects. This observation also appears to be in line with findings presented by Vogelaar and Kramer (2004) with respect to mission command.

- Finally, it is worth mentioning that in Kosovo the recordkeeping system of the German CIMIC company does not allow a reliable correlation between total costs and projects conducted. There are spreadsheets stating which donor provided how much funding for which project. But focusing on overhead, it is impossible to identify how much time soldier X has spent in dealing with CIMIC project Y, or to determine in retrospect how many kilometers were driven in total in order to supervise the reconstruction of a school, for example. As a result controlling and evaluations are hard to conduct.

In connection with the described problems it is of basic interest to determine whether CIMIC projects result in a truly improved situation for the local population (Byman 2001: 108ff.) and whether the military really achieves force protection through CIMIC. Of course it is clear also that identifying and measuring explanatory variables with a firm empirical and theoretical basis constitutes a real problem under the working conditions of a conflict or post-conflict scenario. Yet, further research and especially project evaluations must be conducted in order for these questions to be answered properly.

Conclusion

This chapter on the German Armed Forces' theoretical CIMIC approach and contemporary practice yields five broad conclusions.

First, as of yet there is no true CIMIC formula integrating all stakeholders' concerns. This is mainly due to the rapid structural as well as conceptual development that CIMIC has undergone within the Bundeswehr during the last roughly 15 years. Military as well as civilian protagonists have to keep pace. But the process itself is evidence of the growing importance that military leaders as well as politicians attach to this specific field of activity. However, the overall political interest with regard to CIMIC has to be unmistakably stated to answer the question of how far military forces should be employed outside their traditionally mandated roles and why. This requires a coordinated process to reach an agreement between all involved ministries and governmental departments, which should substantiate the rather general wording used in the White Paper 2006 (BMVg 2006).

Second, despite a number of nebulous statements it has not yet been proven whether the German military really achieves force protection through CIMIC. Further scientific research with respect to the outcomes of CIMIC measures and their efficiency has to be conducted to answer this important question. Whether or not winning the hearts and minds really works should be carefully investigated.

Third, the experience and results of research in related areas such as development policy, economics or sociology have not yet been properly included into the military's conception. The resulting inadequacies in conducting CIMIC projects and missing guidelines for CIMIC as part of post-conflict reconstruction efforts can cause – and partly have already led to – erroneous, albeit well-intended decisions at the outset of a scenario, which could have wide-ranging, long-lasting consequences.

Fourth, since any action in connection with the Armed Forces as a public institution affects the taxpayer, a more efficient use of resources should be a top priority. Rather than more or less relying on improvised measures, it would be in the Bundeswehr's best interest to intensify its endeavors to completely understand what is required from the military's point of view to handle matters in the aftermath of conflict. Also, the identification and execution of projects and general communication with other key players in a PSO must be improved. To cite Kaplan, "it is effectiveness that justifies a humanitarian mission and not whether it is conducted by soldiers or civilians" (2003: 7).

Fifth, there are problems with the selection and training of personnel, and the granting of adequate doses of autonomy for functional specialists. CIMIC staff in general must in all respects be able to fulfill military orders without neglecting the subsidiary goal of reconstructing conflict-ridden or war-torn societies.

In summary, what is needed is an integrated approach in order to come up with a concept that works and satisfies *any* requirement. The Bundeswehr would be well-advised to accept findings from scientific research and incorporate them into its doctrine, and the Armed Forces should not resist efforts to undertake scientific evaluations of CIMIC projects in order to identify and benefit from lessons learned. At the same time, German scholars have to become less hesitant to conduct research in conjunction with the military. Main effort should be put on solving the dilemma of competition between CIMIC as tactical procedure for military operations to create force protection based on the commander's intent on one hand, and CIMIC as political contribution to overall state-building efforts based on the respective national interest on the other. But only true civil–military cooperation will lead to outcomes that help to understand how to improve force-protection requirements and conduct state-of-the-art post-conflict reconstruction and state-building at the same time.

Notes

1 The author would like to thank Maj. Gen. (retired) Christian E.O. Millotat, Deputy Commander (DCOM) Kosovo Force (KFOR) from September 2001 to October 2002, Mr. Axel von Hoerschelmann, Head of Division, State Chancellery of the Federal State of Brandenburg, Mr. Peter Welling, Project Manager, German Technical Cooperation (GTZ), Kosovo, Mr. Tobias Pietz, Researcher, Bonn International Center for Conversion (BICC), and Prof. Dr. von Cramon-Taubadel, Chair of Agricultural Policy, Georg-August-University, Göttingen, for their suggestions and valuable comments on earlier drafts of this chapter.
2 Note the dynamic approach, which implicitly alludes to the perceived inadequateness of current measures.
3 The S5 officer deals with all matters concerning CIMIC.
4
> The Liaison and Observation Team (LOT) is a group of soldiers who do not live in a military camp but in civilian accommodations among the local population providing the dynamic, responsive and locally-based 'public face' of [the international troops]. The purpose of LOT is to be more accessible to citizens and authorities […]
>
> (NATO 2004b)

5
> At local level, KFOR Liaison Monitoring Team's goal is TO liaise closely with the local administrations, community leaders and relevant individuals and organizations through regular meetings and also increase the local confidence. […] LMTs are a tool dedicated to operate in addition to Intel assets as force multiplier.
>
> (NATO 2005)

6 The civilian element of the PRT – comprising representatives of the Ministry of Foreign Affairs, the Ministry of the Interior and the Ministry of Economic Cooperation and Development – engages in diplomatic efforts, police training and reconstruction efforts etc. The military component is tasked to build up a stakeholder network and to provide an environment in which civilian efforts can be conducted securely (Jakobsen 2005; Klingebiel and Roehder 2004: 23–27).
7 Note that the terms "generalists" or "CIMIC generalists" are sometimes used as synonyms for "all rounders" in this context.
8 Branches in staff headquarters (G5) and joint staff headquarters (J9) which deal with all matters concerning CIMIC (NATO 2003: Para 501).
9 Not surprisingly, in trying to find a way to generate more funding for their projects, CIMIC personnel from the reserve force contact individuals who they know from their civilian life, hoping that these individuals or institutions they belong to will contribute substantially. This is another interesting aspect of civil–military cooperation that deserves closer analysis.
10 Interestingly, this is called "support to the civil environment". However, one could argue that it really is to the advantage of the Armed Forces.
11 In May 2004, Germany's then Minister of Defense, Dr. Peter Struck, stressed that "CIMIC has become an inherent part of the nation-building process […]" (BMVg 2004b). Furthermore, the Bundeswehr explicitly states in one CIMIC directive that

consulting services of CIMIC personnel are a "[...] contribution to create national structures (nation-building)" (EinsFüKdoBw 2004: 10).

12 In this context, Traub (2004: 32) states: "If there is such a thing as a state-of-the-art peacekeeping, it would be the NATO–United Nations operation in Kosovo [...]" and Mockaitis (2004: v) stresses: "The NATO deployment in Kosovo provides a unique opportunity to study the effectiveness of civil–military cooperation in humanitarian interventions and other stability and support operations."

13 Millotat (2004: 8 ff.) criticises that UN Resolution No. 1244 does not give explicit post-conflict reconstruction guidelines assigning clear tasks for KFOR and UNMIK. As the primary reason for the complex and still unfavorable situation in Kosovo, Millotat specifies missing the chance of implementing a true joint transitional administration at the very beginning of the operation in 1999. An orchestration of the overall reconstruction of the province instead of the multitude of uncoordinated single actions would have rapidly improved the situation and could have saved a lot of money, according to Millotat (2003: 419ff.).

14 The CIMIC Centre in Prizren celebrated its fifth anniversary in July 2004. Since it opened in 1999, more than 100,000 visitors have asked for help and assistance in various matters. Altogether, the costs of the measures taken by the CIMIC Centre personnel amounts to more then _2,000,000.

15 As a result, everything related to wine, its production or sale is officially considered a "no go" issue for German CIMIC personnel in Kosovo today.

16 Nevertheless, the Armed Forces Office says in a publication for reservists: "To dispel a very widespread error in judgement: Soldiers in CIMIC missions do not compete with humanitarian relief organisations, so-called NGOs" (SKA 2003: 5).

17 It was only recently, that the Bundeswehr Operations Headquarters began asking for the expertise of academic institutions. For instance, in 2005, the author was requested to prepare an expert report on a CIMIC project designed to strengthen human capital in the agricultural sector, and in 2006, he has compiled an evaluation study of the German CIMIC unit's agricultural reconstruction projects in Kosovo for the Bundeswehr Operations Headquarters J9 branch.

References

Akerlof, G. (1970) "The market for 'lemons': quality, uncertainty and the market mechanism", *The Quarterly Journal of Economics* 84(3): 488–500.

Anderson, G. E. (2004) "Winning the Nationbuilding War", *Military Review,* September–October 2004 (English Edition): 47–50.

Auswärtiges Amt (AA) (2000) *Fünfter Bericht der Bundesregierung über ihre Menschenrechtspolitik in den auswärtigen Beziehungen.* Online, available at: www.-auswaertiges-amt.de/www/de/aussenpolitik/menschenrechte/mr_inhalte_ziele/mrb/kap itel_3_html#anfang (accessed 8 March 2005).

Berchthold H. and Leppig, G. (1980) "Zivil-Militärische Zusammenarbeit (ZMZ) – (Kernfunktion der Gesamtverteidigung)", in Reinfried, H. and Walitschek, H. F. (eds) *Die Bundeswehr – Eine Gesamtdarstellung,* Regensburg: Walhalla Praetoria Verlag.

Braunstein, P. (2000) "CIMIC 2000 – Zivil-militärische Kooperation", *Europäische Sicherheit* 12: 47–50.

Braunstein, P., Meyer, C. W. and Vogt, M. J. (2001) "Zivil-militärische Zusammenarbeit der Bundeswehr im Balkan-Einsatz", *Aus Politik und Zeitgeschichte* (APuZ), 20: 37–46.

von Bredow, W. (1995) "Die Zukunft der Bundeswehr – Gesellschaft und Streitkräfte im Wandel", in Wewer, G. (ed.) *Analysen: Politik – Gesellschaft – Wirtschaft,* Opladen: Verlag Leske + Budrich.

Bundesministerium für Verteidigung (BMVg) (2001) *Teilkonzeption Zivil-Militärische Zusammenarbeit der Bundeswehr (TK ZMZ Bw)* (restricted – release by BMVg-FüSKB I (5)), Berlin.

—— (2003) *Verteidigungspolitische Richtlinien (VPR) für den Geschäftsbereich des Bundesministeriums der Verteidigung*, Berlin.

—— (2004a) *Aktuelle Einsätze: Kosovo (KFOR)*. Online, available at: www.einsatz.bundeswehr.de/einsatz_aktuell/kfor/ueberblick/kfor_ueb.php (accessed 25 April 2004).

—— (2004b) *CIMIC: Grundlagen, Ziele und eine Bilanz*. Online, available at: www.bundeswehr.de/forces/grundlagen/einsatz/print/040518_cimic_bm.php (accessed 21 May 2004).

—— (2006) *Weißbuch 2006 zur Sicherheitspolitik Deutschlands und zur Zukunft der Bundeswehr*, Berlin. Online, available at: www.weissbuch2006.de/ (accessed 16 December 2006).

Bundesministerium für wirtschaftliche Zusammenarbeit und Entwicklung (BMZ) (ed.) (1989) *Überprüfen und Handeln – Erfolg durch Erfolgskontrolle? Querschnittsauswertung der im Jahre 1987 durchgeführten Evaluierungen*, Bonn.

—— (2004) "BMZ-Diskurs – Zum Verhältnis von entwicklungspolitischen und militärischen Antworten auf neue sicherheitspolitische Herausforderungen", BMZ discussion paper no. 002, Bonn, May 2004.

Bundesregierung (2004) *Aktionsplan "Zivile Krisenprävention, Konfliktlösung und Friedenskonsolidierung"*, Berlin.

Büsching, M. (2005) "Neue Aufgaben – Reservisten – Pilotprojekt für die Zivil-Militärische Zusammenarbeit in Mecklenburg-Vorpommern", *aktuell – Zeitung für die Bundeswehr*, 40 (4): 10. Online, available at: www.bundeswehr.de/misc/pdf/service/bundeswehr_aktuell/2005/050131_ausgabe_04.pdf (accessed 15 February 2005).

Byman, D. L. (2001) "Uncertain Partners: NGOs and the Military", *Survival* 43(2): 97–114.

Chesterman, S., Ignatieff, M. and Thkur, R. (eds) (2005) *Making States Work: State Failure and the Crisis of Government*, Tokyo, New York, Paris: United Nations University Press.

CIMIC Centre of Excellence (CCOE) (2006) *History of the Civil–Military Co-operation Centre of Excellence*. Online, available at: www.cimicgroupnorth.org/smartsite.dws?id=775 (accessed 18 December 2006).

Danish Refugee Council (ed.) (2002) "Forgotten Humanitarian Crises", paper presented at the Conference on the Role of the Media, Decision-makers and Humanitarian Agencies, Copenhagen, 23 October 2002. Online, available at: ics.leeds.ac.uk/papers/pmt/exhibits/1999/ForgottenCrises-oct02.pdf (accessed 12 March 2005).

Dersch, T. (2005) *Vor neuen Herausforderungen – Das CIMIC Bataillon 100 in Nienburg an der Weser*. Online, available at: www.streitkraeftebasis.de/C1256C290043532F/FrameDocName/rep_cimic_100 (accessed 16 January 2005).

Diering, C. (2004) "Mit Sicherheit", *Die Welt*, 18 March 2004.

Dobbins, J., McGinn, J. G., Crane, K., Jones, S. G., Lal, R., Rathmell, A., Swanger, R. and Timilsina, A. (2003) *America's Role in Nation-Building – From Germany to Iraq*, Santa Monica: RAND.

Douglas, S. (2002) *Toward a Comprehensive Canadian CIMIC Doctrine: Interagency Cooperation and the Influence of Allies in the Balkan*. Online, available at: www.cdacdai.ca/symposia/2002/douglas.htm (accessed 5 April 2004).

Echterling, J. (2003a) *Zusammenarbeit, "ZMZ-Aufgaben"*. Online, available at:

www.streitkraeftebasis.de/C1256C290043532F/vwContentFrame/569AB306EDE7F93
9C1256DD300568E43 (accessed 15 February 2005).
—— (2003b) "CIMIC – Zivil-Militärische Zusammenarbeit der Bundeswehr im
Ausland", *Europäische Sicherheit* 52(10): 32–37.
—— (2004) "Rolle der Zivil-Militärischen Zusammenarbeit in Deutschland bei Hilfeleis-
tungen der Bundeswehr", in Forschungsinstitut der Deutschen Gesellschaft für
Auswärtige Politik (DGAP) (ed.) *Homeland Security: Die Bedrohung durch den
Terrorismus als Herausforderung für eine gesamtstaatliche Sicherheitsstruktur*,
Berlin.
Einsatzführungskommando der Bundeswehr (EinsFüKdoBw) (2003) *Fachliche Weisung
für die Planung und Durchführung der Zivil-Militärischen Zusammenarbeit Ausland
(ZMZ A) bei Einsätzen der Bundeswehr im Rahmen der Internationalen Krisenbewälti-
gung* (resticted – release by BMVg-FüSKB I (5)), Potsdam.
—— (2004) *Fachliche Weisung für die Planung und Durchführung von Unter-
stützungsaktivitäten im Rahmen der Zivil-Militärischen Zusammenarbeit bei Einsätzen
der Bundeswehr im Ausland*, Potsdam.
Enders, T. (2003) "Herausforderung 'Homeland Security' für die Industrie", *Europäische
Sicherheit*, 52(10): 8–11.
Forsteneichner, G. F. C. (2002) *Friedlose Welt – Bewaffnete Konflikte und das Ringen um
Konfliktlösung und Frieden*, Bonn.
Fritz-Vannahme, J. (2003) "Kindergarten: Die Lehren aus Bosnien – Wiederaufbau und
Demokratisierung: Was der Westen auf dem Balkan und in Afghanistan falsch
gemacht hat", *Die Zeit*, 17: 21.
Fukuyama, F. (2004) *State Building – Governance and World Order in the Twenty-First
Century*, London: Profile Books.
Georgi, A. (2003) "Steckt mehr dahinter", *Y. – Magazin der Bundeswehr*, 3(8): 100–101.
Hardegger, S. (2003) *Cimic-Doktrin im Spannungsfeld zwischen humanitärer Hilfe und
militärischer Krisenintervention*, Beiträge No. 41, January 2003, Zürich:
Forschungsstelle für Internationale Beziehungen, Zentrum für internationale Studien,
Eidgenössische Technische Hochschule.
Heinemann-Grüder, A., Lipp, D. and Pietz, T. (2004) "Entwicklungs- und Militärkompo-
nenten in Nachkonfliktlagen", in: Meyer, C. W. and Vogt, M. J. (eds) *CIMIC-Faktoren
V: Arenen*, Speyerer Arbeitsheft No. 159, Speyer: Deutsche Hochschule für Verwal-
tungswissenschaften Speyer.
Höft, H. (2004) "'Lachen Helfen' verbessert die Lebenssituation der Menschen im
Kosovo", *MAZ&More – Feldzeitung der Bundeswehr für das Kosovo und Mazedonien*,
271: 7.
von Hoerschelmann, A. (2004a) "Mehr Mut im Kosovo auch ohne Politik", *MAZ&More
– Feldzeitung der Bundeswehr für das Kosovo und Mazedonien*, 270: 7.
—— (2004b) "Wir versuchen, auch an den Dörfern dranzubleiben", *MAZ&More –
Feldzeitung der Bundeswehr für das Kosovo und Mazedonien*, 273: 2.
—— (2004c) "Gespräche über Kühe als vertrauensbildende Maßnahme", *MAZ&More –
Feldzeitung der Bundeswehr für das Kosovo und Mazedonien*, 273: 3.
—— (2004d) "Johanniter ermöglichen Ambulanz-Anbau", *MAZ&More – Feldzeitung
der Bundeswehr für das Kosovo und Mazedonien*, 274: 4.
—— (2004e) "Armut ist nicht gleich Chaos", *MAZ&More – Feldzeitung der Bundeswehr
für das Kosovo und Mazedonien*, 274: 4.
Huntington, S. P. (1996) *The Clash of Civilizations and the Remaking of World Order*,
New York: Simon & Schuster.

Ignatieff, M. (2003) *Empire Lite: Nation-Building in Bosnia, Kosovo, Afghanistan*, London: Random House.

Jakobsen, P. V. (2005) "PRTs in Afghanistan: successful but not sufficient", *DIIS Report 2005: 6*, Copenhagen: Danish Institute for International Studies (DIIS).

Kaplan, R. D. (2003) "Supremacy by Stealth", *The Atlantic Monthly*, 292(1): 66–83; reprinted in German as "Die Welt sicher machen für die Demokratie – Was wir jetzt tun müssen. Die zehn Regeln für das amerikanische Imperium des 21. Jahrhunderts" in *Die Literarische Welt*, 172: 6–8.

Klingebiel, S. and Roehder, K. (2004) *Entwicklungspolitisch-militärische Schnittstellen – Neue Herausforderungen in Krisen und Post-Konflikt-Situationen*, Berichte und Gutachten 3/2004, Bonn: Deutsches Institut für Entwicklungspolitik.

Knack. S. and Rahman, A. (2004) "Donor Fragmentation and Bureaucratic Quality in Aid Recipients", World Bank Policy Research Working Paper 3186, Washington, DC: The World Bank.

Lange, S. (2005) *Neue Bundeswehr auf altem Sockel – Wege aus dem Dilemma*, SWP-Studie S2, January 2005, Berlin: Stiftung Wissenschaft und Politik and Deutsches Institut für Internationale Politik und Sicherheit. Online, available at: www.swp-berlin.org/common/get_document.php?id=1154 (accessed 03 February 2005).

Longhurst, G. (2004) "Civil–Military Cooperation – The Inukshuk", *The Bulletin*, 10:1: 1–8.

Maase, A. (2005) "Militärischer Führungsprozess und zivil-militärische Zusammenarbeit bei Friedenmissionen", *Österreichische Militärische Zeitschrift* (ÖMZ), 43(2): 155–166.

Merchet, J.-D. (2002) "Les organisations humanitaires sont devenues un business", *Libération*, 7 March 2002.

Mertins, J. (2006) *Startschuß für das CIMIC-Zentrum*. Online, available at: www.streitkraeftebasis.de/portal/a/streitkraeftebasis/kcxml/04_Sj9SPykssy0xPLMnMz0vM0Y_QjzKLt4g3cQsBSUGYwfqRMLGglFR9b31fj_zcVP0A_YLciHJHR0VFACDw1Fg!/delta/base64xml/L2dJQSEvUUt3QS80SVVFLzZfOF80SkQ!?yw_contentURL=%2F01DB040000000001%2FW26PH8X4229INFODE%2Fcontent.jsp (accessed 18 December 2006).

Messner, P. (2004) "Einsatz in einem Land mit zwei Gesichtern", *Die Bundeswehr – Magazin des Deutschen Bundeswehr Verbandes*, 12: 14–17.

Mey, H. H. (2002) "Herausforderungen für die Bundeswehr", *APuZ*, 24: 3–5.

Meyer, C. W. (1998) "Ein Modell für die Zukunft", *Truppenpraxis/Wehrausbildung*, 42(12): 782–786.

—— (2003) "CIMIC-Konzeption der Bundeswehr", in Meyer, C. W. and Vogt, M. J. (eds) *CIMIC-Faktoren I: Militärische Aspekte*, Speyerer Arbeitsheft No. 155, Speyer: Deutsche Hochschule für Verwaltungswissenschaften Speyer.

Millotat, C. E. O. (2003) "Fortschritt im Kosovo 2003", *ÖMZ*, 41(4): 419–428.

—— (2004) "Neue Wege bei Planung und Durchführung von militärischen Einsätzen bei Friedensmissionen", *Europäische Sicherheit*, 53(10): 8–11.

—— (2005) "Neue Wege bei Planung und Durchführung von militärischen Einsätzen im Rahmen von Friedensmissionen", *ÖMZ*, 43(2): 217–220.

Mockaitis, T. R. (2004) *Civil–Military Cooperation in Peace Operations: The Case of Kosovo*, Carlisle, PA: Strategic Studies Institute, U.S. Army War College. Online, available at: www.carlisle.army.mil/ssi/pdffiles/PUB583.pdf (accessed 19 January 2005).

Münkler, H. (2004) *Die neuen Kriege*, Reinbek near Hamburg: Rowohlt.

North Atlantic Treaty Organisation (1991: *The Alliance's Strategic Concept Agreed by the Heads of State and Government Participating in the Meeting of the North Atlantic Council*, Rome, 8 November 1991. Online, available at: www.nato.int/docu/basictxt/b911108b.htm (accessed 22 March 2005).

—— (2001) *MC 411/1: NATO Military Policy on Civil–Military Co-operation*, 17 July 2001, Brussels. Online, available at: www.nato.int/ims/docu/mc411-1-e.htm (accessed 27 April 2004).

—— (2003) *AJP-9 NATO Civil–Military Co-operation (CIMIC) Doctrine*, June 2003, Brussels. Online, available at: www.nato.int/ims/docu/AJP-9.pdf (accessed 28 April 2004).

—— (2004a) *International Military Staff, Civil–military Co-operation*, 27 April 2004. Online, available at: www.nato.int/ims/docu/cimic.htm (accessed 28 April 2004).

—— (2004b) *Liaison and Observation Teams of SFOR*, September 2004. Online, available at: www.nato.int/sfor/factsheet/lot/t040909a.htm (accessed 4 March 2005).

—— (2005) *Inside KFOR. Commander KFOR Press Conference*, 10 June 2005. Online, available at: www.nato.int/kfor/inside/2005/06/i050613b.htm (accessed 18 December 2006).

Peace Through Law Education Fund (PTLEF) (2002) *A Force for Peace and Security – U.S. and Allied Commanders' Views of the Military's Role in Peace Operations and the Impact on Terrorism of States in Conflict*. Online, available at: ftp.ptlef.org/A%20Force%20for%20Peace%20&%20Security.pdf (accessed 28 April 2004).

Platzer, C. (2005) "Taktik im Kosovo: Konsequenzen nach den Märzunruhen", *Truppendienst*, no. 282. Online, available at: www.bmlv.gv.at/truppendienst/ausgaben/artikel.php?id=325 (accessed 30 May 2005).

Pollick, S. (2000) "Civil–Military Cooperation: A New Tool for Peacekeepers", *Canadian Military Journal*, 1(3): 57–63.

Pradetto, A. (2004) "Von der Anarchie zur Zivilisation – Deutschlands neue internationale Rolle", lecture at the 49th General Conference of Protestant Military Chaplains in Bad Honnef, *zur sache.bw – Evangelische Kommentare zu Fragen der Zeit*, 5: 4–11.

Pugh, M. (2000) "Civil–Military Relations in the Kosovo Crisis: An Emerging Hegemony?", *Security Dialogue*, 31(2): 229–242.

Pütger, T. (2002) "Für alle Ethnien – KFOR – Das Bürgerbüro des CIMIC Bataillons in Prizren blickt auf eine mehr als sechsmonatige Erfolgsgeschichte zurück", *aktuell – Zeitung für die Bundeswehr*, 38(22): 12. Online, available at: www.bundeswehr.de/C1256EF40036B05B/vwContentByKey/N264JF8C821MMISDE/$File/BWAKTUELL_0222.PDF (accessed 9 March 2005).

von Randow, G. and Stelzenmüller, C. (2000) "Zivis fürs Grobe", *Die Zeit*, 12: 15–17.

Rehse, P. (2004) *CIMIC: Concepts, Definitions and Practice*, Hamburger Beiträge zur Friedensforschung und Sicherheitspolitik, Heft 136, Hamburg: Institut für Friedensforschung und Sicherheitspolitik an der Universität Hamburg (IFSH). Online, available at: www.ifsh.de/pdf/publikationen/hb/hb136.pdf (21 March 2005).

Reinhardt, K. (2002) *KFOR – Streitkräfte für den Frieden – Tagebuchaufzeichnungen als deutscher Kommandeur im Kosovo*, 2nd edn, Frankfurt (Main): Verlag der Universitätsbuchhandlung Blazek und Bergmann seit 1891.

Rollins, J. W. (2001) "Civil–Military Cooperation (CIMIC) in Crisis Response Operations: The Implications for NATO", *International Peacekeeping*, 8(1): 122–129.

Rosenbauer, C. and Kreis, M. (2005) "Neue Wege der Bundeswehr in der Zivil-Militärischen Zusammenarbeit im Inland", *Europäische Sicherheit*, 54(12): 42–46.

Schneiderhan, W. (2005) "Ziel der Transformation ist die Verbesserung der Einsatzfähigkeit", *Europäische Sicherheit* 54(2): 22–32.

Siegel, A. B. (2000) "Postconflict Problems", *Marine Corps Gazette*, February 2000: 36–38.

—— (2001) "Eyewitness: Associating Development Projects with Military Operations: Lessons from NATO's First Year of Operations in Bosnia-Herzegovina", *International Peacekeeping* 8(3): 99–114.

Stelzenmüller, C. (2002) "Frieden, Freiheit, Horoskope – Schreiben statt Panzer fahren: Im Kosovo machen deutsche Soldaten eine Zeitung auf Albanisch – und werben so für die Demokratie", *Die Zeit* 26: 74.

Streitkräfteamt (SKA) (2003) "Streitkräftebasis: Verstärkung der aktiven Truppe im Auslandseinsatz der Bundeswehr – Reservisten als Fachkräfte in der CIMIC-Organisation", in BMVg (ed.) *Informationsdienst für Reservisten*, 1: 5.

Studer, M. (2000) "Co-operation between civilians and military during humanitarian crises in a historical and political context", paper presented at the Caritas Europa – APRODEV Workshop "The role of the military and the role of humanitarian aid organizations in emergencies", Norway, 8 May 2000.

Study Group on Europe's Security Capabilities (2004) "A Human Security Doctrine for Europe", The Barcelona Report of the Study Group on Europe's Security Capabilities presented to the EU High Representative for Common Foreign and Security Policy Javier Solana, Barcelona, 15 September 2004.

Svensson, J. (2005) "Absorption Capacity and Disbursement Constraints", paper prepared for the 2005 Agence Française de Développement (AFD) – European Development Research Network (EUDN) Conference "Financing Development: What Are the Challenges in Expanding Aid Flows?", Paris, 14 December 2005. Online, available at: www.eudnet.net/download/Svensson.pdf (accessed 19 December 2006).

Tarry, S. (2002) "Demystifying Non-Governmental Organizations in Peace Support Operations", *Canadian Military Journal*, 3(4): 33–38.

Thürnau, J. (2005a) *Hilfe zur Selbsthilfe – Der Agrarwirtschaftstrupp berät Landwirte*, 28 January 2005. Online, available at: www.deutschesheer.de/redaktionen/heer/internet/Contentbase2.nsf/docname/B41A20455631A3DAC1256F7A00447864 (accessed 3 February 2005).

—— (2005b) *DRITARJA und PROZOR – Soldaten der Multinationalen Brigade Süd-West informieren die Zivilbevölkerung*, 28 January 2005. Online, available at: www.deutschesheer.de/redaktionen/heer/internet/Contentbase2.nsf/docname/7146A252AF795181C1256F7A004821F0 (accessed 15 February 2005).

Traub, J. (2004) "Making Sense of the Mission", *New York Times Magazine*, Late Edition – Final, 11 April 2004: 32.

Vogelaar, A. L. W. and E. H. Kramer (2004) "Mission Command in Dutch Peace Support Missions", *Armed Forces and Society*, 30(3): 409–431.

Voget, B. G. (2004a) "Im Flecktarn zum Düngerstreuen – CIMIC-Kompanie hilft beim Aufbau eines Agrarinformationszentrums im Kosovo", *MAZ&More – Feldzeitung der Bundeswehr für das Kosovo und Mazedonien*, 278: 5.

—— (2004b) "In Eintracht stark: Sieben auf den ersten Streich – Erste Genossenschaftsgründungen im Kosovo sind rechtsgültig", *MAZ&More – Feldzeitung der Bundeswehr für das Kosovo und Mazedonien*, 282: 4.

Voll, H.-J. (2005) "Das neue Heer – Chancen und Zukunftsfähigkeit im Rahmen des Transformationsprozesses", *Strategie und Technik*, March 2005: 20–24.

Vorhofer, P. (2003) "Civil–Military Cooperation – Zur Evolution einer neuen Aufgabe in der Krisenbewältigung", *ÖMZ*, 41(6): 753–759.

Widder, W. (2002) "Auftragstaktik and Innere Führung: Trademarks of German Leadership", *Military Review*, September–October 2002 (English Edition): 3–9.

Yrayzoz, J. (2003) "MNB Southwest distributes 35,000 magazines", *KFOR Chronicle*, 31 October 2003. Online, available at: www.nato.int/kfor/chronicle/2003/chronicle_01/10.htm accessed (17 February 2005).

8 CIMIC on the edge

Afghanistan and the evolution of civil–military operations

*Michael McNerney**

Introduction

September 14, 2001: The Pentagon smoldered. Officials inside planned for war. Yet US Secretary of Defense Donald Rumsfeld also emphasized to some of his senior staff that day the important role humanitarian assistance would play in the impending operations in Afghanistan.

The United Nations World Food Program stated in July 2001 that Afghanistan was facing a famine and millions of lives were at risk (UN WFP). A National Intelligence Council report from early September 2001 described a humanitarian emergency in Afghanistan, estimating that five million Afghans were in need of assistance (NIC, pp. 5–6). US military success in Afghanistan might be a Pyrrhic victory if Afghanistan's humanitarian situation were to deteriorate further. For both strategic and moral reasons, the United States could not ignore (or worse, exacerbate) the plight of millions of civilians during the conduct of a military operation. In this context, military and humanitarian activities could not be separate or sequential.

The conventional wisdom of war and assistance is that civilian assistance providers undertake humanitarian activities after combat operations have ceased. In Afghanistan, both military and civilian assistance providers would work simultaneously – if not always side by side. At the height of coalition bombing, the United Nations vaccinated five million Afghan children against polio. Military forces dropped food aid as well as bombs. Later, civilian government officials (diplomats, development experts, and agriculture experts) lived and worked with soldiers (civil affairs, special forces, infantry) in remote and dangerous towns around Afghanistan.

Welcome to the non-linear battlefield

NATO defines civil–military cooperation (CIMIC) as "the co-ordination and co-operation, in support of the mission, between the NATO Commander and civil actors ..." (NATO MC 411/1, p. 1). US military doctrine defines Civil Military Operations (CMO) in a similar if slightly more military-centric fashion: "the activities of a commander that establish, maintain, influence, or exploit relations between military forces ... civilian organizations...and the civilian populace" (JP 3–57, p. I–1). The American term CMO is often simply considered inter-changeable with CIMIC, as NATO and US doctrine do not make comparisons of these terms. While there are in fact differences between these terms in theory and practice, this chapter will focus primarily on the evolution of CMO and how CIMIC and CMO must continue to evolve for the twenty-first century non-linear battlefield.

US military doctrine categorizes four operational phases of war: Deter/ Engage (pre-conflict), Seize Initiative (start of operation), Decisive Operations, and Transition (Post-Conflict). CIMIC and CMO apply to all four phases of war and to "military operations other than war." Moreover, they apply to a non-linear battlefield like Operation Enduring Freedom in Afghanistan, in which the phases of war are blurred (NATO AJP 9, pp. 1–1 to 1–3 & 3–1; JP 3–57, pp. I–1 to I–2). Nevertheless, the perception in the 1990s was that CIMIC and CMO focused on supporting the host nation in the post-conflict phase, and were nor-mally conducted on the basis of a formal agreement related to the cessation of hostilities. Operation Enduring Freedom shattered that perception.

The concept of "CIMIC on the edge" is really about civil military operations in extremely fluid and relatively insecure environments. The Commandant of the US Marine Corps in 1997, General Charles Krulak, articulated the concept of the "three block war" to describe a situation that occurs all too frequently on the non-linear battlefield: "... our service members will be ... providing humanitar-ian assistance ... conducting peacekeeping operations and ... fighting a highly lethal mid-intensity battle – all on the same day, all within three city blocks.... It is an environment born of change" (Krulak, pp. 139–141. See also Collins, p. 2). The commander of Operation Iraqi Freedom, General John Abizaid, told House Armed Services Committee members in March 2005: "We have to design our armed forces for the 360-degree battlefield and not the linear battlefield" (Grier). Though it uses less colorful language, US joint military doctrine reflects these concepts, as well (JP 3–0, p. I–4). Counter-insurgency is the most obvious illus-tration of a non-linear battlefield, but the conflict in Afghanistan – starting with its Special Forces-coordinated uprisings throughout the country – has been non-linear since it began in October 2001.

Many CIMIC approaches used in traditional peace operations like those in the Balkans must be adjusted for the non-linear battlefield. As the United States and its coalition partners experienced in Afghanistan and Iraq, conflicts in the twenty-first century will increasingly be asymmetric and take place on a non-linear battlefield (Metz). Doctrinal distinctions between the Decisive Operations phase and Post-Conflict missions and operations are far less relevant when western powers engage in combat with failed or rogue states. Why? (1) Western powers – for political and moral reasons – often must conduct humanitarian operations simultaneously with combat operations and have strong interests in quickly initiating reconstruction activities in their adversary's country; and (2) asymmetric combat can quickly lead to insurgency situations, since this is the only viable strategy for an outmatched foe. Insurgency is a political phenomenon, not just a military one, and its center of gravity is not a combat force but the general population. Insurgency plays havoc with terms like "decisive operation" and "post-conflict," and it blurs the lines between warfighters, peacekeepers/stabilization forces, civilian government officials, and non-governmental assistance-providers.

Two principles that are also important on more linear battlefields must guide CMO on the non-linear battlefield: decentralization and integration. Decentralization means putting people close to the action and enabling them to be decisive and assertive. Change and insecurity dominate the non-linear battlefield, so those on that battlefield must constantly adapt while remaining bold in their actions. Integration means maximizing the degree to which military and civilian actors plan and execute their missions jointly. Unity of effort is a core principle for CIMIC and CMO doctrine (NATO AJP-9 p. 2–1 and JP 3–57 pp. I–1 to I–7). Yet in practice unity of effort in the civil–military context usually means military and civilian leaders take cautious, parallel steps toward common goals, while emphasizing information-sharing. Cautious, parallel efforts on the non-linear battlefield are a recipe for failure.

An analysis of CMO in Afghanistan provides important insights into the need for more innovative and complex approaches than those pursued in military operations in the 1990s. The 1991 Gulf War was the model for the preferred American way of war: short, straightforward, and linear. Operation Enduring Freedom would be none of those things. At the end of 2001, Afghanistan had suffered generations of warlords, ethnic tensions, and factionalism; 23 years of war; five years of Taliban repression and mismanagement; and four years of drought. Military operations and civilian-led humanitarian and reconstruction activities would require boldness and an extraordinary degree of integration. Although breaking the Taliban's hold on Afghanistan would prove relatively easy, providing humanitarian assistance, security, and good governance to the Afghan people presented a foreign policy challenge more difficult than anything America had faced since Vietnam.

This chapter will illustrate the evolution of US civil–military operations in the past 15 years, culminating with CMO on the non-linear battlefield of Afghanistan. First, it will review CIMIC and CMO experiences and doctrine from the 1990s. The 1990s taught important CMO lessons about the importance of coordination, logistics, perseverance, balancing goals and force commitment, and a clear definition of roles and responsibilities. In addition, painful lessons relevant to CMO on the non-linear battlefield were learned while experiencing the differences between peacekeeping and peace enforcement. Second, the chapter will describe and assess civil–military planning and operations on the non-linear battlefield of Afghanistan particularly from 2001–2004 at the strategic, operational, and tactical levels. Third, the chapter's conclusion will review CMO lessons from Afghanistan in light of the future security environment and provide some recommendations for policy-makers and for future research. A common mistake is to look at CMO in the context of CMO rather than in the broader context of politics, military strategy, and the operating environment itself. CMO is a strategic, operational, and tactical tool. Understanding how this tool should be used is ultimately far more important than the details of the tool itself. The question, "how can we improve CMO performance?" is less important than "how can we make CMO more relevant to achieving the overall goal?"

CIMIC/CMO experiences and doctrine in the 1990s

Despite the fact that the dawn of the 1990s presented the United States with combat operations, the decade was, for the most part, the decade of peace operations. The United States led such operations in Somalia, Haiti, Bosnia, and Kosovo, and played smaller roles in United Nations peacekeeping efforts around the world.

The US military combat plan for its December 1989 invasion of Panama, "Just Cause," was well planned and well executed (Donnelly *et al.* pp. 398–400). The CMO plan "Blind Logic," which focused on post-conflict reconstruction, was poorly planned and poorly executed (See Shultz, Joint History Office, pp. 71–72, and Donnelly *et al.* pp. 374–379 and 400–401). The commander-in-chief ("CINC") of US military operations in Latin America, General Maxwell R. Thurman, stated "I did not even spend five minutes on Blind Logic during my briefing as the incoming CINC in August" (Shultz, p. 16.). The weaknesses of CMO in supporting the post-conflict reconstruction effort in Panama were quickly forgotten by most US and international observers, however. There was no humanitarian crisis or insurgency. Most importantly, because the Panama operation did not take place in the context of a global threat to US vital interests, the stakes in Panamanian state-building were not perceived to be high. "Hit and run" military operations seemed to be the recipe for success.

The February 1991 Gulf War, Operation Desert Storm, reinforced the perception that US-led wars in the new world order would be fast, clean, and linear (See Gordon and Trainor). There would be plenty of post-conflict reconstruction to be done, but for the most part it was not a job for the military. Commanding General Norman Schwarzkopf's deputy, Lieutenant General John Yeosock, recalled the end of combat operations: "The impetus became, how fast can you get (American troops) out of there, and are we going to get them all back for the Washington parade..." Because troops were "fighting in a big sandbox, clearly out of population centers," CMO in Desert Storm was relatively straightforward and limited to the post-conflict phase (Donnelly, 2004, pp. xiv–xv). US civil affairs soldiers played an important role assisting in Kuwait's recovery from the end of February through the end of April 1991 (Scales, p. 337). But their role was short-lived, as civilian authorities and the private sector quickly took over.

In April 1991, with hundreds of thousands of Kurdish refugees trapped between Saddam Hussein's military and a closed Turkish border, the United States first air-dropped food and relief supplies and then – under pressure from Turkey, the United Kingdom, and France – established a militarily protected enclave for the Kurds in northern Iraq (DiPrizio, pp. 22 and 39). Operation Provide Comfort eventually involved 20,000 troops from six countries and provided humanitarian relief and security for Kurds throughout northern Iraq, including 500,000 refugees in 43 camps operated by coalition forces (FM 100–23, p. 10 and FM 41–10, para. 1–3). CMO played a major role in Operation Provide Comfort, but because of the relatively secure environment and straightforward humanitarian mission, CMO was mostly about logistics – transporting and distributing supplies, organizing camps, etc.[1]

The CMO lessons from Panama and Iraq in the early 1990s fit well with US military doctrine. Overwhelming force led to quick and clear military victories, followed by assistance efforts that transitioned rapidly to civilian organizations. The United Nations also had reasons for optimism in the early 1990s, leading successful peacekeeping operations in Namibia, El Salvador, Cambodia, and Mozambique between 1989 and 1993 (Dobbins 2005, pp. xvi–xvii). The lessons of Somalia would prove to be far more complex – and painful – for both organizations.

Operation Restore Hope in Somalia was a humanitarian mission but included 28,000 American troops to successfully establish a secure environment for providing assistance. Military and civilian actors worked effectively together throughout the operation. One of the most important CMO initiatives was the establishment of the Civil–Military Operations Center (CMOC), "the key coordinating point between the task force and humanitarian relief organizations" (NDU p. 69). Less than five months later, however, the humanitarian assistance mission became something else – a feeble peace enforcement mission perhaps, and a limited disarmament, demobilization and reintegration campaign. The international community gave the UN a broader mandate but fewer troops – mostly poorly-equipped Pakistanis. Using three separate chains of command, the United States contributed a CMO/logistics force, a quick-reaction force, and later a special operations force to capture the Mogadishu warlord Mohamed Farah Aideed, who was responsible for attacks on UN peacekeepers. A more aggressive mandate with fewer troops and confusing chains of command proved to be a recipe for disaster. The relatively successful, "traditional" CMO in Panama and Iraq had limited utility in the context of Somalia, where the security situation and extent of the humanitarian problem were quite different. Moreover, even effective CMO was irrelevant in a political context that combined ambitious goals with insufficient commitment.

The United States followed the same strategy in its 1994 Haiti intervention – Operation Uphold Democracy – as it did for Restore Hope: apply overwhelming force against limited objectives for a short period of time. But this time, there would be no "mission creep" similar to what happened in Somalia. US-led forces quelled the violence, restored the deposed President Aristide, and helped oversee elections. They conducted CMO, supporting disarmament, police and judicial reform, infrastructure repair, and health and sanitation projects. In light of its effectiveness in Somalia, the military established a Civil–Military Operations Center to coordinate actions of the UN, NGOs, and military. Civil affairs units were decentralized, operating in ten areas of the country. They also supported capacity-building, assigning soldiers to various ministries to provide advice on governance issues (Dobbins 2003, pp. 74–77, Weiss, pp. 186–187, and DiPrizio, p. 93). Despite these initial successes, CMO efforts were fruitless because the overall mission was ultimately unsuccessful. Operation Restore Democracy focused more on short-term stability than the root causes of Haiti's problems: weak democratic institutions and endemic corruption. As US involvement waned, Haiti reverted back to poor governance and lawlessness. Nevertheless, at the time the US government considered the operation to be a success: "The mission was clearly defined. An exit strategy was identified and adhered to. Transfer to UN authority occurred according to schedule. Interagency political–military planning occurred at a higher and more integrated level than in any earlier similar operation" (NDU 1996, p. 48).

Experiences in Panama, northern Iraq, Somalia, and Haiti were improving US CMO capabilities. Interagency coordination was improving at the strategic level and civil–military operations centers and other innovations were improving tactical coordination. But these improvements occurred in a US political context that sought to minimize risk through overwhelming force and narrowly-defined, short missions, or – preferably – avoiding missions completely that did not directly threaten US vital interests. Doctrine also improved. In 1994, the United States published Field Manual 100–23, Peace Operations, which included important distinctions between peacekeeping and peace enforcement, as well as guidance on the role of civil–military operations centers. Doctrine for civil–military operations overall, however, remained limited, particularly in its ability to describe a non-linear operating environment (FM 100–23).

While the United States focused on Somalia and Haiti, the UN and European Commission (EC) were learning painful lessons about the difference between peacekeeping and peace enforcement in the former Yugoslavia. While war raged from 1992 to 1995, EC-led UN peacekeepers witnessed numerous atrocities but lacked the authority and capability to take effective action. The UN force of fewer than 10,000 troops may have proved useful in a peacekeeping operation, in which there was consent between the warring parties to end the conflict. But they were helpless in a peace enforcement situation. Because CIMIC efforts must advance the larger strategic mission and are not an end in themselves, they were of limited value in an environment of strategic impotence.

The US military argued forcefully against any involvement in this period, estimating the need for over 500,000 troops to protect aid and enforce peace effectively. The US government consistently resisted sending American troops into a high-risk, conflict-ridden environment (Weiss, pp. 109–110 and DiPrizio pp. 103 and 119). But as human suffering worsened and public awareness grew, the US government decided to lead a more robust military and diplomatic effort to end the fighting. The combination of more effective Croatian and Bosnian military operations and US-led NATO airstrikes, forced the Serbs to the bargaining table. For all its weaknesses, the Dayton Accord and subsequent deployment of 60,000 troops stopped the fighting and created an environment conducive to CMO and reconstruction activities (Dobbins 2003, p. 95).

CMO and CIMIC doctrine and approaches developed tremendously in Bosnia in terms of sophistication. CMO depends perhaps more than anything else on the strategic context in which it takes place. For all the continuing problems there, perhaps the greatest reason for Bosnia's relative success was the US abandonment of short deadlines. A critical lesson of Bosnia that allowed CMO to be effective was that "instead of obsessing about the exit, planners should concentrate on the strategy" (Rose, p. 56). Both US and European forces undertook countless CMO/CIMIC activities in Bosnia, and their approaches and principles were in many ways similar: create conditions that support strategic objectives, avoid duplication of effort with civilian organizations, maximize the use of civil resources, improve civilian perceptions of the military force, understand local culture, establish common goals, clearly define roles and responsibilities, and make every effort to maintain consent and communicate clearly. These principles shaped much of current US and NATO CMO/CIMIC doctrine and policy (JP 3–57 and NATO AJP-9).

There was, however, one important difference between US and European styles that can best be described as attitude. One US military commander summarized the American attitude in a review of his Bosnia deployment: "It is always a combat mission" (Scaparrotti, p. 78). At the most basic level, the US military conducted CMO – and its other operations – with more of a "war-fighting" attitude than their European counterparts. This US attitude impeded the mission at times, with US forces being perceived by Bosnian civilians as unapproachable and threatening, compared to European troops. Moreover, some US commanders were instructed that "if mission and force protection are in conflict, then we don't do the mission" (Boot, p. 326). Stereotypes emerged of grim-faced American soldiers in full battle gear (mocked by some Europeans as "ninja turtles") contrasted with British soldiers in "soft caps" kicking soccer balls with local children. While US troops approached this peacekeeping mission as if it were a peace enforcement operation, many US allies had shown the opposite tendency: approaching peace enforcement operations as if they were peacekeeping (Cassidy, pp. 2 and 231–233). CMO requires a war-fighting attitude (and capability) that manifests itself – paradoxically – in a humane, sensitive, "peace-building" approach to the local population. The US military improved (though by no means perfected) its ability to balance a war-fighting attitude and peace-building approach in Bosnia, thanks in part to the long duration of its involvement there. The British military, because of its experiences with small wars and as evidenced by its relative successes in Afghanistan (see below) perhaps manages this balance best (Author's interviews, Cassidy, pp. 12–13, and 231–233, and Martin, 2003). Such a balance is even more important on the non-linear battlefield, as Operations Enduring Freedom and Iraqi Freedom would show.

The United States would lead another long-term NATO intervention in the Balkans, starting in March 1999 with a 78-day bombing campaign. Almost 900,000 Kosovar Albanians fled Kosovo for neighboring countries during the bombing. US-led forces executed combat operations and humanitarian assistance simultaneously in Kosovo, just as they would in Afghanistan in 2001. Yet,

Kosovo – like Panama, Iraq, Haiti, and post-Dayton Bosnia – was a relatively linear battlefield. The military conducted CMO to assist Kosovar refugees during the bombing, but only in neighboring countries (and in the US state of New Jersey, where Kosovar refugees admitted to America were processed). NATO deployed a robust security force of 50,000 troops into Kosovo, but only after reaching an agreement with Serbian President Slobodan Milosevic. CMO took place in the context of clear combat/post-combat phases and secure operating environments (PKI, pp. 2–4, Daalder and O'Hanlon, pp. 124–125, and Dobbins 2003, pp. 111–112).

US CMO was extensive in Bosnia and Kosovo. For example, the US Army reported a typical week in Kosovo included 6–7 medical/dental projects, 8–10 civil affairs/humanitarian assistance projects, 7,500–9,000 information products distributed, 19 radio and 2 TV shows, 1,043 security patrols, and 50–55 contacts with local leaders or officials from the UN, NGOs, or the Kosovo Force (PKI, p. 6). While CMO doctrine and activities were clearly improving by the end of the 1990s, they remained far from perfect. Although the use of civil–military operations centers improved communication between the military and civilian organizations, coordination remained problematic. CMO doctrine was still inadequate and not fully in synch with NATO doctrine. Military education and training regarding CMO was also weak. Most importantly, CMO was consistently under resourced (PKI, pp. 32 and 36).

Despite these weaknesses, US CMO in Kosovo – as in Bosnia – was ultimately effective for three reasons: (1) CMO activities reinforced strategic goals, supporting peace accord terms and post-conflict governance structures; (2) civil and military efforts have been sustained over a long period of time; and (3) US forces conducted peacekeeping operations but were prepared for peace enforcement. This third reason – a reflection of the war-fighting attitude described earlier – meant that the US force in Kosovo was robust and equipped to fight. The advantages of this attitude were evident to the author during a visit to Kosovo a few weeks after extensive and violent ethnic riots in March 2004. Witnesses described how US soldiers were proactive and forceful in the face of rioting, pre-empting more severe violence, while other observers noted that a number of military units from other countries were passive and ineffective (Author's discussions. See also Donald, p. 127, HRW, and Amnesty).

This war-fighting attitude must always be balanced with a peace-building approach, however. As in Bosnia, the US military in Kosovo over-emphasized force protection, particularly in the first few years of the operation. Only the UK established an extensive presence and information network in its Balkans operations, using small teams to conduct frequent "soft cap" foot patrols. The UK, therefore, had better situational awareness and stronger influence with local communities and leaders (Donald, p. 127).

Another key difference between US and European approaches is the US use of specialized civil affairs units, primarily reservists, and the propensity of most European militaries to conduct CIMIC with general purpose forces and view their personnel as "all-rounders." Specialized units have the advantage of bringing greater expertise to their activities, particularly when members of these units bring relevant experiences to bear from their civilian careers. As this chapter will discuss, however, civil affairs units risk creating an impression that CMO is basically separate from the primary war-fighting mission. This risk can become particularly problematic in non-linear, hostile environments like Afghanistan.

At the close of the 1990s, the United Nations took a hard look at its perform-ance in peace operations and proposed a number of improvements relevant to CMO. The August 2000 Report of the Panel on United Nations Peace Opera-tions (the "Brahimi Report") included recommendations to improve rapid deployment capability, improve the effectiveness of UN Civilian Police, and develop an exportable legal code to be used during the law and order gap between the cessation of major combat and reconstruction. Brahimi argued, "no amount of good intentions can substitute for the fundamental ability to project credible force," but also noted that "force alone cannot create peace..." (Brahimi). Despite some initial momentum and a few structural changes in the UN, the Brahimi process stalled after the fall of the World Trade Center Towers. Following the US-led Coalition's toppling of the Taliban government, UN Secretary General Kofi Annan appointed Lakhdar Brahimi to be his Special Representative for Afghanistan. But most of Brahimi's proposed reforms had not yet taken hold, and the UN did not use Afghanistan as the place to experi-ment with a significant military and bureaucratic presence.

Understanding and countering the conventional military capabilities of states that might threaten vital interests is not sufficient in the twenty-first century threat environment. The non-linear battlefield requires that the military achieve success not only in high-intensity combat, but across the full spectrum of mili-tary operations. This full spectrum includes CMO missions, which traditionally have been considered to be of secondary importance: providing humanitarian assistance; liaising with local leaders and other civilians; conducting psychologi-cal operations; assessing regional political actors and events; and advising, train-ing, and liaising with foreign militaries. The experiences of the 1990s partially prepared us for the non-linear battlefield, as exhibited by enhanced military doc-trine, improvements in CMO execution, and the Brahimi Report, but there remained tremendous room for improvement at the start of Operation Enduring Freedom in Afghanistan.

Afghanistan is different from every US military operation in the 1990s because of the combination of vital interests, the role of CMO, and the non-linearity of the battlefield. Although there were powerful arguments behind each of America's military operations in the 1990s, none addressed vital national interests comparable to Operation Enduring Freedom: America's response to a direct attack on the homeland. CMO should have been a critical component of all the operations reviewed here – Panama, Northern Iraq, Somalia, Haiti, Bosnia, and Kosovo. In Panama, CMO was important on the ground but strategically neglected. In Northern Iraq and Somalia, CMO was integral but basically limited to humanitarian efforts. In Haiti, CMO was important but ulti-mately futile. Only in Bosnia and Kosovo was CMO truly critical. And only in

Somalia did the United States get a clear preview of just how challenging the twenty-first century non-linear battlefield would be.

CMO in Afghanistan

> The first, the supreme, the most far-reaching act of judgment that the statesman and commander have to make is to establish ... the kind of war on which they are embarking.
>
> (Clausewitz p.88)

Because of the experiences of the 1990s, CIMIC/CMO is sometimes misperceived – perhaps even by some governments and individual military personnel – as "humanitarianism in military uniforms." But, as both NATO and US doctrine emphasizes, CIMIC/CMO is first and foremost about building relationships between military commanders and civilian actors, in support of the overall political–military mission. Those civilian actors include government and UN officials, NGOs, and – most importantly for the non-linear battlefield – the local population. Humanitarian activities are just one important tool to help CMO and CIMIC practitioners build those relationships. There is no question that Secretary Rumsfeld was deeply concerned about the humanitarian impact of impending Coalition military operations when he ordered that humanitarian assistance be a central component of planning for Operation Enduring Freedom. But the goal of Operation Enduring Freedom was not to provide humanitarian assistance. The goal was to eliminate the Taliban government and al-Qaeda and help Afghanistan establish a stable, democratic government. CMO would be a means to that end – a military and political end, not a humanitarian end. CMO would play crucial and very visible roles from the start of the US-led bombing campaign through the insurgency that followed.

CMO success, however, was mixed. Clausewitz would perhaps argue that statesmen and commanders alike embarked upon a war in Afghanistan that required greater attention to post-Taliban stabilization and reconstruction. Recalling the four operational phases of war (Deter/Engage, Seize Initiative, Decisive Operations, and Transition/Post-conflict), one might argue that the phases were not only blurred in Afghanistan, but were transformed relative to traditional thinking about what each phase entails. The US Marine Corps Small Wars Manual states, "Adversaries will avoid fighting on terms that would allow them to be attrited into submission by overwhelming force – the prototypical American way of fighting conventional wars ...." Therefore, "...if our political objectives can only be accomplished after a successful stability phase, then the stability phase is, de facto, the decisive phase." Army doctrine is consistent with this concept, though most people still equate Decisive Operations with major combat (USMC pp. 4–5 and FM 3–07 ch.1 p. 3).

CMO until the fall of the Taliban government

With only about three weeks to plan before the October 7, 2001 start of military operations in Afghanistan, the US government established an interagency team to set a strategic framework for humanitarian assistance activities, including civil–military operations. The United States was embarking on a war in which successful CMO was critical to the mission and the mission was critical to national security (For a detailed assessment of CMO in Afghanistan during the first year of military operations, see Flavin. For a look at the interactions between military and civilian assistance providers in the first few months of the conflict, see Oliker *et al.* and Collins and McNerney).

The interagency team met daily and included representatives from the National Security Council, Office of the Secretary of Defense (including the author), Joint Staff, State Department, and US Agency for International Development (USAID). They established goals of minimizing the impact of combat operations on humanitarian efforts and civilians and facilitating the provision of humanitarian assistance by every feasible means. They tracked the humanitarian situation and ongoing relief efforts and made sure humanitarian issues remained a high priority for the US leadership. But perhaps their most important decision was to avoid micromanagement of CMO and allow the center of gravity for decision-making to quickly shift to the operational level – US Central Command (CENTCOM).

By early October 2001, CENTCOM established an unprecedented cell of advisors from the military, State Department, USAID, UN, and non-governmental organization (NGO) community to enhance civil–military cooperation prior to and during combat in Afghanistan. The Department of Defense had published joint doctrine on CMO in February 2001, which provided guidance for creating a Joint Civil Military Operations Task Force (JCMOTF) (JP 3–57 pp. II–17 to II–21). CENTCOM's army component – US Army Forces Central Command – established a JCMOTF (which later evolved into a Coalition Joint Civil Military Operations Task Force or CJCMOTF), and it was tied closely to this cell of advisors. To future historians, it may appear that the new doctrine drove this enhanced level of cooperation among military and civilian communities. As is often the case, however, much of the innovation derived from "bright ideas" developed in random conversations, e.g.: "We should send some of our interagency team from Washington to CENTCOM.... You should call your colleague at the UN and see if he'd be willing to go to CENTCOM..."

Thus, thanks partly to doctrine and partly to spontaneous innovation, the two principles of "CIMIC on the edge" – decentralization and integration – were implemented extremely well at CENTCOM. There were three roles planned for CENTCOM's CMO during the impending combat in Afghanistan: (1) direct provision of humanitarian assistance ("retail" assistance), (2) transportation of relief supplies on behalf of aid providers ("wholesale" assistance), and (3) coordination.

Direct assistance came in the form of 2.4 million humanitarian daily rations (HDRs) and other supplies dropped by US Air Force C-17 aircraft. Initial HDR deliveries served two purposes: feed hungry people and deliver the message that America was at war with terrorists and the Taliban, not the Afghan people. Within the first few weeks, US Special Forces soldiers began guiding the air-drops of HDRs and relief supplies and organized local communities to retrieve them, thereby accomplishing a third objective: building relationships with Afghans (See Collins and McNerney, pp. 192–193).

CMO also included "wholesale" assistance in support of USAID and the UN, using the military's airlift capacity to transport supplies to points of entry along the borders of Afghanistan. In October and November 2001, the US military delivered tens of thousands of blankets, tons of biscuits, and rolls of plastic sheeting to Afghanistan's borders, at which point private contractors and NGOs working for USAID and the UN took the supplies and distributed them within Afghanistan (Ibid). Wholesale assistance like this is fairly rare, since private sector airlift capacity is extensive and cheaper than military airlift. Moreover, while this assistance results in positive press coverage, it does nothing to help CMO implementers build goodwill and trust among local populations. Such goodwill can be a useful benefit in a disaster scenario but is absolutely critical for a non-linear battlefield.

Perhaps the US military's greatest CMO success was in its coordination efforts, which were barely noticed by most outside observers. From Operation Blind Logic in Panama through CMO operations in the 1990s, CMO planning was rarely well integrated with the rest of the military's plans. But from September 2001 until the collapse of the Taliban in December 2001, CMO planners and executers supporting Operation Enduring Freedom in Afghanistan were better integrated not only with the rest of the military but also with civilian actors. The UN was able to deliver historic levels of food aid into Afghanistan, even as the US-led coalition's bombing campaign reached its most intense period in November and December. UNICEF vaccinated five million children for polio in the same period. This level of success would have been impossible without the civil–military coordination that took place at CENTCOM, ensuring that military operations did not hamper relief activities and vice versa. Civilian relief experts provided a perspective and an instant source of information that military oper-ators would otherwise have lacked. These advisors had access to the top military commanders and tied the warfighters to assistance providers far more effectively than in past operations when civilians remained in Washington, DC and New York and coordination took place through occasional visits and phone calls. Although the UN and NGO representatives at CENTCOM left soon after the collapse of the Taliban government, US government civilian agencies continued to maintain representatives at CENTCOM.

Civil–military coordination at the operational level will never be the same, thanks to the CMO successes at the end of 2001. More broadly, the Defense Department has pursued greater civil–military integration at the operational level through the creation of Joint Interagency Coordination Groups. The US military is also working on developing conduits for multinational civil–military coordination at the operational level (JFCOM).

At the tactical level, the United States established a CMOC on October 11, 2001 in Islamabad, Pakistan to facilitate CMO in the field. This group focused initially on monitoring the humanitarian situation, facilitating relief efforts, and serving as a conduit for sharing information on military and humanitarian activities. They served as the eyes, ears, and hands of CENTCOM's CJCMOTF and civil–military advisory cell. But CMO decision-making stayed primarily at CENTCOM until the fall of the Taliban.

CMO during counter-insurgency operations

The Taliban fled Kabul and Kandahar in November 2001. By December, the CMO center of gravity shifted to Kabul. CENTCOM deployed its CJCMOTF to Kabul with the primary task of conducting quick impact projects to accomplish three objectives: minimize the negative effects of combat operations; enhance the credibility of Coalition forces with the Afghan people; and enhance the credibility of the interim Afghan Government (Flavin, p. 19). All three of these objectives centered on building relationships with Afghans, building their trust and confidence in the Coalition and the new government.

Civil Affairs teams set up eight Coalition Humanitarian Liaison Cells (CHLCs) in major towns throughout Afghanistan and began contracting with local workers to implement dozens of assistance projects, e.g. school and medical clinic repairs, well and irrigation digging, and bridge and road repairs. Each CHLC was quite small, with only six to eight Civil Affairs soldiers co-located with Special Forces teams to improve force protection. The Office of the Secretary of Defense provided Overseas Humanitarian Disaster and Civic Aid (OHDACA) funds and guidance on use of the funds, but devolved decision-making authority for individual projects to CENTCOM, which then provided the authority to the field. The CHLCs worked with USAID and later the UN and Afghan Government to ensure the projects did not conflict with civilian agency efforts. For the most part, the CMO effort rested on the relatively small number of civil affairs soldiers in Kabul and at the CHLCs and their OHDACA funds, which were limited to humanitarian activities like school-building and well-drilling and could not be used in support of broader reconstruction efforts like building police stations, providing training, improving communications infrastructure, etc.

The CHLCs looked nothing like the coordination-oriented CMOCs, which had been a key component of CMO since Somalia. While eager to assist Afghan communities and avoid duplication with civilian relief efforts, the CHLCs could not serve as a hub for military-NGO-UN interaction. The CHLCs were part of a combatant force in an insurgency environment. While the CHLCs did develop low-key working relationships with many NGOs, there always remained some distance (and tensions) between the military and NGO communities, given NGO principles of impartiality, and independence. While NGOs might remain independent, the CMO effort had to be integrated with the efforts of the rest of the Coalition military, US Government, UN, and Afghan Government.

By the summer of 2002, it was clear that the Afghan insurgency was not going to fade away. The Coalition military headquarters began to slowly change its focus from combat operations with humanitarian assistance support to stability operations and building the capacity of Afghan institutions. It began to recognize the situation in Afghanistan as a CMO problem that would require a long-term, sustained approach. The CJCMOTF established Civil Affairs Ministerial Teams to advise officials in various Afghan ministries, thereby executing an important CMO (and counter-insurgency) activity that had been previously been ignored (Flavin, p. 22). The CHLCs were too isolated from the rest of the military, political, and economic actors in Afghanistan, too limited in their scope of operations, too few, too small, and too poor. The Provincial Reconstruction Teams (PRTs) first established in December 2002 tried to address these problems, and perhaps epitomize "CIMIC on the edge." The PRTs essentially replaced the CHLCs with teams of 60–100 soldiers plus (eventually) Afghan advisors and representatives from civilian agencies (in the US case, the State Department, USAID, and Department of Agriculture). They reinforced the CIMIC on the edge principles of decentralization and integration, operating remotely but assertively because they combined military, civilian, and host nation actors on a single team (For a detailed discussion of PRTs, see McNerney).

The PRTs were born in an environment of change, so it is not surprising that their mission evolved over time. In addition, each PRT's composition varied over time and depending on its location. A November 2002 briefing from the Coalition headquarters (Coalition Joint Task Force-180) planning cell was vague in its description of the mission: (1) "Monitor..." (2) "Assist ... coordinating bodies" (3) "Facilitate cooperation..." (4) "Facilitate ... extending ITGA (Islamic Transitional Government of Afghanistan) influence through interaction ..." (5) "Provide expert advice...". Its initial organizational chart focused on the military structure, with a dotted line connecting to "Afghan Government, government organizations (e.g. USAID), State Department, NGOs, and UN" actors lumped together at the far end of the page (CJTF-180).

After many months of limited operations, the PRT mission coalesced around three basic objectives: enhancing security, strengthening the reach of the Afghan central government, and facilitating reconstruction. Though they could not simply "create security," they eventually helped diffuse factional fighting, supported deployments of the Afghan National Army and police, conducted patrols, and reinforced security efforts during the disarmament, demobilization, and reintegration process. They strengthened the reach of the Afghan government through Afghan government representatives serving on the PRTs and by providing monitoring, registration, and security support for events like the constitutional convention ("Loya Jirga") and elections. They facilitated reconstruction by funding projects like school repairs or, more importantly over time, by helping the State, USAID, and Department of Agriculture representatives at the PRTs to implement civilian-funded projects.

As they got a better focus and a stronger contingent of civilian representation, the PRTs began to have an impact far greater than the CHLCs. Lieutenant General David Barno recognized the importance of the PRTs when he took over Coalition forces in November 2003. He sped up the establishment of new PRTs, increasing their number from eight to fourteen in less than a year. He also changed the strategic context in ways that made PRTs – and CMO overall – more effective. He adopted a more classic counter-insurgency strategy for his combat forces, dispatching units as small as 40 soldiers to live in Afghan villages rather than conducting raids from the large coalition base at Bagram. He also moved his military headquarters to Kabul to facilitate the integration of military, political, and economic efforts (Schmitt, 2004).

The PRTs, perhaps unintentionally, also served to integrate Coalition efforts with those of the UN and the International Security Assistance Force (ISAF). The UN adopted a "light footprint" approach in Afghanistan, emphasizing its role as one of supporting the Afghan government, not directing international assistance efforts. UN and Coalition officials shared information, but in-depth and open collaboration – so critical at CENTCOM during combat operations in Fall 2001 – was quite limited until UN, Afghan, and Coalition officials began coordinating on issues surrounding the PRTs in 2003. The UN-mandated ISAF deployed to Kabul in January 2002 in what was essentially a peace operations role. For about a year, ISAF limited its contact with Coalition forces because of the latter's status as a combatant.

As the Coalition shifted more of its operations toward stabilization and capacity-building, however, the two military forces began to enhance their coordination. Coordination grew increasingly close as the following events took place in 2003: NATO took over leadership of ISAF in August; the UN authorized expansion of ISAF beyond Kabul in October; and ISAF took over the PRT in Konduz under German leadership in December. NATO recognized the PRTs as an innovative approach to advancing stabilization and CIMIC/CMO goals. NATO used the PRTs to extend ISAF's operations to northern Afghanistan, operating five PRTs by October 2004, and to western Afghanistan with four additional PRTs by September 2005. By July 2006 NATO was operating four PRTs in southern Afghanistan and by November 2006 NATO was operating twelve PRTs in the east. Because PRTs emphasized flexibility in approach, their structure and operations could vary depending on their location and leadership, yet their activities were integrated with Afghanistan's broader political, military, and economic goals.

Assessment

Afghanistan clearly illustrated "CIMIC on the edge" – US Special Forces organizing communities to collect air-dropped relief supplies; food convoys and polio vaccinations proceeding in the midst of a bombing campaign; PRTs funding school repairs by day and repelling rocket attacks by night; soldiers living with civilian government relief experts far from the host nation capital. CMO efforts were innovative (and therefore, because they challenged traditional approaches, controversial) and tried to meet the CIMIC on the edge principles of decentralization and integration. Yet results were mixed.

While by no means perfect (and no good soldier or defense analyst expects perfection), CMO in Afghanistan before the fall of the Taliban government was, overall, an unequivocal success. The degree of coordination between military and civilian actors was unprecedented for an operational command directing combat. With Afghanistan facing famine conditions, this coordination facilitated UN deliveries of historic levels of food assistance at the height of the Coalition bombing campaign.

Airdrops of HDRs and relief supplies built goodwill among many Afghan communities, particularly once Special Forces soldiers supported distribution on the ground. The overall humanitarian benefits of the HDRs were small, yet they fed some Afghans who for a time had no other access to food assistance. Controversies about the utility of food-drops and the color of their packaging (which was changed upon realization that the HDRs were similar in color – though different in size and shape – to a type of cluster bomb submunition the US Air Force was dropping) negated some but certainly not all of the global public relations benefits. (For a full assessment of HDRs, see Oliker *et al.* pp. 41–44.) Military logistical support for USAID and the UN played a small but important role in the relief effort and also resulted in positive press coverage.

CMO success (and relevance) was far more elusive as major combat and humanitarian relief blurred into counter-insurgency and reconstruction. There were strategic, operational, and institutional reasons for CMO shortcomings in Afghanistan. At the strategic level, the UN and United States both adopted a light footprint approach, hoping to avoid the overdependence on external assistance seen in the Balkans and wary of Afghanistan's bloody history with foreign powers in their country. From a practical standpoint, a robust presence in a country as large and rugged as Afghanistan would have required manpower and financial commitments no one in the international community seemed willing to make. Blanketing the country with foreign troops and assistance providers would have been counter-productive and impractical, but the light footprint was too light and caused problems for CMO. Following the CIMIC on the edge principles of decentralization and integration allows small teams to have a disproportionately large impact in their area of operations. But the overly light footprint meant that there were far too few teams and too few civilian officials to work with the military on these teams.

Second, providing humanitarian assistance is just one component of CMO. US leadership strongly supported the humanitarian aspects of CMO during major combat in Afghanistan and for small quick-impact projects thereafter. But CMO-related guidance and funding did not go far beyond DoD's OHDACA account, which is limited to humanitarian activities and should have only been a small component of any CMO effort. This is not to argue that CMO should have led the nation-building effort in Afghanistan, but rather that CMO should have been better integrated into the international community's broader reconstruction and capacity-building efforts. The perception of soldiers in the field, however, was that they were to stay completely out of anything that looked like nation-building (Author's discussions).

Third, the military strategy remained focused for many months on direct action against remnants of Taliban and al-Qaeda fighters rather than shifting to a counter-insurgency approach, which would have placed greater emphasis on CMO. In fact, counter-insurgency and peace operations, which both require a central role for CMO, are more similar than many people would care to admit. The US Marine Corps 2004 *Small Wars Manual* notes that the principles for military operations other than war are "remarkably similar to Sir Robert Thompson's five basic principles of counter-insurgency" (USMC, p. 38). The strategic leaders continued to approach post-Taliban Afghanistan with a combat mindset, even though they were engaged in a war that military doctrine at the time might have considered (ironically) a "military operation other than war."

At the operational level, planners did not follow their own doctrine, which emphasized "the transition from a primarily CA (civil affairs) approach to the broader and over-arching concept of CMO," which should be integrated into overall military planning and operations. Maneuver units are supposed to deploy with civil affairs units attached, but they did not. In fact, initial US divisions deployed to Afghanistan were told their mission was combat and not to expect to come into contact with locals. Particularly in 2002–2003, commanders continued to view CMO as a "civil affairs thing," very much separate from the "main effort" of fighting Taliban and al-Qaeda remnants. The CHLCs implemented their assistance projects, built relationships with local leaders, and achieved real success in improving the attitudes of locals but were almost completely isolated from maneuver units. A notable exception was a Canadian battalion operating with the 101st Airborne Division in Kandahar that conducted its own CIMIC operations and coordinated activities with the Kandahar CHLC with great success (Flavin, pp. 36–37, 40 and JP 3–57 pp. I–3 to I–4). As discussed earlier, specialized units like civil affairs can bring tremendous experience to bear, but only when properly integrated into the overall mission. The "all-rounder" approach of the Canadian military may have given its battalion in Kandahar an advantage over its American counterparts in that instance.

Because CMO was incorrectly perceived as a civil affairs job and of secondary importance, CMO efforts were woefully under-resourced. Since each of the (only) eight CHLCs consisted of a handful of civil affairs and special forces soldiers (who often had their own work to do) with a couple of vehicles and poor communications equipment, their area of impact was extremely limited. The establishment of PRTs improved the situation, but only over the course of many months. Transportation and communications initially remained extremely limited. Civilian agency participants were slow to arrive and upon arrival were often seen at best as advisors and sources of money to help the military accomplish its mission. At worst, they were seen as burdens on an overstretched operations budget. The civilians themselves were often unclear about their mission and ill-equipped to play a strong role. By comparison, the UK-led PRT in

Mazar-e Sharif was relatively well-equipped, had strong representation from multiple agencies, and worked as a team to support both military and civilian objectives. The CHLC/PRT quick impact projects played an important role in building positive relationships with local Afghans, but they were often not "quick" at all. Contracting restrictions and bureaucracy within the Coalition headquarters in Afghanistan often created delays in accessing the funds. Moreover, these OHDACA-funded projects should have been one small part of a much larger and diverse CMO effort. For example, while the UK-led PRT in Mazar-e Sharif made it a priority to support police training, DDR (disarmament, demobilization, and reintegration) and other security sector reform efforts, the PRT in Gardez resisted initial State Department requests for police training assistance. Eventually, PRTs played important roles in security sector reform, elections, and other issues but "OHDACA addiction" limited the scope of CMO efforts in 2002 and 2003.

Institutional limitations were, perhaps, the greatest challenge to effective CMO in Afghanistan. The best operational plans and crisis decision-making are not enough if military and civilian agencies are not organized to succeed. At the risk of abusing one of Secretary Rumsfeld's famous laments, you conduct CMO with the government you have, not the one you wish you had. While CMO doctrine improved after the 1990s, the US military failed to educate and train its (non-CA) forces adequately for CMO. And although doctrine emphasizes that CMO is the responsibility of every commander, there is precious little guidance explaining what that means. NATO and European Union (EU) CIMIC doctrine does a better job in this regard (NATO AJP-9 and EU). In addition, there are lessons to be learned from US allies. For example, the UK and Canadian militaries don't have separate civil affairs specialists but have done a particularly good job making CIMIC integral to their overall operations. This is not to argue that the US military should abandon civil affairs as the core of its CMO efforts, but rather that CMO is far more useful to the overall political and military mission when the rest of the military understands CMO and knows how to use it.

US CMO doctrine must evolve to a new level and take on an interagency perspective, not just a military perspective. The CIMIC on the edge principle of integration does not mean integrating civilian actors into military operations, but rather integrating civilian and military actors to reinforce each other's operations on behalf of a unified political–military mission. A number of US civilians complained that the military often ignored or ran roughshod over other actors. One retired army colonel argued that the attitude of many in the US military was "we are not here to support other agencies – we know how to do this better than you" (Author's interviews).

Unfortunately, civilian agencies have even farther to go to integrate effectively with the military. In Afghanistan, there were far too few civilian officials to carry out their mission. Fewer still had any experience training or planning with the military. The State Department's Coordinator for Stabilization and Reconstruction – appointed in 2004 – is working on improving the ability of civilian agencies to train, plan, and deploy for missions where CMO plays a central role, including (perhaps most importantly) the non-linear battlefield (See State).

Institutionally, CMO must begin to take place in the context of "interagency jointness." The 1986 Goldwater–Nichols Act improved jointness among the US Army, Navy, Air Force, and Marine Corps by redesigning how military personnel were organized, trained, commanded, and employed. The Center for Strategic and International Studies 2004 report "Beyond Goldwater Nichols" argued that the post 9/11 security environment "demands that we extend our notion of 'jointness' beyond the Military Services to the interagency and coalition levels" (Murdock, *et al.* p. 61). The UK PRT in Mazar-e Sharif, whose civilian and military members were trained, deployed, and supported as a team, set the modern standard for interagency jointness in the field. The CORDS program in Vietnam (see below) integrated civilian and military efforts on a larger scale than the PRT model, with soldiers serving directly under civilians, and vice versa, at all levels (Komer, p. 115).

Conclusion

CMO activities and doctrine evolved and improved over the 1990s and in Afghanistan. Those who did CMO generally did it well. The real issue was CMO's relevance to the broader US and international political and military objectives in Afghanistan. CMO in the 1990s primarily meant supporting civilian agency efforts, sharing information, and sometimes building the capacity of the host nation. Occasionally it included military-directed quick impact assistance projects, though they usually took place in clear post-conflict environments in which the military acted in a peace operations role. Despite the disintegration of the Taliban government in November 2001, the operating environment in Afghanistan remained insecure – far more so than most CMO environments in the 1990s. Thus, Afghanistan posed greater challenges for effective CMO and required a creative and robust approach.

Why did ISAF operate only around Kabul for almost two years? Although there were a number of factors – including initial US reluctance to expand ISAF beyond the Afghan capital – the primary reason had to do with an unwillingness and unpreparedness to execute adequate stabilization and CIMIC missions "on the edge." The non-linear battlefield in Afghanistan was too fluid and dangerous (and big) for many countries that preferred to conduct CIMIC in the context of peacekeeping. And it was too dispersed, subtle, and political for a US military that preferred major combat to CMO-intensive stability operations. The UK, whose military approaches small wars like a fish in water, was (justifiably) unwilling to go it alone.

Many of the lessons required for success in Afghanistan, Iraq, the Global War on Terror, and future non-linear battlefields come not from the 1990s but from counter-insurgency operations in the Philippines, Vietnam, and elsewhere. Contrary to what many critics think, the US military has been building schools and clinics – for military and political ends – for over 100 years. For example, to defeat the Philippine insurrection from 1899–1902, the United States used over 500 small garrisons (up from 53 in 1900) throughout the Philippines. The personnel from these garrisons lived and worked in local communities, fought insurgents, built rapport with the populace, and implemented civil works projects. The US military, with a field strength of 24,000–44,000, defeated an insurgent force estimated at 80,000–100,000 (Deady, pp. 55 and 57).

Failure also provides important lessons – lessons beyond simply "never again." For example, Robert Komer's seminal RAND report on Vietnam argued, "Instead of adapting our response to the unique circumstances of Vietnam, we fought the enemy our way – at horrendous cost and with tragic side effects – because we lacked the incentive and much existing capability to do otherwise." Komer stated that the costly US "search and destroy" (or attrition) strategy was ineffective because of the enemy's ability to control his losses by evading contact and using sanctuaries and to replace much of his losses by further recruitment. The United States did adapt toward the end of its involvement in Vietnam, but it was too little, too late. The Central Intelligence Agency and Army Special Forces developed a 50,000-man Civilian Irregular Defense Group, and the Army deployed 353 Mobile Advisory Teams to give on-the-job training to Vietnamese security forces. The US Marines deployed "only" (Komer lamented) 114 Combined Action Platoons, each composed of 12 US Marines and 24 Popular Force militiamen, to live in local villages thereby building relationships and enhancing security. Finally, the CORDS program (Civil Operations and Revolutionary Development Support) deployed unified civil–military teams to all 250 districts and 44 provinces in Vietnam. Perhaps PRTs are not as unique as many people think. (Komer, pp. vii, 108–109, and 114–117. For more on Combined Action Platoons, see West.)

Since Vietnam, it has been especially true that the US military "ostensibly worships Clausewitz as the principal philosopher/oracle of war on the one hand, but on the other hand it exhibits a Jominian predilection to divorce the political from the military when the shooting starts" (PK in the Abyss, p. 121). The Prussian strategist Clausewitz emphasized that war was an extension of politics and spoke of the fog and friction of war. But the Swiss theorist Antoine-Henri Jomini looked at war more as a scientific puzzle that could be solved with fundamental principles, the right calculations, and an effective decision-making process. Jomini's view on the non-linear battlefield was that a military should simply avoid it (Shy pp. 169–173). To this day, impediments to innovation required to effectively conduct complex operations remain a result of the US military's cultural preference for maneuver warfare and high-tech weapon systems.

The non-linear battlefield will become more common, given the overwhelming conventional military advantages of the United States and the ability of future enemies – particularly ethnic, ideological, and religious extremists – to fight asymmetrically. NGOs express concern about blurring the lines between humanitarians and military personnel, particularly when the latter are involved in providing assistance rather than focusing exclusively on "creating" security. The harsh reality, however, is that the non-linear battlefield blurs many lines. The lines separating humanitarian assistance, "post-conflict" reconstruction, development, security sector reform, combat, and complex operations (i.e. stability operations, peace operations, counter-insurgency, irregular warfare, and counter-terrorism) are all blurred. How does one draw lines between warlords, governors, and local leaders? Why were some NGOs concerned that Afghans would be confused between NGOs and Coalition troops when both build schools, yet showed little concern about confusion over ISAF troops conducting a CIMIC school-building project? Are Afghans ignorant of the difference between civilians and military but quite sophisticated about which military forces are operating under a UN mandate?

So how and when did the United States draw the line between Decisive Operations and Transition/Post-conflict in Afghanistan? There seemed to be little consideration of the idea that major combat could transition to stability operations within the Decisive Operations phase. The conventional wisdom was that Decisive Operations would end when major combat was declared over. The timing for moving to Transition/Post-conflict was a much-discussed point in Washington, at CENTCOM, and at Coalition headquarters in Afghanistan. Decision-makers considered but rejected the idea of moving to Transition/Post-conflict in the north and west but not in the south and east. After Operation Anaconda in March 2002, no clear breakpoint ever arose. Eventually, the United States declared major combat operations over both in Afghanistan and Iraq in May 2003, primarily because it would appear strange to shift to Transition/Post-conflict in Iraq before Afghanistan. Is the reality that Afghanistan is still in the Decisive Operations phase, or were the successful October 2004 presidential elections perhaps the transition point? Perhaps there is no way to know until years after the fact. Unfortunately, decision-makers do not have the luxury of time given to journalists, much less historians. The shift to the Transition/Post-conflict phase was equally problematic for Iraq (Author's discussions).

In fact, events in Iraq make an even stronger case for why governments must be prepared for the non-linear battlefield. Despite the commitment by the United States of far greater resources for combat, CMO, and civilian reconstruction efforts, insurgents in Iraq have been more successful than insurgents in Afghanistan. Are Afghanistan and Iraq anomalies? No. Future enemies have learned the lesson that direct, high-intensity combat with America and its allies is futile. Insurgency, terrorism, and other asymmetric tactics – against which US-led coalitions have had greater difficulty – will surely be the preferred method of fighting the United States for the foreseeable future. Of course, more traditional peace operations with clear post-conflict phases and more secure operating environments will continue, as well. But to train, plan, and equip only for Balkan-like CIMIC operations or to simply relegate CMO completely to a small group of specialist soldiers risks leaving troops ill-prepared to address more chaotic, fluid, and dangerous environments in the twenty-first century.

So how can CMO/CIMIC be more effective and more relevant to political and military efforts on the non-linear battlefields of the twenty-first century?

- CMO/CIMIC must have the ability to be flexible and tough, i.e. effective in many different operating environments. Practitioners must be prepared to work alongside maneuver units or in relative isolation. They must be prepared to fight. They must balance a warfighter attitude with a sensitive, peace-building approach to the local populace.
- CMO/CIMIC must go beyond information-sharing and be able to integrate its actions with the rest of the military effort and more closely coordinate with civilian actors. Beyond that, it must be able to establish field-level "interagency jointness" between the military and government civilians.
- Doctrine must integrate US CMO and NATO/EU CIMIC approaches and incorporate an interagency perspective.
- Military personnel and their civilian partners must be educated, trained, and equipped for the non-linear battlefield, and the role of CMO/CIMIC on that battlefield, not six weeks before deployment but over entire careers.
- CMO/CIMIC need better measures of effectiveness. After action reports far too often focus on outputs (e.g. schools built, coordination meetings) or – worse – inputs (e.g. dollars spent, personnel assigned to a task) rather than outcomes, which require polling data and more rigorous analysis of cause (e.g. clinic repair, interactions with community leaders) and effect (e.g. reduction in rocket attacks).
- More research and dialogue is needed among the military, civilian government agencies, UN, NGO community, and private sector regarding CMO/CIMIC and the non-linear battlefield. The principles of humanitarianism (independence, neutrality, and impartiality) constrain NGOs from integrating their actions with broader political and military efforts. Are these principles appropriate or feasible for the non-linear battlefield? Should all other efforts be integrated, while NGOs doing humanitarian work remain separate – and what about reconstruction or developmental work? Are private contractors more appropriate for the non-linear battlefield? According to the Geneva Conventions of 1949, humanitarian assistance by military combatants is legal and "nothing exceptional," but the "delivery of assistance by nongovernmental relief organizations ... as a legal concept at least in international armed conflicts, is the exception rather than the rule" (Spieker, pp. 220–221).

In the book, *Nation-Building Unraveled*, the authors argue, "there can be no doubt that the history of external interventions in complex crises will be divided into pre-September 11 and post-September 11 periods" (Donini, *et al.* p. 2). CMO improved throughout the 1990s, but the post-9/11 security environment presents challenges not only for CMO practitioners but also for military commanders and civilian leaders for whom CMO is one tool among many. The principles of decentralization and integration are critical as governments use

CIMIC/CMO increasingly "on the edge" in coming years. Decentralized action without integration of efforts makes CMO less relevant. Integrated efforts that are overly centralized make CMO less effective. Afghanistan was the first, but not the last, post-9/11 challenge, and it provides many important lessons for how governments must adapt to achieve CMO – and overall – success on the non-linear battlefield.

Notes

* The views in this chapter do not necessarily represent the views of the US Department of Defense.
1 Then-Major General Jay Garner, who later directed the Office of Reconstruction and Humanitarian Assistance for Operation Iraqi Freedom, was responsible for securing the region. Among his commanders was then-Lieutenant Colonel John Abizaid, later the top military commander for Operation Iraqi Freedom.

References

Amnesty (Amnesty International), *Serbia and Montenegro (Kosovo/Kosova).*
The March Violence: KFOR and UNMIK's failure to protect the rights of the minority communities, July 2004. Online, available at: web.amnesty.org/library/Index/ENGEUR700162004?open&of=ENG-YUG.
Boot, Max, *The Savage Wars of Peace* (New York: Basic Books, 2002).
Brahimi, Lakhdar, *Report of the Panel on United Nations Peace Operations* (New York: United Nations, 2000). Online, available at: www.un.org/peace/reports/peace_operations.
Cassidy, Robert M. *Peacekeeping in the Abyss* (Westport, CT: Praeger, 2004).
CJTF-180 (Coalition Joint Task Force-180) CJ5 briefing "The Joint Regional Team Concept," November 21, 2002. Unpublished.
Clausewitz, Carl von, *On War*, trans. Michael Howard and Peter Paret (Princeton, NJ: Princeton University Press, 1989).
Collins, Joseph J., "Afghanistan: Winning a Three Block War," Paper submitted for the Conference on the Three Block War, Canadian Army and the Centre for Conflict Studies, University of New Brunswick, October 21–23, 2004.
Collins, Joseph J. and McNerney, Michael J., "Security and Humanitarian Assistance: The US Experience in Afghanistan," in Dennis Dijkzeul (ed.) *Between Force and Mercy: Military Action and Humanitarian Aid* (Berlin: Berliner Wissenschafts-Verlag, 2004).
Daalder, Ivo H. and O'Hanlon, Michael E., *Winning Ugly: NATO's War to Save Kosovo* (Washington, DC: The Brookings Institution, 2000).
Deady, Timothy K., "Lessons from a Successful Counterinsurgency: The Philippines, 1899–1902," *Parameters*, Spring 2005 (Carlisle, PA: US Army War College).
DiPrizio, Robert C., *Armed Humanitarians: U.S. Interventions from Northern Iraq to Kosovo* (Baltimore, MA: The Johns Hopkins University Press, 2002).
Dobbins, James *et al.*, *America's Role in Nation-Building: From Germany to Iraq* (Santa Monica, CA: RAND Corporation, 2003).
Dobbins, James *et al.*, *The UN's Role in Nation-Building: From the Congo to Iraq* (Santa Monica, CA: RAND Corporation, 2005).

Donald, Dominic, "The Doctrine Gap: The Enduring Problem of Contemporary Peace Support Operations Thinking," in Colin McInnes and Nicholas J. Wheeler (eds) *Dimensions of Western Military Intervention* (London: Frank Cass Publishers, 2002).

Donini, Antonio, Niland, Norah and Wermester, Karin, *Nation-Building Unraveled? Aid, Peace and Justice in Afghanistan* (Bloomfield, CT: Kumarian Press, 2004)

Donnelly, Thomas, *Operation Iraqi Freedom: A Strategic Assessment* (Washington, DC: AEI Press, 2004).

Donnelly, Thomas, Roth, Margaret and Baker, Caleb, *Operation Just Cause: The Storming of Panama* (New York: Maxwell Macmillan International, 1991).

EU (European Union Military Committee) *CIMIC Concept*, Brussels, DOC 06/02.

Krulak (National Press Club) *Vital Speeches of the Day*, 15 December 1997.

Flavin, William, *Civil Military Operations: Afghanistan, Observations on Civil Military Operations During the First Year of Operation Enduring Freedom* (Carlisle, PA: US Army War College, 2004).

FM 3–07, *Stability Operations and Support Operations* (Washington, DC: Department of the Army, 2003). Online, available at: www.dtic.mil/doctrine/jel/service_pubs/fm3_07.pdf.

FM 41–10, *Civil Affairs Operations* (Washington, DC: Department of the Army, 2000). Online, available at: www.globalsecurity.org/military/library/policy/army/fm/41–10_2000.

FM 100–23, *Peace Operations* (Washington, DC: Department of the Army, 1994).

Gall, Carlotta, "Afghan Officials Urge Donors to Shift Focus", *New York Times*, 5 April 2005.

Gordon, Michael R. and Trainor, Bernard E., *The General's War* (Boston, MA: Little, Brown and Company, 1995).

Grier, Paul, Christian Science Monitor, "A Changed Military Emerges from Iraq War," 21 March 2005.

JOC (Joint Operations Concepts) (Washington, DC: US Joint Staff, November 2003). Online, available at: www.dtic.mil/jointvision.

HRW (Human Rights Watch) *Failure to Protect: Anti-Minority Violence in Kosovo March 2004*, July 2004. Online, available at: hrw.org/reports/2004/kosovo0704/kosovo0704.pdf.

JFCOM (Joint Forces Command) Information Papers. Online, available at: www.jfcom.mil/about/fact_ciacg.htm; www.jfcom.mil/about/fact_jiacg.htm.

JP 3–0 (Joint Chiefs of Staff, Joint Publication 3–0). (Washington, DC: US Joint Staff, 10 September 2001).

JP 3–57 (Joint Publication 3–57), *Joint Military Doctrine for Civil–Military Operations*, 8 February 2001.

Joint History Office (Ronald H. Cole), *Operation Just Cause: The Planning and Execution of Joint Operations in Panama, February 1998 to January 1990* (Washington, DC: Office of the Joint Chiefs of Staff, 1995).

Komer, R.W., *Bureaucracy Does Its Thing: Institutional Constraints on US–GVN Performance in Vietnam*, Report R-967-ARPA (Santa Monica, CA: The RAND Corporation, 1972). Republished as *Bureaucracy at War* in 1985.

Martin, Paul, "British Tactics in Basra Praised," *Washington Times*, 3 April 2003.

McNerney, Michael, "Stabilization and Reconstruction in Afghanistan: Are PRTs a Model or a Muddle?" *Parameters*, Winter 2005–06 (Carlisle, PA: US Army War College).

Metz, Steven and Johnson, Douglas V., *Asymmetry and US Military Strategy: Definition,*

Background, and Strategic Concepts, Carlisle, PA: Strategic Studies Institute, US Army War College, January 2001.

Murdock, Clark, Flournoy, Michele, Williams, Christopher and Campbell, Kurt, "Beyond Goldwater-Nichols: Defense Reform for a New Strategic Era" (Washington, DC: Center for Strategic and International Studies 2004). Online, available at: www.csis.org/isp/bgn.

NATO AJP-9, "NATO Civil–Military Co-Operation Doctrine," Allied Joint Publication 9, June 2003, Brussels.

NATO MC 411/1, "NATO Military Policy on Civil–Military Co-operation," NATO International Military Staff, January 2002, Brussels. Online, available at: www.nato.int/ims/docu/mc411-1-e.htm.

NDU (Kenneth Allard), *Somalia Operations: Lessons Learned* (Washington, DC: National Defense University Press, 1995). Online, available at: permanent.access. gpo.gov/websites/nduedu/www.ndu.edu/inss/books/books%20-%201990%20to%201995/ Somalia%20Lessons%20Learned%20Jan%2095/SOLL.pdf.

NDU (Margaret Daly Hayes and RAdm Gary F. Wheatley, USN (Ret.)), *Interagency and Political–Military Dimensions of Peace Operations: Haiti – A Case Study* (Washington, DC: National Defense University, 1996).

NIC, "Global Humanitarian Emergencies: Trends and Projections, 2001–2002," National Intelligence Council report NIC 2001–04, September 2001.

Oliker, Olga, *et al.*, *Aid During Conflict: Interaction Between Military and Civilian Assistance Providers in Afghanistan, September 2001 to June 2002* (Santa Monica, CA: RAND Corporation, 2004).

PKI (US Army Peacekeeping Institute), *Kosovo After Action Review* (Carlisle, PA: US Army Peacekeeping Institute, 2001).

Rose, Gideon, "The Exit Strategy Delusion," *Foreign Affairs*, Jan./Feb. 1998.

Scales: Brigadier General Robert H., *Certain Victory: The US Army in the Gulf War* (Washington, DC: United States Army, 1993).

Scaparrotti, Lieutenant Colonel Curtis M., "The Blue Falcons in Bosnia," in Douglas V. Johnson (ed.) *Warriors in Peace Operations* (Carlisle, PA: US Army War College, 1999).

Schmitt, Eric, "US General Maps New Tactic To Pursue Taliban and Qaeda," *New York Times*, 18 February 2004.

Shultz, Richard H. Jr., *In the Aftermath of War: US Support for Reconstruction and Nation-Building in Panama Following Just Cause* (Alabama: Air University Press, 1993).

Shy, John "Jomini," in Peter Paret (ed.) *Makers of Modern Strategy: From Machiavelli to the Nuclear Age* (Princeton, NJ: Princeton University Press, 1986).

Spieker, Heike, "The International Red Cross and Red Crescent and Military-Humanitarian Relationships," in Dennis Dijkzeul (ed.) *Between Force and Mercy: Military Action and Humanitarian Aid* (Berlin: Berliner Wissenschafts-Verlag, 2004).

State, "Strengthening US Reconstruction and Stabilization Capabilities." Online, available at: www.state.gov/s/crs.

UN WFP (United Nations World Food Program) In-Depth Report, "Afghanistan Facing Famine; Millions of Lives at Risk," 3 July 2001. Online, available at: www.wfp.org/newsroom/in_depth/afghanistan.html.

USMC (United States Marine Corps) *Draft Small Wars Manual*, January 2004. Online, available at: www.smallwars.quantico.usmc.mil.

Weiss, Thomas G. Weiss, *Military–Civilian Interactions: Intervening in Humanitarian Crises* (Lanham, MD: Rowman & Littlefield Publishers, Inc., 1999).

West: F.J., *The Village* (New York: Harper & Row, 1972).

Part III
Extensions

9 Medical aspects of civil–military operations

The challenges of military health support to civilian populations on operations

Susan J. Neuhaus

Introduction

Changing role of the military

The fundamental role of military medical support on operations is to conserve military force strength. Historically, military operations have focused on military health support to combatant casualties during high-intensity warfare. However, this pattern of health care delivery is changing and modern military forces provide health support to a growing category of 'Stability and Reconstruction Operations' (S&R), including operations whose primary focus is provision of humanitarian aid. Recent operations have demonstrated that the vast preponderance of casualties treated by Western militaries on operations are now civilian patients.[1,2,3]

This changing nature of Western militaries has resulted in new complexities for the interactions between military and civilian health-care providers. Traditionally, there has been a clear distinction between the roles of military and non-military organisations and similar distinction between health care provided to combatants and non-combatants. However, in recent years, tasks which have historically belonged exclusively within the domain of international and non-government organisations are increasingly being performed by the military. This new set of challenges has implications for military planning, command and interaction with civil agencies.

Lack of policy and doctrine

As Western militaries have increasingly become involved in Stability and Reconstruction Operations a doctrinal gap has emerged. In particular there is scant doctrine to facilitate planning and conduct of health support to civilians during complex emergencies (stability, humanitarian/disaster relief, peace support or service protected evacuation operations).[4] This lack of policy and doctrine creates anxiety and uncertainty between military health care providers and other stakeholder organisations (international organisations and non-government organisations).[5]

Humanitarian and military providers of health care have significantly different organisational structures, philosophies, objectives and working methods. The different mandates, characteristics and nature of the diverse providers of health care must be clearly understood in order to prevent competition, avoid role confusion, minimise inconsistencies and promote restoration of civil health infrastructure and return to normalcy.

The aim of this chapter is to discuss the principles, confounding issues and practical considerations that affect provision of military health support to civilian populations. In particular it will address the complex relationships between military and non-government providers of health care in an operational setting.

Principles and concepts

Medical consequences of current and emerging operations

Complex emergencies

Complex emergencies can be defined by the requirement to simultaneously engage in humanitarian assistance, internal security and combat operations. Complex emergencies, whether these are 'stability operations' or responses to humanitarian crises or natural disasters, represent a fundamental public health crisis with break down of civilian health infrastructure (Table 1). Inevitably there will be a period following military intervention in which the security environment is not permissive to non-government agencies (NGOs) and international aid workers. During this time the military must take primacy of responsibility, sometimes as the Occupying Power.

Health service delivery and improving access to poor and vulnerable members of society is an important component of stabilising a country emerging from conflict. Health facilities are usually the first to be destroyed and the last to be rehabilitated.[6] Public health needs must be addressed and include re-establishment of transportation, and communication.[7]

Humanitarian issues are likely to occur in the early phases of any complex operation: a collapsed state may generate an internally displaced or refugee population with acute medical needs, while war-fighting will generate civilian casualties as 'collateral damage' from direct military action and indirect effects of living in a country at war. These patients include elderly, pregnant women and children and those with existing chronic illnesses. In such operations greater than 70 per cent of victims are civilians, primarily children and adolescents.[8] This represents a significant change from historical conflicts. For example Second World War estimates of civilian casualties were only 19 per cent.[9]

Medical responses to complex operations need to be individualised as each occurs in a different geopolitical setting with different injury and illness pat-

Table 9.1 Health consequences of complex emergencies

(Modified from Burkle, F. Lessons learnt and future expectations of complex emergencies. *British Medical Journal* 1999:319 (7207)422–6).

- High levels of violence, especially between ethnic groups.
- Disruption/destruction of health infrastructure and loss of local health-care providers. HN health-care providers either become displaced with the population or may be targeted.
- Human rights violations.
- Competition for limited health assets.
- Refugees or internally displaced populations with consequent rise in malnutrition, infectious disease, increased infant and maternal mortality, etc.
- Disruption to water supply, sanitation.
- Rise in international drug cartels.

terns. The nature of the medical challenges will vary with the nature and intensity of the fighting, weapons used, and the existing health infrastructure and transportation facilities.[10]

In modern intra- and inter-state violence, most injuries are caused by fragments and mine injuries rather than bullets. The use of improvised weapons is common and improvised bombs, grenades and mortars can produce unpredictable patterns of injury. In addition a frequent collateral problem in managing victims of such conflicts is due to the large mass movement of people, either as refugees or internally displaced populations (IDPs).

Refugee populations and IDPs create a unique subset of medical problems with high mortality rates due to violence, deprivation and disease.[11] Those who are most vulnerable are women, the elderly and children. Wars kill and injure more children than soldiers.[12] High fertility rates in many affected countries make a predominant workload of children under the age of five,[13] with death occurring due to direct trauma, neonatal deaths due to lack of obstetric care, disease and indirect effects (e.g. playing with landmines). These require specialist skills and equipment which most militaries, unlike their humanitarian counterparts, are not configured to provide.

Disease epidemics,[14] infectious disease, dysentery, and malnutrition predominate in refugee camps and require commitment of environmental health assets such as vector control, childhood immunisations (to prevent secondary disease outbreaks) and engineering assets (i.e. clean water, road repairs for access to rural areas[15]). Military forces may have a role in providing or assisting in this area, particularly with the use of engineering assets.

Complex emergencies are also characterised by high levels of psychiatric problems resulting from violence, dislocation, rape or torture. This is beyond the mandate and capability of most military health services. Despite this a significant percentage of the patients presenting themselves to a military medical facility will have these problems in addition to other medical conditions, and contingencies must therefore be made to address such issues or transfer the responsibility to an alternative agency.

Impact of terrorism/counterterrorism

The current increase in global terrorist activities poses significant and new health-care challenges. The management of mass casualties, in particular large numbers of burns patients, is beyond the capability of most health facilities, civilian or military. Military health-care providers may therefore be required in the early response phase to provide triage and immediate casualty care. There is also a need in such incidents to integrate care with multiple non-health agencies including investigative, fire and police. There may be an additional requirement for large scale and rapid response forensic and identification facilities.[16]

Increasingly humanitarian aid workers, relief convoys and health facilities are seen as 'legitimate' targets for insurgency operations. This has recently been evidenced by the targeting of an ICRC hospital in Baghdad in 2003, ambushes of NGO convoys and the kidnapping of NGO personnel. Such deliberate targeting of health facilities and staff undermines confidence, creates fear and uncertainty and encourages NGO agencies to withdraw services. It is increasingly apparent that security can no longer be guaranteed and NGOs are facing increasing bills for provision of contract security.

Security concerns affect not only civilian health (e.g. rape, massacres, kidnapping) but also providers of health care. Terrorist and insurgency operations have increased insecurity for both military and NGO health-care providers. The inability to distinguish between 'combatants' (insurgents) and civilian members of the community places medical facilities at risk both in terms of security and also their perception of neutrality. Commanders must therefore determine what level of risk is acceptable to medical staff when providing care to civilian populations.

Recent distinctions between humanitarian and reconstruction operations have particular relevance to health care provision. Throughout most of the 1990s and pre-'9/11', interventions were primarily humanitarian. In contrast, most current deployments are focused on reconstruction, counterinsurgency or anti-terrorism and there is a decreased emphasis on impartiality. Appropriate medical support to this second category of operations may not be impartial or even humanitarian in nature – e.g. it may be of the 'Special forces' patrol medic type, which is specifically designed to alienate one group while supporting another. Similarly, commanders may choose to use provision of free health care to 'draw' certain populations back into a particular area or foster confidence in a military administration. This unique (and controversial) use of health care as a 'weapon of war' at either strategic or tactical levels has considerable implications for medical ethics which are discussed further below.

With an increasing trend to urban operations, military counterinsurgency (COIN) operations are likely to be small group, highly mobile, operations in built-up areas. Therefore support to displaced populations and civilians is less likely to be considered part of military mandate. An exception to this is the use of 'Special forces' patrol medics. In this setting impartial support is less likely, with provision of health care being utilised as a tool to influence local populations. Furthermore, the feasibility for terrorists to acquire nuclear, biological and chemical weapons poses unique health care challenges. Few organisations other than militaries are capable of responding to such a crisis.

Disaster relief operations

While disaster relief operations are considered a form of complex emergency, the challenges for military health support are qualitatively different. Disaster relief operations are usually low threat situations requiring an immediate health response.[17] Frequently military support is requested in the initial phase as Defence forces are often the only organisations capable of rapid deployment of highly trained personnel at a high level of readiness, with sophisticated medical assets, logistic support and an inbuilt redundancy into an unfamiliar geopolitical landscape.

Health care responses will vary with the nature and magnitude of the disaster. Guidelines developed by the World Health Organisation (WHO) and Pan-American Health Organisation (PAHO)[18] imply the usefulness of hospital level facilities is limited to the provision of acute trauma care in the first 48 hours, with benefit from secondary trauma management (i.e. management of complications and general medical conditions) up to two weeks following the incident. They recommend that unless a field hospital can be functionally deployed within five days of a disaster its deployment should be delayed until a detailed health needs analysis has been performed. Beyond the first week following the incident, the greatest benefit is likely to be from provision of preventive health, environmental health care. Because of the benign threat environment that accompanies most natural disasters, transfer of responsibility to humanitarian agencies is rarely a problem, enabling the military to disengage early.

Legal and ethical basis for military provision of health support to civilian populations

Two bodies of law, the Geneva Conventions of 1949 and the Hague Convention of 1899, form the cornerstone of law relating to the conduct of individuals and nations in wartime.[19] In adhering to the requirements of the Geneva Conventions, medical personnel accept a responsibility not to engage in acts of war, to care to for sick and wounded impartially and to speak out against atrocities committed by either side.[20] Traditionally this has largely been limited to provision of health care to combatants of two warring parties.

However, the requirements of International Humanitarian Law (IHL) also dictate that support to non-combatant civilian populations must be provided *by the military* when that military organisation is either the intervening force or has effective control over a territory or when humanitarian aid organisations are unable or reluctant to operate.[21] The latter is particularly the case when security considerations preclude freedom of action of humanitarian aid organisations. The military therefore has a clear duty of care to *all* casualties, combatant and non-combatant alike. Further, the UN Convention on the Rights of the Child also states that signatory parties must take all feasible measures to ensure the protection and care of children affected by armed conflict.[22] Sick and injured children are therefore automatic dependencies in any military intervention if the participating nations are signatories.

While the laws governing wars between nations are clearly defined, the application of these principles across the spectrum of conflict, particularly in intra-state violence is less clearly defined. However, the overarching consideration in each of these layers of IHL is the need for 'universal provision of emergency care' to all casualties of conflict regardless of their combatant or civilian status.

Existing CIMIC doctrine

Civil–military cooperation (CIMIC) is concerned with successful achievement of a military mission and the ability to create and sustain the conditions that support a long term solution. Different concepts of CIMIC exist. For example, while the UN definition focuses on the humanitarian objectives of CIMIC:

> the essential dialogue and interaction between civilian and military actors in humanitarian emergencies that is necessary to protect and promote humanitarian principles, avoid competition, minimise inconsistency, and when appropriate pursue common goals.[23]

NATO definitions are mission orientated: '... the co-ordination and co-operation, in support of the mission, between the [NATO] commander and civil populations...

The extent of civil–military co-operation and co-ordination will vary significantly between missions and may range from co-existence in the area of operations, co-operation between agencies to full integration of civilian and military assets.

CIMIC health doctrine

The UN Office for the Co-ordination of Humanitarian Affairs (UNOCHA) provides 'Guidelines for the Use of Military and Civil Defence Assets to Support United Nations Humanitarian Activities in Complex Emergencies.[24] NATO 'Principles of Operational Medical Support' also provide guidance for 'International Disaster Relief Operations'[25] but detailed guidance for the management of non-combatants in other operations is not covered.

Doctrine of most professional military forces distinguish between Humanitarian Disaster Relief Operations (HDRO) in which humanitarian aid provision is the primary military focus and Humanitarian Assistance (HA) in which military operations retain primacy.[26] Almost universally however, there is little detail regarding the planning and conduct of health operations or guidelines to facilitate inter-action with non-military agencies, particularly in the setting of intervention in intra-state conflict and stability operations.[27] Specific aspects of inter-agency co-operation and co-ordination are discussed below.

Nature of military health support to civilian populations

Military objectives: why neutrality is a myth

The medical profession is focused on prevention and alleviation of human suffering. The key tenets of ethical health care are based on the principles of neutrality, equality and autonomy. Of these, autonomy is the least well understood. Autonomy implies 'freedom from coercion', and applies to both the patient and the medical practitioner, who should be free to treat patients based on medical need, not military priorities. However, this creates ethical dilemmas for military health-care providers who must balance professional ethics with military imperatives and constraints.[28]

Militaries do not enter into humanitarianism or altruism for its own sake; they are instruments of state and therefore cannot be apolitical. Similarly, militaries do not provide impartial humanitarian aid – great selectivity is employed in accordance with national strategic political imperatives. Military health-care providers cannot, by definition, be neutral because they form part of a system that imposes its national or coalition values on another country. Therefore health provision by the military must strike a balance between a pragmatic and a principled response.

Furthermore, military health care cannot be impartial because in situations of great humanitarian need, health care assets would be paralysed in less than 24 hours by overwork and fixed in location thereby undermining the commander's freedom of manoeuvre. Regardless of the mission, the fundamental role of military health support is support to the deployed military force and this is at all times an overriding consideration.

Most Western military forces have highly sophisticated health care assets which can be rapidly deployed in support of a military operation. However, the inevitable rationalisation that has occurred over the last two decades means that few are adequately equipped or staffed to manage a broad spectrum of non-combatant medical emergencies. Military health facilities are configured for the treatment of predominantly young fit male trauma victims and not for obstetric or paediatric emergencies or for dealing with chronic health problems across a broad population, which is the principal humanitarian dependency.

Although there is general acceptance from both military and humanitarian communities that the primary role of the military is *not* humanitarian medical assistance, such assistance is becoming a significant component of current military operations.[29] Increasingly militaries, either through 'coalitions of the willing' or via the United Nations, are being called upon to intervene in humanitarian crises. The shift towards 'whole of government' responses to international conflict and catastrophe also implies much greater integration between civil and military assets than has been seen in the past; health care is no exception to this.

While many humanitarian agencies resent military involvement in provision of humanitarian health care,[30] most also accept that the military has an important role in securing a permissive environment to enable them to operate freely. Humanitarian agencies must be able to obtain access to all vulnerable populations in all areas. Such agencies have legitimate concerns that cooperating with militaries will lead to a progressive loss of access to communities that oppose the military force, thereby limiting their freedom of action. Inevitably, for reasons of security or logistic support, there will be circumstances in which military health assets are better placed to meet certain health needs.

A further factor is the now pervasive international media attention focused on the welfare of civilian populations. This creates a strategic imperative to fulfill the 'hearts and minds' requirements of both the international media/public and the local population in any military operation and health care is an important asset to achieve this aim. Media coverage may provide an opportunity to focus public attention on the humanitarian needs of a particular mission. This can have valuable spin offs in terms of public support and aid donations and assist meeting strategic and political goals of both the host nation and the intervening nation or coalition. Moreover, given the casualty aversion of Western societies, medical care has a key strategic role in preventing deaths that could undermine popular support for a campaign.[31]

Humanitarian providers of health care

International conflicts and catastrophes are characterised by the presence of multiple health-care providers. These include various international government organisations (IGOs) such as UN agencies and the International Committee of the Red Cross (ICRC) and non-government organisations (NGOs). Some of these agencies are very professional, complex multinational organisations with clear mandates and vast field experience. Others comprise groups of enthusiastic individuals often without resources or logistic support. Only a limited number of these facilities can provide a full range of medical support (e.g. surgical capabilities) and virtually none can meet the sophistication, logistic support and rapid deployability of the military. Humanitarian efforts must also consider any existing host nation medical framework. Local health-care providers may still be operating in some areas but their services may be inadequate due to lack of facilities or resources.[32] Alternately local health-care providers may themselves have become targets of violence or be displaced with the population.

Non Government Organisations (NGOs)

Recent years have seen a dramatic increase in the number of NGOs providing relief, advocacy, medical and humanitarian assistance. There are now over 5000 such organisations.[33] NGOs vary tremendously in size, capability, experience and support but most tend to have a 'Western' ideology. In contrast to the UN organisations and the ICRC, each NGO determines its own mandate and is accountable to its members and sponsors. They are supported by institutional and public donors and often heavily influenced by donor philosophies and the need to answer to donor scrutiny. Not all NGO health providers can be considered 'neutral' as some consider an advocacy role an important part of their mandate.[34]

Most NGOs are reluctant to engage with the military and are concerned about compromising integrity and security.[35] The reasons for this are complex but include the fear that by association with the military their neutrality and safety will be threatened. Historically, IGOs and NGOs have depended for their security on a perception of neutrality. This is derived from delivery of impartial health care to predominantly non-combatant populations. In the current age of asymmetric warfare and terrorism, neutrality no longer appears to hold protection and NGOs are increasingly concerned about being targeted for political or terrorist advantage. Examples include the attack on the ICRC hospital in Chechnya in 1996 in which six humanitarian workers were killed, and the kidnapping and (presumed) execution of CARE aid worker Margaret Hassan in Iraq.

Frequently the effect of so many organisations on the ground is often to create confusion, misunderstanding and competition. This is underpinned by frequent misunderstandings of each other's capabilities, suspicions of underlying agendas, fundamental philosophical differences and security concerns. Friction between agencies (both interagency and NGO-military) is common to most operations due to misunderstanding of intention and purpose.[36] This is exemplified by Bernard Kouchner, the founder of Médicins Sans Frontières who described: '... wars [between philanthropists] as the worst of all ... quarrelling amongst themselves for control of victims of disaster ... [they] fight to death amongst themselves having risked their lives together'.[37]

While friction between military and humanitarian agencies is understandable, given their often opposing political and philosophical views, many of the NGO criticisms of the military in provision of humanitarian health care are valid. These include 'military short term vision' and a focus on 'high end' sophisticated health support.

In order to avoid prolonged commitment militaries tend to focus on short term 'projects' rather than long term redevelopment and restoration 'programmes'. This renders the military subject to suggestions of 'tokenism' and propagandaism. However, such projects can have long-term effects. An example would be surgical repair of congenital facial defects such as cleft palate. The benefits of the surgery are life long, re-establish the individual's place in their society and foster immediate goodwill with the family, relatives and friends.[38]

Military health care is usually trauma focused and therefore delivers 'curative' health interventions for a minority of the population (e.g. surgery) rather than on restoration of 'health' and prevention of disease. This is also a reflection of the short-term nature of many deployments. Disease prevention programmes (such as public health interventions, vaccination programmes) are usually long-term developmental and capacity building projects which are beyond the resources of military health-care providers.

By virtue of operational considerations and the use of 'spare capacity' only for humanitarian intervention, military focus also tends to be on the treatment of limited numbers of personnel, i.e. focus on 'hundreds' rather than millions (e.g. refugee populations).

There are also some significant cultural values that must be addressed. Military culture is often an anathema to NGO personnel and its command and control arrangements and operational focus may result in a perception of inflexibility. NGOs may feel compromised and threatened in an insecure environment and this can lead to resentment of the apparent security and sophisticated resources available to military medical personnel.

Practical considerations

Interactions with non-military stakeholders

The existence of multiple players within the area of operations can lead to role confusion and conflict. Relationships vary from tacit co-existence to (rarely) full co-operation and integration of military and civilian health care resources, depending on the nature of the mission. However, it is essential that, at the very least, formal communication channels exist between agencies and that co-ordination of activities is achieved.

Co-ordination (who should lead)

A major challenge within all aspects of CIMIC is to foster collaboration between otherwise competing organisations.[39] Civil military co-ordination is imperative across the operational spectrum. Lack of communication between agencies, competition and inadequate communication, has the ability to paralyse operations and undermine operational effectiveness. The level of co-ordination and co-operation will vary with different operations and depend on the state of host nation (HN) health resources, locally available logistic and administrative support, availability of NGOs and other health-care providers, and the security situation.

UN based operations

Guidance on co-ordination exists for UN based operations where the UN should be the lead agency.[40] The UN Office of the Co-ordination for Humanitarian Affairs (UN OCHA) has a mandated role for co-ordination in emergency humanitarian situations. UN capability includes the facility to field a UN Disaster Assessment and Coordination (UNDAC) team and On-site Operations Co-ordination Centre (OSOCC) or Humanitarian Operations Centre (HOC).

Overall co-ordination and leadership lies with the Humanitarian Co-ordinator, usually the UN Development Programme representative of the Host Nation. In complex emergencies the Humanitarian Co-ordinator may be an external UN appointment. The UN OCHA or its derivative will be required to co-ordinate all UN agencies in the operational area and establish liaison and communication with IGOs, NGOs and the military. These UN agencies will generally have primacy in the area of operations and should be the main point of contact for all CIMIC activity. Military health planners need to be represented within this framework.

Non-UN operations

Non-UN operations, and operations undertaken by ad hoc coalitions are more complex to co-ordinate. It is always preferable for civilian or national government to lead this process. Generally it is to be advised that the military avoid a clear leadership role in the co-ordination activities but, they can have a role in facilitation, particularly standardised health reporting information and administrative support. However, in many situations, particularly in the early phase of a mission, there may be a vacuum in which the military must assume the primacy.

Co-operation with humanitarian medical providers

There is general acceptance that co-operation between military and humanitarian agencies is essential – particularly to share information and co-ordinate resources – and should be encouraged whenever security considerations allow it. In particular the care of civilians needs to be co-ordinated between agencies.

A key aspect of interaction between agencies is to provide clarity on capabilities and areas of responsibility. For example, the military facility may have responsibility for Level 3 (surgical) care, while the NGO organisation has primary responsibility for refugee and development programmes and primary health care. Formalised understandings need to be developed concerning patient referral systems, inter-agency transfers and a focus developed on empowerment of local health facilities, rather than isolated provision of care.

Humanitarian and HN health care agencies need clear guidelines as to which personnel can be treated in a military facility and what restrictions are placed on access (see below). Referral systems should be formalised and ideally all referrals to military facilities should be triaged through Humanitarian and HN health care agencies. Depending on the capabilities of each organisation it may be appropriate for different facilities to accept 'role specific' tasks. For example it may be appropriate for all paediatric medical emergencies to be treated at an NGO, rather than military, hospital. Similarly, although the military may provide a surgical capability to deal with life threatening emergencies, patients may require transfer back to local facilities for postoperative care and rehabilitation.

There are areas in which military health-care providers can combine efforts to restore confidence in local health facilities. This includes needs assessments, opportunities for clinical updates and servicing of medical equipment.

Ideally health planning for a complex operation should include relevant government and humanitarian agencies prior to any deployment. Integrated health planning is controversial but offers the opportunity to raise awareness of each others' activities and mandates, share heath intelligence, mobilise appropriate health assets and structure responses to a meet a common vision. However, integrated mission planning may also draw NGOs into the political process, which may not be in their (or their sponsors') interests.

An example of effective co-operation is the British based NGO-Military Contact Group (NMCG) which was established in 2000 to facilitate communication between the military and aid organisations.[41] The NMCG is convened by the British Red Cross Society and includes members from the military, joint CIMIC Group, UK Ministry of Defence (MOD), UK Department for International Development (DFID) and several NGOs. It also serves as a forum to improve mutual understanding and resolve perception differences between the various agencies. Another British agency is the International Conflict Prevention Fund, which is an interagency organisation with pooled funds available to different organisations in the pre-crisis phase. It must be accepted however that while some NGOs are willing to participate in integrated planning, education or training, some will not be willing to participate in this process and will remain outside of the influence of any co-ordinating group.

Planning considerations

Understanding the problem and defining the mission

Traditional military medical planning for operations focuses on complex predictions of combat casualties and provides for the treatment of prisoners of war (POWs) in accordance with the Geneva conventions. Treatment of local non-combatant populations is not always appreciated as a significant part of the casualty estimate process, but it is almost inevitable that they will enter the military casualty chain and therefore need to be included in the planning process. 'Non-combatants' include not only members of the local population but also an increasing number of own national civilians within the operational area. This includes media, contractors, own nation personnel attached to UN agencies and potentially own nation humanitarian aid workers. It is imperative that planning incorporates health staffs and an appreciation of the full extent of the dependency. This is particularly evident when military health facilities expect to encounter significant paediatric, obstetric or refugee patients.

Equally important is the need to fully assess the civilian health infrastructure and determine the quality and availability of resources and services. This can be achieved using internationally accepted guidelines such as the NAOMI guidelines (NATO Assessment of Medical Indicators) or SPHERE Guidelines (see below).[42]

Equipment and manning

Most Western militaries have restructured over the previous decades in response to primarily medical needs of the military force and are therefore focused on provision of acute trauma services, ranging from first aid, resuscitation through to initial trauma surgery. Few are structured to provide for the range of medical conditions found in civilian emergencies. In particular, rapidly deployable paediatric and obstetric facilities are rare in Western militaries and yet, in the situations outlined above, deployment without such a capability may render that nation in breach of the UN Conventions on the Rights of the Child.[43]

Such rationalisations and narrowing of military responsibilities over time have also threatened the ability of developed nations to undertake national mobilisation in a crisis, for example a major terrorist incident. Most civilian planners assume military doctors and hospitals can be set-up as needed to supplement civilian capabilities – not realising that 'spare' assets no longer exist. Many developed countries are dependent on the use of reservists to provide key health personnel. These health providers have 'real-time' civilian hospital jobs which will demand their presence under the very circumstances where we might also be needed for counter-terrorist consequence management.

Similarly, significant training gaps are evident when military health providers engage in humanitarian activities. Further, recent trends in medicine to 'subspecialisation' means that many military doctors may have limited or no experience in dealing with patients with obstetric emergencies, children, or patients with a range of diseases attributable to pre-existing chronic conditions or epidemic outbreaks. This has significant implications for the ability to meet minimum international standards of health care provision (see below). Military planners must decide if this capability gap is to be met by further training of military personnel, by reserve specialists or contract civilian professionals.

Military health-care providers frequently find themselves called upon to provide essential equipment or pharmaceutical items to civilian, and sometimes NGO, facilities. It is not the responsibility of the military to provide drugs, disposables or other medical equipment to civilian medical services. If provided, they should be commensurate with current WHO and Pharmacies san Frontiéres schedules, to avoid introducing new and unsustainable drugs/equipment into the civilian health service.

Avoiding mission expansion and population dependence

Medical mission expansion ('mission creep') is a consequence of poor planning and medical command. Mission creep encourages disconnection of strategic intentions from tactical actions, encourages population dependence and hampers disengagement. It usually comes about because either the mission is wrong or has not been adequately articulated. The dangers of mission expansion are that not only does it threaten strategic objectives, it consumes resources intended for military personnel and creates ethical and political dilemmas over the management of patients.[44] Medical planners have a responsibility to ensure that assets are not over-extended and jeopardise the treatment of military personnel. At the same time however, there needs to be flexibility to allow for 'mission shift' as the situation on the ground changes. This may occur in response to a change in strategic imperatives or through changes at the tactical level such as withdrawal of a key humanitarian provider or large scale movement of IDPs.

Frequently mission expansion is contributed to by the ethical and professional frustrations of medical staff in over-resourced and under-utilised military facilities, i.e. force preservation assets sitting idle while civilians die for lack of 'civic action' assets. False expectations are easily created, either among the medical staff (who may have deployed to 'do good' rather than 'to support the military') or among the community. 'Perception management' is therefore an important task of any military medical commander. This is aggravated by the reality that in many peacekeeping operations the volume of medical work is low.[45]

Conduct of operations

What level of health care should the military provide?

Level of care refers to the capability provided by the military in support of health care to the civilian community. This may range from health advice, primary health care and environmental support, first aid, initial resuscitation and evacuation to non-military health facilities to provision of fully integrated hospital services with surgery and intensive care capabilities. What level of care should be provided is governed by clinical need and underpinned by the Geneva Conventions and the Laws of Armed Conflict. Once patients have arrived at a military medical facility they can no longer be distinguished as own/enemy/civilian and must ethically be treated on the basis of medical priority alone, therefore if military health assets are to be limited or 'rationed' this must occur prior to casualties arriving at that facility.

The military must normally provide emergency treatment of life threatening conditions and meet the requirements of 'universal provision of care' (see above). In deciding what level of care will be provided to non-combatant/civilian populations, medical planners must take into account:

* Laws of Armed Conflict
* Obligations for the universal provision of acute emergency care
* Health requirements of the military force
* Tactical and strategic military imperatives
* Availability and capability of non-military health assets
* Primacy of clinical need
* The rights of the child
* Duty and standards of care.

The level of care provided needs to be affordable and achievable and must not interfere with provision of health care to the military force, nor should it be led by the presence of a sophisticated asset on the ground which is allowed to 'draw' casualties. An exception to this is in a counter-insurgency operation where that may be precisely the commanders intent to achieve a politico–strategic objective. Further, levels of care need to be sustainable in the HN following military withdrawal. Care needs to be taken not to create a culture of dependency, reliant on a transient medical facility with a vacuum of resource and skills once the force disengages, nor should it undermine confidence in existing health infrastructure. Inevitably this creates friction as there will be significant differences between the level of care provided by a sophisticated first world military medical facility and the local health services or those provided by IGOs/NGOs depending on the assets they have available and the austerity of the operating conditions.

Almost universally, provision of primary health care and environmental health resources (e.g. water and sanitation services) has a greater ability to influence the health and wellbeing of the population, compared to 'high end' hospital facilities. Where possible the military should avoid providing hospital level capabilities unless that capability cannot be provided by existing civilian assets.

Health capabilities also need to be culturally sensitive. This includes requirements to provide accommodation for relatives/carers, particularly for children and translators. There may also be local sensitivities about social or religious values such as reluctance of female patients to be seen by male doctors. There is an ethical responsibility to provide consent to medical procedures in their own language. This implies the need for the establishment to incorporate either military or contract translators.

Whenever possible, military medical planners should be encouraged to utilise civilian assets for the treatment of non-military personnel. The military should particularly avoid provision of rehabilitation or management of chronic health problems. Military patients with these problems are repatriated. Civilian patients with these problems should be the responsibility of humanitarian and HN agencies.

Standards of care

Standards of care refer to the standard of clinical decision-making and treatment within a health institution in accordance with 'best clinical practice'. However, it is not feasible to meet sophisticated care values of developed societies when providing health services to local communities, nor should it be encouraged as it raises unrealistic expectations within communities and is not sustainable beyond the length of military deployment. Whenever possible health care should be provided to a standard compatible with 'best practice' in the pre-conflict HN health service. This is emotive and standards of care need to be clearly defined as part of the planning process. NATO provides a useful definition: '... medical support must meet standards acceptable to both the participating nations and the receiving country. The aim is to provide treatment outcomes as far as possible equivalent to the normal peacetime standards of the receiving country'.[46]

However, defining an 'appropriate' standard of care is ethically fraught and open to widely varying interpretations.[47] The principle that 'some care is better than none' is no longer consistent with contemporary medical ethics or professionalism. Normal rules of accountability and clinical governance also apply on operations and they apply equally regardless of the patients' combatant or civilian status.[48] Providers of care must be adequately trained to the task and must carry out their clinical duties with competence.

The recent development of international consensus standards for minimal performance in humanitarian missions by SPHERE[49] has done much to clarify what constitutes 'acceptable' practice. SPHERE was launched in 1997 as a collaboration between humanitarian NGOs and the Red Cross and Red Crescent movements to provide consensus standards of humanitarian accountability and improve effectiveness of humanitarian operations. The strict adherence to accepted local/NGO treatment protocols when treating civilian patients facilitates standardisation of treatments within the operational area, minimises perceptions of differential standards of care and facilitates transfer of patients from military to civilian health facilities. It is also important to accept that the practicalities of the operating environment mean there will inevitably be some differences between the management of military and civilian patients. This is particularly evident when military and civilian patients are being treated at the same facility. Evacuation policies and protocols for military casualties mean that these patients will be evacuated beyond the immediate operational area to sophisticated 'home nation' medical facilities. This option is not available for non-designated civilian personnel. Therefore considerations of appropriate 'post hospital' management must be taken in the context of local health facilities. For example it may be inappropriate to attempt limb salvage in a civilian patient with no access to intensive long-term rehabilitation and physiotherapy, when the standard management of such injuries in that community is amputation. If not previously developed, these treatment protocols need to be negotiated between health providers as part of the CIMIC co-ordination process.

Control of entry into and exit from the military medical system

It is inevitable that civilians will enter the military health system during complex operations. If however this is not regulated, the system risks becoming rapidly overloaded. Once *in* the military system any patient becomes the military's responsibility and, in the absence of an effective HN medical infrastructure or co-operative humanitarian agency, it is very difficult to offload that responsibility.

Requirements for 'gatekeeping' do not just occur on arrival at a medical facility but must be taken into account when constructing policy for pre-hospital or field medical staff. This needs to be appropriate, e.g. military pre-hospital teams will frequently institute intensive care (ICU) measures such as mechanical ventilation which cannot be supported by ICRC or other humanitarian facilities.[50] This automatically compromises the ability to transfer such patients to a non-military hospital and creates a host of ethical and political dilemmas.

A particular problem is created when military facilities provide care *above* the level of care normally encountered in the pre-conflict HN, e.g. ICU facilities. ICU is a special example as it is a highly limited, expensive and specialist resource. Use of ICU beds by non-designated patients creates competition for resources that could threaten the ability to deal with military casualties. It is also fraught with ethical difficulties. Military patients requiring ICU usually undergo strategic casualty evacuation (CASEVAC) to a sophisticated ICU beyond the operational area within 72 hours. However, without a comparable HN facility to transfer civilian patients to, they must either remain a military responsibility or their treatment must be withdrawn. While this could be overcome by transfer of patients to outside of the operational area to first world health facilities, this policy is unsustainable, creates divisions and can undermine local facilities and staff. In addition, recent experience from Iraq has demonstrated the potential to create a raft of political problems such as asylum issues.

Once within the military health chain, it is also necessary to manage the length of stay, appropriateness of resource use, and egress from the system. This can only occur in the setting of mutual assistance between humanitarian, HN and military medical staff, underpinning the requirement for formalised CIMIC arrangements. There is a need to assess and monitor the length of civilian admission and identify any 'discharge blocks' that may require negotiation at combined civil–military meetings. Discharge blocks can be created by lack of a competent humanitarian or host nation health facility or reluctance on behalf of the military to transfer the patients to a suitable facility.

Lack of a competent humanitarian or HN health facility does not imply a requirement for a humanitarian or HN health facility that is the *same* standard of care as the military facility, but one which is to an 'acceptable standard' and one that is consistent with the pre-conflict HN capability (see above). Reluctance may exist on behalf of either the military medical staff or the staff of the receiving health facility. Military medical staff may be unwilling to accept that there may be some diminution of patient care standards following patient transfer, and thereby prolong the military admission until the patient is 'completely well'.[51] Alternatively, humanitarian or HN health facilities may be reluctant to accept patients (e.g. in the post-operative phase) perceiving that the military is avoiding its ongoing responsibilities. Therefore, in long term engagements with a fragile security situation it may be necessary for the military to contribute to rebuilding civilian health infrastructure to facilitate medical disengagement.

Concept of Medical Rules of Engagement (M-ROE)

The concept of Medical Rules of Engagement (M-ROE) has been developed by the British military.[52] Their purpose is to define the population that is entitled to treatment *prior* to their arrival at a military health facility and to provide transparency in medical treatment policies. The underlying premise of M-ROE is that it is inevitable that civilians will enter the medical treatment and evacuation chain. If operational policy is not to treat civilians then access to the military medical system must be denied. If the operational policy is to treat only limited 'entitled' groups then this too, must be articulated and promulgated. The construction of M-ROE is a *political*, not a medical responsibility. Medical practitioners must not be expected to abrogate their ethical responsibilities to treat all casualties based solely on medical need.

M-ROE need to be operation specific and will require revision at different phases of the mission. Operational commanders must articulate specific definitions of 'entitled and non-entitled' patients *and* conditions. The broad panacea of treating 'life or limb threatening emergences' is inadequate and open to vast differences in interpretation. If the guidelines for treating military personnel differ from those for treating civilians these need to be documented and promulgated by senior medical personnel. This is a command and political decision.

M-ROE effectively provide clarity of the 'gatekeeping' criteria. They must be based on clinical need, capability and security considerations and need to be widely promulgated to both military and non-military health providers. Care must be taken to ensure that access to the military health system is equitable and based on need and reflects the capacity, and willingness, of humanitarian or HN health facilities to accept patients excluded by the military.

M-ROE may provide clear distinction between 'designated' and 'non-designated personnel' and clearly define any 'rationing' of military health resources. For example, there may be limited access to investigational facilities, ward accommodation, high dependency nursing and intensive care, surgical intervention and use of blood products for non designated personnel. Alternatively, CASEVAC policy may dictate provision of first aid only with transfer of all non-designated 'conditions' (e.g. pregnant women, non-trauma problems) to a local, rather than a military, facility.

The advantages of such an approach include an unambiguous definition of dependency, the ability to resist mission expansion, clarity for HN and humanitarian agencies about what care the military will and will not provide, and reduction in the frustrations of clinical staff when dealing with patients that they are not trained, equipped or resourced to deal with and cannot effectively manage.

It is imperative when implementing M-ROE that health-care providers understand this is a command and political policy formulated in conjunction with senior medical staff. The policy must not be subject to ad hoc alterations, on-site interpretation and must avoid operational inconsistency. In longer campaigns however, there may be a requirement to revise the guidance as the campaign matures and as planners gain a better understanding of the environment.

Table 9.2 Avoiding mission expansion and facilitating disengagement

---

- Adequately define the mission
  - Plan early for stated or implied requirements to treat civilian populations.
  - Identify end states and exit strategies as part of the planning process.
- Provide clear guidelines for standards of care (M-ROE)
  - Define entitled vs non-entitled personnel.
  - Have a clearly established evacuation policy for civilian patients.
  - Avoid using spare capacity to draw additional civilian workload beyond provision of emergency care.
  - Avoid provision of rehabilitation to civilians.
- Foster an environment where humanitarian and HN agencies have freedom of action
- Foster coordination with humanitarian and HN agencies
  - Integrated mission planning.
  - Utilise non-military health assets for civilian patients whenever possible.
- Identify and address discharge blocks
  - Facilitate early transfer of responsibility for civilians to IGO/NGOs as soon as possible.

Measuring effectiveness of health care provision

Measuring the effectiveness of health care provision on operations is frequently overlooked. The health sector is often assumed to be 'doing good' with little objective supporting evidence. While 'health heroism' gains good press it must be accepted that any military involvement in complex operations has limited ability to impact on the health of the population at large. Reporting and analysis is frequently limited, projects are poorly linked with other projects and the lessons are lost to the wider military and civilian medical communities.[53]

More effective CIMIC requires:

> developing specific written purpose, criteria and quantifiable measures, coordinating the purpose, criteria and measures with all involved, including donor and host nation officials, all other providers (expatriates, private volunteers, non government organisations) and beneficiaries and documenting then analysing results to compare outcomes with project purpose and international consensus standards for minimal performance in humanitarian assistance.[54]

In particular, it is necessary to critically appraise the value of medical assistance given and to disseminate this information and lessons learned into the international humanitarian community. Measures of health effectiveness need to take into account the relevance and impact of any health interventions. Post-deployment reports tend to focus on the number of patients treated in a facility, but this is inadequate without measures of how the intervention changed the health status of the patients or populations.[55] For example if equipment donations were undertaken, relevant effectiveness indicators include whether the equipment was needed, used, and if any problems were experienced with maintenance and education. Surrogate markers of effectiveness, such as mortality and complication rates, adverse outcomes can also be useful indicators of effectiveness.

Conclusions/recommendations

Military health-care providers are increasingly being required to provide humanitarian support to civilian populations in complex emergencies. Militaries have provided excellent care to civilian populations under difficult and austere conditions and have helped many individuals and communities. However, as demand for health care increases in complex emergencies and military stabilisation and reconstruction operations, there is a need to better manage these finite resources. Reliance on military providers of humanitarian health care is not sustainable. Effectiveness can only be enhanced by all humanitarian medical providers complimenting each others' contribution to build host nation health care capability.

To provide effective and meaningful care to civilian populations on operations within a strategic military context, health planners need to clearly define the boundaries and responsibilities of the medical service for treating civilians on operations. In a militarily benign environment this is best managed by civilian and humanitarian agencies; in a militarily insecure environment the military must accept responsibility for these tasks and plan accordingly. Robust strategies should be developed to minimise dependence of local communities on military health assets and to facilitate early disengagement. This includes treating civilians in HN or humanitarian medical facilities whenever possible and focusing on transferable skills (such as – training of local staff, provision of safe water supplies and sanitation) rather than provision of sophisticated surgical capability. Improved co-ordination and co-operation with humanitarian agencies providing health care will significantly enhance outcomes for civilian patients and support the wider campaign.

While the *raison d'etre* of the military health service is to support warfighting, it must retain the flexibility to adapt to increasingly encountered operational conditions requiring new skill sets, interactions with other agencies and the ability to balance ethical principles with a pragmatic response.

Notes

1 Kenward, G., Jain, T.N. and Nicholson, K. Mission creep: an analysis of accident and emergency room activity in a military facility in Bosnia-Herzegovina. *Journal Royal Army Medical Corps* 2004; 150(1): 20–23.
2 Neuhaus, S.J. Post Vietnam – three decades of Australian military surgery. *Australian Defence Force Health* 2004; 5: 16–21.
3 Grosso, S.M. US Army surgical experience during the NATO peacekeeping mission in Bosnia-Herzegovina, 1995 to 1999: lessons learned. *Military Medicine* 2001; 166: 587–592.
4 Deployable Medical Capability Study: Role/Echelon 3 Support for Civilians on Operations? November 2003. Available at Defence Medical Services Department website. www.dmsd.mod.uk.
5 Civil and Military Humanitarianism in Complex Political Emergencies: Desirability and Possibilities of a Cooperation. March 2003. Online, available at: www.psw.ugent.be/ctws/publicates/deroos/pdf.

6 Coupland, R.M. Epidemiological approach to surgical management of the casualties of war. *British Medical Journal* 1994; 308: 1693–1697.
7 Burkle, F. Lessons learnt and future expectations of complex emergencies. *British Medical Journal* 1999; 319 (7207) 422–426.
8 Burkle, F. Lessons learnt and future expectations of complex emergencies. *British Medical Journal* 1999; 319 (7207) 422–426.
9 Plunkett, M. and Southall, D., War and Children. *Archives of Diseases in Childhood* 1998; 78: 72–77.
10 Lepaniemi, A.K. Medical Challenges of Internal Conflicts. *World Journal of Surgery* 1998; 22; 1197–1201.
11 Division of Emergency and Humanitarian Action. *Applied health research in emergency settings.* Geneva: World Health Organisation; Melbourne; Macfarlane Burnet Centre for Medical Research, 1999.
12 Machel, G. Impact of Armed Conflict on Children. Report of the Secretary General of United Nations. New York 1996, United Nations.
13 Burkle, F. Pediatric Issues in Complex Emergencies. *Ambulatory Child Health* 2001; 7: 119–126.
14 Mandalakas, A. The Greatest Impact of War and Conflict. *Ambulatory Child Health* 2001; 7; 97–103.
15 Noji, E. Public Health Interventions. In: Leaning, J *et al. Humanitarian Crisis: The Medical and Public Health Response.* London 1999, Harvard University Press.
16 Hampson, G.V., Cook, S.P. and Fredricksen, SR. Operation Bali Assist – the Australian Defence Force response to the Bali bombing, 12 October 2002. *Medical Journal of Australia* 2002; 177: 620–623.
17 Taylor, P.R.F., Edmonson, D.L. and Schlommer, J.E. Operation Shaddock – the Australian Military Defence Force response to the tsunami disaster in Papua New Guinea. *Medical Journal of Australia* 1998; 169: 602–606.
18 WHO-PAHO Guidelines for the Use of Foreign Field Hospitals in the Aftermath of Sudden-Impact Disasters. PAHO 2003.
19 Leaning, J. Medicine and international humanitarian law. *British Medical Journal* 1999; 319: 7207: 393–394, see also First Geneva Convention, Articles 12 and 15; Second Convention, Articles 12 and 18: Protocol 1, Article 10 and Protocol 2, Article 7.
20 This is also a requirement under Chapter 7 of the United Nations Charter (coordination and monitoring of human rights violations) so health professionals must understand their obligations to document such abuses that occur in times of conflict.
21 Geneva Conventions 1949, and two Additional Protocols 1977.
22 United Nations General Assembly. Conventions on the Rights of the Child. New York 1989, United Nations.
23 United Nations Office for the Co-ordination of Humanitarian Affairs (UNOCHA). Guidelines on the Use of Military and Civil Defence Assets to Support United Nations Humanitarian Activities in Complex Emergencies. UN March 2003.
24 United Nations Office for the Co-ordination of Humanitarian Affairs (UNOCHA). Guidelines on the Use of Military and Civil Defence Assets to Support United Nations Humanitarian Activities in Complex Emergencies. UN March 2003.
25 MC 326/2. NATO Principles and Policies of Operational Medical Support. Draft 6 (23 September 2003).
26 JWP 0–01 British Defence Doctrine.
27 Medical Capability Study: Role/Echelon 3 Support for Civilians on Operations? November 2003. Available at Defence Medical Services Department website. www.dmsd.mod.uk.
28 Neuhaus, S.J., Bridgewater, F. and Kilcullen, D.J. Military Medical Ethics: Issues for 21st Century Operations. *Australian Defence Force Journal* 2001; 151: 49–58.
29 Ford, N. Afghanistan: humanitarian aid and military intervention don't mix. *British Journal General Practice* 2001; 51: 946.

30 An example is included in: MSF rejects link of humanitarian and military actions. Press release, Islamabad, October 8, 2001. Online, available at: www.msf.org. countries.
31 Neuhaus, S.J., Bridgewater, F. and Kilcullen, D.J. Military Medical Ethics: Issues for 21st Century Operations. *Australian Defence Force Journal* 2001; 151: 49–58.
32 Rushbach, R. The International Committee of the Red Cross and Health. *International Review of the Red Cross* 1987; 260: 513–522.
33 Ryan, J. *et al.* Conflict and Catastrophe Medicine. London 2002, Springer.
34 Civil and Military Humanitarianism in Complex Political Emergencies: Desirability and Possibilities of a Cooperation. March 2003 Online, available at: www.psw.ugent. be/ ctws/publicates/deroos/pdf.
35 Weissman, F. Humanitarian action and military intervention: temptations and possibilities. *Disasters*. 2004 June; 28(2): 205–215.
36 Civil and Military Humanitarianism in Complex Political Emergencies: Desirability and Possibilities of a Cooperation. March 2003 Online, available at: www.psw.ugent. be/ctws/publicates/deroos/pdf.
37 Zelden, T. *An Intimate History of Humanity*. New York 1994, HarperCollins.
38 An example of such a project is 'Operation Smile'. See Drifmeyer, J, Llewellyn, C. Toward More Effective Humanitarian Assistance. *Military Medicine* 2004: 169(3); 161–168.
39 Burkle, F. Lessons learnt and future expectations of complex emergencies. *British Medical Journal* 1999; 319(7207): 422–426.
40 United Nations Office for the Co-ordination of Humanitarian Affairs (UNOCHA). Guidelines on the Use of Military and Civil Defence Assets to Support United Nations Humanitarian Activities in Complex Emergencies. UN March 2003.
41 NGO members include Action Aid, OXFAM, Save the Children, International Alert, Merlin and Médicins san Frontières. Online, available at: www.mod.uk/jdcc/pso.htm, accessed April 30, 2005.
42 Sphere Humanitarian Charter and Minimum Standards in Disaster Response. October 2003. Online, available at: www.sphereproject.org.
43 UN Charter on Rights of the Child stipulates that care to children should be provided by someone with specialist paediatric training.
44 Kenward, G., Jain, T.N. and Nicholson, K. Mission creep: an analysis of accident and emergency room activity in a military facility in Bosnia-Herzegovina. *Journal Royal Army Medical Corps*. 2004; 150(1): 20–23.
45 Neuhaus, S.J. Post Vietnam – three decades of Australian military surgery. *Australian Defence Force Health* 2004; 5: 16–21.
46 MC326/2 NATO Principles and Policies of Operational Medical Support.
47 Rumbaugh, J.R. Operation Pacific Haven: Humanitarian Medical Support for Kurdish Evacuees. *Military Medicine* 1998; 163: 269–271.
48 Burkle, F. *et al.* Complex Humanitarian Emergencies III. Measures of Effectiveness. *Pre-hospital and Disaster Medicine* 1995; 10: 48–56.
49 Sphere Humanitarian Charter and Minimum Standards in Disaster Response. October 2003 (4th edition). Online, available at: www.sphereproject.org.
50 Dufour, D. *et al. Surgery for Victims of War*. Geneva 1988. The International Committee of the Red Cross.
51 Kenward, G., Jain, T.N. and Nicholson, K. Mission creep: an analysis of accident and emergency room activity in a military facility in Bosnia-Herzegovina. *Journal Royal Army Medical Corps*. 2004; 150(1): 20–23.
52 Deployable Medical Capability Study: Role/Echelon 3 Support for Civilians on Operations? November 2003. Available at Defence Medical Services Department website. www.dmsd.mod.uk.
53 Drifmeyer, CL. Overview of Overseas Humanitarian, Disaster and Civic Aid Programmes. *Military Medicine* 2003; 168(12): 975–980.

54 Drifmeyer, J. and Llewellyn, C. Toward More Effective Humanitarian Assistance. *Military Medicine* 2004: 169(3); 161–168.
55 Drifmeyer, C.L. Overview of Overseas Humanitarian, Disaster and Civic Aid Programmes. *Military Medicine* 2003; 168 (12): 975–980.

Bibliography

Burkle, F. Lessons learnt and future expectations of complex emergencies. *British Medical Journal* 1999; 319 (7207) 422–426.

Burkle, F. Pediatric issues in complex emergencies. *Ambulatory Child Health* 2001; 7: 119–126.

Burkle, F.M. Jr. Complex, humanitarian emergencies: I. Concept and participants. *Pre-hospital and Disaster Medicine* 1995 Jan–Mar; 10(1): 36–42.

Burkle, F.M. Jr., McGrady, K.A., Newett, S.L., Nelson, J.J., Dworken, J.T., Lyerly, W.H. Jr., Natsios, A.S. and Lillibridge, S.R. Complex humanitarian emergencies III. Measures of effectiveness. *Pre-hospital and Disaster Medicine* 1995; 10: 48–56.

Civil–Military Relationships in Complex Emergencies: An Interagency Standing Committee Working Groups Reference Paper. June 2004. United Nations Office for the Coordination of Humanitarian Affairs.

Civil and Military Humanitarianism in Complex Political Emergencies: Desirability and Possibilities of a Cooperation. March 2003. Online, available at: www.psw.ugent.be/ctws/publicates/deroos/pdf.

Coupland, R.M. Epidemiological approach to surgical management of the casualties of war. *British Medical Journal* 1994; 308: 1693–1697.

Deployable Medical Capability Study: Role/Echelon 3 Support for Civilians on Operations? November 2003. Available at Defence Medical Services Department website. www.dmsd.mod.uk.

Division of Emergency and Humanitarian Action. *Applied health research in emergency settings*. Geneva: World Health Organisation; Melbourne; Macfarlane Burnet Centre for Medical Research, 1999.

Drifmeyer, C.L. Overview of overseas humanitarian, disaster and civic aid programmes. *Military Medicine* 2003; 168(12): 975–980.

Drifmeyer, J. and Llewellyn, C. Toward more effective humanitarian assistance. *Military Medicine* 2004; 169(3): 161–168.

Dufour, D., Jensen, S. K., Owen-Smith, M., Salmela, J., Stening, G. F., and Zetterström, B. *Surgery for Victims of War*. Geneva 1988, The International Committee of the Red Cross.

Ford, N. Afghanistan: humanitarian aid and military intervention don't mix. *Br J General Practice* 2001; 51: 946.

Grosso, S.M. US Army surgical experience during the NATO peacekeeping mission in Bosnia-Herzegovina, 1995 to 1999: lessons learned. *Military Medicine* 2001; 166: 587–592.

JWP 0–01 *British Defence Doctrine*.

Hampson, G.V., Cook, S.P. and Fredricksen, S.R. Operation Bali Assist – the Australian Defence Force response to the Bali bombing, 12 October 2002. *Medical Journal of Australia* 2002; 177: 620–623.

International Committee of the Red Cross. *The Fundamental Principles of the Red Cross and Red Crescent Movements*. Geneva 1990. International Committee of the Red Cross.

Kenward, G., Jain, T.N. and Nicholson, K. Mission creep: an analysis of accident and emergency room activity in a military facility in Bosnia-Herzegovina. *Journal Royal Army Medical Corps.* 2004; 150(1): 20–23.

Leaning, J. Medicine and international humanitarian law. *British Medical Journal* 1999; 319(7207): 393–394.

Geneva Conventions 1949, and two Additional Protocols 1977.

Lepaniemi, A.K. Medical challenges of internal conflicts. *World Journal of Surgery* 1998; 22: 1197–1201.

Machel, G. Impact of armed conflict on children. Report of the Secretary General of United Nations. New York 1996, United Nations.

Mandalakas, A. The greatest impact of war and conflict. *Ambulatory Child Health* 2001; 7: 97–103.

MC326/2 NATO Principles and Policies of Operational Medical Support.

Médicins Sans Frontières. Refugee health. *An Approach to Emergency Situations.* London 1997. Macmillan.

Neuhaus, S.J., Bridgewater, F. and Kilcullen, D.J. Military Medical ethics: issues for 21st century operations. *Australian Defence Force Journal* 2001; 151: 49–58.

Neuhaus, S.J. Post Vietnam – three decades of Australian military surgery. *Australian Defence Force Health* 2004; 5: 16–21.

Noji, E. Public Health Interventions. In: Leaning, J., Briggs, S. and Chen, L. *Humanitarian Crisis: The Medical and Public Health Response.* London 1999, Harvard University Press.

Plunkett, M. and Southall, D. War and children. *Archives of Diseases in Childhood* 1998; 78: 72–77.

Rushbach, R. The international committee of the Red Cross and health. *International Review of the Red Cross.* 1987; 260: 513–522.

Rumbaugh, J.R. Operation Pacific Haven: humanitarian medical support for Kurdish evacuees. *Military Medicine* 1998; 163: 269–271.

Ryan, J., Mahoney, P., Greaves, I., and Bowyer, G. (eds) *Conflict and Catastrophe Medicine.* London 2002, Springer.

Sphere Humanitarian Charter and Minimum Standards in Disaster Response. October 2003 (4th edition). Online, available at: www.sphereproject.org.

Taylor, P.R.F, Edmonson, D.L. and Schlommer, J.E. Operation Shaddock – the Australian Military Defence Force response to the tsunami disaster in Papua New Guinea. *Medical Journal of Australia* 1998; 169: 602–606.

United Nations General Assembly. *Conventions on the Rights of the Child.* New York 1989, United Nations.

United Nations Office for the Co-ordination of Humanitarian Affairs (UNOCHA). *Guidelines on the Use of Military and Civil Defence Assets to Support United Nations Humanitarian Activities in Complex Emergencies.* UN March 2003.

WHO-PAHO *Guidelines for the Use of Foreign Field Hospitals in the Aftermath of Sudden-Impact Disasters.* PAHO 2003.

Weissman, F. Humanitarian action and military intervention: temptations and possibilities. *Disasters.* 2004 June; 28(2): 205–215.

Zelden, T. *An Intimate History of Humanity.* New York 1994, HarperCollins.

MSF rejects link of humanitarian and military actions. Press release, Islamabad, October 8, 2001. Online, available at: www.msf.org.countries.

10 At a crossroads or a dead-end?

Considering the civil–military relationship in times of armed conflict

Raj Rana

The violence directed against humanitarian aid workers has come in a context in which the US backed coalition has consistently sought to use humanitarian aid to build support for its military and political ambitions. MSF denounces the coalition's attempts to co-opt humanitarian aid and use it to "win hearts and minds". By doing so, providing aid is no longer seen as an impartial and neutral act, endangering the lives of humanitarian volunteers and jeopardizing the aid to people in need. Only recently, on May 12th 2004, MSF publicly condemned the distribution of leaflets by the coalition forces in southern Afghanistan in which the population was informed that providing information about the Taliban and al Qaeda was necessary if they wanted the delivery of aid to continue.

(Statement by MSF, 28 July 2004)

"We need to put more military effort into [Afghanistan]," he added. "We must apply ourselves more energetically for one more year in order to win." "Military effort alone" was not enough to win the battle, General Richards said. "Our civilian partners must improve the speed and scale of their reconstruction and development effort, sufficient to keep pace with the people's expectations," he added.

(BBC News, 22 January 2007)

The 1990s saw the beginnings of a tighter integration of political and military efforts in multinational efforts towards conflict management and resolution, and a new trend of multinational military forces being given humanitarian roles and mandates. In both Bosnia-Herzegovina and Somalia, there was a high risk that these trends would weaken the perception and reality of impartial, independent and neutral humanitarian action in the eyes of both the belligerents and beneficiaries. Humanitarian agencies were able to be neutral and independent only with difficulty when they used, for example, the logistical assets of peacekeeping forces which ultimately became belligerents in the conflicts they were meant to mitigate.

Armed forces were previously unwilling or unable to rise to the "humanitarian" challenge of the Balkans or Somalia with their existing doctrine and training. But by the time NATO took military action in Kosovo in 1999, the "humanitarian" practice of armed forces had adapted to the challenge. Under enormous pressure from their home governments to be seen as "doing good", NATO military forces were prompt to act in the face of a humanitarian crisis. They were as rapid as humanitarian agencies in the delivery of food to refugees in Albania, interposed themselves into the coordination of humanitarian aid and attempted to position their military operations as being a "humanitarian intervention". As humanitarian actors followed the NATO-led ground forces into Kosovo, the blurring of roles between humanitarian actors and the military had reached its high-water mark.

As the introductory quotes suggest, the realities have moved even further from what might be termed the "Kosovo crossroads". The practice of multinational military missions bartering humanitarian assistance against intelligence is a difficult reality for a civilian humanitarian agency to accept. If humanitarian assistance is perceived and used as part of the military mission, then is MSF not co-opted into the conflict itself? General Richards pushes the logic onwards from the standoff at the crossroads, and potentially heads towards an intellectual dead-end. From his frame or logic, the failure of the military mission in Afghanistan was in fact a civilian (humanitarian and development) one. If humanitarian actors had done a better job of satisfying the Afghan people's expectations, effectively winning their hearts-and-minds, then perhaps we wouldn't face such a security crisis in the country? As such contrasting perspectives co-exist, this chapter attempts to survey whether the relationship between military and humanitarian actors is at a crossroads, or if it has headed towards a dead-end.

In 2001, the ICRC adopted Guidelines for Civil–Military Relations (CMR), based on the organization's experiences of the previous decade. While a relationship with armed forces is natural for an organization that works in contexts of armed conflict, there was a particular need to address both the complexity of multidimensional peacekeeping operations and the growing trend towards integrating the efforts of political, military and humanitarian actors. The ICRC's Guidelines (see Annex) address the risks and threats posed by multinational military missions engaging in humanitarian activities or deployed under a humanitarian mandate, while potentially becoming an active participant in hostilities.

Contemporary contexts such as Afghanistan and Iraq confirm the validity and persistence of the earlier fundamental issues and concerns. Some indications of the more recent developments:

- Humanitarian operations have become a mainstream, non-combat function of armed forces, employed equally in combat, stabilization operations or as part of nation-building agendas. Providing assistance to the civilian population, or influencing the humanitarian and reconstruction efforts of others, is considered as a means of "force multiplication" or "force protection". Political authorities expect their armed forces to have improved their civil–military capacities so as to meet their obligations under international humanitarian law (IHL), in addition to becoming part of the integral post-conflict political and reconstruction efforts of local authorities, State civilian agencies, humanitarian organizations and others.

- The phenomenon of armed forces engaging in humanitarian action in the 1990s was a new and evolving concept without a road map, and there was room for humanitarian agencies to contest the perceived "militarization" of humanitarian assistance. Today, military and political actors are more certain of how they want to intervene, and consider every armed intervention as a fresh opportunity to test new integrated and comprehensive approaches to conflict management, peace-building and stabilization. Humanitarian organizations that fail to align themselves with these integrated approaches are perceived as being entrenched behind the inflexibility of their mandates, or simply out of step with the times.

- At both national and regional levels, there are active efforts to streamline and merge State and military capacities in carrying out future armed interventions. The concept image of the latter is one in which the military is able to jump from waging war to peacekeeping, to humanitarian assistance on the same day, at times within the same city. Civilian experts will be embedded into military structures to provide support for policing, civil administration and political reform, and to act as advisors to military forces and even as donors to humanitarian, reconstruction and private sector actors.

This chapter examines the ICRC's view of the civil–military relationship in contemporary humanitarian environments and is based on recent reconsideration of the ICRC's civil–military relations strategy. While the guidelines adopted in 2001 remain unchanged, it is clearly necessary to reconsider the analytical framework within which they are relevant. From the tentative attempts of the 1990s to conduct humanitarian activities, armed forces have now moved on to consider such tasks as their mainstream responsibilities in all contexts.

There is a need for creative liberty in considering the relationship between multinational military missions and humanitarian actors in time of armed conflict, the current trends and the potential consequences. It is no longer sufficient to limit the discussion to how humanitarian agencies and multinational military missions might cooperate or coordinate. Humanitarian actors are obliged to understand the evolving non-combat doctrine, operations and aims of the military forces with whom they are obliged to share their working environment and their "humanitarian space". Most importantly, civil–military relations can no longer be considered as a subject in isolation. In order to understand the effects today – and more importantly, in the next five to ten years – the evolution of how armed forces see their capacity to take on civilian roles and tasks has to be understood within broader trends of nation-building and integrated approaches to conflict management, peace-building and stability.

The first section of this chapter examines how the military sees its role in taking on civilian (non-combat) tasks, and the doctrine that determines it. Concrete examples are given of such military non-combat operations that the ICRC encounters in the field are used to illustrate this. The second section situates these developments within broader trends of multinational armed interventions and the conduct of hostilities. The third section takes a critical look at how neutral, independent humanitarian action is being perceived by armed forces audiences, and outlines possible considerations of increasing importance for the ICRC in maintaining its relevance. The chapter starts from the position that the narrowing down of the humanitarian environment and the increasing security concerns for humanitarian workers, must in part be attributed to the involvement of multinational military missions taking on roles that go beyond providing security or engaging in combat.

How does the military see its role?

There are a wealth of texts that describe the relationship between the military and humanitarian actors in time of armed conflict. The subjects covered include the humanitarian and political aspects of the relationship, the cultural differences between the humanitarian and military worlds and some of the persistent issues that the two groups must resolve at the field level. The latter includes greater coordination to avoid duplication of efforts, the sensitivities of exchanging security information, or the basic "reach out" efforts to overcome the reticence of both actors that share the same working environment.

Interestingly, there is relatively little written about how armed forces understand their role in assuming civilian tasks. However, without closer consideration of how the military understands its evolving role in humanitarian activities, humanitarian agencies are unclear about whom exactly they are dealing with. Furthermore, within the complex military world of hierarchy and acronyms it is prerequisite to understand how the military interface with humanitarian agencies fits into broader military operations. The following therefore is an examination of some definitions of the military practice of non-combat functions, including the provision of humanitarian assistance by armed forces, and attempts to understand their significance for the present debate.

"Civil–military cooperation" (CIMIC) and "Civil affairs" (CA) are the names used by NATO and the United States Armed Forces (USAF) respectively, to describe those non-combat functions of their armed forces that deal with civilian functions, or involve armed forces taking on tasks typically performed by civilian authorities, NGOs or international humanitarian organizations. In order to avoid confusion with the military terms, the ICRC deliberately chose the term "civil–military relations" (CMR) to describe the relationship between humanitarian organizations and multinational military missions in situations associated with armed conflict.

It has to be imagined that armed forces have developed such doctrine with a view to improve their capacity to meet their obligations towards the civilian population as laid down by international humanitarian law (IHL). International humanitarian law does not expressly address the issue of civil–military relations or the delivery of assistance by armed forces, nor does it preclude a party to a conflict or an occupying power from meeting the needs of the civilian population by means of its armed forces. Specifically, Parties to a conflict and/or occupying powers have the obligation to ensure that the civilian population under their control are adequately supplied with food, medical supplies, clothing, bedding means of shelter and other supplies essential to its survival. The key IHL issue in considering CIMIC/CA lies in assessing whether the civilian population is being provided with these basic supplies in an impartial manner, without any adverse distinction.

It must be emphasized that neither civil–military cooperation nor civil affairs are new phenomena. Both have been part of the major military operations of the twentieth century. For example, the Provincial Reconstruction Teams set up in Afghanistan in 2004 have their roots in the Strategic Hamlet Project implemented by the United States Armed Forces during the Vietnam War. In the latter example, Special Forces personnel were deployed alongside USAID civilian representatives in a hearts-and-minds campaign to provide development assistance while waging a counter-insurgency campaign. The post-Cold War period has seen the importance of CIMIC/CA rise and become more of a mainstream capacity of armed forces.

Their respective military definitions are the following:

- "CIMIC (civil–military cooperation) is the coordination and cooperation, in support of the mission, between the NATO Commander and civil populations, including national and local authorities, as well as international, national and non-governmental organizations and agencies."
- "Civil Affairs (CA) are those interrelated military activities that embrace the relationship between military forces and civil authorities and populations. CA missions include civil–military operations and civil administration (…) CA encompasses the activities that military commanders take to establish and maintain relations between their forces and the civil authorities and general population, resources, and institutions in friendly, neutral, or hostile areas where their forces are employed. Commanders plan and conduct CA activities to facilitate military operations and help achieve politico-military objectives derived from US national security interests. Establishing and maintaining military-to-civil relations may entail interaction between US, multinational and indigenous security forces, and governmental and non-governmental agencies as part of missions tasked to a JFC [Joint Forces Command]. These activities may occur before, during, subsequent to or in the absence of other military actions."

There are clearly differences in scope between the civil–military cooperation and the civil affairs doctrine. NATO foresaw civil–military cooperation as the interface intended first and foremost to improve coordination and reduce overlap with civilian organizations and authorities. There was no explicit call to "conduct" humanitarian projects within the doctrine; there was also no strict "exclusion" of such projects, provided that they support the military mission.

The civil affairs approach of the United States Armed Forces described above is more difficult to categorize. It promotes an approach that seeks to influence the civilian environment in support of their armed forces. This can take the form of trying to win hearts-and-minds, or of applying tactics to break the morale of the enemy or reduce the support they receive from the civilian population. Civil Affairs operations can consciously substitute for civilian authorities and organizations, if such practice supports the commander's intent (and objectives) with regard to the civilian population. Civil Affairs staff and operations bring skills and approaches that can be seen as oriented towards occupation, or for winning the civilian population's hearts-and-minds in order to combat an insurgency.

The two approaches are broadly moving towards convergence, or at least share sufficient common ground to be compatible. The "Cold Warrior" generation of NATO officers who defended the limited interface role of civil–military cooperation is being replaced by a generation of officers whose formative years have been spent operating within the complexities of the Balkans, Sierra Leone, Somalia and Afghanistan. The current generation of multinational military missions practising civil–military cooperation and civil affairs see no contradiction in a fighting force actively conducting humanitarian operations, or fulfilling this role in what they perceive as a "humanitarian vacuum" in contexts such as Iraq.

Civil–military cooperation and civil affairs should not be considered as a completely benign military function or one that can be considered in isolation from combat and intelligence gathering. With the restructuring of armed forces over the last decade, CIMIC/CA is bundled together with the bulk of non-combat operations that are part of a commander's range of tools for waging war – globally referred to as "information operations" (InfoOps). Civil–military cooperation and civil affairs are complementary to the other public function of "media operations" (MediaOps), while "psychological operations" (PsyOps) and "electronic warfare" are often undertaken in support of intelligence objectives. As such, there can be no complete separation between military humanitarian activities and intelligence gathering. This trend equally extends to armed forces involved in UN mandated peace operations.

The concepts of Civil–military cooperation and civil affairs are starting to spread. Within western armed forces, they are no longer limited to a small cadre of specialists. Particularly with the USAF, combat forces in general are becoming active in the provision of assistance. In Asia, some national armed forces are seeing Civil–military cooperation and civil affairs as one of the three pillars of their doctrine, together with intelligence gathering and combat. In Africa, civil–military cooperation doctrine is developing along the lines of "traditional" 1990s peace operations, but will inevitably adopt "humanitarian" operations as a standard complement to the security and stability roles of armed forces.

To humanitarian actors, civil–military cooperation and civil affairs can be understood as follows:

- it is the interface to facilitate unity of effort between military forces and the relevant civilian entities including local, national or regional authorities, NGOs and international organizations;
- it serves as the focal point within the military for monitoring and influencing the general and humanitarian situation facing the civilian population;
- civil–military cooperation and civil affairs staff play the role of humanitar-

ian diplomat and conscience of their commander, though as a combat support function and not as operational decision makers;

- civil–military cooperation and civil affairs is part of a broader range of non-combat tools that a commander employs to dominate whatever landscape is faced – the media (national/international), the civilian population (winning support for his forces/denying support to the enemy), intelligence, and in support of broader political objectives (nation-building, integrated approach, etc.);

- current civil–military cooperation and civil affairs humanitarian projects are almost identical in implementation to those of humanitarian organizations. The modus operandi of CIMIC/CA teams includes needs assessments, definition of projects, securing of financing (military or national donors), finding implementing partners or contractors and evaluating the impact of their projects.

The following examples attempt to put a face to the civil–military cooperation and civil affairs operations that humanitarian actors have to contend with in contemporary contexts.

Afghanistan: Provincial Reconstruction Teams (PRTs)

USAID describes Provincial Reconstruction Teams (PRTs) as: "Joint Civil Military units, which strengthen the reach of the central government through improved security and the facilitation of reconstruction and development efforts."

Provincial Reconstruction Teams can be seen as a sort of civilian–military annex to a military force, and are oriented towards a nation-building role as part of both military strategy and political aims. They are employed equally by NATO forces under the UN mandated International Stability Force (ISAF), and by Coalition Forces involved in Operation Enduring Freedom. There are civilian State and donor representatives permanently based in the PRTs who maintain some authority over projects and approach

With over US$180 million available to finance ten Provincial Reconstruction Teams in 2004, they have substantial influence and means. Functioning as a sort of security platform from which civilian representatives select projects, implementation is then undertaken by the International Organization for Migration (IOM – covering northern Afghanistan) and UNOPs (southern Afghanistan). Projects are largely infrastructure-oriented and include roads, offices and schools. Only a fraction of the financing is for direct provision of humanitarian assistance by combat troops.

UN Mission in Liberia (UNMIL): Quick Impact Projects (QIP)

To cite the words of the Commander of the Pakistani UNMIL garrison in Voinjama, Liberia: "For the sake of humanity and as a goodwill gesture, we distributed some bags of rice and clothing to the local people we met here to ease their suffering." UNMIL's military contingents show that UN mandated military missions are also providing humanitarian assistance as an integral task. A variety of Quick Impact Projects with small budgets are implemented by armed forces as goodwill gestures and presumably integrated into the broader relief efforts of other humanitarian actors. Additionally, as active participants to the Disarmament, Demobilization, and Reintegration process, the various military contingents of UNMIL have been implementing a food/cash exchange for weapons programme, with mixed results (for example, riots by would-be demobilized soldiers and ensuing security concerns for the civilian population).

Some aspects of the relationship with humanitarian agencies mirror the issues of the 1990s, particularly the lack of coordination between military and humanitarian actors. In one example, an UNMIL battalion unilaterally decided to provide medical assistance to a hospital where the ICRC was already working. The ICRC ultimately chose to abandon its programme to avoid duplication of effort, and leave the support of the civilian hospital to UN troops.

Despite not having an explicit mandate from the United Nations to conduct humanitarian operations, there is apparently US$1 million available at the UN Department of Peacekeeping Operations for the various UN military contingents in Liberia to conduct local humanitarian projects.

Situating civil–military relations within broader trends

In the last decade, the relationship between humanitarian agencies and multinational military missions was one that could be understood with a fairly narrow examination of the differences and complementarities of the two groups at times performing similar roles. Today, a broader view must be taken to understand the complexity of the environment in which humanitarian actors work and the associated risks.

Civil–military cooperation and civil affairs, and military non-combat operations more generally, are only a subset of broader trends in the humanitarian environment within which the ICRC is concerned about the civil–military relationship. In the following projection of current trends an outline is given of future conflict environments that are likely to be characterized by a further blurring of functions, roles and mandates. It is this type of environment that humanitarian agencies will have to contend with in the future.

The growing sophistication of armed forces

In one moment in time our service members will be feeding and clothing displaced refugees – providing humanitarian assistance. In the next moment, they will be holding two warring tribes apart – peacekeeping. Finally, they will be fighting a highly lethal mid-intensity battle. All in the same day, all within three city blocks.

Armed forces will train and fight in a way adapted to the complexity that General Krulak describes here. Even lower-level combat commanders will have to place growing emphasis on peacekeeping/stability operations and humanitarian assistance. Non-combat functions will be seen as core tasks in all contexts, including situations of armed conflict. Armed forces' media operations (information campaign) will further dominate the public realm, obscuring the realities and human costs of war with sound bites about their humanitarian and reconstruction efforts. The military will continue to use the image and symbol of their assistance/reconstruction efforts as a way of winning support locally, regionally and often most importantly, back home.

Despite its efforts to further professionalize armed forces to equal the challenge of multi-faceted operations, the military will still depend upon the integration of civilian functions and specialists into its military structures. Embedded civilians will take on further importance, with State civilian advisors for humanitarian, reconstruction or political matters, private contractors in traditional combat support functions, and as in-house State donor representatives.

To keep pace with the evolving realities of conflict, the ICRC will have to draw the attention of a broader spectrum of actors with regard to their IHL obligations in conflict. It will not be sufficient to address only States Parties to a conflict, greater investment will also be required in constructive dialogue with, for example, private military or security companies, private contractors, police forces, trainers and other relevant players.

There could be some positive aspects to civilian integration into armed forces. Civilians might advocate for greater cultural sensitivity of armed forces, lobby for greater awareness of the effects of conflict on civilian populations, provide both technical and political advice and ensure awareness of humanitarian needs and action in the waging of war. The inclusion of civilian and contracted experts and support resources in armed forces might enhance the fulfilment of IHL responsibilities by States, but the contrary could also be the case.

Instrumentalizing humanitarian and reconstruction assistance

When armed forces (and political decision makers) perceive that there is an "humanitarian vacuum", they may try to fill it themselves or find short-term solutions that further their own military aims. This response will probably be based upon their experiences in contexts such as Afghanistan and Iraq, where humanitarian agencies are unable to function for lack of adequate security or in accordance with their modus operandi. The growing belief that humanitarian assistance is a tool that they can utilize may become a prevailing consideration on the part of armed forces.

While humanitarian agencies will largely continue to impartially provide needs-based assistance to those affected by conflict, armed forces will at times employ humanitarian assistance as a means to attain a strategic or tactical military goal. Armed forces might use tactics of bartering assistance to the civilian population in exchange for intelligence, to improve the protection of their own force, for the winning of hearts-and-minds, or as a means of coercing or reward-ing cooperation. There is consequently a risk of cohabitation of incompatible approaches to humanitarian assistance in contexts of armed conflict. Humanitar-ian actors may be forced to revise their respective policies on assistance or to reconsider withdrawing from contexts that are too politically sensitive or too insecure for them to function effectively, thus leaving the task of humanitarian assistance to the military forces who are, in fact, partly or wholly responsible for the insecurity and the perceived partiality of those very agencies.

> Barno [USAF Commander of Operation Enduring Freedom in Afghanistan] suggested that it was time for relief groups to accept that they could not be neutral after a stream of deliberate attacks on de-miners and well-diggers (…) "They probably have to, and they are, realizing that they are now oper-ating in a different world", he said.

For conflicts in the media spotlight, parties to a conflict will use heavy lever-age on the press, engaging in activities traditionally conducted by civilian agen-cies and each competing to market a "with us or against us" relationship with humanitarian actors.

Nation-building and integrated approaches to conflict management

The UK government has proposed:

> the setting up of the Post Conflict Reconstruction Unit (PCRU) working closely with the Foreign and Commonwealth Office and the Ministry of Defence. The PCRU will include staff from DFID [Department for Inter-national Development], FCO [Foreign and Commonwealth Office] and MoD [Ministry of Defence]. It will plan and implement strategies, including civil-ian deployment, for post-conflict reconstruction and military-to-civilian trans-ition, which will involve the recruitment, training, deployment and management of skilled civilian staff and appropriate resources. A Senior Offi-cials' Steering Group will provide strategic policy and operational direction.

Multinational armed interventions and peace operations will steadily become a more sophisticated endeavour. As seen in Afghanistan, multinational military forces (both ISAF and CF) will find broadening synergies with national authori-ties and UN political bodies. Cooperation may range from coordination of the information campaign to support of election processes and cementing the authority of a new government. While not a new phenomenon, the distinction between civilian agencies and military actors will increasingly cease to be rele-vant in the eyes of the population and authorities. Humanitarian organizations and personnel will simply be expected to integrate into the broader efforts made by the international community, regardless of the threats to neutrality or independence.

In the specific relationship between humanitarian actors and multinational military missions, there is a risk that the gap between policy and practice will grow. Some humanitarian actors will, with difficulty, resist political and financial pressures to integrate into broader efforts. Others will simply accept that they are not neutral or independent, and adapt their modus operandi to the realities of the situation. Collective and constructive dialogue on the civil–military relationship might become difficult for a community of humanitarian agencies with divergent mandates.

Outsourcing of tasks in armed conflict

Two highly complex and vitally important post-conflict reconstruction projects – the Loya Jirga Elections and the National Currency Exchange Program – were planned and executed by the company [Global Risk Strategies – Private Security Company] on behalf of the UN and the US and Afghan Governments. Controlling and utilizing a range of aircraft, vehicles, communications and logistics equipment, and liaising in over thirty locations across the country with all levels of national and local Government and military, company personnel ensured that these vital developments were a success.

Particularly in the case of Iraq, the absence of humanitarian workers because of security concerns is cementing the military perception that humanitarian organizations lack the will to "face the dangers". Key States, armed forces and possibly humanitarian actors will push for even greater use of civilian contractors to carry out humanitarian and reconstruction activities, thus outsourcing risks, roles and responsibilities.

State civilian agencies (departments of foreign affairs, development, etc.) will also embrace the notion of outsourcing their programmes to the private sector. This approach will allow greater political control of implementation and choice of projects and target populations, and will inductively limit responsibility and accountability. By extension, humanitarian organizations risk becoming implementing agencies to the private sector, particularly in large-scale structural development programmes and even in contexts that are still qualified as armed conflicts.

Old recipes for a new world?

In these typically difficult times it is better for us to focus our humanitarian minds on engagement and not complaint. Instead of lamenting about the forces ranged against us, we should be planning and preparing, making relationships and building alliances, persuading or outwitting our opponents. We need to get tactical: to win where we can and to retreat where we cannot. Now is not the time, as some are advocating, to invest in yet more interminable debates that pander to a culture of complaint and seek to re-define humanitarian action from first principles once again. Nor is it the time to form a square and defend humanitarian values. They are simply not that threatened. Instead, it is the time to get decisive about where we can and cannot operate and to get innovative about how we do things. It is the time to be creative about humanitarian agency rather than to wallow in humanitarian agony.

Hugo Slim has pinpointed the challenges facing humanitarian actors in the complexity of contexts such as Afghanistan and Iraq today, and prescribes a simple remedy of renewed engagement. The call to, "win where one can, and retreat where one cannot", perhaps all too sadly describes the modus operandi imposed on such organizations in these two contexts. Faced with armed forces who will continue to take on traditionally civilian roles in contexts of armed conflict, and whose "humanitarian intent" will at times be at odds with those of civilian humanitarian actors, there will be questions of how far pragmatism might go.

While there is much credence to the pragmatism of humanitarian organizations choosing contexts in which they work, or finding innovative solutions to old problems, there are also fixed limits to how far the ICRC or other humanitarian organizations can "bend the rules" to face new challenges. For an organization like the ICRC – that is mandated to impartially protect and assist victims of conflict, without any distinction based on nationality, race, religion, politics or other criteria – the choice of where to work is dictated above all by where the victims are found. Thus, the issue is perhaps not how humanitarian organizations might adapt to the realities, but whether they should in the first place.

This final section takes a look at how the ICRC and its particular brand of humanitarian action are being perceived by military audiences, in light of the evolutions in doctrine and the environment for humanitarian action. The ICRC and its strict adherence to neutrality and independence are something of an anachronism to armed forces audiences being trained to better understand and integrate all political, military and humanitarian action, whatever their assignment.

The following paraphrases the relationship of the ICRC with multinational military missions. For this relationship the ICRC advocates:

- maintaining its independence of decision making and action;
- keeping a clear distinction between humanitarian, political and military roles and actors in times of armed conflict; and
- maintaining a dialogue at all times, and at all levels, with multinational military missions, whatever their status in the conflict.

Not surprisingly, in light of the evolution of military CIMIC/CA doctrine and operations and the broader trends in peace operations and conflict management, some State and other armed forces often perceive the ICRC as stubbornly resistant to change or simply outdated. Whatever their perception, the ICRC's position is limited by principles that exclude closer cooperation, or subordination of the ICRC's brand of humanitarian action to broader political goals or new trends in warfare and multinational interventions. It does not, however, exclude dialogue and engagement.

The ICRC has a Unit for Relations with Armed and Security Forces, a group of military and police specialists who guide the organization through its liaising with armed, security and police forces throughout the world. The Unit works steadily to make the specific role and identity of the ICRC known to armed forces worldwide, particularly to those armed forces deploying on missions abroad, to senior levels of command and to people who are influential in policy and training at strategic levels.

To use western European contexts as a barometer of perception, the reaction to such ICRC dissemination efforts is increasingly animated. This is largely due to the fact that armed forces have a growing operational experience in contexts shared with humanitarian actors, and a wealth of personal experience – both positive and negative – of the possibilities for coordination and complementarity between military and humanitarian action. These are some examples of common reactions by armed forces to ICRC presentations:

- often there is some surprise when confronted with the ICRC's strict advocacy for neutrality and independence. There is scepticism among officers who are being asked by their political authorities to conduct "Three Block Warfare" (i.e. war fighting, peacekeeping and providing humanitarian assistance within three city blocks) – only to find that not all civilian organizations are comfortable moving into areas made "permissive" (in a security sense) by the military. Some of the more thoughtful audiences begin to question the very essence of humanitarian action, and respond that their military missions and role are also guided by principles of neutrality, independence and impartiality;
- Reluctance to accept that if "we" are all working towards the same goals, then why can't "we" work together? Armed forces often assume that there is a desired end state to the military mission they have been entrusted – stability, security, elections, etc. "Joint Integrated Approaches", or the unity of effort of military, diplomatic and economic power are ways in which armed forces understand their niche in the broader integrated approaches to nation-building. Interestingly, their approach is often to focus their strategic aim and end state on the same target population – victims of war. It is difficult to explain that the ICRC has the same unremitting interest in assisting the victims of conflict, though without the necessity to integrate into the political–military strategy and all the while conscious of the efforts of others.

The crux of the matter can be summarized thus:

You [ICRC] are afraid we [armed forces] will exploit you for intelligence purposes, you would prefer us to stay out of the humanitarian business, you want to work towards the same goal of helping the people, but not with us – what do you want us to do?

Understandably, there is a certain frustration with an organization that can be perceived as asking for everything and its opposite. On the one hand, the ICRC expects a fixed relationship and a discussion on topics that are of concern to armed forces whatever their status in the conflict – ICRC access to victims, detention by armed forces, etc. The organization is equally concerned that the blurring of roles and actors will create the perception of having taken sides in the conflict and thus place it and its staff at risk. There is no one way to clarify how the ICRC and its position are perceived.

Key considerations for the way forward

The concepts of neutrality and independence are increasingly misunderstood and/or distorted to fit other agendas. The challenge for the future will be for the ICRC to find the means that distinguish it from all other actors. Some of the key considerations as to the relationship with multinational military missions – and indeed advocated by the ICRC beyond the scope of the civil–military relationship – include the following:

- In a world becoming ever more polarized, the need for neutral and independent humanitarian action as provided by the ICRC is essential in limiting the means employed in warfare and the human cost of war and armed violence. There remains a need for neutral and independent humanitarian actors in times of armed conflict; neutrality is a pivotal aspect of humanitarian action and is not a concept that can be abandoned and reinstated at will.
- It is critical to maintain a distinction between humanitarian activity and politically motivated aid.
- While there is room for divergent approaches to providing humanitarian and reconstruction assistance in time of armed conflict, all players must understand that their actions affect all those with whom they share the same geographic and humanitarian environment. Engagement and dialogue are the core remedy.
- It is essential to gain the acceptance and trust of all parties to a conflict regardless of their status within it, in order to have access to the people affected by the conflict and be able to provide them with protection and assistance. Whether the ICRC's brand of humanitarian action is accepted or not, the ICRC needs to maintain the perception of its neutrality and independence that enables it to protect and assist on all sides of the existing or potential frontlines.

Conclusion

The conclusion to be drawn is in many ways epitomized by the ICRC Guidelines on civil–military relations which continue to govern the organization's relations with multinational military missions in time of armed conflict despite the continuing changes taking place in that environment. Some closing points however need to be added.

Today, the narrowing down of the humanitarian environment felt by the ICRC in both Afghanistan and Iraq can in part be attributed to the involvement of multinational armed forces assuming roles that go beyond providing security or engaging in combat. In both contexts, armed forces are increasingly active in roles typically filled by civilians. The distinction between humanitarian, political and military action becomes blurred when armed forces are perceived as being humanitarian actors, when civilians are embedded into military structures, and when the impression is created that humanitarian organizations and their personnel are merely tools within integrated approaches to conflict management.

If Afghanistan and Iraq are a new benchmark for the civil–military relations challenges facing the ICRC, there should be concern that the issues facing humanitarian agencies in such situations, if not the situations themselves, will only increase in the years to come. Political and military decision-makers are consolidating the lessons they have learned and proposing even more extensive synergies of political, humanitarian and military action.

Civil–military cooperation and civil affairs, and the greater issue of improving synergy between military and civilian efforts in multinational interventions, will be a key priority for both States and armed forces. Concepts of future operations will have military forces working closely with their national civilian counterparts towards a form of "integrated approach" at the national, regional and inter-governmental levels.

The challenges of the civil–military relationship today cannot be resolved by consultation solely between humanitarian and military actors; a more comprehensive approach to an influential and diverse range of political leaders and opinion makers is necessary. While perhaps neither side of the debate will allow itself to be persuaded to adopt the principles of the "adversary", each must understand and respect the notion of complementarity and distinction.

11 Conclusion

Joined up or messed up? CIMIC and the future

Christopher Ankersen

Thematic connections

Even a cursory reading of the chapters in this volume reveals the emergence of several related themes. Not all authors (here or elsewhere) agree on the significance of these themes, nor do they share normative positions with regard to them. Nevertheless, the themes are cross-cutting, and emerge regardless of the country under observation, the nature of the mission studied, or the specific CIMIC activity examined.

CIMIC is about relationships

While de Coning and Rietjens address the issue of partnership and cooperation most explicitly, several other contributors comment on the importance of the relationships which CIMIC entails. Whether seen as true 'cooperation' or as coordination, collaboration, or competition, CIMIC is about actors from different fields of endeavour working, if not together, then at least side-by-side. In some cases, partners are carefully chosen, according to rational (albeit not always transparent) criteria. In other cases, soldiers and humanitarians find themselves thrust on each other. Several strategies are possible, ranging from engagement (as promoted by de Coning) to awareness (promoted by Rietjens) to distinction (promoted by Rana).

CIMIC is about effectiveness, but does not always deliver

In each case, it is assumed that CIMIC, as a strategy, is designed to achieve some goal. This is one area in which the contributors do not share a normative perspective, but each seem to agree that CIMIC is about producing results (even if those results are deemed to be one-sided and selfish, rather than genuinely motivated by humanitarian impulses). Knight believes that, in some cases, and within limits, CIMIC can deliver: it can help create 'freedom from want' and 'freedom from fear'. However, it is not clear that, even with such an instrumental foundation, CIMIC is as effective as it could be. Savage and McNerney demonstrate that Canadian and American efforts in Afghanistan have come up short of either improving lives, or pacifying populations. Voget's assessment of German CIMIC activities in Kosovo reveals similar problems. Neuhaus cautions that medical CIMIC has limitations and should not be seen as medicine for every ailment.

CIMIC is about coherence, but is often inconsistent

Born, at least partially, of the desire to tackle complex emergencies in an integrated manner, avoiding function 'silos' or 'stovepipes' CIMIC is meant to provide both a 'whole of government' and a 'multidimensional' solution. In the case of Canada, Savage locates CIMIC as part of the government's '3D' policy, one that ties together diplomacy, development, and defence. In reality, though, the expected coherence has not materialized. Rana believes this is due to the differences in priorities between government departments *and* between state-based and non-governmental actors. More often than not what we see is 'CIMIC at random', military projects disconnected from any countrywide strategy.

There is another dimension to coherence which effects CIMIC: coherence of purpose. How congruent is it for militaries to engage in activities that have been regarded as the remit of humanitarian organizations? Can 'warfighters' properly be 'aid providers'? Surely there is something paradoxical in relief delivered from the barrel of a gun? Voget is confident that CIMIC has nothing to do with humanitarianism at all; Savage seems to agree. Knight states that CIMIC fits inside the context of human security and 'responsibility to protect', but recognizes that this context does not bind military activity completely. McNerney, recognizing the lack of 'altruism' in CIMIC, does not see a problem with such a juxtaposition, while Neuhaus carefully pares notions of medical humanitarianism from military medicine. Rana calls for the demarcations between soldiers and humanitarians to be strengthened, not blurred. It is not clear, at the end of the debate, to determine whether the goal of coherence makes sense (based on efficiency gains). Perhaps such expectations ignore too many important differences; coherence might be homogenization in sheep's clothing.

Next steps

Rana's 'dead end' for CIMIC is probably premature. The pressures which have brought it to the fore in the international arena are not likely to disappear any time soon. Indeed, as America embarked on its 2007 'surge' in Iraq, it considered 'reconstruction' a key element of its strategy for victory. That being said, it is prudent to identify areas that are deserving of further study.

What does CIMIC look like in other contexts, with different actors?

A few countries have been examined here, and there are good case studies which examine the performance of others (Jakobsen 2005; Gordon 2006). More and more countries are becoming involved in CIMIC, in places other than the

Balkans and Afghanistan. What does CIMIC look like in Africa, performed by countries other than those from the Anglosphere and Western Europe?

Case studies are important and will definitely continue. However, case studies, to be as valuable as possible, must have a theoretical or thematic core. Description abounds, but for scholars to be seen as more than 'slow journalists' analysis is critical.

How does CIMIC affect the identities of those who carry it out?

As soldiers carry out relief and reconstruction activities, and aid workers find themselves 'integrated' into military campaigns, one might expect there to be noticeable changes in how these actors perceive of their roles, the professions, and, ultimately, themselves. In other words, how does CIMIC affect the 'warrior spirit'? It might be possible to trace a dual movement of a 'humanization of war' as well as a 'militarization of aid'. Christopher Coker speaks of war as an existential concept, one that would 'only end when warriors no longer need it to affirm their own humanity' (Coker 2004, 6). What if warriors find affirmation through CIMIC, rather than combat? Does something similar exist within the humanitarian community? More work on this aspect of CIMIC would make a welcome addition to the field.

Dead-end, or U-turn?

I will end this book with an image of what could come to pass for CIMIC, rather than solid conclusion. What if, due to its inconclusive record on effectiveness and the ambiguous virtue of coherence, the relationships that lie at the heart of CIMIC, start to pull apart? What if actors decide *not* to cooperate? What if, beyond the kind of functional division of labour suggested by Rana, aid and reconstruction works in complex emergencies become completely disconnected, creating 'anarchical relief', where the silos and uni-dimensional approaches of the past come back to haunt the 'humanitarian space'? Would the affected populations in war-torn corners of the globe be better off in a world where the international response to crises were to be 'un-joined up'? There are signs of a shift away from CIMIC as cooperation and to straightforward 'relief delivery by the military' that does not involve cooperation. Money is simply provided to military units and they are directed to 'reconstruct'. Indeed, familiarity with the provision of relief may be spawning contempt, not with the activity, but with the need to partner in order to get it done. According to one military officer involved in CIMIC in Lebanon: 'Our training in Spain is always for war fighting ... but you don't need specific skills here – we rely on our Spanish character. We share a drink with the people, sing and dance' (Blanford 2007). What is clear is that CIMIC is still an under-studied and under-appreciated field. As Minear states in his Foreword to this volume, 'the recurrence of a consistent set of critical but unresolved policy issues in successive conflicts suggests that the process of lessons-learning and institutional change is a lethargic and halting one'. CIMIC is too important to be marred by such a process.

References

Blanford, N. 2007. 'UN shifts toward aid projects in Lebanon,' *Christian Science Monitor.* 8 February.

Jakobsen, P.V. 2005. 'PRTs in Afghanistan: successful but not sufficient,' DIIS Report 2005: 6. (Copenhagen: Danish Institute of International Studies).

Gordon, S. 2006. 'Exploring the civil–military interface and its impact on European strategic and operational personalities: "civilianisation" and limiting military roles in stabilisation operations?' *European Security* (15.3): 339–361.

Index

eBooks

eBooks – at www.eBookstore.tandf.co.uk

A library at your fingertips!

eBooks are electronic versions of printed books. You can store them on your PC/laptop or browse them online.

They have advantages for anyone needing rapid access to a wide variety of published, copyright information.

eBooks can help your research by enabling you to bookmark chapters, annotate text and use instant searches to find specific words or phrases. Several eBook files would fit on even a small laptop or PDA.

NEW: Save money by eSubscribing: cheap, online access to any eBook for as long as you need it.

Annual subscription packages

We now offer special low-cost bulk subscriptions to packages of eBooks in certain subject areas. These are available to libraries or to individuals.

For more information please contact webmaster.ebooks@tandf.co.uk

We're continually developing the eBook concept, so keep up to date by visiting the website.

www.eBookstore.tandf.co.uk